Suzuki GSF600 & 1200 Bandit Fours
Service and Repair Manual

Matthew Coombs

Models covered

(3367-264-12Y2)

GSF600 (Bandit N 600) 599cc. UK 1995-on
GSF600S (Bandit S 600) 599cc. UK and US 1996-on
GSF1200 (Bandit N 1200) 1157cc. UK 1996-on
GSF1200S (Bandit S 1200) 1157cc. UK 1996-on, US 1997

© Haynes Publishing 2000

ABCDE
FGHIJ
KLMNO

Printed by **J H Haynes & Co Ltd, Sparkford, Nr Yeovil, Somerset BA22 7JJ, England**

A book in the **Haynes Service and Repair Manual Series**

Haynes Publishing
Sparkford, Nr Yeovil, Somerset BA22 7JJ, England

Haynes North America, Inc
861 Lawrence Drive, Newbury Park, California 91320, USA

Editions Haynes S.A.
Tour Aurore - La Défense 2, 18 Place des Reflets,
92975 PARIS LA DEFENSE Cedex, France

Haynes Publishing Nordiska AB
Box 1504, 751 45 UPPSALA, Sweden

ISBN **1 85960 367 X**

British Library Cataloguing in Publication Data
A catalogue record for this book is available from the British Library.

Library of Congress Catalogue Card Number 97-72742

Contents

LIVING WITH YOUR SUZUKI BANDIT

Introduction

Daily (pre-ride) checks

MAINTENANCE

Routine maintenance and servicing

Contents

REPAIRS AND OVERHAUL

REFERENCE

Suzuki Every Which Way

by Julian Ryder

From Textile Machinery to Motorcycles

Suzuki were the second of Japan's Big Four motorcycle manufacturers to enter the business, and like Honda they started by bolting small two-stroke motors to bicycles. Unlike Honda, they had manufactured other products before turning to transportation in the aftermath of World War II. In fact Suzuki has been in business since the first decade of the 20th-Century when Michio Suzuki manufactured textile machinery.

The desperate need for transport in post-war Japan saw Suzuki make their first motorised bicycle in 1952, and the fact that by 1954 the company had changed its name to Suzuki Motor Company shows how quickly the sideline took over the whole company's activities. In their first full manufacturing year, Suzuki made nearly 4500 bikes and rapidly expanded into the world markets with a range of two-strokes.

Suzuki didn't make a four-stroke until 1977 when the GS750 double-overhead-cam across-the-frame four arrived. This was several years after Honda and Kawasaki had established the air-cooled four as the industry standard, but no motorcycle epitomises the era of what came to be known as the Universal Japanese motorcycle better than the GS. So well engineered were the original fours that you can clearly see their genes in the GS500 twins that are still going strong in the mid-1990s. Suzuki's ability to prolong the life of their products this way means that they are often thought of as a conservative company. This is hardly fair if you look at some of their landmark designs, most of which have been commercial as well as critical successes.

Two-stroke Success

Early racing efforts were bolstered by the arrival of Ernst Degner who defected from the East German MZ team at the Swedish GP of 1961, bringing with him the rotary-valve secrets of design genius Walter Kaaden. The new Suzuki 50 cc racer won its first GP on the Isle of Man the following year and winning the title easily. Only Honda and Ralph Bryans interrupted Suzuki's run of 50 cc titles from 1962 to 1968.

The T500 two-stroke twin

The arrival of the twin-cylinder 125 racer in 1963 enabled Hugh Anderson to win both 50 and 125 world titles. You may not think 50 cc racing would be exciting - until you learn that the final incarnation of the thing had 14 gears and could do well over 100 mph on fast circuits. Before pulling out of GPs in 1967 the 50 cc racer won six of the eight world titles chalked up by Suzuki during the 1960s as well as providing Mitsuo Itoh with the distinction of being the only Japanese rider to win an Isle of Man TT. Mr Itoh still works for Suzuki, he's in charge of their racing program.

Europe got the benefit of Suzuki's two-stroke expertise in a succession of air-cooled twins, the six-speed 250 cc Super Six being the most memorable, but the arrival in 1968 of the first of a series of 500 cc twins which were good looking, robust and versatile marked the start of mainstream success.

So confident were Suzuki of their two-stroke expertise that they even applied it to the burgeoning Superbike sector. The GT750 water-cooled triple arrived in 1972. It was big, fast and comfortable although the handling and stopping power did draw some comment. Whatever the drawbacks of the road bike, the engine was immensely successful in Superbike and Formula 750 racing. The roadster has its devotees, though, and is now a sought-after bike on the classic Japanese scene. Do not refer to it as the Water Buffalo in such company. Joking aside, the later disc-braked versions were quite civilised, but the audacious idea of using a big two-stroke motor in what was essentially a touring bike was a surprising success until the fuel crisis of the mid-'70s effectively killed off big strokers.

The same could be said of Suzuki's only real lemon, the RE5. This is still the only mass-produced bike to use the rotary (or Wankel) engine but never sold well. Fuel consumption in the mid-teens allied to frightening complexity and excess weight meant the RE5 was a non-starter in the sales race.

Development of the Four-stroke range

When Suzuki got round to building a four-stroke they did a very good job of it. The GS fours were built in 550, 650, 750, 850 1000 and 1100 cc sizes in sports, custom, roadster and even shaft-driven touring forms over many years. The GS1000 was in on the start of Superbike racing in the early 1970s and the GS850 shaft-driven tourer was around nearly 15 years later. The fours spawned a line of 400, 425, 450 and 500 cc GS twins that were essentially the middle half of the four with all their reliability. If there was ever a criticism of the GS models it was that with the exception of the GS1000S of 1980, colloquially known as the ice-cream van, the range was visually uninspiring.

They nearly made the same mistake when they launched the four-valve-head GSX750 in 1979. Fortunately, the original twin-shock

One of the later GT750 'kettle' models with front disc brakes

The GS400 was the first in a line of four-stroke twins

The GS750 led the way for a series of four cylinder models

version was soon replaced by the 'E'-model with Full-Floater rear suspension and a full set of all the gadgets the Japanese industry was then keen on and has since forgotten about, like 16-inch front wheels and anti-dive forks. The air-cooled GSX was like the GS built in 550, 750 and 1100 cc versions with a variety of half, full and touring fairings, but the GSX that is best remembered is the Katana that first appeared in 1981. The power was provided by an 1000 or 1100 cc GSX motor, but wrapped around it was the most outrageous styling package to come out of Japan. Designed by Hans Muth of Target Design, the Katana looked like nothing seen before or since. At the time there was as much anti feeling as praise, but now it is rightly regarded as a classic, a true milestone in motorcycle design. The factory have even started making 250 and 400 cc fours for the home market with the same styling as the 1981 bike.

Just to remind us that they'd still been building two-strokes for the likes of Barry Sheene, in 1986 Suzuki marketed a road-going version of their RG500 square-four racer which had put an end to the era of the four-stroke in 500 GPs when it appeared in 1974. In 1976 Suzuki not only won their first 500 title with Sheene, they sold RG500s over the counter and won every GP with them - with the exception of the Isle of Man TT which the works riders boycotted. Ten years on, the RG500 Gamma gave road riders the nearest experience they'd ever get to riding a GP bike. The fearsome beast could top 140 mph and only weighed 340 lb - the other alleged GP replicas were pussy cats compared to the Gamma's man-eating tiger.

The RG only lasted a few years and is already firmly in the category of collector's item; its four-stroke equivalent, the GSX-R, is still with us and looks like being so for many years. You have to look back to 1985 and its launch to realise just what a revolutionary step the GSX-R750 was: quite simply it was the first race replica. Not a bike dressed up to look like a race bike, but a genuine racer with lights on, a bike that could be taken straight to the track and win.

The first GSX-R, the 750, had a completely new motor cooled by oil rather than water and an aluminium cradle frame. It was sparse, a little twitchy and very, very fast. This time Suzuki got the looks right, blue and white bodywork based on the factory's racing colours and endurance-racer lookalike twin headlights. And then came the 1100 - the big GSX-R got progressively more brutal as it chased the Yamaha EXUP for the heavyweight championship.

And alongside all these mould-breaking designs, Suzuki were also making the best looking custom bikes to come out of Japan, the Intruders; the first race replica trail bike, the DR350; the sharpest 250 Supersports, the RGV250; and a bargain-basement 600, the Bandit. The Bandit proved so popular they went on to build 1200 and 750 cc versions of it. I suppose that's predictable, a range of four-stroke fours just like the GS and GSXs. It's just like the company really, sometimes predictable, admittedly - but never boring.

Suzuki's GSX-R range represented their cutting edge sports bikes

Power to the people

The Bandits big and small shouldn't really be any good. After all, they are simply warmed over versions of old motors - used to keep costs down - bolted into a simple tubular steel chassis and fitted with suspension that could not be described as state-of-the-art. Such was the impact the 600 Bandit made on its launch at the 1994 Cologne Show that it hardly rated a mention in reports, but when the roadtesters got to ride it the result was unanimous amazement. The commonest comparison was with the old Power Valve Yamaha RD350LC, here was a bike that was serious fun and, in most markets, much, much cheaper than the opposition. The 600 Bandit turned out to be much more than the sum of its parts.

The oil-cooled motor was lifted from the curiously styled GSX600F, but tuned almost exclusively for more mid-range and low-down power and torque, with carbs shrunk by one mil to 32mm and given more downdraft, plus revised cams and ignition timing. The chassis was all new, a tubular steel twin cradle with aluminium swinging arm. The whole front end - forks, brakes and mudguard - came straight out of the RF600 parts bin, the rear wheel off the Japan-only 400 cc Bandit.

So far so good, but the styling proved a vital ingredient. Suzuki spent money where it mattered, the scalloped tank, four-into-one exhaust and slightly sporty riding position give the bike a sparse, modern look thankfully unadorned by the acid-house graphics that still afflicted some of the range. Some bikes in this sector are forever tagged with the 'retro'

Suzuki Bandit S 600

badge but the Bandit could never be accused of looking remotely old-fashioned. Or performing in anything other than a manner comparable with much more expensive and higher-tech middleweights.

The 1200 Bandit followed the same recipe, this time using the old oil-cooled GSX-R1100 motor as opposed to the current water-cooled version. Suzuki departed from the naked-bike class standard by making the big Bandit small - you have to check the numbers on the tail unit to work out whether it's a 600 or 1200. Compare the 1200 Bandit's all-up weight of 228 kg with the Honda CB1000's 261 kg or the Yamaha XJR1200's 245 kg for evidence. Also, despite using the same motor as the old GSX-R1100, the 1200 Bandit's wheelbase is 50 mm shorter.

The result on both the 600 and 1200 is tons of fun for your money. There is no evidence at

all of the parts bin special nature of the components, the whole thing works so much better than it should if all you read is the spec sheet. On the 600 you get loads more power than the other naked 600s allied to truly stomping mid-range - not something you associate with a performance middleweight. On the 1200 you get that good old GSX-R1100 power and speed - lots of it - but you get it in a surprisingly compact and useable package. For a few extra kilos you can have the 600 S or 1200 S models which have the added luxury of a surprisingly effective half-fairing.

The smaller Bandit can't be claimed to outperform long-time class benchmark the Honda CBR600, but it can lay claim to being the most useable bike in its class and the one that sets the standard that matters - how much fun you get for your money.

Acknowledgements

Our thanks are due to Bridge Motorcycle World of Exeter who supplied the GSF600 and 1200 featured in the photographs throughout this manual and to Pete Trott who carried out the mechanical work. We would also like to thank the Avon Rubber Company, who kindly supplied information and technical assistance on tyre fitting, and NGK Spark plugs (UK) Ltd for information on spark plug maintenance and electrode conditions.

Thanks are also due to Redcat Marketing and Kel Edge for supplying colour transparencies. The introduction, " Suzuki - Every Which Way" was written by Julian Ryder.

About this Manual

The aim of this manual is to help you get the best value from your motorcycle. It can do so in several ways. It can help you decide what work must be done, even if you choose to have it done by a dealer; it provides information and procedures for routine maintenance and servicing; and it offers diagnostic and repair procedures to follow when trouble occurs.

We hope you use the manual to tackle the work yourself. For many simpler jobs, doing it yourself may be quicker than arranging an appointment to get the motorcycle into a dealer and making the trips to leave it and pick it up. More importantly, a lot of money can be saved by avoiding the expense the

shop must pass on to you to cover its labour and overhead costs. An added benefit is the sense of satisfaction and accomplishment that you feel after doing the job yourself.

References to the left or right side of the motorcycle assume you are sitting on the seat, facing forward.

We take great pride in the accuracy of information given in this manual, but motorcycle manufacturers make alterations and design changes during the production run of a particular motorcycle of which they do not inform us. No liability can be accepted by the authors or publishers for loss, damage or injury caused by any errors in, or omissions from, the information given.

Professional mechanics are trained in safe working procedures. However enthusiastic you may be about getting on with the job at hand, take the time to ensure that your safety is not put at risk. A moment's lack of attention can result in an accident, as can failure to observe simple precautions.

There will always be new ways of having accidents, and the following is not a comprehensive list of all dangers; it is intended rather to make you aware of the risks and to encourage a safe approach to all work you carry out on your bike.

Asbestos

● Certain friction, insulating, sealing and other products - such as brake pads, clutch linings, gaskets, etc. - contain asbestos. Extreme care must be taken to avoid inhalation of dust from such products since it is hazardous to health. If in doubt, assume that they do contain asbestos.

Fire

● Remember at all times that petrol is highly flammable. Never smoke or have any kind of naked flame around, when working on the vehicle. But the risk does not end there - a spark caused by an electrical short-circuit, by two metal surfaces contacting each other, by careless use of tools, or even by static electricity built up in your body under certain conditions, can ignite petrol vapour, which in a confined space is highly explosive. Never use petrol as a cleaning solvent. Use an approved safety solvent.

● Always disconnect the battery earth terminal before working on any part of the fuel or electrical system, and never risk spilling fuel on to a hot engine or exhaust.

● It is recommended that a fire extinguisher of a type suitable for fuel and electrical fires is kept handy in the garage or workplace at all times. Never try to extinguish a fuel or electrical fire with water.

Fumes

● Certain fumes are highly toxic and can quickly cause unconsciousness and even death if inhaled to any extent. Petrol vapour comes into this category, as do the vapours from certain solvents such as trichloro-ethylene. Any draining or pouring of such volatile fluids should be done in a well ventilated area.

● When using cleaning fluids and solvents, read the instructions carefully. Never use materials from unmarked containers - they may give off poisonous vapours.

● Never run the engine of a motor vehicle in an enclosed space such as a garage. Exhaust fumes contain carbon monoxide which is extremely poisonous; if you need to run the engine, always do so in the open air or at least have the rear of the vehicle outside the workplace.

The battery

● Never cause a spark, or allow a naked light near the vehicle's battery. It will normally be giving off a certain amount of hydrogen gas, which is highly explosive.

● Always disconnect the battery ground (earth) terminal before working on the fuel or electrical systems (except where noted).

● If possible, loosen the filler plugs or cover when charging the battery from an external source. Do not charge at an excessive rate or the battery may burst.

● Take care when topping up, cleaning or carrying the battery. The acid electrolyte, evenwhen diluted, is very corrosive and should not be allowed to contact the eyes or skin. Always wear rubber gloves and goggles or a face shield. If you ever need to prepare electrolyte yourself, always add the acid slowly to the water; never add the water to the acid.

Electricity

● When using an electric power tool, inspection light etc., always ensure that the appliance is correctly connected to its plug and that, where necessary, it is properly grounded (earthed). Do not use such appliances in damp conditions and, again, beware of creating a spark or applying excessive heat in the vicinity of fuel or fuel vapour. Also ensure that the appliances meet national safety standards.

● A severe electric shock can result from touching certain parts of the electrical system, such as the spark plug wires (HT leads), when the engine is running or being cranked, particularly if components are damp or the insulation is defective. Where an electronic ignition system is used, the secondary (HT) voltage is much higher and could prove fatal.

Remember...

✗ **Don't** start the engine without first ascertaining that the transmission is in neutral.

✗ **Don't** suddenly remove the pressure cap from a hot cooling system - cover it with a cloth and release the pressure gradually first, or you may get scalded by escaping coolant.

✗ **Don't** attempt to drain oil until you are sure it has cooled sufficiently to avoid scalding you.

✗ **Don't** grasp any part of the engine or exhaust system without first ascertaining that it is cool enough not to burn you.

✗ **Don't** allow brake fluid or antifreeze to contact the machine's paintwork or plastic components.

✗ **Don't** siphon toxic liquids such as fuel, hydraulic fluid or antifreeze by mouth, or allow them to remain on your skin.

✗ **Don't** inhale dust - it may be injurious to health (see Asbestos heading).

✗ **Don't** allow any spilled oil or grease to remain on the floor - wipe it up right away, before someone slips on it.

✗ **Don't** use ill-fitting spanners or other tools which may slip and cause injury.

✗ **Don't** lift a heavy component which may be beyond your capability - get assistance.

✗ **Don't** rush to finish a job or take unverified short cuts.

✗ **Don't** allow children or animals in or around an unattended vehicle.

✗ **Don't** inflate a tyre above the recommended pressure. Apart from overstressing the carcass, in extreme cases the tyre may blow off forcibly.

✔ **Do** ensure that the machine is supported securely at all times. This is especially important when the machine is blocked up to aid wheel or fork removal.

✔ **Do** take care when attempting to loosen a stubborn nut or bolt. It is generally better to pull on a spanner, rather than push, so that if you slip, you fall away from the machine rather than onto it.

✔ **Do** wear eye protection when using power tools such as drill, sander, bench grinder etc.

✔ **Do** use a barrier cream on your hands prior to undertaking dirty jobs - it will protect your skin from infection as well as making the dirt easier to remove afterwards; but make sure your hands aren't left slippery. Note that long-term contact with used engine oil can be a health hazard.

✔ **Do** keep loose clothing (cuffs, ties etc. and long hair) well out of the way of moving mechanical parts.

✔ **Do** remove rings, wristwatch etc., before working on the vehicle - especially the electrical system.

✔ **Do** keep your work area tidy - it is only too easy to fall over articles left lying around.

✔ **Do** exercise caution when compressing springs for removal or installation. Ensure that the tension is applied and released in a controlled manner, using suitable tools which preclude the possibility of the spring escaping violently.

✔ **Do** ensure that any lifting tackle used has a safe working load rating adequate for the job.

✔ **Do** get someone to check periodically that all is well, when working alone on the vehicle.

✔ **Do** carry out work in a logical sequence and check that everything is correctly assembled and tightened afterwards.

✔ **Do** remember that your vehicle's safety affects that of yourself and others. If in doubt on any point, get professional advice.

● If in spite of following these precautions, you are unfortunate enough to injure yourself, seek medical attention as soon as possible.

Frame and engine numbers

The frame serial number is stamped into the right-hand side of the steering head. The engine number is stamped into the top of the right-hand side of the crankcase behind the cylinder block. Both of these numbers should be recorded and kept in a safe place so they can be furnished to law enforcement officials in the event of a theft. There is also a carburettor identification number on the side of each carburettor body.

The frame serial number, engine serial number and carburettor identification number should also be kept in a handy place (such as with your driver's licence) so they are always available when purchasing or ordering parts for your machine.

The procedures in this manual identify the models by name (eg GSF1200S), and where necessary also by suffix letter (eg GSF1200SV); the suffix letter is linked to the production year and will be necessary when ordering parts for your bike.

UK models

To determine the suffix letter, refer to the frame numbers in the following table. The first part of the frame number is the model code (eg GN77A), followed by the actual serial number. Note that the date of first registration will not necessarily coinside with the production year.

Model	Year	Suffix letter	Initial frame number
600	1995	S	GN77A-100001 on
600	1996	T	GN77A-103184 on
600	1997	V	GN77A-111124 on
1200	1996	T	JS1GV75A-000500001 on
1200	1997	V	JS1GV75A-000510752 on

The frame number is stamped on a plate on the right-hand frame spar . . .

. . . as well as on the steering head

US models

On US models the suffix letter is included in the frame number. The first part of the frame number is the model code (JS1GN77A - 600 models, JS1GV75A - 1200 models), followed by the suffix letter (see below), then the actual frame number.

Year	Suffix letter
1996	T
1997	V

The engine number is stamped into the top of the crankcase behind the cylinder block

Buying spare parts

Once you have found all the identification numbers, record them for reference when buying parts. Since the manufacturers change specifications, parts and vendors (companies that manufacture various components on the machine), providing the ID numbers is the only way to be reasonably sure that you are buying the correct parts.

Whenever possible, take the worn part to the dealer so direct comparison with the new component can be made. Along the trail from the manufacturer to the parts shelf, there are numerous places that the part can end up with the wrong number or be listed incorrectly.

The two places to purchase new parts for your motorcycle - the accessory store and the franchised dealer - differ in the type of parts they carry. While dealers can obtain virtually every part for your motorcycle, the accessory dealer is usually limited to normal high wear items such as shock absorbers, tune-up parts, various engine gaskets, cables, chains, brake parts, etc. Rarely will an accessory outlet have major suspension components, cylinders, transmission gears, or cases.

Used parts can be obtained for roughly half the price of new ones, but you can't always be sure of what you're getting. Once again, take your worn part to the breaker (wrecking yard) for direct comparison.

Whether buying new, used or rebuilt parts, the best course is to deal directly with someone who specialises in parts for your particular make.

1 Engine/transmission oil level

Before you start

✔ Take the motorcycle on a short run to allow it to reach normal operating temperature.

 Warning: Do not run the engine in an enclosed space such as a garage or workshop.

✔ Stop the engine and support the motorcycle in an upright position on level ground. Position the motorcycle on its centrestand (where fitted) or on an auxiliary stand. Allow it to stand undisturbed for a few minutes to allow the oil level to stabilise.

✔ The oil level is viewed through the window in the clutch cover on the right-hand side of the engine. Wipe the glass clean before inspection to make the check easier.

Bike care:

● If you have to add oil frequently, you should check whether you have any oil leaks. If there is no sign of oil leakage from the joints and gaskets the engine could be burning oil (see *Fault Finding*).

The correct oil

● Modern, high-revving engines place great demands on their oil. It is very important that the correct oil for your bike is used.
● Always top up with a good quality oil of the specified type and viscosity and do not overfill the engine.

Oil type	API grade SF or SG
Oil viscosity	SAE 10W40

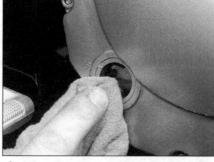

1 Wipe the oil level window in the clutch cover so that it is clean.

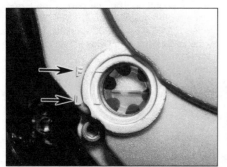

2 With the motorcycle held vertical, the oil level should lie between the F and L lines (arrows).

3 If the level is below the L line, remove the filler cap from the top of the clutch cover ...

4 ... and top the engine up with the recommended grade and type of oil, to bring the level up to the F line on the window.

2 Clutch fluid level (GSF1200 and GSF1200S)

Before you start:

✔ Position the motorcycle on its stand, and turn the handlebars until the top of the clutch fluid reservoir is as level as possible.

✔ Make sure you have the correct hydraulic fluid - DOT 4 is recommended. Wrap a rag around the reservoir to ensure that any spillage does not come into contact with painted surfaces.

Bike care:

● If the fluid reservoir requires repeated topping-up this is an indication of a hydraulic leak somewhere in the system, which should be investigated immediately.
● Check for signs of fluid leakage from the hydraulic hose and components - if found, rectify immediately.
● Check the operation of the clutch; if there is evidence of air in the system (spongy feel to the lever), bleed the clutch as described in Chapter 2.

 Warning: Brake and clutch hydraulic fluid can harm your eyes and damage painted surfaces, so use extreme caution when handling and pouring it and cover surrounding surfaces with rag. Do not use fluid that has been standing open for some time, as it absorbs moisture from the air which can cause a loss of clutch effectiveness.

1 The clutch fluid level is checked via the sightglass in the reservoir - it must be above the LOWER level mark (arrow).

2 If the level is below the LOWER level mark, remove the two screws (arrows) to free the reservoir cover, then remove the cover, diaphragm plate and diaphragm. Top up as described for the front brake in Section 3.

3 Brake fluid levels

> **Warning: Brake and clutch hydraulic fluid can harm your eyes and damage painted surfaces, so use extreme caution when handling and pouring, cover surrounding surfaces with rag. Do not use fluid that has been standing open for some time, as it absorbs moisture from the air which can cause a dangerous loss of braking effectiveness.**

Before you start:

✔ Position the motorcycle on its stand, and turn the handlebars until the top of the front brake master cylinder is as level as possible. Remove the seat and side panels (see Chapter 7) to top up the rear brake fluid reservoir - fluid level can be checked through a hole in the side panel.

✔ Make sure you have the correct hydraulic fluid - DOT 4 is recommended. Wrap a rag around the reservoir being worked on to ensure that any spillage does not come into contact with painted surfaces.

Bike care:

● The fluid in the front and rear brake master cylinder reservoirs will drop slightly as the brake pads wear down.

● If either fluid reservoir requires repeated topping-up this is an indication of an hydraulic leak somewhere in the system, which should be investigated immediately.

● Check for signs of fluid leakage from the hydraulic hoses and components - if found, rectify immediately.

● Check the operation of both brakes before taking the machine on the road; if there is evidence of air in the system (spongy feel to lever or pedal), it must be bled as described in Chapter 6.

1 The front brake fluid level is checked via the sightglass in the reservoir - it must be above the LOWER level mark (arrow).

2 If the level is below the LOWER level mark, remove the two screws (arrows) to free the reservoir cover, then remove the cover, diaphragm plate and diaphragm.

3 Top up with new clean hydraulic fluid of the recommended type, until the level is above the LOWER mark. Take care to avoid spills (see **Warning** above).

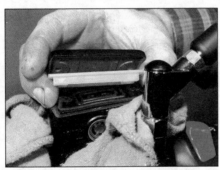

4 Ensure that the diaphragm is correctly seated before installing the plate and cover.

5 The rear brake fluid level can be seen through the translucent body of the reservoir via the hole in the left-hand side panel. The fluid must lie between the LOWER and UPPER level marks (arrows). If necessary, remove the side panels (see Chapter 7) and top up the fluid level using the same procedure for the front brake reservoir (see Steps 2, 3 and 4), noting that there is no diaphragm plate between the cover and the diaphragm.

4 Suspension, steering and drive chain

Suspension and steering:

● Check that the front and rear suspension operates smoothly without binding.

● Check that the suspension is adjusted as required.

● Check that the steering moves smoothly from lock-to-lock.

Drive chain:

● Check that the drive chain slack isn't excessive, and adjust if necessary (see Chapter 1).

● If the chain looks dry, lubricate it (see Chapter 1).

5 Tyres

The correct pressures:

● The tyres must be checked when **cold**, not immediately after riding. Note that low tyre pressures may cause the tyre to slip on the rim or come off. High tyre pressures will cause abnormal tread wear and unsafe handling.

● Use an accurate pressure gauge.

● Proper air pressure will increase tyre life and provide maximum stability and ride comfort.

Tyre care:

● Check the tyres carefully for cuts, tears, embedded nails or other sharp objects and excessive wear. Operation of the motorcycle with excessively worn tyres is extremely hazardous, as traction and handling are directly affected.

● Check the condition of the tyre valve and ensure the dust cap is in place.

● Pick out any stones or nails which may have become embedded in the tyre tread. If left, they will eventually penetrate through the casing and cause a puncture.

● If tyre damage is apparent, or unexplained loss of pressure is experienced, seek the advice of a tyre fitting specialist without delay.

Tyre tread depth:

● At the time of writing UK law requires that tread depth must be at least 1 mm over 3/4 of the tread breadth all the way around the tyre, with no bald patches. Many riders, however, consider 2 mm tread depth minimum to be a safer limit. Suzuki recommend a minimum of 1.6 mm on the front and 2 mm on the rear.

● Many tyres now incorporate wear indicators in the tread. Identify the triangular pointer, or TWI marking, on the tyre sidewall to locate the indicator bar and replace the tyre if the tread has worn down to the bar.

1 Check the tyre pressures when the tyres are **cold** and keep them properly inflated.

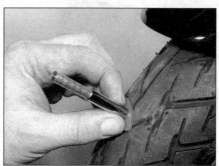

2 Measure tread depth at the centre of the tyre using a tread depth gauge.

3 Tyre tread wear indicator bar and its location marking (usually an arrow, triangle or the letters TWI) on the sidewall (arrows).

Model	Front	Rear
GSF600 and GSF600S	33 psi (2.25 Bar)	36 psi (2.50 Bar)
GSF1200 and GSF1200S	36 psi (2.50 Bar)	36 psi (2.50 Bar)

6 Legal and safety checks

Lighting and signalling:

● Take a minute to check that the headlight, tail light, brake light, instrument lights and turn signals all work correctly.

● Check that the horn sounds when the switch is operated.

● A working speedometer is a statutory requirement in the UK.

Safety:

● Check that the throttle grip rotates smoothly and snaps shut when released, in all steering positions. Also check for the correct amount of freeplay (see Chapter 1).

● On GSF600 and GSF600S models, check that the clutch lever operates smoothly and with the correct amount of freeplay (see Chapter 1).

● Check that the engine shuts off when the kill switch is operated.

● Check that sidestand return spring holds the stand securely up when retracted. The same applies to the centrestand (where fitted).

● Check that the engine cannot be started when the sidestand is down and the engine is in gear.

● Check that the engine cuts out if the sidestand is lowered when the engine is running and in gear.

● Check that the engine cuts out if a gear is selected when the engine is running and the sidestand is down.

Fuel:

● This may seem obvious, but check that you have enough fuel to complete your journey. If you notice signs of fuel leakage - rectify the cause immediately.

● Ensure you use the correct grade unleaded or low-lead fuel - see Chapter 3 Specifications.

Chapter 1
Routine maintenance and servicing

Contents

1

Degrees of difficulty

| Easy, suitable for novice with little experience | | Fairly easy, suitable for beginner with some experience | | Fairly difficult, suitable for competent DIY mechanic | | Difficult, suitable for experienced DIY mechanic | | Very difficult, suitable for expert DIY or professional | |

Engine

Valve clearances (COLD engine)
Intake valves	0.10 to 0.15 mm
Exhaust valves	0.18 to 0.23 mm

Spark plugs
GSF600 and GSF600S
  Type
Standard	NGK CR9EK or Nippondenso U27ETR
For cold climate (below 5°C)	NGK CR8EK or Nippondenso U24ETR
For extended high speed riding	NGK CR10EK or Nippondenso U31ETR
Electrode gap	0.6 to 0.7 mm

GSF1200 and GSF1200S
  Type
Standard	NGK JR9B
For cold climate (below 5°C)	NGK JR8B
For extended high speed riding	NGK JR10B
Electrode gap	0.6 to 0.7 mm

Engine idle speed
US GSF1200 and GSF1200S	1200 ± 50 rpm
All other models	1200 ± 100 rpm

Clutch release mechanism screw (GSF600 and GSF600S)	1/4 to 1/2 a turn out

Cylinder compression
GSF600 and GSF600S
Standard	142 to 213 psi (10 to 15 Bar)*
Minimum	114 psi (8 Bar)*
Maximum difference between cylinders	28 psi (2 Bar)*

GSF1200 and GSF1200S
Standard	178 psi (12.5 Bar)*
Minimum	124 psi (8.75 Bar)*
Maximum difference between cylinders	28 psi (2 Bar)*

Oil pressure (with engine warm)	43 to 85 psi (3.0 to 6.0 Bar) at 3000 rpm, oil at 60°C

*Note: If all cylinders record less than the standard psi (Bar), overhaul is required (see text). If only one cylinder records less than standard psi (Bar), then the engine is good as long as that cylinder is not below the minimum psi (Bar) and the difference between any two cylinders is less than 28 psi (2 Bar).

Miscellaneous

Freeplay adjustments
Clutch lever (GSF600 and GSF600S)	10 to 15 mm

  Throttle cables
Accelerator cable	0.5 to 1.0 mm

    Decelerator cable
GSF600 and GSF600S	0 freeplay
GSF1200 and GSF1200S	0.5 to 1.0 mm

Drive chain
  Freeplay
GSF600 and GSF600S	25 to 35 mm
GSF1200 and GSF1200S	20 to 30 mm
Stretch limit (21 pin length - see text)	319.4 mm

Brake pedal height
GSF600 and GSF600S	40 to 50 mm
GSF1200 and GSF1200S	50 to 60 mm

Tyre pressures (cold)	Front	Rear
GSF600 and GSF600S	33 psi (2.25 Bar)	36 psi (2.50 Bar)
GSF1200 and GSF1200S	36 psi (2.50 Bar)	36 psi (2.50 Bar)

Torque settings

Cylinder head 10 mm domed nuts	38 Nm
Cylinder head 6 mm bolt	10 Nm
Cylinder block nut	9 Nm
Exhaust downpipe clamp bolts	23 Nm
Front silencer bolt	23 Nm
Rear silencer bolt	
GSF600 and GSF600S	23 Nm
GSF1200 and GSF1200S	29 Nm
Valve clearance adjuster locknut	10 Nm
Oil drain plug	23 Nm
Rear axle nut	100 Nm
Steering stem nut	65 Nm
Fork clamp bolts (top yoke)	23 Nm
Suspension linkage rod bolts	
GSF600 and GSF600S	76 Nm
GSF1200 and GSF1200S	78 Nm
Suspension linkage arm bolt	77 Nm
Shock absorber mounting bolts	50 Nm
Swingarm pivot nut	100 Nm

Recommended lubricants and fluids

Drive chain lubricant	Heavy motor oil (40 or 50 weight)
Engine/transmission oil type	API grade SF or SG motor oil
Engine/transmission oil viscosity	SAE 10W40
Engine/transmission oil capacity	
Oil change	3.3 litres
Oil and filter change	3.5 litres
Following engine overhaul - dry engine, new filter	4.6 litres
Brake and clutch fluid	DOT 4
Fork oil type	SAE 10W fork oil
Fork oil capacity	
GSF600 and GSF600S	
UK models	521 cc
US models	522 cc
GSF1200 and GSF1200S	
UK models	516 cc
US models	514 cc
Fork oil level*	
GSF600 and GSF600S	
UK models	97 mm
US models	96 mm
GSF1200 and GSF1200S	
UK models	99 mm
US models	101 mm

Oil level is measured from the top of the tube with the fork spring removed and the leg fully compressed.

Miscellaneous	
Wheel bearings	Multi-purpose grease
Rear suspension bearings	Multi-purpose grease
Steering head bearings	Multi-purpose grease
Cables, lever and stand pivot points	Motor oil
Throttle grip	Multi-purpose grease or dry film lubricant

1

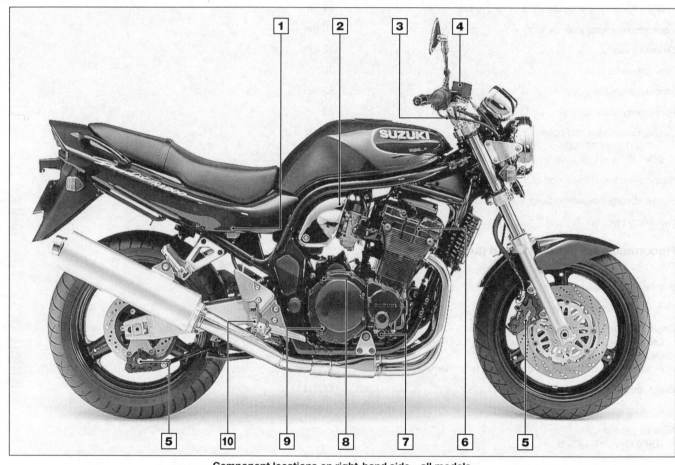

Component locations on right-hand side - all models

1 Rear brake fluid reservoir
2 Air filter
3 Throttle cable upper adjusters
4 Front brake fluid reservoir
5 Brake pads
6 Valves and spark plugs
7 Oil pressure take-off point
8 Engine oil filler cap
9 Engine oil level window
10 Rear brake pedal height adjuster

Component locations on left-hand side - 600 models

1 Clutch cable upper adjuster
2 Steering head bearings
3 Fuel tap filter

4 Carburettor synchronisation screws
5 Idle speed adjuster
6 Battery

7 Drive chain
8 Engine oil drain plug
9 Clutch cable lower adjuster

10 Clutch mechanism adjuster
11 Engine oil filter

Component locations on right-hand side - 1200 models

1 Clutch fluid reservoir
2 Steering head bearings
3 Fuel tap filter

4 Carburettor synchronisation screws
5 Idle speed adjuster

6 Battery
7 Drive chain

8 Engine oil drain plug
9 Engine oil filter

1

Note: *The daily (pre-ride) checks outlined at the beginning of this manual cover those items which should be inspected on a daily basis. Always perform the pre-ride inspection at every maintenance interval (in addition to the procedures listed). The intervals listed below are the intervals recommended by the manufacturer for each particular operation during the model years covered in this manual. Your owner's manual may have different intervals for your model.*

Daily (pre-ride)
☐ See *'Daily (pre-ride) checks'* at the beginning of this manual.

After the initial 600 miles (1000 km)
Note: *This check is usually performed by a Suzuki dealer after the first 600 miles (1000 km) from new. Thereafter, maintenance is carried out according to the following intervals of the schedule.*

Every 600 miles (1000 km)
☐ Clean and lubricate the drive chain (Section 1).
☐ Check and adjust drive chain freeplay (Section 2).

Every 3700 miles (6000 km) or 12 months
Carry out all the items under the Daily (pre-ride) checks and the 600 mile (1000 km) check, plus the following:
☐ Clean the air filter element (Section 3).
☐ Tighten the cylinder head nuts and exhaust pipe bolts - GSF600 and GSF600S (Section 4).
☐ Check the valve clearances - GSF600 and GSF600S (Section 5).
☐ Check the spark plug gaps (Section 6).
☐ Check the fuel hoses and system components (Section 7).
☐ Change the engine oil (Section 8).
☐ Check and adjust the engine idle speed (Section 9).
☐ Check throttle/choke cable operation and freeplay (Section 10).
☐ Check the operation of the clutch (Section 11).
☐ Check for drive chain wear and stretch (Section 12).
☐ Check the brake pads for wear (Section 13).
☐ Check the operation of the brakes, and for fluid leakage (Section 14).
☐ Check the tyre and wheel condition, and the tyre tread depth (Section 15).
☐ Check the tightness of all nuts and bolts (Section 16).

Every 7500 miles (12,000 km) or two years
Carry out all the items under the 3700 mile (6000 km) check, plus the following:
☐ Check the valve clearances - GSF1200 and GSF1200S (Section 17).
☐ Tighten the exhaust pipe bolts - GSF1200 and GSF1200S (Section 18).
☐ Replace the spark plugs (Section 19).

Every 7500 miles (12,000 km) or two years (continued)
☐ Replace the engine oil filter - GSF600 and GSF600S (Section 20).
☐ Check the front and rear suspension (Section 21).
☐ Check the steering head bearing freeplay (Section 22).
☐ Check carburettor synchronisation - GSF1200 and GSF1200S (Section 23).

Every 11,000 miles (18,000 km) or three years
Carry out all the items under the 3700 mile (6000 km) check, plus the following:
☐ Replace the air filter (Section 24).
☐ Replace the engine oil filter - GSF1200 and GSF1200S (Section 25).

Every two years
☐ Change the brake fluid (Section 26).
☐ Change the clutch fluid - GSF1200 and GSF1200S (Section 27).

Every four years
☐ Replace the brake hoses (Section 28).
☐ Replace the fuel hoses and EVAP hoses (California models only) (Section 29).
☐ Replace the clutch hose - GSF1200 and GSF1200S (Section 30)

Non-scheduled maintenance
☐ Check carburettor synchronisation - GSF600 and GSF600S (Section 31).
☐ Check the headlight aim (Section 32).
☐ Check the wheel bearings (Section 33).
☐ Check and lubricate the stands, lever pivots and cables (Section 34).
☐ Change the front fork oil (Section 35).
☐ Check the cylinder compression (Section 36).
☐ Check the engine oil pressure (Section 37).
☐ Re-grease the steering head bearings (Section 38).
☐ Re-grease the swingarm and suspension linkage bearings (Section 39).
☐ Replace the brake master cylinder and caliper seals (Section 40).

Introduction

1 This Chapter is designed to help the home mechanic maintain his/her motorcycle for safety, economy, long life and peak performance.

2 Deciding where to start or plug into the routine maintenance schedule depends on several factors. If the warranty period on your motorcycle has just expired, and if it has been maintained according to the warranty standards, you may want to pick up routine maintenance as it coincides with the next mileage or calendar interval. If you have owned the machine for some time but have never performed any maintenance on it, then you may want to start at the nearest interval and include some additional procedures to ensure that nothing important is overlooked. If you have just had a major engine overhaul, then you may want to start the maintenance routine from the beginning. If you have a used machine and have no knowledge of its history or maintenance record, you may desire to combine all the checks into one large service initially and then settle into the maintenance schedule prescribed.

3 Before beginning any maintenance or repair, the machine should be cleaned thoroughly, especially around the oil filter, spark plugs, valve cover, side panels, carburettors, etc. Cleaning will help ensure that dirt does not contaminate the engine and will allow you to detect wear and damage that could otherwise easily go unnoticed.

4 Certain maintenance information is sometimes printed on decals attached to the motorcycle. If the information on the decals differs from that included here, use the information on the decal.

Every 600 miles (1000 km)

1 Drive chain - cleaning and lubrication

1 Place the machine on its centre stand (where fitted), or support the machine on an auxiliary stand so that the rear wheel is off the ground. Rotate the rear wheel whilst cleaning and lubricating the chain to access all the links.

2 Wash the chain in paraffin (kerosene), then wipe it off and allow it to dry, using compressed air if available. If the chain is excessively dirty it should be removed from the machine and allowed to soak in the paraffin (see Chapter 5).

Caution: Don't use petrol (gasoline), solvent or other cleaning fluids which might damage the internal sealing properties of the chain. Don't use high-pressure water. The entire process shouldn't take longer than ten minutes - if it does, the O-rings in the chain rollers could be damaged.

3 The best time to lubricate the chain is after the motorcycle has been ridden, because when the chain is warm the lubricant penetrates the joints between the side plates better than when cold.

4 Apply the specified lubricant (see Specifications at the beginning of the Chapter) to the area where the side plates overlap - not to the middle of the rollers **(see illustration)**. After applying the lubricant, let it soak in for a few minutes before wiping off any excess.

Caution: If one of the commercial aerosol chain lubricants is used, make sure it is marked as being suitable for O-ring chains.

> **HAYNES HINT** *Apply lubricant to the top of the lower chain run - centrifugal force will work it into the chain when the bike is moving.*

2 Drive chain - freeplay check and adjustment

Check

1 A neglected drive chain won't last long and can quickly damage the sprockets. Routine chain adjustment will ensure maximum chain and sprocket life.

2 To check the chain, shift the transmission into neutral and make sure the ignition switch is OFF. Place the machine on its sidestand.

3 Measure the amount of freeplay on the chain's bottom run, at a point midway between the two sprockets, then compare your measurement to the value listed in this Chapter's Specifications **(see illustration)**. Since the chain will rarely wear evenly, rotate the rear wheel so that another section of chain can be checked; do this several times to check the entire length of chain. In some cases where lubrication has been neglected, corrosion and galling may cause the links to bind and kink, which effectively shortens the chain's length. If the chain is tight between the sprockets, rusty or kinked, or if any of the pins are loose or the rollers damaged, it's time to replace it with a new one. If you find a tight area, mark it with felt pen or paint, and repeat the measurement after the bike has been ridden. If the chain's still tight in the same area, it may be damaged or worn. Because a tight or kinked chain can damage the transmission output shaft bearing, it's a good idea to replace it.

Adjustment

4 Rotate the rear wheel until the chain is positioned with the tightest point at the centre of its bottom run, then place the machine on its sidestand.

5 On US models, remove the split pin from the rear axle nut, then on all models slacken the axle nut **(see illustration)**.

1

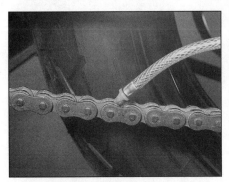

1.4 Apply the specified lubricant to the overlap between the sideplates

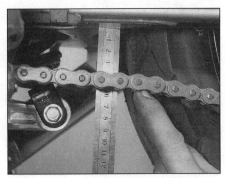

2.3 Measuring drive chain freeplay

2.5 Remove the split pin (where fitted), then slacken the axle nut

2.6a Adjust the chain tension by turning the bolts in the ends of the swingarm

2.6b The cut-out on each adjuster (arrow) must be in the same position relative to the notches in the swingarm

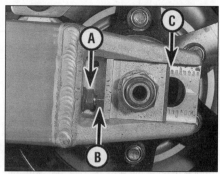

2.7 Slacken each locknut (A), then adjust the chain tension by turning each bolt (B) - back of each adjuster block must be in the same position relative to the notches in the swingarm

6 On GSF600 and GSF600S models, turn the chain adjusting bolt on the end of each side of the swingarm evenly until the amount of freeplay specified at the beginning of the Chapter is obtained at the centre of the bottom run of the chain (see illustration). Following chain adjustment, check that the cut-out on the top of each chain adjuster is in the same position in relation to the marks on the swingarm (see illustration). It is important that each adjuster aligns with the same mark; if not, the rear wheel will be out of alignment with the front.

7 On GSF1200 and GSF1200S models, slacken the adjuster locknut on each side of the swingarm, then turn the adjuster bolts evenly until the amount of freeplay specified at the beginning of the Chapter is obtained at the centre of the bottom run of the chain (see

illustration). Following chain adjustment, check that the back of each chain adjuster block is in the same position in relation to the marks on the swingarm. It is important each adjuster aligns with the same notch; if not, the rear wheel will be out of alignment with the front.

8 If there is a discrepancy in the chain adjuster positions, adjust one of the chain adjusters so that its position is exactly the same as the other. Check the chain freeplay as described above and readjust if necessary. Wheel alignment can be checked as described in Chapter 6.

9 Tighten the axle nut to the torque setting specified at the beginning of the Chapter, then tighten both chain adjuster bolts (600 models) or the adjuster locknuts (1200 models) securely (see illustration). On US models, fit a new split pin to secure the axle nut.

2.9 Tighten the axle nut to the specified torque setting

Every 3700 miles (6000 km) or 12 months

3 Air filter - cleaning

Caution: If the machine is continually ridden in dusty conditions, the filter should be cleaned more frequently.

1 Remove the fuel tank (see Chapter 3).
2 Unscrew the two screws securing the air filter cover to the filter housing (see illustration). Move the breather hoses aside, noting their routing, and remove the cover. Withdraw the filter from the housing (see illustration).
3 Tap the filter on a hard surface to dislodge

any dirt. If compressed air is available, use it to clean the element, directing the air from the inside (see illustration). If the element is torn or extremely dirty, replace it with a new one.
4 Install the filter by reversing the removal procedure. Make sure the filter is properly seated and the tabs on the bottom of the

3.2a The air filter cover is secured by two screws (arrows)

3.2b Remove the cover and lift out the filter

3.3 Clean the element using compressed air directed from the inside

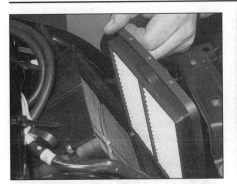

3.4a Make sure the filter is installed the right way round . . .

3.4b . . . then fit the cover . . .

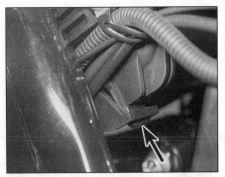

3.4c . . . locating its tabs in the slots in the housing (arrow)

3.5 Remove the plug and allow any fluid to drain

4.3a Slacken the cylinder head front bolt (arrow)

cover locate into the slots in the housing **(see illustrations)**.

5 Trace the air filter housing drain hose from the base of the housing and remove the drain plug from its end **(see illustration)**. Allow any fluid to drain, then install the plug.

4 Cylinder head nuts and exhaust system bolts - check (GSF600 and GSF600S)

1 Suzuki recommend that the cylinder head

nuts and exhaust pipe bolts are checked to ensure they are tightened to their correct torque settings. The engine must be completely cool for these maintenance procedures, so let the machine sit overnight before beginning.

Cylinder head nuts

2 Remove the valve cover (see Chapter 2).
3 The cylinder head is secured by eight 10 mm domed nuts, four 10 mm plain nuts and one 6 mm bolt. Slacken the bolt at the front of

the cylinder head **(see illustration)**. The nuts are numbered for identification **(see illustrations)**. Slacken them evenly and a little at a time in a **reverse** of their numerical sequence until they are all slack.

4 Using a torque wrench, tighten the domed nuts evenly and a little at a time in the numerical sequence to the torque setting specified at the beginning of the Chapter **(see illustrations 4.3b and c)**.

5 When the nuts are correctly torqued, tighten the plain bolt at the front of the cylinder head to the specified torque setting

1

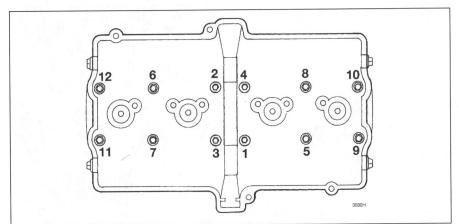

4.3b Cylinder head TIGHTENING sequence

12 6   2 4   8 10

11 7   3 1   5 9

0530H

4.3c The cylinder head nut tightening sequence numbers are cast into the head next to the nuts; loosen from the highest number to the lowest, and tighten from the lowest to the highest

4.5 Tighten the cylinder head bolt and the cylinder block nut to the specified torque settings

4.7a Tighten the downpipe clamp bolts . . .

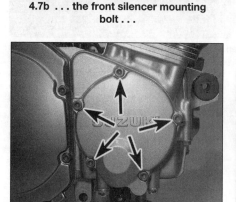

4.7b . . . the front silencer mounting bolt . . .

4.7c . . . and the rear silencer mounting bolt to the specified torque settings

5.4 The pulse generator coil assembly cover is secured by five bolts (arrows)

5.5 Turn the rotor using a spanner until it is aligned with the pick-up coil as shown

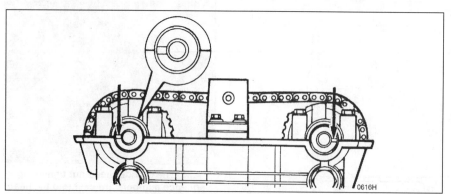

5.6a When correctly positioned for the first stage of valve clearance adjustment, the camshaft notches (arrows) should point away from each other - if they don't, turn the engine another full turn

(see illustration). Also check that the nut securing the front of the cylinder block to the crankcase is tightened to the specified torque.
6 Install the valve cover (see Chapter 2).

Exhaust pipe bolts

7 Using a torque wrench, check that the eight exhaust downpipe clamp bolts and the silencer mounting bolts are tightened to the torque settings specified at the beginning of the Chapter **(see illustrations)**.

5 Valve clearances - check and adjustment (GSF600 and GSF600S)

1 The engine must be completely cool for this maintenance procedure, so let the machine sit overnight before beginning.
2 Remove the plug caps from the spark plugs.
3 Remove the valve cover (see Chapter 2). Remove the spark plugs (see Section 6).
4 Unscrew the five bolts securing the pulse generator coil assembly cover to the right-hand side of the engine **(see illustration)**.
5 Turn the crankshaft in a clockwise direction with a 19 mm spanner or socket on the large hex of the signal generator rotor until the T mark is aligned with the protrusion on the pickup coil **(see illustration)**. Alternatively, place the motorcycle on its centrestand or an auxiliary stand, select a high gear and rotate the rear wheel by hand in its normal direction of rotation to turn the engine.
Caution: DO NOT use the signal generator Allen bolt to turn the crankshaft - it may snap or strip out. Also be sure to turn the engine in its normal direction of rotation.
6 The notches in the ends of the camshafts should now be pointing away from each other and aligned with the gasket mating surface on the cylinder head **(see illustration)**. Also check the position of the no. 1 cylinder cam lobes - they should be in one of the acceptable positions for valve adjustment **(see illustrations)**. If the camshafts aren't

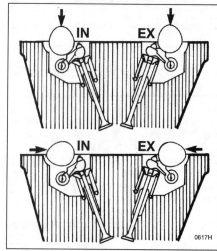

5.6b Acceptable cam lobe positions for valve adjustment

5.8 Check the valve clearance using a feeler gauge

5.9 Loosen the locknut and adjust the clearance by turning the screw using a pair of pliers

positioned correctly, rotate the engine one full turn more, until the rotor T mark again lines up with the protrusion on the pick-up coil. The camshafts should now be positioned correctly.

7 With the engine in this position, the following valves can be checked:
  a) no. 1, intake and exhaust valves
  b) no. 2, exhaust valves
  c) no. 3, intake valves

8 Start with the no. 1 intake valve clearance. Insert a feeler gauge of the thickness listed in this Chapter's Specifications between each valve stem and cam lobe adjuster screw **(see illustration)**. Pull the feeler gauge out slowly - you should feel a slight drag. If there's no drag, the clearance is too loose. If there's a heavy drag, or the gauge will not fit, the clearance is too tight.

9 If the clearance is incorrect, loosen the adjuster screw locknut with a spanner and turn the adjuster screw in or out as needed until the specified clearance is obtained **(see illustration)**.

10 Hold the adjuster screw (to keep it from turning) and tighten the locknut. Recheck the clearance on both intake valves to make sure nothing has changed.

11 Now adjust the remaining valves listed in Step 7, following the same procedure you used for the no. 1 cylinder intake valves. Make sure you use a feeler gauge of the specified thickness - intake and exhaust valve clearances differ.

12 Rotate the crankshaft one full turn and again align the T mark on the rotor with the protrusion on the pickup coil **(see illustration 5.5)**. The notches in the ends of the camshafts should now point toward each other **(see illustration)**.

13 Check and adjust the following valves as described in Steps 8, 9 and 10 **(see illustrations 5.8 and 5.9)**:
  a) no. 2, intake valves
  b) no. 3, exhaust valves
  c) no. 4, intake and exhaust valves

14 Install all disturbed components in a reverse of the removal sequence. Use a new gasket on the pulse generator cover, and

make sure the sealing washer is installed with the top bolt **(see illustrations)**.

6 Spark plug gaps -
check and adjustment

1 Make sure your spark plug socket is the correct size before attempting to remove the

plugs - a suitable one is supplied in the motorcycle's tool kit which is stored under the seat.

2 Remove the seat (see Chapter 7) and disconnect the battery negative (-) lead.

3 Clean the area around the plug caps to prevent any dirt falling into the spark plug channels.

4 Check that the cylinder location is marked on each plug lead, then pull the spark plug

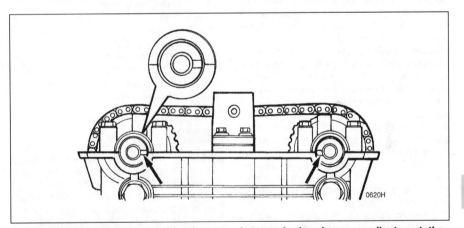

5.12 When correctly positioned for the second stage of valve clearance adjustment, the camshaft notches (arrows) should face each other - if they don't, turn the engine another full turn

5.14a Install the cover using a new gasket . . .

5.14b . . . and make sure the sealing washer is installed on the top bolt

1

6.4a Remove the spark plug cap . . .

6.4b . . . then unscrew the spark plug

cap off each spark plug **(see illustration)**. Using either the plug removing tool supplied in the bike's toolkit or a socket type wrench, unscrew the plugs from the cylinder head **(see illustration)**. Lay each plug out in relation to its cylinder; if any plug shows up a problem it will then be easy to identify the troublesome cylinder.

5 Inspect the electrodes for wear. Both the centre and side electrodes should have square edges and the side electrodes should be of uniform thickness. Look for excessive deposits and evidence of a cracked or chipped insulator around the centre electrode. Compare your spark plugs to the colour spark plug reading chart at the end of this manual. Check the threads, the washer and the ceramic insulator body for cracks and other damage.

6 If the electrodes are not excessively worn, and if the deposits can be easily removed with a wire brush, the plugs can be re-gapped and re-used (if no cracks or chips are visible in the insulator). If in doubt concerning the condition of the plugs, replace them with new ones, as the expense is minimal.

7 Cleaning spark plugs by sandblasting is permitted, provided you clean the plugs with a high flash-point solvent afterwards.

8 Before installing the plugs, make sure they are the correct type and heat range and check the gap between each outer electrode and the centre electrode **(see illustration)**. Compare the gap to that specified and adjust as necessary. If the gap must be adjusted, bend the side electrodes only and be very careful not to chip or crack the insulator nose **(see illustration)**. Make sure the washer is in place before installing each plug.

9 Since the cylinder head is made of aluminium, which is soft and easily damaged, thread the plugs into the heads by hand **(see illustration)**. Once the plugs are finger-tight, the job can be finished with the tool supplied or a socket. Tighten the spark plugs to the specified torque setting - do not over-tighten them.

> **HAYNES HiNT**
> *As the plugs are quite recessed, slip a short length of hose over the end of the plug to use as a tool to thread it into place. The hose will grip the plug well enough to turn it, but will start to slip if the plug begins to cross-thread in the hole - this will prevent damaged threads.*

10 Reconnect the spark plug caps, making sure they are securely connected to the correct cylinder. Install all components previously removed.

> **HAYNES HiNT**
> *Stripped plug threads in the cylinder head can be repaired with a Heli-Coil insert - see 'Tools and Workshop Tips' in the Reference section.*

7 Fuel system - check

> ⚠ *Warning: Petrol (gasoline) is extremely flammable, so take extra precautions when you work on any part of the fuel system. Don't smoke or allow open flames or bare light bulbs near the work area, and don't work in a garage where a natural gas-type appliance is present. If you spill any fuel on your skin, rinse it off immediately with soap and water. When*

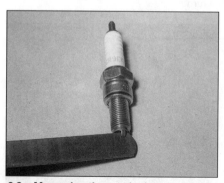

6.8a Measuring the spark plug gaps using a feeler gauge

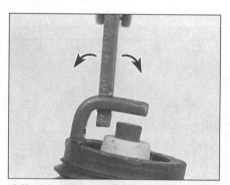

6.8b Adjust the electrode gap by bending the side electrode only, as indicated by the arrows

6.9 Thread the plug in as far as possible by hand

you perform any kind of work on the fuel system, wear safety glasses and have a fire extinguisher suitable for a Class B type fire (flammable liquids) on hand.

Check

1 Remove the fuel tank (see Chapter 3) and check the tank, the fuel tap, and the fuel hoses for signs of leakage, deterioration or damage; in particular check that there is no leakage from the fuel hoses. Replace any hoses which are cracked or deteriorated.
2 If the fuel tap is leaking, remove the tap and tighten the assembly screws on the back of the tap (see Chapter 3). If leakage persists unscrew the screws and disassemble the tap, noting how the components fit. Inspect all components for wear or damage. If any of the components are worn or damaged, a new tap must be fitted.
3 If the carburettor gaskets are leaking, the carburettors should be disassembled and rebuilt using new gaskets and seals (see Chapter 3).

Filter cleaning

4 Cleaning or replacement of the fuel filter is advised after a particularly high mileage has been covered. It is also necessary if fuel starvation is suspected.
5 The fuel filter is mounted in the tank and is integral with the fuel tap. Remove the fuel tank and the fuel tap (see Chapter 3). Clean the gauze filter to remove all traces of dirt and fuel sediment. Check the gauze for holes. If any are found, a new filter should be fitted (check for availability - it may be necessary to replace the whole tap). Check the condition of the O-ring and replace it if it is in any way damaged or deteriorated.

8 Engine/transmission - oil change

 Warning: Be careful when draining the oil, as the exhaust pipes, the engine, and the oil itself can cause severe burns.

1 Consistent routine oil and filter changes are the single most important maintenance

procedure you can perform on a motorcycle. The oil not only lubricates the internal parts of the engine, transmission and clutch, but it also acts as a coolant, a cleaner, a sealant, and a protectant. Because of these demands, the oil takes a terrific amount of abuse and should be replaced often with new oil of the recommended grade and type. Saving a little money on the difference in cost between a good oil and a cheap oil won't pay off if the engine is damaged. The oil filter should be changed with every second oil change on 600 models (see Section 20), and with every third change on 1200 models (see Section 25).
2 Before changing the oil, warm up the engine so the oil will drain easily.
3 Put the motorcycle on its centrestand (where fitted), or support it upright using an auxiliary stand, and position a clean drain tray below the engine. Unscrew the oil filler cap on the clutch cover to vent the crankcase and to act as a reminder that there is no oil in the engine **(see illustration)**.
4 Next, unscrew the oil drain plug from the bottom of the engine and allow the oil to flow into the drain tray **(see illustrations)**. Discard the sealing washer on the drain plug as it should be replaced whenever the plug is removed.
5 When the oil has completely drained, fit a new sealing washer over the drain plug. Fit the plug to the sump and tighten it to the torque setting specified at the beginning of the Chapter. Avoid overtightening, as damage to the sump will result.
6 Refill the crankcase to the proper level using the recommended type and amount of oil (see Specifications). Check the oil level as described in Daily (pre-ride) checks. Start the engine and let it run for two or three minutes (make sure that the oil pressure light extinguishes after a few seconds). Shut it off, wait a few minutes, then recheck the oil level and add more oil if necessary. Check around the drain plug for leaks.

 HAYNES HiNT *Saving a little money on the difference between good and cheap oils won't pay off if the engine is damaged as a result.*

7 The old oil drained from the engine cannot be re-used and should be disposed of properly. Check with your local refuse disposal company, disposal facility or environmental agency to see whether they will accept the used oil for recycling. Don't pour used oil into drains or onto the ground.

 **HAYNES HiNT** *Check the old oil carefully - if it is very metallic coloured, then the engine is experiencing wear from break-in (new engine) or from insufficient lubrication. If there are flakes or chips of metal in the oil, then something is drastically wrong internally and the engine will have to be disassembled for inspection and repair. If there are pieces of fibre-like material in the oil, the clutch is experiencing excessive wear and should be checked.*

OIL CARE *FOLLOW THE CODE*
OIL BANK LINE
0800 66 33 66

Note: It is antisocial and illegal to dump oil down the drain. To find the location of your local oil recycling bank, call this number free.

In the USA, note that any oil supplier must accept used oil for recycling

9 Idle speed - check and adjustment

1 The idle speed should be checked and adjusted before and after the carburettors are synchronised (balanced) and when it is obviously too high or too low. Before adjusting the idle speed, make sure the valve clearances and spark plug gaps are correct. Also, turn the handlebars back-and-forth and see if the idle speed changes as this is done. If it does, the throttle cable may not be adjusted correctly, or may be worn out. This is

1

8.3 Unscrew the oil filler cap

8.4a Unscrew the oil drain plug (arrow) . . .

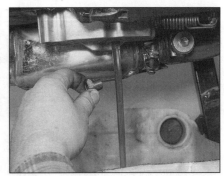

8.4b . . . and allow the oil to drain

a dangerous condition that can cause loss of control of the bike. Be sure to correct this problem before proceeding.

2 The engine should be at normal operating temperature, which is usually reached after 10 to 15 minutes of stop and go riding. Place the motorcycle on its centrestand (where fitted), or support it upright using an auxiliary stand, and make sure the transmission is in neutral.

3 With the engine idling, adjust the idle speed by turning the throttle stop screw in or out until the idle speed listed in this Chapter's Specifications is obtained. The throttle stop screw is located centrally under the carburettors (see illustration).

4 Snap the throttle open and shut a few times, then recheck the idle speed. If necessary, repeat the adjustment procedure.

5 If a smooth, steady idle can't be achieved, the fuel/air mixture may be incorrect (see Chapter 3) or the carburettors may need synchronising (see Section 23).

10 Throttle and choke cables - check

Throttle cables

1 Make sure the throttle grip rotates easily from fully closed to fully open with the front

wheel turned at various angles. The grip should return automatically from fully open to fully closed when released.

2 If the throttle sticks, this is probably due to a cable fault. Remove the cables (see Chapter 3) and lubricate them (see Section 34). Install the cables, making sure they are correctly routed. If this fails to improve the operation of the throttle, the cables must be replaced. Note that in very rare cases the fault could lie in the carburettors rather than the cables, necessitating the removal of the carburettors and inspection of the throttle linkage (see Chapter 3).

3 With the throttle operating smoothly, check for a small amount of freeplay in the cables and compare the amount to that listed in this Chapter's Specifications (see illustration). If it's incorrect, adjust the cables to correct it.

4 Freeplay adjustments can be made at the throttle end of the cable. Loosen the locknut on the accelerator cable where it leaves the handlebar (see illustration). Turn the adjuster until the specified amount of freeplay is obtained (see this Chapter's Specifications), then retighten the locknut.

5 If the cable can't be adjusted within specifications, reset the adjuster at the carburettor end (see Chapter 3). Otherwise, replace the cable (see Chapter 3).

6 Adjust the decelerator cable in the same manner until the specified amount of freeplay is obtained (see illustration 10.4).

⚠️ **Warning: Turn the handlebars all the way through their travel with the engine idling. Idle speed should not change. If it does, the cable may be routed incorrectly. Correct this condition before riding the bike.**

7 Check that the throttle twistgrip operates smoothly and snaps shut quickly when released.

Choke cable

8 If the choke does not operate smoothly this is probably due to a cable fault. Remove the cable (see Chapter 3) and lubricate it (see Section 34). Install the cable, routing it so it takes the smoothest route possible.

9 Check for a small amount of freeplay in the cable and adjust it if necessary using the adjuster at the lever end of the cable, using the method described in Step 4 above for the throttle cables (see illustration). If this fails to improve the operation of the choke, the cable must be replaced. Note that in very rare cases the fault could lie in the carburettors rather than the cable, necessitating the removal of the carburettors and inspection of the choke valves (see Chapter 3).

11 Clutch - check

GSF600 and GSF600S

Cable adjustment

1 Periodic adjustment of the clutch cable is necessary to compensate for wear in the clutch plates and stretch of the cable. Check that the amount of freeplay at the clutch lever end is within the specifications listed at the beginning of the Chapter (see illustration). If adjustment is required, it can be made at either the lever end of the cable or at the clutch end.

2 To adjust the freeplay at the lever, pull back the rubber cover, then loosen the locking ring and turn the adjuster in or out until the

9.3 Throttle stop screw (arrow)

10.3 Throttle cable freeplay is measured in terms of the amount of outer cable movement in the adjuster

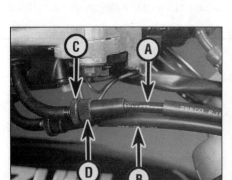

10.4 Accelerator cable (A), decelerator cable (B), locknut (C) and adjuster (D)

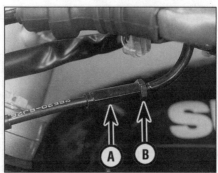

10.9 Choke cable adjuster (A) and locknut (B)

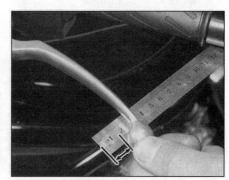

11.1 Measuring clutch lever freeplay

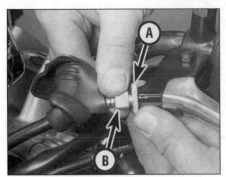

11.2 Locking ring (A), adjuster (B) at clutch lever end

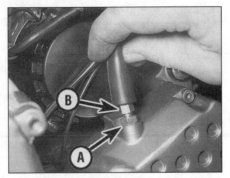

11.4 Lift the rubber cover to expose the locknut (A) and adjuster (B) at the lower end of the clutch cable

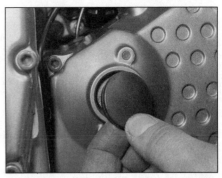

11.5 Remove the rubber cover to expose the release mechanism

required amount of freeplay is obtained **(see illustration)**. To increase freeplay, turn the adjuster clockwise. To reduce freeplay, turn the adjuster anti-clockwise. Tighten the locking ring securely and slip the rubber cover into place.

3 If all the adjustment has been taken up at the lever, reset the adjuster (turn it fully clockwise) to give the maximum amount of freeplay, then set the correct amount of freeplay using the adjuster at the clutch end of the cable. Subsequent adjustments can then be made using the lever adjuster only.

4 To adjust the freeplay at the clutch end of the cable, pull up the rubber cover on the top of the engine sprocket cover, then loosen the locknut and turn the adjuster until the required amount of freeplay is obtained **(see illustration)**. To increase freeplay, turn the adjuster clockwise. To reduce freeplay, turn the adjuster anti-clockwise. Tighten the locknut securely and slip the rubber cover into place.

Release mechanism adjustment

5 Remove the rubber cover from the clutch release mechanism set in the engine sprocket cover **(see illustration)**.

6 Pull back the rubber cover on the adjuster at the lever end of the cable, then fully slacken the locking ring and screw the adjuster fully in **(see illustration 11.2)**. This creates slack in the cable.

7 Slacken the locknut on the release

mechanism, then unscrew the adjuster screw a few turns. Now turn the adjuster screw in until resistance is felt, then back it off 1/4 to 1/2 a turn **(see illustration)**.

8 Hold the adjuster screw steady and tighten the locknut **(see illustration)**. Replace the rubber cover.

9 Pull up the rubber cover on the adjuster on the top of the sprocket cover, then loosen the locknut and turn the adjuster until the specified amount of freeplay is obtained **(see illustration 11.4)**. Tighten the locknut and slip the rubber cover into place. Check that the locking ring on the adjuster at the lever end of the cable is tight and slip the rubber cover into place.

GSF1200 and GSF1200S

10 These models are fitted with an hydraulic clutch, for which there is no method of adjustment.

11 Check the fluid level in the reservoir (see *Daily (pre-ride) checks*).

12 Inspect the hose and its connections for signs of fluid leakage, cracking, deterioration and wear. The clutch fluid should be changed every two years (see Section 27), and the hoses replaced every four years (see Section 30), irrespective of their condition at that stage.

13 Check the operation of the clutch; if there is evidence of air in the system (spongy feel to the lever), bleed the clutch as described in Chapter 2.

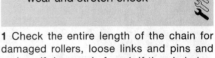

12 Drive chain -
wear and stretch check

1 Check the entire length of the chain for damaged rollers, loose links and pins and replace if damage is found. If the chain has reached the end of its adjustment, it must be replaced.

2 The amount of chain stretch can be measured and compared to the stretch limit specified at the beginning of the Chapter. On US models, remove the split pin from the rear axle nut, then on all models slacken the axle nut. On 1200 models, slacken the adjuster locknuts, then on all models turn the chain adjusting bolts on each side of the swingarm evenly until the chain is tight. Measure along the bottom run the length of 21 pins (from the centre of the 1st pin to the centre of the 21st pin) and compare the result with the service limit specified at the beginning of the Chapter **(see illustration)**. Rotate the rear wheel so that several sections of the chain are measured, then calculate the average. If the chain exceeds the service limit it must be replaced (see Chapter 5). **Note:** *It is good practice to replace the chain and sprockets as a set.*

3 Check the teeth on the engine sprocket and the rear wheel sprocket for wear (see Chapter 5).

4 Inspect the drive chain slider on the swingarm for excessive wear and replace it if necessary (see Chapter 5).

1

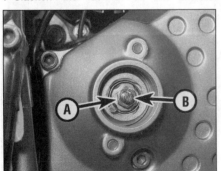

11.7 Slacken the locknut (A) and turn the adjuster screw (B) on the release mechanism

11.8 Counter-hold the adjuster while tightening the locknut

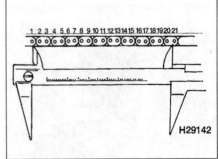

H29142

12.2 Measure the distance between the 1st and 21st pins to determine drive chain stretch

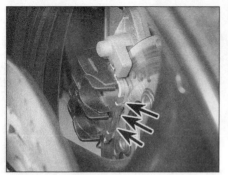

13.1a Front brake pad wear indicator grooves - pad installed . . .

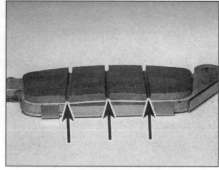

13.1b . . . and pad removed (600 models . . .

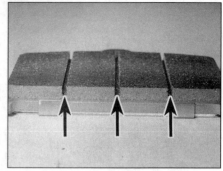

13.1c . . . and 1200 models)

13.1d Rear brake pad wear indicator line and groove shown installed . . .

13.1e . . . and removed

13 Brake pads - wear check

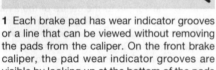

1 Each brake pad has wear indicator grooves or a line that can be viewed without removing the pads from the caliper. On the front brake caliper, the pad wear indicator grooves are visible by looking up at the bottom of the pads **(see illustrations)**. On the rear brake caliper, the pad wear indicator is visible by looking down onto the bottom of the pads **(see illustrations)**.
2 If the pads are worn to or beyond the base of the grooves, they must be replaced. If the pads are dirty or if you are in doubt as to the amount of friction material remaining, remove them for inspection (see Chapter 6). **Note:** *Some after-market pads may use different indicators to those on the original equipment as shown.*
3 Refer to Chapter 6 for details of pad replacement.

14 Brake system - check

1 A routine general check of the brake system will ensure that any problems are discovered and remedied before the rider's safety is jeopardised.
2 Check the brake lever and pedal for loose connections, improper or rough action, excessive play, bends, and other damage. Replace any damaged parts with new ones (see Chapter 6).
3 Make sure all brake fasteners are tight. Check the brake pads for wear (see Section 13) and make sure the fluid level in the reservoirs is correct (see *Daily (pre-ride) checks*). Look for leaks at the hose connections and check for cracks in the hoses. If the lever or pedal is spongy, bleed the brakes (see Chapter 6).
4 Make sure the brake light operates when the front brake lever is depressed. The front brake light switch is not adjustable. If it fails to operate properly, check it (see Chapter 8).
5 Make sure the brake light is activated just before the rear brake pedal takes effect. If adjustment is necessary, hold the switch and turn the adjusting nut on the switch body until the brake light is activated when required **(see illustration)**. If the switch doesn't operate the brake light, check it (see Chapter 8).
6 Check the position of the brake pedal. The distance between the top of the end of the brake pedal and the top of the rider's footrest should be as specified at the beginning of the Chapter **(see illustration)**. If the pedal height is incorrect, slacken the locknut on the master cylinder pushrod, then turn the pushrod adjuster until the pedal is at the correct height **(see illustration)**. Tighten the locknut securely. Adjust the rear brake light switch after adjusting the pedal height (see Step 5).

14.5 Rear brake light switch adjuster nut (arrow)

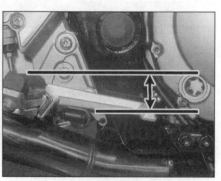

14.6a Measuring rear brake pedal height

14.6b Master cylinder pushrod locknut (A) and adjuster (B)

7 The front brake lever has a span adjuster which alters the distance of the lever from the handlebar **(see illustration)**. Pull the lever away from the handlebar and turn the adjuster dial until the setting which best suits the rider is obtained. There are four positions.

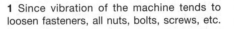
14.7 Adjusting the front brake lever span

15 Wheels and tyres - general check

Tyres

1 Check the tyre condition and tread depth thoroughly - see *Daily (pre-ride) checks*.

Wheels

2 Cast wheels are virtually maintenance free, but they should be kept clean and checked periodically for cracks and other damage. Also check the wheel runout and alignment (see Chapter 6). Never attempt to repair damaged cast wheels; they must be replaced with new ones. Check the valve rubber for signs of damage or deterioration and have it replaced if necessary. Also, make sure the valve stem cap is in place and tight.

16 Nuts and bolts - tightness check

1 Since vibration of the machine tends to loosen fasteners, all nuts, bolts, screws, etc.

should be periodically checked for proper tightness.
2 Pay particular attention to the following:

Spark plugs
Engine oil drain plug
Gearshift pedal bolt
Footrest and stand bolts
Engine mounting bolts
Shock absorber mounting bolts and suspension linkage bolts
Handlebar bolts
Front axle nut and clamp bolt
Front fork clamp bolts (top and bottom yoke)
Rear axle nut
Swingarm pivot nut
Brake caliper mounting bolts
Brake hose banjo bolts and caliper bleed valves
Brake disc bolts and rear sprocket nuts
Exhaust system bolts/nuts

3 If a torque wrench is available, use it along with the torque specifications at the beginning of this, or other, Chapters.

Every 7500 miles (12,000 km) or two years

Carry out all the items under the 3700 mile (6000 km) check, plus the following:

17 Valve clearances - check and adjustment (GSF1200 and GSF1200S)

1 The procedure for checking and adjusting the valve clearances is the same as for the 600 models (see Section 5).

18 Exhaust system bolts - tightness check (GSF1200 and GSF1200S)

1 Using a torque wrench, check that the exhaust downpipe clamp bolts and the silencer mounting bolts are tightened to the

torque settings specified at the beginning of the Chapter **(see illustrations 4.7a, b and c)**.

19 Spark plugs - replacement

1 Remove the old spark plugs as described in Section 6 and install new ones.

20 Engine/transmission - oil filter replacement (GSF600 and GSF600S)

Note: *This procedure should be carried out in conjunction with the routine oil change (see Section 8).*

1 Drain the engine oil (see Section 8, Steps 1 to 4).
2 Position the oil drain tray so that it is below the oil filter, which is located behind the exhaust downpipes on the front of the engine. Using an oil filter removal tool (there are several types commercially available at low cost), unscrew the filter **(see illustrations)**. Clean the filter thread and housing on the crankcase using clean rag. Wipe off any remaining oil from the filter sealing area.
3 When the oil has completely drained, apply a smear of clean engine oil to the rubber sealing ring on the new filter, then install the filter onto the engine and thread it on until the gasket just touches the engine **(see illustrations)**. Tighten the filter two full turns from the initial contact using the method employed on removal **(see**

1

20.2a Remove the oil filter with a chain or strap wrench ...

20.2b ... or a special socket

20.3a Smear clean engine oil onto the sealing ring ...

20.3b . . . then install the filter . . .

20.3c . . . and tighten it the specified amount with a special socket or filter wrench - a strap-type wrench like this one can be used

21.3a Lever off the fork dust seal . . .

illustration). Do not overtighten the filter as the seal will be damaged and the filter will leak.

4 Follow steps 5 to 7 in Section 8.

21 Suspension - check

1 The suspension components must be maintained in top operating condition to ensure rider safety. Loose, worn or damaged suspension parts decrease the motorcycle's stability and control.

Front suspension

2 While standing alongside the motorcycle, apply the front brake and push on the handlebars to compress the forks several times. See if they move up-and-down smoothly without binding. If binding is felt, the forks should be disassembled and inspected (see Chapter 5).

3 Inspect the area above the dust seal for signs of oil leakage, then carefully lever off the dust seal using a flat-bladed screwdriver and inspect the area around the fork seal **(see illustrations)**. If leakage is evident, the seals must be replaced (see Chapter 5).

4 Check the tightness of all suspension nuts and bolts to be sure none have worked loose.

Rear suspension

5 Inspect the rear shock for fluid leakage and tightness of its mountings. If leakage is found, the shock should be replaced (see Chapter 5).

6 With the aid of an assistant to support the bike, compress the rear suspension several times. It should move up and down freely without binding. If any binding is felt, the worn or faulty component must be identified and replaced. The problem could be due to either the shock absorber, the suspension linkage components or the swingarm components.

7 Position the motorcycle on its centrestand (where fitted), or support it using an auxiliary stand so that the rear wheel is off the ground. Grab the swingarm and rock it from side to side - there should be no discernible movement at the rear **(see illustration)**. If there's a little movement or a slight clicking can be heard, inspect the tightness of all the rear suspension mounting bolts and nuts, referring to the torque settings specified at the beginning of the Chapter, and re-check for movement. Next, grasp the top of the rear wheel and pull it upwards - there should be no discernible freeplay before the shock absorber begins to compress **(see illustration)**. Any freeplay felt in either check indicates worn bearings in the suspension linkage or swingarm, or worn shock absorber mountings. The worn components must be replaced (see Chapter 5).

8 To make an accurate assessment of the swingarm bearings, remove the rear wheel (see Chapter 6) and the bolt securing the suspension linkage rods to the linkage arm (see Chapter 5). Grasp the rear of the swingarm with one hand and place your other hand at the junction of the swingarm and the frame. Try to move the rear of the swingarm from side-to-side. Any wear (play) in the bearings should be felt as movement between the swingarm and the frame at the front. If there is any play, the swingarm will be felt to move forward and backward at the front (not from side-to-side). Next, move the swingarm up and down through its full travel. It should move freely, without any binding or rough spots. If any play in the swingarm is noted or if the swingarm does not move freely, the bearings must be removed for inspection or replacement (see Chapter 5).

22 Steering head bearings - freeplay check and adjustment

1 This motorcycle is equipped with tapered roller steering head bearings which can become dented, rough or loose during normal use of the machine. In extreme cases, worn or loose steering head bearings can cause steering wobble - a condition that is potentially dangerous.

21.3b . . . and check for signs of oil leakage

21.7a Checking for play . . .

21.7b . . . in the rear suspension assembly

22.4 Checking for play in the steering head bearings

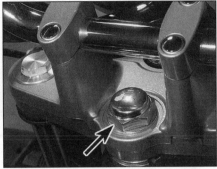

22.5a Slacken the steering stem nut (arrow) . . .

22.5b . . . and each fork clamp bolt (arrow)

Check

2 Place the motorcycle on its centrestand. Raise the front wheel off the ground either by having an assistant push down on the rear or by placing a support under the engine.

3 Point the front wheel straight-ahead and slowly move the handlebars from side-to-side. Any dents or roughness in the bearing races will be felt and the bars will not move smoothly and freely.

4 Next, grasp the fork sliders and try to move them forward and backward **(see illustration)**. Any looseness in the steering head bearings will be felt as front-to-rear movement of the forks. If play is felt in the bearings, adjust the steering head as follows.

> **HAYNES HiNT** *Freeplay in the fork due to worn fork bushes can be misinterpreted for steering head bearing play - do not confuse the two.*

Adjustment

5 Although not essential, it is wise to remove the fuel tank (see Chapter 3) to avoid the possibility of damage should a tool slip while adjustment is being made. Slacken the steering stem nut, then slacken the fork clamp bolts in the top yoke **(see illustrations)**. **Note:** *Depending on the tools available, it may be necessary to displace the handlebars in order to provide enough clearance (see Chapter 5).*

6 Using a suitable drift located in one of the notches in the adjuster ring, slacken the adjuster ring slightly by tapping the drift with a hammer, until pressure is just released, then tighten it until all freeplay in the forks is removed, yet the steering is able to move freely from side to side **(see illustration)**. The object is to set the adjuster ring so that the bearings are under a very light loading, just enough to remove any freeplay.

Caution: Take great care not to apply excessive pressure because this will cause premature failure of the bearings.

7 If the bearings cannot be set up properly, or if there is any binding, roughness or notchiness, they will have to be removed for inspection or replacement (see Chapter 5).

8 With the bearings correctly adjusted, tighten the steering stem nut and the fork clamp bolts to the torque settings specified at the beginning of the Chapter. **Note:** *Depending on the tools available, it may be necessary to displace the handlebars in order to provide enough clearance for a socket and torque wrench (see Chapter 5).*

9 Check the bearing adjustment as described above and re-adjust if necessary.

23 Carburettors - synchronisation (GSF1200 and GSF1200S)

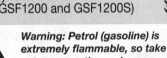

> ⚠ *Warning: Petrol (gasoline) is extremely flammable, so take extra precautions when you work on any part of the fuel system. Don't smoke or allow open flames or bare light bulbs near the work area, and don't work in a garage where a natural gas-type appliance is present. If you spill any fuel on your skin, rinse it off immediately with soap and water. When you perform any kind of work on the fuel system, wear safety glasses and have a fire extinguisher suitable for a Class B type fire (flammable liquids) on hand.*
> *Warning: Take great care not to burn your hand on the hot engine unit when accessing the gauge take-off points on the intake manifolds. Do not allow exhaust gases to build up in the work area; either perform the check outside or use an exhaust gas extraction system.*

1 Carburettor synchronisation is simply the process of adjusting the carburettors so they pass the same amount of fuel/air mixture to each cylinder. This is done by measuring the vacuum produced in each cylinder. Carburettors that are out of synchronisation will result in decreased fuel mileage, increased engine temperature, less than ideal throttle response and higher vibration levels. Before synchronising the carburettors, make sure the valve clearances are properly set.

2 To properly synchronise the carburettors, you will need a set of vacuum gauges or calibrated tubes to indicate engine vacuum.

22.6 Adjust the bearings using a drift located into one of the notches in the adjuster ring

The equipment used should be suitable for a four cylinder engine and come complete with the necessary adapters and hoses to fit the take off points. **Note:** *Because of the nature of the synchronisation procedure and the need for special instruments, most owners leave the task to a Suzuki dealer.*

3 Start the engine and let it run until it reaches normal operating temperature, then shut it off.

4 Remove the fuel tank (see Chapter 3).

5 Disconnect the fuel tap vacuum hose from the vacuum take-off stub on no. 3 carburettor (1200 models) or no. 4 carburettor (600 models) and remove the blanking caps from the take-off stubs of the remaining carburettors **(see illustration)**.

6 Connect the gauge hoses to the take-off adapters. Make sure they are a good fit

23.5 Remove the vacuum hose and the blanking caps

1

because any air leaks will result in false readings.

7 Arrange a temporary fuel supply, either by using a small temporary tank or by using extra long fuel pipes to the now remote fuel tank. Alternatively, position the tank on a suitable base on the motorcycle, taking care not to scratch any paintwork, and making sure that the tank is safely and securely supported.

8 Start the engine and increase the idle speed to 1750 rpm using the throttle stop screw under the carburettors. If using vacuum gauges fitted with damping adjustment, set this so that the needle flutter is just eliminated but so that they can still respond to small changes in pressure.

9 The vacuum readings for all of the cylinders should be the same. If the vacuum readings vary, proceed as follows.

10 The carburettors are adjusted by turning the synchronising screws situated in-between each carburettor, in the throttle linkage **(see illustration 31.1)**. Note: *Do not press down on the screws whilst adjusting them, otherwise a false reading will be obtained.* First synchronise no. 3 carburettor to no. 4 until the readings are the same. Then synchronise no. 1 carburettor to no. 2. Finally synchronise nos. 1 and 2 carburettors to nos. 3 and 4 using the centre synchronising screw. When all the carburettors are synchronised,

open and close the throttle quickly to settle the linkage, and recheck the gauge readings, readjusting if necessary.

11 When the adjustment is complete, recheck the vacuum readings, then adjust the idle speed by turning the throttle stop screw until the idle speed listed in this Chapter's Specifications is obtained. Stop the engine.

12 Remove the gauge hoses, then install the vacuum hose onto no. 3 carburettor (1200 models) or no. 4 carburettor (600 models) and the take-off blanking caps onto the other carburettors.

13 Detach the temporary fuel supply and install the fuel tank (see Chapter 3).

Every 11,000 miles (18,000 km) or three years

Carry out all the items under the 3700 mile (6000 km) check:

24 Air filter - replacement

1 Remove the old air filter as described in Section 3 and install a new one.

25 Engine/transmission - oil filter replacement (GSF1200 and GSF1200S)

Note: *This procedure should be carried out in conjunction with the routine oil change (see Section 8).*

1 The procedure for replacing the oil filter is the same as for the 600 models (see Section 20).

Every two years

26 Brakes - fluid change

1 The brake fluid should be replaced at the prescribed interval or whenever a master cylinder or caliper overhaul is carried out. Refer to the brake bleeding section in Chapter 6, noting that all old fluid must be pumped from the fluid reservoir and hydraulic line before filling with new fluid.

 HAYNES HINT *Old brake fluid is invariably much darker in colour than new fluid, making it easy to see when all old fluid has been expelled from the system.*

27 Clutch - fluid change (GSF1200 and GSF1200S)

1 The clutch fluid should be replaced at the prescribed interval or whenever a master cylinder or release cylinder overhaul is carried out. Refer to the clutch bleeding section in Chapter 2, noting that all old fluid must be pumped from the fluid reservoir and hydraulic line before filling with new fluid (see **Haynes Hint**).

Every four years

28 Brake hoses - replacement

1 The hoses will in time deteriorate with age and should be replaced regardless of their apparent condition.

2 Refer to Chapter 6 and disconnect the brake hoses from the master cylinders and calipers. Always replace the banjo union sealing washers with new ones.

29 Fuel hoses - replacement

 Warning: Petrol (gasoline) is extremely flammable, so take

extra precautions when you work on any part of the fuel system. Don't smoke or allow open flames or bare light bulbs near the work area, and don't work in a garage where a natural gas-type appliance is present. If you spill any fuel on your skin, rinse it off immediately with soap and water. When you perform any kind of work on the fuel system, wear safety glasses and have a fire extinguisher suitable for a Class B type fire (flammable liquids) on hand.

1 The fuel delivery and vacuum hoses should be replaced regardless of their condition. On California models, also renew the emission control system hoses.

2 Remove the fuel tank (see Chapter 3). Disconnect the fuel hoses from the fuel tap and from the carburettors, noting the routing of each hose and where it connects (see

Chapter 3 if required). It is advisable to make a sketch of the various hoses before removing them to ensure they are correctly installed.

3 Secure each new hose to its unions using new clamps. Run the engine and check for leaks before taking the machine out on the road.

30 Clutch - hose replacement (GSF1200 and GSF1200S)

1 The hose will in time deteriorate with age and should be replaced regardless of its apparent condition.

2 Refer to Chapter 2 and disconnect the clutch hose from the master cylinder and release cylinder. Always replace the banjo union sealing washers with new ones.

Non-scheduled maintenance

31 Carburettors - synchronisation (GSF600 and GSF600S)

1 Although not specified as a regular maintenance item on the 600 models, carburettor synchronisation should be carried out periodically to ensure the smooth running of the engine. The procedure for synchronising the carburettors is the same as for the 1200 models described in Section 23 **(see illustration)**.

32 Headlight aim - check and adjustment

Note: *An improperly adjusted headlight may cause problems for oncoming traffic or provide poor, unsafe illumination of the road ahead. Before adjusting the headlight aim, be sure to consult with local traffic laws and regulations - for UK models refer to MOT Test Checks in the Reference section.*

1 The headlight beam can adjusted both horizontally and vertically. Before making any adjustment, check that the tyre pressures are correct and the suspension is adjusted as required. Make any adjustments to the headlight aim with the machine on level ground, with the fuel tank half full and with an assistant sitting on the seat. If the bike is usually ridden with a passenger on the back, have a second assistant to do this.

GSF600 and GSF1200

2 Horizontal adjustment is made by turning the adjuster screw in the headlight rim **(see illustration)**. Turn it clockwise to move the beam to the right, and anti-clockwise to move it to the left.

3 Vertical adjustment is made by slackening the headlight mounting bolts and guide plate bolt and tilting the light up or down as required **(see illustration)**. Tighten the bolts securely after the adjustment has been made.

GSF600S and GSF1200S

4 Horizontal adjustment is made by turning the adjuster screw on the upper right-hand side on the back of the headlight **(see illustration)**. Turn it clockwise to move the beam to the right, and anti-clockwise to move it to the left.

5 Vertical adjustment is made by turning the adjuster screw on the lower left-hand side on the back of the headlight **(see illustration 32.4)**. Turn it clockwise to move the beam down, and anti-clockwise to move it up.

33 Wheel bearings - check

1 Wheel bearings will wear over a period of time and result in handling problems.

2 Place the motorcycle on its centrestand (where fitted) or support it upright using an auxiliary stand. Check for any play in the bearings by pushing and pulling the wheel against the hub **(see illustration)**. Also rotate the wheel and check that it rotates smoothly.

3 If any play is detected in the hub, or if the wheel does not rotate smoothly (and this is not due to brake or transmission drag), the wheel bearings must be removed and inspected for wear or damage (see Chapter 6).

1

31.1 Carburettor synchronisation screws (arrows)

32.2 Headlight beam horizontal adjuster (arrow)

32.3 Headlight mounting bolt (A) and guide plate bolt (B)

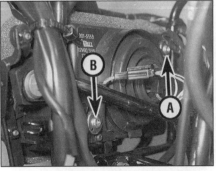

32.4 Horizontal adjuster (A), vertical adjuster (B) - S models

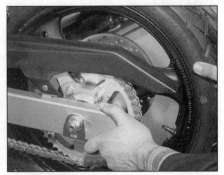

33.2 Checking for play in the wheel bearings

34.3a Lubricating a cable with a pressure lubricator. Make sure the tool seals around the inner cable

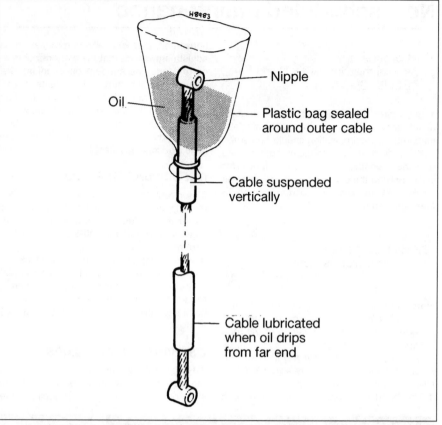

34.3b Lubricating a cable with a makeshift funnel and motor oil

34 Stands, lever pivots and cables - lubrication

1 Since the controls, cables and various other components of a motorcycle are exposed to the elements, they should be lubricated periodically to ensure safe and trouble-free operation.
2 The footrests, clutch and brake levers, brake pedal, gearshift lever linkage and stand pivots should be lubricated frequently. In order for the lubricant to be applied where it will do the most good, the component should be disassembled. However, if chain and cable lubricant is being used, it can be applied to the pivot joint gaps and will usually work its way into the areas where friction occurs. If motor oil or light grease is being used, apply it sparingly as it may attract dirt (which could cause the controls to bind or wear at an accelerated rate). **Note:** *One of the best lubricants for the control lever pivots is a dry-film lubricant (available from many sources by different names).*
3 To lubricate the cables, disconnect the relevant cable at its upper end, then lubricate the cable with a pressure adapter, or if one is not available, using the set-up shown **(see illustrations)**. See Chapter 3 for the choke and throttle cable removal procedures, and Chapter 2 for the clutch cable (GSF600 and GSF600S).
4 The speedometer and tachometer cables should be removed (see Chapter 8) and the inner cable withdrawn from the outer cable and lubricated with motor oil or cable lubricant. Do not lubricate the upper few inches of the cable as the lubricant may travel up into the instrument head.

35 Front forks - oil change

1 Fork oil degrades over a period of time and loses its damping qualities. The forks fitted to these machines are not equipped with drain

plugs, necessitating that they be removed from the yokes and the oil drained by removing the top plugs and inverting the fork.
2 Refer to Chapter 5 for front fork removal, oil draining and refilling.

36 Cylinder compression - check

1 Among other things, poor engine performance may be caused by leaking valves, incorrect valve clearances, a leaking head gasket, or worn pistons, rings and/or cylinder walls. A cylinder compression check will help pinpoint these conditions and can also indicate the presence of excessive carbon deposits in the cylinder heads.
2 The only tools required are a compression gauge and a spark plug wrench. A compression gauge with a threaded end for the spark plug hole is preferable to the type which requires hand pressure to maintain a tight seal. Depending on the outcome of the initial test, a squirt-type oil can may also be needed.
3 Make sure the valve clearances are correctly set (see Section 5) and that the cylinder head nuts are tightened to the correct torque setting (see Section 4).
4 Refer to *Fault Finding Equipment* in the

Reference section for details of the compression test.

37 Engine - oil pressure check

1 The oil pressure warning light should come on when the ignition (main) switch is turned ON and extinguish a few seconds after the engine is started - this serves as a check that the warning light bulb is sound. If the oil pressure light comes on whilst the engine is running, low oil pressure is indicated - stop the engine immediately and carry out an oil pressure check. **Note:** *Check first that the fault is not caused by a low engine/transmission oil level (see Daily (pre-ride) checks).*
2 An oil pressure must be carried out if the warning light comes on (Step 1), but can also provide useful information about the condition of the engine's lubrication system.
3 To check the oil pressure, a suitable gauge and adapter piece (which screws into the crankcase) will be needed. Suzuki provide a kit (part nos. 09915-74510 and 09915-74540) for this purpose.
4 Warm the engine up to normal operating temperature then stop it.

37.5 Remove the oil pressure take-off plug (arrow) and screw the adapter in its place

5 Unscrew the plug below the right-hand crankcase cover and swiftly screw the adapter into the crankcase threads **(see illustration)**. Connect the gauge to the adapter.

6 Start the engine and increase the engine speed to 3000 rpm whilst watching the gauge reading. The oil pressure should be similar to that given in the Specifications at the start of this Chapter.

7 If the pressure is significantly lower than the standard, either the pressure regulator is stuck open, the oil pump is faulty, the oil strainer or filter is blocked, or there is other engine damage. Begin diagnosis by checking the oil filter, strainer and regulator, then the oil pump (see Chapter 2). If those items check out okay, chances are the bearing oil clearances are excessive and the engine needs to be overhauled.

8 If the pressure is too high, either an oil passage is clogged, the regulator is stuck closed or the wrong grade of oil is being used.

9 Stop the engine and unscrew the gauge and adapter from the crankcase.

10 Install the crankcase plug using a new sealing washer, and tighten it securely. Check the oil level (see *Daily (pre-ride) checks*).

38 Steering head bearings - lubrication

1 Over a period of time the grease will harden or may be washed out of the bearings by incorrect use of jet washes.

2 Disassemble the steering head for re-greasing of the bearings. Refer to Chapter 5 for details.

39 Rear suspension bearings - lubrication

1 Over a period of time the grease will harden or dirt will penetrate the bearings.

2 The suspension components are not equipped with grease nipples. Remove the swingarm and the suspension linkage as described in Chapter 5 for greasing of the bearings.

40 Brake caliper and master cylinder seals - replacement

1 Brake seals will deteriorate over a period of time and lose their effectiveness, leading to sticking operation or fluid loss, or allowing the ingress of air and dirt. Refer to Chapter 6 and dismantle the components for seal replacement.

1

Notes

Chapter 2
Engine, clutch and transmission

Contents

Degrees of difficulty

Easy, suitable for novice with little experience	**Fairly easy,** suitable for beginner with some experience	**Fairly difficult,** suitable for competent DIY mechanic	**Difficult,** suitable for experienced DIY mechanic	**Very difficult,** suitable for expert DIY or professional

Specifications

GSF600 and GSF600S

General

Type	Four-stroke in-line four
Capacity	599 cc
Bore	62.6 mm
Stroke	48.7 mm
Compression ratio	11.3 to 1
Clutch	Wet multi-plate
Transmission	Six-speed constant mesh
Final drive	Chain

2

Camshafts and rocker arms

GSF600 and GSF600S

Camshaft
  Intake lobe height
    Standard . . . . 33.13 to 33.17 mm
    Service limit (min) . . . . 32.83 mm
  Exhaust lobe height
    Standard . . . . 32.85 to 32.89 mm
    Service limit (min) . . . . 32.55 mm
  Journal diameter . . . . 21.959 to 21.980 mm
  Journal holder diameter . . . . 22.012 to 22.025 mm
  Journal oil clearance
    Standard . . . . 0.032 to 0.066 mm
    Service limit (max) . . . . 0.15 mm
  Runout (max) . . . . 0.10 mm
Rocker arm bore ID . . . . 12.000 to 12.018 mm
Rocker arm shaft OD . . . . 11.973 to 11.984 mm

Cylinder head

Warpage (max) . . . . 0.20 mm

Valves, guides and springs

Valve clearances . . . . See Chapter 1
Intake valve
  Head diameter . . . . 23 mm
  Stem diameter . . . . 4.965 to 4.980 mm
  Guide bore diameter . . . . 5.000 to 5.012 mm
  Stem-to-guide clearance . . . . 0.020 to 0.047 mm
  Stem deflection (max) - see text . . . . 0.35 mm
  Face thickness (min) . . . . 0.5 mm
  Seat width . . . . 0.9 to 1.1 mm
  Valve lift . . . . 7.8 mm
  Head runout (max) . . . . 0.03 mm
  Stem runout (max) . . . . 0.05 mm
  Stem length above collet groove (min) . . . . 2.5 mm
Exhaust valve
  Head diameter . . . . 20 mm
  Stem diameter . . . . 4.955 to 4.970 mm
  Guide bore diameter . . . . 5.000 to 5.012 mm
  Stem-to-guide clearance . . . . 0.030 to 0.057 mm
  Stem deflection (max) - see text . . . . 0.35 mm
  Face thickness (min) . . . . 0.5 mm
  Seat width . . . . 0.9 to 1.1 mm
  Valve lift . . . . 7.3 mm
  Head runout (max) . . . . 0.03 mm
  Stem runout (max) . . . . 0.05 mm
  Stem length above collet groove (min) . . . . 2.5 mm
Valve springs (intake and exhaust)
  Free length limit (min)
    Inner spring . . . . 35.0 mm
    Outer spring . . . . 38.4 mm
  Spring tension
    Inner spring . . . . 28.0 mm with 5.6 to 6.6 kg load
    Outer spring . . . . 31.5 mm with 12.8 to 15.0 kg load

Cylinder block

Bore
  Standard . . . . 62.600 to 62.615 mm
  Service limit (max) . . . . 62.690 mm
Warpage (max) . . . . 0.20 mm
Cylinder compression . . . . see Chapter 1

Pistons

Piston diameter (measured 15.0 mm up from skirt, at 90° to piston pin axis)
  Standard . . . . 62.555 to 62.570 mm
  Service limit (min) . . . . 62.480 mm
1st oversize . . . . + 0.5 mm
2nd oversize . . . . + 1.0 mm

Pistons (continued)

GSF600 and GSF600S

Piston-to-bore clearance
    Standard . . . . 0.040 to 0.050 mm
    Service limit (max) . . . . 0.120 mm
Piston pin diameter
    Standard . . . . 17.996 to 18.000 mm
    Service limit (min) . . . . 17.98 mm
Piston pin bore diameter in piston
    Standard . . . . 18.002 to 18.008 mm
    Service limit (max) . . . . 18.03 mm

Piston rings

Ring end gap (free)
    Top ring
        Standard . . . . 8.60 mm (approx.)
        Service limit (min) . . . . 6.90 mm
    2nd ring
        Standard . . . . 6.70 mm (approx.)
        Service limit (min) . . . . 5.40 mm
Ring end gap (installed)
    Top ring
        Standard . . . . 0.10 to 0.30 mm
        Service limit (max) . . . . 0.70 mm
    2nd ring
        Standard . . . . 0.30 to 0.50 mm
        Service limit (max) . . . . 0.70 mm
Ring thickness
    Top ring . . . . 0.77 to 0.79 mm
    2nd ring . . . . 0.97 to 0.99 mm
Ring groove width in piston
    Top ring . . . . 0.81 to 0.83 mm
    2nd ring . . . . 1.01 to 1.03 mm
    Oil ring . . . . 2.01 to 2.03 mm
Ring-to-groove clearance
    Top ring (max) . . . . 0.18 mm
    2nd ring (max) . . . . 0.15 mm
Oversize ring identification
    Top and second rings
        1st oversize 50
        2nd oversize 100
    Oil ring (standard uncoloured)
        1st oversize . . . . Red
        2nd oversize . . . . Yellow

Clutch

Friction plate
    Quantity 8
    Thickness
        Standard . . . . 2.65 to 2.95 mm
        Service limit . . . . 2.35 mm
    Tab width (min) . . . . 15.0 mm
Plain plate
    Quantity 7
    Warpage (max) . . . . 0.1 mm
Spring free length (min) . . . . 69.5 mm
Release mechanism screw . . . . 1/4 to 1/2 a turn out

Transmission

Gear ratios (no. of teeth)
    Primary reduction . . . . 1.744 to 1 (75/43T)
    Final reduction
        UK models . . . . 3.133 to 1 (47/15T)
        US models . . . . 3.200 to 1 (48/15T)
    1st gear . . . . 3.083 to 1 (37/12T)
    2nd gear . . . . 2.062 to 1 (33/16T)
    3rd gear . . . . 1.647 to 1 (28/17T)
    4th gear . . . . 1.400 to 1 (28/20T)
    5th gear . . . . 1.227 to 1 (27/22T)
    6th gear . . . . 1.095 to 1 (23/21T)

2

Selector drum and forks

GSF600 and GSF600S

Selector fork-to-groove clearance
    Standard . . . . 0.1 to 0.3 mm
    Service limit (max) . . . . 0.5 mm
Selector fork end thickness
    Nos. 1 and 3 . . . . 4.6 to 4.7 mm
    No. 2 . . . . 4.8 to 4.9 mm
Selector fork groove width
    Nos. 1 and 3 . . . . 4.8 to 4.9 mm
    No. 2 . . . . 5.0 to 5.1 mm

Crankshaft and bearings

Journal diameter . . . . 31.976 to 32.000 mm
Main bearing oil clearance
    Standard . . . . 0.020 to 0.044 mm
    Service limit (max) . . . . 0.08 mm
Runout (max) . . . . 0.05 mm
Thrust bearing clearance . . . . 0.04 to 0.09 mm
Inner thrust bearing thickness . . . . 2.445 to 2.465 mm

Connecting rods

Small-end internal diameter
    Standard . . . . 18.010 to 18.018 mm
    Service limit (max) . . . . 18.040 mm
Big-end side clearance
    Standard . . . . 0.1 to 0.2 mm
    Service limit (max) . . . . 0.3 mm
Big-end width . . . . 20.95 to 21.00 mm
Crankpin width . . . . 21.10 to 21.15 mm
Crankpin diameter . . . . 33.976 to 34.000 mm
Big-end oil clearance
    Standard . . . . 0.032 to 0.056 mm
    Service limit (max) . . . . 0.08 mm

Lubrication system

Oil pressure . . . . see Chapter 1

Torque settings

Engine mounting bolts
    Engine rear mounting bolts (upper and lower) . . . . 75 Nm
    Engine front and lower mounting bolts . . . . 55 Nm
    Right-hand side frame downtube bolts . . . . 32 Nm
    Left-hand side engine front mounting bracket-to-frame bolts . . . . . . 32 Nm
Oil cooler mounting bolts . . . . 10 Nm
Oil cooler hose banjo bolts . . . . 28 Nm
Oil cooler hose union bolts . . . . 10 Nm
Oil hose union bolts . . . . 10 Nm
Valve cover standard bolts . . . . 14 Nm
Valve cover banjo bolts . . . . 16 Nm
Cam chain tensioner mounting bolts . . . . 7 Nm
Cam chain tensioner spring cap bolt . . . . 35 Nm
Top cam chain guide mounting bolts . . . . 10 Nm
Camshaft sprocket bolts . . . . 25 Nm
Camshaft journal cap bolts . . . . 10 Nm
Rocker shaft locking bolt . . . . 9 Nm
Rocker shaft plug . . . . 28 Nm
Cylinder head 10 mm nuts . . . . 38 Nm
Cylinder head 6 mm bolt . . . . 10 Nm
Cylinder block nut . . . . 9 Nm
Clutch nut . . . . 90 Nm
Clutch pressure plate bolts . . . . 12 Nm
Starter clutch bolt . . . . 150 Nm
Oil pressure regulator . . . . 28 Nm
Oil sump bolts . . . . 14 Nm
Crankcase 6 mm bolts and nuts . . . . 13 Nm
Crankcase 8 mm bolts . . . . 22 Nm
Main oil gallery plug . . . . 40 Nm
Cylinder studs . . . . 15 Nm
Oil pump mounting bolts . . . . 10 Nm
Connecting rod cap nuts
    Initial setting (see text) . . . . 20 Nm
    Final setting . . . . 35 Nm

GSF1200 and GSF1200S

General

Type	Four-stroke in-line four
Capacity	1157 cc
Bore	79.0 mm
Stroke	59.0 mm
Compression ratio	9.5 to 1
Clutch	Wet multi-plate
Transmission	Five-speed constant mesh
Final drive	Chain

Camshafts and rocker arms

Camshaft

Intake lobe height	
Standard	33.58 to 33.62 mm
Service limit (min)	33.28 mm
Exhaust lobe height	
Standard	33.41 to 33.45 mm
Service limit (min)	33.11 mm
Journal diameter	21.959 to 21.980 mm
Journal holder diameter	22.012 to 22.025 mm
Journal oil clearance	
Standard	0.032 to 0.066 mm
Service limit (max)	0.15 mm
Runout (max)	0.10 mm
Rocker arm bore ID	12.000 to 12.018 mm
Rocker arm shaft OD	11.973 to 11.984 mm

Cylinder head

Warpage (max)	0.20 mm

Valves, guides and springs

Valve clearances	See Chapter 1
Intake valve	
Head diameter	28.5 mm
Stem diameter	4.965 to 4.980 mm
Guide bore diameter	5.000 to 5.012 mm
Stem-to-guide clearance	0.020 to 0.047 mm
Stem deflection (max) - see text	0.35 mm
Face thickness (min)	0.5 mm
Seat width	0.9 to 1.1 mm
Valve lift	Not available
Head runout (max)	0.03 mm
Stem runout (max)	0.05 mm
Stem length above collet groove (min)	2.5 mm
Exhaust valve	
Head diameter	25 mm
Stem diameter	4.945 to 4.960 mm
Guide bore diameter	5.000 to 5.012 mm
Stem-to-guide clearance	0.040 to 0.067 mm
Stem deflection (max) (see text)	0.35 mm
Face thickness (min)	0.5 mm
Seat width	0.9 to 1.1 mm
Valve lift	Not available
Head runout (max)	0.03 mm
Stem runout (max)	0.05 mm
Stem length above collet groove (min)	2.5 mm
Valve springs (intake and exhaust)	
Free length limit (min)	
Inner spring	35.0 mm
Outer spring	37.8 mm
Spring tension	
Inner spring	28.0 mm with 5.3 to 6.5 kg load
Outer spring	31.5 mm with 13.1 to 15.1 kg load

Cylinder block

Bore

Standard	79.000 to 79.015 mm
Service limit (max)	79.080 mm
Warpage (max)	0.20 mm
Cylinder compression	see Chapter 1

2

Pistons

GSF1200 and GSF1200S

Piston diameter (measured 15.0 mm up from skirt, at 90° to piston pin axis)
Standard	78.945 to 78.960 mm
Service limit (min)	78.880 mm
Oversize	+ 0.5 mm

Piston-to-bore clearance
Standard	0.040 to 0.070 mm
Service limit (max)	0.120 mm

Piston pin diameter
Standard	19.996 to 20.000 mm
Service limit (min)	19.98 mm

Piston pin bore diameter in piston
Standard	20.002 to 20.008 mm
Service limit (max)	20.03 mm

Piston rings

Ring end gap (free)

Top ring
Standard	10.0 mm (approx.)
Service limit (min)	8.0 mm

2nd ring
Standard	12.0 mm (approx.)
Service limit (min)	9.60 mm

Ring end gap (installed)

Top ring
Standard	0.20 to 0.35 mm
Service limit (max)	0.50 mm

2nd ring
Standard	0.30 to 0.50 mm
Service limit (max)	1.00 mm
Ring thickness (top and 2nd rings)	0.97 to 0.99 mm

Ring groove width in piston
Top and 2nd rings	1.01 to 1.03 mm
Oil ring	2.01 to 2.03 mm

Ring-to-groove clearance
Top ring (max)	0.18 mm
2nd ring (max)	0.15 mm

Oversize ring identification
Top ring	50
2nd ring	50
Oil ring	Blue (standard Red)

Clutch

Friction plate
Quantity	10
Thickness	2.92 to 3.08 mm
Tab width (min)	13.0 mm

Plain plate
Quantity	9
Warpage (max)	0.1 mm
Diaphragm spring free height (min)	2.9 mm
Master cylinder bore diameter	14.000 to 14.043 mm
Master cylinder piston diameter	13.957 to 13.984 mm
Release cylinder bore diameter	35.700 to 35.762 mm
Release cylinder piston diameter	35.650 to 35.675 mm

Transmission

Gear ratios (no. of teeth)
Primary reduction	1.565 to 1 (72/46T)
Final reduction	3.000 to 1 (45/15T)
1st gear	2.384 to 1 (31/13T)
2nd gear	1.631 to 1 (31/19T)
3rd gear	1.250 to 1 (25/20T)
4th gear	1.045 to 1 (23/22T)
5th gear	0.913 to 1 (21/23T)

Selector drum and forks

GSF1200 and GSF1200S

Selector fork-to-groove clearance
    Standard .... 0.1 to 0.3 mm
    Service limit (max) .... 0.5 mm
Selector fork end thickness .... 4.8 to 4.9 mm
Selector fork groove width .... 5.0 to 5.1 mm

Crankshaft and bearings

Journal diameter .... 35.976 to 36.000 mm
Main bearing oil clearance
    Standard .... 0.020 to 0.044 mm
    Service limit (max) .... 0.08 mm
Runout (max) .... 0.05 mm
Thrust bearing clearance .... 0.04 to 0.08 mm
Inner thrust bearing thickness .... 2.420 to 2.440 mm

Connecting rods

Small-end internal diameter
    Standard .... 20.010 to 20.018 mm
    Service limit (max) .... 20.040 mm
Big-end side clearance
    Standard .... 0.1 to 0.2 mm
    Service limit (max) .... 0.3 mm
Big-end width .... 20.95 to 21.00 mm
Crankpin width .... 21.10 to 21.15 mm
Crankpin diameter .... 37.976 to 38.000 mm
Big-end oil clearance
    Standard .... 0.032 to 0.056 mm
    Service limit (max) .... 0.08 mm

Lubrication system

Oil pressure .... see Chapter 1

Torque settings

Engine mounting bolts
    Engine rear mounting bolts (upper and lower) .... 88 Nm
    Engine front and lower mounting bolts .... 55 Nm
    Engine lower mounting bolt bracket-to-frame/downtube bolts ..... 23 Nm
    Engine front mounting bolt bracket-to-frame/downtube bolts ...... 23 Nm
    Engine front mounting bracket joining bolts .... 50 Nm
    Right-hand side frame downtube bolts .... 50 Nm
Oil cooler mounting bolts .... 10 Nm
Oil cooler hose banjo bolts .... 28 Nm
Oil cooler hose union bolts .... 10 Nm
Oil hose union bolts .... 10 Nm
Valve cover standard bolts .... 14 Nm
Valve cover banjo bolts .... 16 Nm
Cam chain tensioner mounting bolts .... 7 Nm
Cam chain tensioner spring cap bolt .... 35 Nm
Rear cam chain guide bolt .... 6 Nm
Camshaft sprocket bolts .... 25 Nm
Camshaft journal cap bolts .... 10 Nm
Rocker shaft locking bolt .... 9 Nm
Rocker shaft plug .... 28 Nm
Cylinder head 10 mm nuts .... 38 Nm
Cylinder head 6 mm bolt .... 10 Nm
Cylinder block nut .... 9 Nm
Clutch nut .... 150 Nm
Clutch master cylinder clamp bolts .... 10 Nm
Clutch hose banjo bolts .... 23 Nm
Clutch release cylinder bleed valve .... 8 Nm
Starter clutch bolt .... 150 Nm
Oil pressure regulator .... 28 Nm
Oil sump bolts .... 14 Nm
Crankcase 6 mm bolts and nuts .... 13 Nm
Crankcase 8 mm bolts .... 22 Nm
Main oil gallery plug .... 40 Nm
Cylinder studs .... 15 Nm
Oil pump mounting bolts .... 14 Nm
Connecting rod cap nuts
    Initial setting (see text) .... 25 Nm
    Final setting .... 50 Nm

2

1 General information

The engine/transmission unit is an air/oil-cooled in-line four. The valves are operated by double overhead camshafts which are chain driven off the crankshaft. The engine/transmission assembly is constructed from aluminium alloy. The crankcase is divided horizontally.

The crankcase incorporates a wet sump, pressure-fed lubrication system which uses a gear-driven, dual-rotor oil pump, an oil filter and by-pass valve assembly, a relief valve and an oil pressure switch. The oil is cooled by a radiator matrix mounted on the frame downtubes.

Power from the crankshaft is routed to the transmission via the clutch, which is of the wet, multi-plate type and is gear-driven off the crankshaft. The 600 models have a conventional cable-operated clutch, whilst the 1200 models have an hydraulically-operated diaphragm spring clutch The transmission is a five-speed (1200 models) or six-speed (600 models) constant-mesh unit. Final drive to the rear wheel is by chain and sprockets.

2 Operations possible with the engine in the frame

The components and assemblies listed below can be removed without having to remove the engine/transmission assembly from the frame. If however, a number of areas require attention at the same time, removal of the engine is recommended.

Oil hoses and cooler
Valve cover
Cam chain tensioner and cam chain guides
Camshafts and rocker arms
Cylinder head
Cylinder block, pistons and piston rings
Ignition rotor and pulse generator coil assembly
Clutch
Gearchange mechanism (external components)
Alternator
Starter clutch and idle gear
Engine sprocket
Oil sump, oil strainer and oil pressure relief valve
Starter motor

3 Operations requiring engine removal

It is necessary to remove the engine/transmission assembly from the frame and separate the crankcase halves to gain access to the following components.

Transmission shafts
Selector drum and forks
Crankshaft and bearings
Connecting rod big-ends and bearings
Oil pump
Cam chain and cam chain tensioner blade

4 Major engine repair - general note

1 It is not always easy to determine when or if an engine should be completely overhauled, as a number of factors must be considered.
2 High mileage is not necessarily an indication that an overhaul is needed, while low mileage, on the other hand, does not preclude the need for an overhaul. Frequency of servicing is probably the single most important consideration. An engine that has regular and frequent oil and filter changes, as well as other required maintenance, will most likely give many miles of reliable service. Conversely, a neglected engine, or one which has not been run in properly, may require an overhaul very early in its life.
3 Exhaust smoke and excessive oil consumption are both indications that piston rings and/or valve guides are in need of attention, although make sure that the fault is not due to oil leakage.
4 If the engine is making obvious knocking or rumbling noises, the connecting rod and/or main bearings are probably at fault.
5 Loss of power, rough running, excessive valve train noise and high fuel consumption rates may also point to the need for an overhaul, especially if they are all present at the same time. If a complete tune-up does not remedy the situation, major mechanical work is the only solution.
6 An engine overhaul generally involves restoring the internal parts to the specifications of a new engine. The piston rings and main and connecting rod bearings are usually replaced and the cylinder walls honed or, if necessary, re-bored during a major overhaul. Generally the valve seats are re-ground, since they are usually in less than perfect condition at this point. The end result should be a like new engine that will give as many trouble-free miles as the original.
7 Before beginning the engine overhaul, read through the related procedures to familiarise yourself with the scope and requirements of the job. Overhauling an engine is not all that difficult, but it is time consuming. Plan on the motorcycle being tied up for a minimum of two weeks. Check on the availability of parts and make sure that any necessary special tools, equipment and supplies are obtained in advance.
8 Most work can be done with typical workshop hand tools, although a number of precision measuring tools are required for inspecting parts to determine if they must be replaced. Often a dealer will handle the

inspection of parts and offer advice concerning reconditioning and replacement. As a general rule, time is the primary cost of an overhaul so it does not pay to install worn or substandard parts.
9 As a final note, to ensure maximum life and minimum trouble from a rebuilt engine, everything must be assembled with care in a spotlessly clean environment.

5 Engine - removal and installation

⚠️ *Warning: The engine is very heavy. Removal and installation should be carried out with the aid of at least one assistant; personal injury or damage could occur if the engine falls or is dropped. If available, an hydraulic or mechanical floor jack can be used to support and lower or raise the engine.*

Removal

1 Position the bike on its centrestand or support it securely in an upright position using an auxiliary stand. Work can be made easier by raising the machine to a suitable working height on a hydraulic ramp or a suitable platform. Make sure the motorcycle is secure and will not topple over (see *Tools and Workshop Tips* in the Reference section).
2 If the engine is dirty, particularly around its mountings, wash it thoroughly before starting any major dismantling work. This will make work much easier and rule out the possibility of caked on lumps of dirt falling into some vital component.
3 Drain the engine oil and, if required, remove the oil filter (see Chapter 1).
4 Remove the seat and the side panels, and on GSF600S and GSF1200S models remove the fairing (see Chapter 7).
5 Disconnect the battery negative (-ve) lead (see Chapter 8). Trace the black/white wire connected to the battery negative lead and disconnect it at its connector **(see illustration)**. Feed the lead through to the engine and coil it on the crankcase, noting its routing.
6 Remove the fuel tank (see Chapter 3).

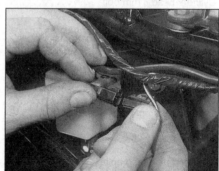

5.5 Disconnect the negative lead wire at the connector

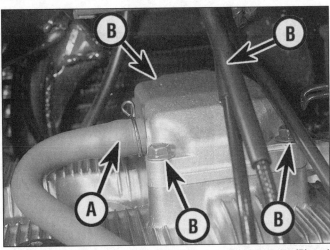

5.9a Detach the breather hose (A), then unscrew the bolts (B) and remove the cover . . .

5.9b . . . and the gasket

7 Remove the carburettors (see Chapter 3). Plug the engine intake manifolds with clean rag.

8 Release the two spark plug leads from the clamp on the valve cover breather, then disconnect all the leads from the plugs and secure them clear of the engine.

9 Disconnect the breather hose from the valve cover breather **(see illustration)**. Unscrew the four bolts securing the breather, noting the lead clamp secured by the right-hand rear bolt, and remove it from the valve cover along with the gasket **(see illustration)**.

10 Pull back the rubber cover on the starter motor terminal and disconnect the lead **(see illustration)**.

11 Trace the ignition pulse generator and oil pressure switch wiring back from its exit hole in the crankcase behind the cylinder block and disconnect it at the connectors **(see illustration)**. Release the wiring from any clips or ties, noting its routing, and coil it on top of the crankcase so that it does not impede engine removal.

12 Trace the alternator wiring and neutral switch wiring back from the top of the crankcase and disconnect it at the connectors

(see illustrations). Release the wiring from any clips or ties, noting its routing, and coil it on top of the crankcase so that it does not impede engine removal. Make sure the sidestand switch wiring is clear of the engine.

13 Unscrew the gearchange lever linkage arm pinch bolt and remove the arm from the shaft, noting any alignment marks on the arm and the shaft **(see illustration)**. If no marks are visible, make your own before removing

the arm so that it can be correctly aligned with the shaft on installation.

14 Remove the front sprocket cover and the front sprocket (see Chapter 5). The sprocket cover can be secured out of the way with the clutch cable (600 models) or release cylinder and hose (1200 models) still connected. Alternatively, separate the cable or release cylinder from the cover (see Section 19 or 21) and remove the cover.

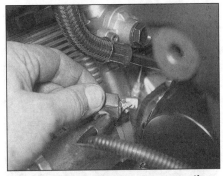

5.10 Pull back the cover to expose the starter motor terminal

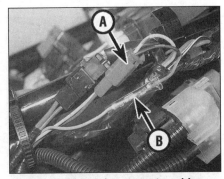

5.11 Ignition pulse generator wiring connector (A), oil pressure switch wiring connector (B)

2

5.12a Alternator wiring connector (arrow) . . .

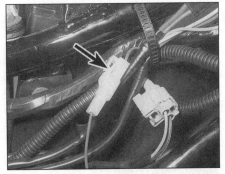

5.12b . . . neutral switch wiring connector (arrow)

5.13 Make alignment marks, then remove the bolt (arrow) and slide gearchange arm off shaft

5.19a Remove the bolts (arrows) . . .

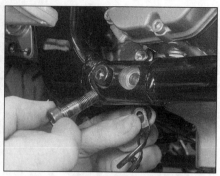

5.19b . . . noting the positions of the breather hose clamp . . .

5.19c . . . and the special nut fitted to the middle engine bolt . . .

5.19d . . . then remove the frame section

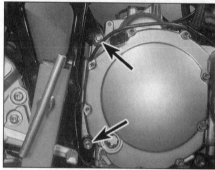

5.20a Unscrew the nuts from the engine rear bolts (arrows) . . .

15 Remove the exhaust system (see Chapter 3).
16 Remove the oil cooler and hoses (see Section 7).
17 On California models, disconnect the PAIR system pipes from the front of the engine (see Chapter 3). Discard the gaskets as new ones must be used.
18 At this point, position an hydraulic or mechanical jack under the engine with a block of wood between the jack head and sump. Make sure the jack is centrally positioned so the engine will not topple in any direction when the last mounting bolt is removed. Take the weight of the engine on the jack.
19 Remove the nuts and bolts which secure the right-hand side frame downtube to the rest of the frame and to the engine, then remove the right-hand side frame downtube **(see illustrations)**. Note where the various nuts and bolts and the breather hose clamp fit as an aid to installation.
20 Make sure the engine is properly supported on the jack, and have an assistant support it as well. Remove the remaining engine mounting nuts and bolts and remove the bracket and spacer **(see illustrations)**. Note where the various nuts, bolts, bracket and spacer fit as an aid to installation.
21 The engine can now be removed from the frame. Check that all wiring, cables and hoses are well clear, then manoeuvre the engine out of the right-hand side of the frame **(see illustration)**.

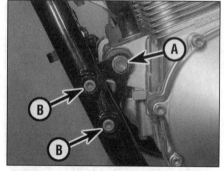

5.20b . . . then remove the engine front bolt (A) and the bracket bolts (B), and remove the bracket

5.20c Remove the engine middle bolt, noting its special nut . . .

5.20d . . . then withdraw the rear mounting bolts (arrows) . . .

5.20e . . . noting how the spacer fits on the top bolt

5.21 Carefully manoeuvre the engine clear of the frame

22 The engine mounting bolt nuts are self-locking, and Suzuki advise that they can only be used once. Discard all the nuts and replace them with new ones on installation.

Installation

23 Installation is the reverse of removal, noting the following points:

a)   Make sure no wires, cables or hoses become trapped between the engine and the frame when installing the engine.

b)   The engine mounting bolts are all of different length. Make sure the correct bolt is installed in its correct location.

c)   Install the long rear engine mounting bolts from the left-hand side. The longer bolt is for the upper rear mounting, and the shorter for the lower rear mounting.

d)   Use new self-locking nuts on the engine mounting bolts. Do not fully tighten any of the bolts until they have all been installed. Make sure the spacer and bracket are correctly positioned.

e)   Tighten the engine mounting bolt nuts, the right side frame downtube bolt nuts and any other bolts and nuts to the torque settings specified at the beginning of the Chapter.

f)   Use new gaskets on the exhaust pipe connections.

g)   Align the marks made on the gearchange lever linkage arm and shaft when installing the arm onto the shaft, and tighten the pinch bolt securely.

h)   Make sure all wires, cables and hoses are correctly routed and connected, and secured by any clips or ties.

i)   Refill the engine with oil (see Chapter 1).

j)   Adjust the drive chain freeplay (see Chapter 1).

k)   Adjust the throttle cable freeplay and idle speed, and on 600 models the clutch freeplay (see Chapter 1).

6 Engine disassembly and reassembly - general information

Disassembly

1 Before disassembling the engine, the external surfaces of the unit should be thoroughly cleaned and degreased. This will prevent contamination of the engine internals, and will also make working a lot easier and cleaner. A high flash-point solvent, such as paraffin (kerosene) can be used, or better still, a proprietary engine degreaser. Use old paintbrushes and toothbrushes to work the solvent into the various recesses of the engine casings. Take care to exclude solvent or water from the electrical components and intake and exhaust ports.

6.4 An engine support made from pieces of 2 x 4 inch wood

 Warning: The use of petrol (gasoline) as a cleaning agent should be avoided because of the risk of fire.

2 When clean and dry, arrange the unit on the workbench, leaving suitable clear area for working. Gather a selection of small containers and plastic bags so that parts can be grouped together in an easily identifiable manner. Some paper and a pen should be on hand to permit notes to be made and labels attached where necessary. A supply of clean rag is also required.

3 Before commencing work, read through the appropriate section so that some idea of the necessary procedure can be gained. When removing components it should be noted that great force is seldom required, unless specified. In many cases, a component's reluctance to be removed is indicative of an incorrect approach or removal method - if in any doubt, re-check with the text.

4 An engine support stand made from short lengths of 2 x 4 inch wood bolted together into a rectangle will help support the engine **(see illustration)**. The perimeter of the mount should be just big enough to accommodate the sump within it so that the engine rests on its crankcase.

5 When disassembling the engine, keep 'mated' parts together (including gears, cylinders, pistons, connecting rods, valves, etc. that have been in contact with each other during engine operation). These 'mated' parts must be reused or replaced as an assembly.

6 Engine/transmission disassembly should

be done in the following general order with reference to the appropriate Sections.

   Remove the valve covers
   Remove the cam chain tensioner and cam chain guide blades
   Remove the camshafts
   Remove the cylinder head
   Remove the cylinder block
   Remove the pistons
   Remove the ignition rotor and pulse generator coil assembly (see Chapter 4)
   Remove the clutch
   Remove the gearchange mechanism external components
   Remove the starter clutch and idle gear
   Remove the alternator (see Chapter 8)
   Remove the starter motor (see Chapter 8)
   Remove the oil sump
   Separate the crankcase halves
   Remove the crankshaft and connecting rods
   Remove the transmission shafts/gears
   Remove the gearchange mechanism internal components
   Remove the oil pump

Reassembly

7 Reassembly is accomplished by reversing the general disassembly sequence.

7 Oil cooler and hoses - removal and installation

Note: *The oil cooler and its hoses can be removed with the engine in the frame. If the engine has been removed, ignore the steps which do not apply.*

Removal

1 Drain the engine oil (see Chapter 1) and, if required for easier access, remove the fairing (where fitted) (see Chapter 7).

2 Unscrew the banjo bolt securing each oil cooler hose to the oil sump just below the oil filter **(see illustration)**. Discard the sealing washers as new ones must be used. If required, unscrew the two bolts securing each hose union to the bottom of the cooler and detach the hoses. Discard the O-rings as new ones must be used. Release the hoses from the clamps on the frame **(see illustration)**.

7.2a Remove the banjo bolts and detach the hoses from the oil sump

7.2b Each hose is secured by a clamp on the frame

7.3a Remove the two cooler mounting bolts . . .

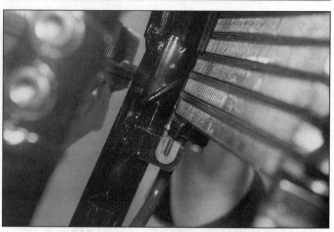

7.3b . . . then lift the cooler out of its lug(s)

7.4a Remove the two bolts securing the hose to the crankcase (arrows) . . .

7.4b . . . and the two bolts (arrows) securing each hose to the valve cover

3 Unscrew the two bolts securing the top of the cooler to the frame, then carefully lift the cooler out of its bottom mounting lug(s) (one on 600 models, two on 1200 models) on the frame downtube(s) **(see illustrations)**. Take care not to lose the U-shaped rubber mount(s) from the lug(s), and replace if brittle, worn or cracked.
4 Unscrew the two bolts securing the oil hose union to the crankcase behind the cylinder block, then unscrew the two bolts securing

each hose union to the valve cover **(see illustrations)**. Manoeuvre the hoses free of the carburettors. Discard the O-rings as new ones must be used.

Installation

5 Installation is the reverse of removal. Always use new sealing washers and O-rings when installing the hoses **(see illustrations)**. Tighten the cooler mounting bolts, the hose banjo bolts and the hose union bolts to the

torque settings specified at the beginning of the Chapter **(see illustration)**.

8 Valve cover - removal and installation

Note: *The valve cover can be removed with the engine in the frame. If the engine has been removed, ignore the steps which do not apply.*

7.5a Use a new O-ring on each hose union . . .

7.5b . . . and new sealing washers on each side of the banjo fittings

7.5c Tighten all of the bolts to the specified torque setting

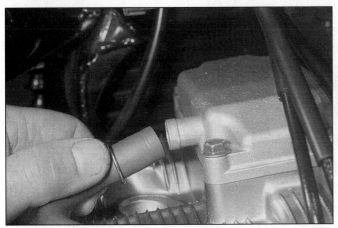

8.3 Detach the hose from the breather

8.6 The valve cover is secured by fourteen bolts (arrows)

Removal

1 Remove the seat and the side panels (see Chapter 7) and disconnect the battery negative (-ve) lead.
2 Remove the fuel tank (see Chapter 3).
3 Disconnect the breather hose from the breather on top of the valve cover **(see illustration)**. For improved clearance if required, unscrew the four bolts securing the breather, noting the lead clamp secured by the right rear bolt, and remove it from the valve cover along with the gasket **(see illustrations 5.9a and b)**.
4 Disconnect the spark plug leads from the plugs and secure them clear of the engine.
5 Unscrew the two bolts securing each oil hose union to the valve cover and displace the hoses **(see illustration 7.4b)**. Discard the O-rings as new ones must be used. If the engine is being disassembled, also unscrew the two bolts securing the oil hose union to the crankcase behind the cylinder block **(see illustration 7.4a)**.
6 The valve cover is secured by fourteen bolts, the four running along the middle of the cover, adjacent to the spark plug holes, being of the banjo type. Unscrew the bolts and remove them along with their sealing washers where fitted, noting the positions of the different types of bolt and washer **(see illustration)**. Check the condition of the

8.9 Make sure both dowels are installed (arrow)

sealing washers and replace them if necessary. It is a good idea to replace them as a matter of course.
7 Lift the valve cover off the cylinder head. If it is stuck, do not try to lever it off with a screwdriver. Tap it gently around the sides with a rubber hammer or block of wood to dislodge it.

Installation

8 Examine the valve cover gasket and the plug hole gaskets for signs of damage or deterioration and replace them if necessary.
9 Clean the mating surfaces of the cylinder head and the valve cover with lacquer thinner,

8.10a The main gasket . . .

acetone or brake system cleaner. Make sure the cover dowels are securely installed **(see illustration)**.
10 If new gaskets are being used, apply a smear of a suitable adhesive (such as Suzuki Bond no. 1207B) into the grooves in the valve cover. Install the gaskets onto the valve cover, making sure they fit correctly into the groove **(see illustrations)**. Apply a sealant to the cut-outs in the cylinder head where the gasket half-circles fit **(see illustration)**.
11 Position the cover on the cylinder head, making sure the gasket stays in place and the cover locates correctly onto the dowels **(see illustration)**. Install the cover bolts, using new

2

8.10b . . . and the plug hole gaskets fit into grooves in the cover

8.10c Apply a sealant to each cut-out in the cylinder head (arrow)

8.11a Position the cover on the head . . .

8.11b . . . then install the banjo bolts . . .

8.11c . . . and the standard bolts . . .

8.11d . . . and tighten them to the specified torque setting

sealing washers if required, and tighten them to the torque settings specified at the beginning of the Chapter, noting the difference between the standard bolts and the banjo bolts **(see illustrations)**.
12 Install the oil hose unions onto the valve cover using new O-rings **(see illustration 7.5a)**. Tighten the union mounting bolts to the specified torque setting.
13 Install the remaining components in the reverse order of removal.

9 Cam chain tensioner and cam chain guide blades - removal, inspection and installation

Note: *The cam chain tensioner and guide blades can be removed with the engine in the frame.*

Cam chain tensioner

Caution: Once you start to remove the tensioner bolts, you must remove the tensioner all the way and reset it before tightening the bolts. The tensioner extends itself and locks in place, so if you loosen the bolts partway and then retighten them, the tensioner or cam chain will be damaged.

Removal

1 Unscrew the tensioner spring cap bolt and withdraw the spring from the tensioner body **(see illustration)**.
2 Unscrew the two tensioner mounting bolts and withdraw the tensioner from the back of the cylinder block **(see illustration 9.1)**.
3 Remove the gasket from the base of the tensioner or from the cylinder block and discard it as a new one must be used.

Inspection

4 Examine the tensioner components for signs of wear or damage.
5 Release the ratchet mechanism from the tensioner plunger and check that the plunger moves freely in and out of the tensioner body **(see illustration 9.8)**.
6 If the tensioner or any of its components are worn or damaged, or if the plunger is seized in the body, they must be replaced. Individual components are available.

Installation

7 Unscrew the five bolts securing the pulse generator coil cover to the right-hand side of the engine **(see illustration)**. Turn the crankshaft in a clockwise direction with a 19 mm spanner or socket on the large hex of the ignition rotor **(see illustration)**. Alternatively, place the motorcycle on its centrestand (where fitted) or support it using an auxiliary stand so that the rear wheel is off the ground, then select a high gear and rotate the rear wheel by hand in its normal direction of rotation. This removes all the slack between the crankshaft and the camshaft in the front run of the chain and transfers it to the

back run where it will be taken up by the tensioner.
Caution: DO NOT use the ignition rotor retaining Allen bolt to turn the crankshaft - it may snap or strip out. Also be sure to turn the engine in its normal direction of rotation.
8 Release the ratchet mechanism and press the tensioner plunger all the way into the tensioner body **(see illustration)**.
9 Place a new gasket on the tensioner body, then install it in the engine **(see illustration)**. Tighten the mounting bolts to the torque setting specified at the beginning of the Chapter.

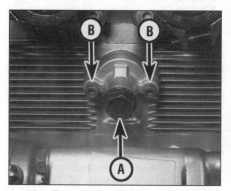

9.1 Tensioner spring cap bolt (A), tensioner mounting bolts (B)

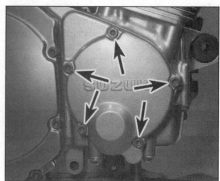

9.7a The pulse generator cover is secured by five bolts (arrows)

9.7b Use a spanner on the rotor to turn the crankshaft

9.8 Release the ratchet and press the tensioner plunger all the way in

9.9 Install the tensioner body in the engine with a new gasket

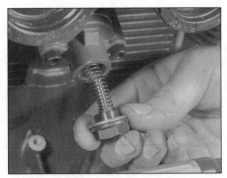

9.10 Install the tensioner spring and cap bolt

9.12a Use a new gasket . . .

10 Install a new sealing washer on the spring cap bolt. Install the spring and cap bolt and tighten the bolt to the torque setting specified at the beginning of the Chapter (see illustration).
11 It is advisable to remove the valve cover (see Section 8) and check that the cam chain is tensioned. If it is slack, the tensioner piston did not release.
12 Install the pulse generator cover using a new gasket, and make sure the sealing washer is installed with the top bolt (see illustrations). If removed, install the valve cover (see Section 8).

Cam chain guide blades

Removal - GSF600 and GSF600S

13 Remove the valve cover (see Section 8).
14 Unscrew the four bolts (see illustration) securing the cam chain top guide to the cylinder head and remove it, noting which way round it fits (look for the arrow on its top surface).
15 To remove the cam chain front guide blade it is necessary to first remove the exhaust camshaft (see Section 11). Lift the front cam chain guide blade out of the front of the cam chain tunnel, noting which way round it fits and how it locates in the cut-outs in the cylinder head (see illustration).

Removal - GSF1200 and GSF1200S

16 Remove the valve cover (see Section 8).
17 To remove the cam chain front guide

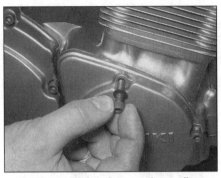

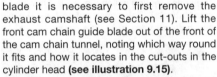

9.12b . . . and make sure the sealing washer is installed on the top bolt

blade it is necessary to first remove the exhaust camshaft (see Section 11). Lift the front cam chain guide blade out of the front of the cam chain tunnel, noting which way round it fits and how it locates in the cut-outs in the cylinder head (see illustration 9.15).
18 The top cam chain guide, located in the valve cover, should be inspected in situ prior to removal, and removed only if necessary. To remove the guide, unscrew the four bolts securing the breather to the top of the valve cover and remove the breather and its gasket. Remove the two screws securing the cam chain top guide to the valve cover and remove the guide, noting which way round it fits.
19 To inspect or remove the rear cam chain guide it is necessary to first remove the intake camshaft (see Section 11). Having done this, the guide can be inspected in situ. To remove

9.14 The cam chain top guide is secured by four bolts (arrows)

the guide, support it with your finger or grasp it with a pair of pliers, using an assistant if required, then unscrew the bolt securing the guide to the cylinder head, taking great care not to allow the guide to fall down the cam chain tunnel and into the crankcase.

Inspection - all models

20 Examine the sliding surface of the guides for signs of wear or damage, and replace them if necessary.

Installation - GSF600 and GSF600S

21 Install the front guide blade into the front of the cam chain tunnel (see illustration 9.15), making sure it locates correctly in its seat and its lugs locate in their cut-outs in the cylinder head (see illustrations). Install the exhaust camshaft (see Section 11).

2

9.15 Lift out the guide noting how it fits

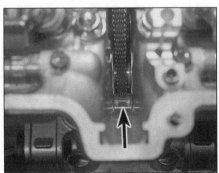

9.21a The bottom of the guide must locate in the seat (arrow) . . .

9.21b . . . and the lugs at the top (arrows) must locate in the cut-out in the head

9.22a Install the top guide . . .

9.22b . . . making sure the arrow points to the front of the engine

Inspection

7 Examine the sliding surface of the tensioner blade for signs of wear or damage, and replace it if necessary. Check the condition of the rubber cushions and replace them if they are damaged or deteriorated.

Installation

8 If removed, install the pin into the end of the blade. Install the tensioner blade into the upper crankcase half, making sure it is the correct way round and its pin locates correctly in the cut-outs. Fit the rubber cushions into the cut-outs with their rounded ends facing away from the tensioner blade pin and with the arrows on the rounded ends facing front and back, not side to side **(see illustration)**.

9 Reassemble the crankcase halves (see Section 26).

22 Install the top guide onto the cylinder head, making sure the arrow on its top faces the front of the engine **(see illustrations)**. Tighten the mounting bolts to the torque setting specified at the beginning of the Chapter.

23 Install the valve cover (see Section 8).

Installation - GSF1200 and GSF1200S

24 Apply a suitable non-permanent thread locking compound to the threads of the cam chain rear guide bolt. Install the rear guide onto the cylinder head, taking great care not to drop it down the cam chain tunnel and into the crankcase, and tighten the bolt to the torque setting specified at the beginning of the Chapter. Install the intake camshaft (see Section 11).

25 If removed, install the cam chain top guide onto the valve cover. Apply a suitable non-permanent thread locking compound to the threads of the guide screws and tighten them securely. If the engine is in the frame, install the breather cover and tighten its bolts securely. If the engine is out of the frame, leave the breather cover off to aid installation of the engine.

26 Install the front guide blade into the front of the cam chain tunnel, making sure it locates correctly in its seat and its lugs locate in their cut-outs in the cylinder head **(see illustrations 9.15, 9.21a and b)**. Install the exhaust camshaft (see Section 11).

27 Install the valve cover (see Section 8).

2 Slip the cam chain off the crankshaft.

Installation

3 Slip the cam chain onto its sprocket on the crankshaft, making sure it is properly engaged.

4 Install the crankshaft (see Section 30).

Cam chain tensioner blade

Removal

5 Separate the crankcase halves (see Section 26).

6 Remove the two rubber cushions from the upper crankcase half, noting which way up and round they fit, then lift the cam chain tensioner blade out of its cut-outs in the crankcase, noting which way round it fits **(see illustrations)**. Take care not to lose the pin which fits into the end of the blade.

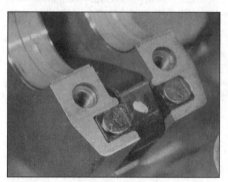

10.6a The tensioner blade is held in place by two cushions

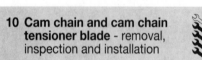

10 Cam chain and cam chain tensioner blade - removal, inspection and installation

Note: *To remove the cam chain and the cam chain tensioner blade the engine must be removed from the frame and the crankcases separated.*

Cam chain

Removal

1 Separate the crankcase halves (see Section 26) and remove the crankshaft (see Section 30).

10.6c . . . then lift out the blade

11 Camshafts, rocker arm shafts and rocker arms - removal, inspection and installation

Note: *The camshafts and rockers can be removed with the engine in the frame.*

Camshafts

Removal

1 Remove the valve cover (see Section 8).

2 Unscrew the five bolts securing the pulse generator coil cover to the right-hand side of the engine **(see illustration 9.7a)**. The engine can be rotated by using a 19 mm spanner or

10.6b To remove the blade, remove the cushions . . .

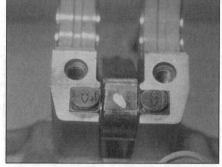

10.8 Make sure the arrows on the cushions point to the front and back of the engine

11.2a Align the ignition rotor with the pulse generator coil protrusion (arrow) . . .

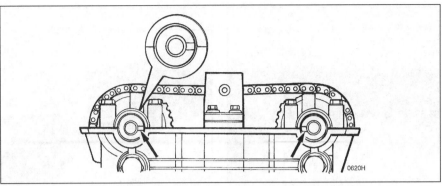

11.2b . . . and make sure the cam notches face each other. If they face away from each other, turn the rotor through 360°

socket on the large hex on the ignition rotor and turning it in a clockwise direction only **(see illustration 9.7b)**.

Caution: DO NOT use the ignition rotor retaining Allen bolt to turn the crankshaft - it may snap or strip out. Also be sure to turn the engine in its normal direction of rotation.

Alternatively, place the motorcycle on its centre stand (where fitted) or support it using an auxiliary stand so that the rear wheel is off the ground, then select a high gear and rotate the rear wheel by hand in its normal direction of rotation. Rotate the engine until the T mark on the rotor aligns with the protrusion in the centre of the pulse generator coil, and so that the notches in the right-hand end of each camshaft face each other and the number 1 arrow on the exhaust camshaft sprocket points at the valve cover gasket mating surface on the cylinder head **(see illustrations)**. Check the positions of the marks on the exhaust and intake sprockets **(see illustration 11.24)**. This is how they should be positioned for installation later.

3 Remove the cam chain tensioner (see Section 9). On GSF600 and GSF600S models, remove the cam chain top guide (see Section 9).

4 Before disturbing the camshaft journal caps, check for identification markings, which should be the letters A, B, C or D, one for each cap, cast into their top surface, on its own or inside either a square or a triangle, and corresponding to the mark on the cylinder head **(see illustration)**. These markings ensure that the caps can be matched up to their original journals on installation. If no markings are visible, mark your own using a felt pen. If necessary, make a sketch of the layout as an aid for installation **(see illustration)**.

5 Unscrew the journal cap bolts for one of the camshafts, evenly and a little at a time, until they are all loose, then unscrew the journal cap bolts for the other camshaft. Remove the bolts and lift off the journal caps **(see illustration)**. Retrieve the dowels from either the cap or the cylinder head if they are loose **(see illustration)**.

11.2c The no. 1 arrow on the exhaust sprocket should point directly at the gasket mating surface

11.4a Each cam journal cap has a letter, either on its own or inside a square or triangle, that indicates its position on the engine

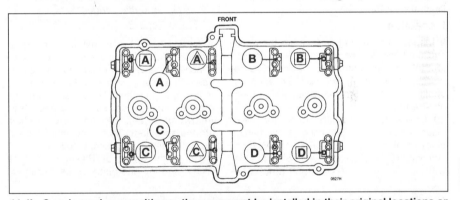

11.4b Cam journal cap positions - the caps must be installed in their original locations or the camshafts may seize

11.5a Lift the caps off the camshaft . . .

11.5b . . . and retrieve the dowels if loose

2

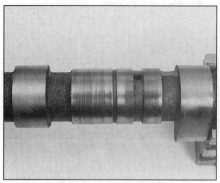

11.9 Check the journal surfaces of the camshaft for scratches or wear

11.10a Check the lobes of the camshaft for wear - here's an example of damage requiring camshaft repair or renewal

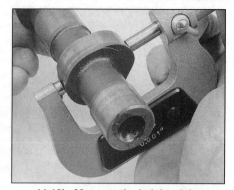

11.10b Measure the height of the camshaft lobes with a micrometer

Caution: If the bearing cap bolts aren't loosened evenly, the camshaft may bind.

6 Pull up on the cam chain and carefully guide one camshaft out. With the chain still held taut, remove the other camshaft. **Note:** *Don't remove the sprockets from the camshafts unless absolutely necessary.*

7 While the camshafts are out, don't allow the chain to go slack - the chain may drop down and bind between the crankshaft and case, which could damage these components. Wire the chain to another component to prevent it from dropping. Also, cover the top of the cylinder head with a rag to prevent foreign objects from falling into the engine.

8 Lift out the cam chain front guide **(see illustration 9.15).**

Inspection

9 Inspect the bearing surfaces of the head and the bearing caps and the corresponding journals on the camshaft. Look for score marks, deep scratches and evidence of spalling (a pitted appearance) **(see illustration).**

10 Check the camshaft lobes for heat discoloration (blue appearance), score marks, chipped areas, flat spots and spalling **(see illustration).** Measure the height of each lobe with a micrometer **(see illustration)** and

compare the results to the minimum lobe height listed in this Chapter's Specifications. If damage is noted or wear is excessive, the camshaft must be replaced. Also, be sure to check the condition of the rocker arms, as described later in this Section.

11 Check the amount of camshaft runout by supporting each end of the camshaft on V-blocks, and measuring any runout using a dial gauge. If the runout exceeds the specified limit the camshaft must be replaced.

HAYNES HiNT *Refer to Tools and Workshop Tips in the Reference section for details of how to read a micrometer and dial gauge.*

12 Next, check the camshaft bearing oil clearances. Clean the camshafts, the bearing surfaces in the cylinder head and the bearing caps with a clean, lint-free cloth, then lay the cams in place in the cylinder head, with the sprocket marks correctly aligned **(see illustration 11.24).** Engage the cam chain with the sprockets, so the camshafts don't turn as the bearing caps are tightened.

13 Cut eight strips of Plastigauge (type HPG-1) and lay one piece on each bearing

journal, parallel with the camshaft centreline **(see illustration).**

14 Make sure the journal cap dowels are installed **(see illustration 11.5b).** Install the journal caps in their proper positions **(see illustration 11.4b)** and install the bolts. Tighten the bolts evenly and a little at a time in a criss-cross pattern, to the torque listed in this Chapter's Specifications. While doing this, DO NOT let the camshafts rotate!

15 Now unscrew the bolts, a little at a time, and carefully lift off the journal caps.

16 To determine the oil clearance, compare the crushed Plastigauge (at its widest point) on each journal to the scale printed on the Plastigauge container **(see illustration).** Compare the results to this Chapter's Specifications. If the oil clearance is greater than specified, either the camshaft journal or journal holder (or both) are worn. Measure the diameter of the camshaft journal with a micrometer **(see illustration).** Measure the journal holder diameter by assembling the journals on the cylinder head without the camshaft in place, and measuring the diameter with an internal micrometer or telescoping gauge. If any measurement is outside of that specified, the camshaft or journal holder/cylinder head must be replaced.

11.13 Place a strip of Plastigauge on each bearing journal

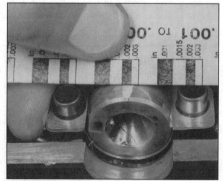

11.16a Compare the width of the crushed Plastigauge to the scale provided with it to obtain the clearance

11.16b Measure the cam bearing journal with a micrometer

11.23a The intake camshaft is marked IN, the exhaust camshaft is marked EX

11.23b Make sure the front run of the chain is taut before laying it on the sprocket

17 Except in cases of oil starvation, the cam chain wears very little. If the chain has stretched excessively, which makes it difficult to maintain proper tension, replace it with a new one (see Section 10).

18 Check the sprockets for wear, cracks and other damage, replacing them if necessary. If the sprockets are worn, the chain is also worn, and also the sprocket on the crankshaft (which can only be remedied by replacing the crankshaft). If wear this severe is apparent, the entire engine should be disassembled for inspection.

19 Check the front chain guide blade and the top and rear chain guides (1200 models only) for wear or damage (see Section 9). If they are worn or damaged, the chain may be worn out or improperly tensioned. Check the operation of the cam chain tensioner (see Section 9).

Installation

20 If removed, install each sprocket onto its camshaft, making sure they are installed with the numbered side of each sprocket facing the notched end of the camshaft and so that the numbers align as shown **(see illustration 11.24)** when the notches are facing each other. Apply a smear of a suitable non-permanent thread locking compound to the sprocket bolts before installing them, and tighten them to the torque setting specified at the beginning of the Chapter.

21 Install the front cam chain guide (see Section 9).

22 Make sure the bearing surfaces in the cylinder head and the journal caps are clean, then apply a light coat of engine oil or moly-based grease to each of them. Apply a coat of moly-based grease to the camshaft lobes.

23 Check that the cam chain is engaged around the lower sprocket teeth on the crankshaft and that the crankshaft is positioned as described in Step 2. Install the exhaust camshaft (identified by EX) through the cam chain **(see illustration)**. Position it so that the notch in its right-hand end faces the right-hand side of the engine and points backwards, and so that the arrow marked 1 on the sprocket points forwards and is flush with the top of the cylinder head mating surface, and the arrow marked 2 points vertically upwards **(see illustration 11.24)**. Keeping the front run of the chain taut engage the chain on the sprocket teeth **(see illustration)**.

24 Starting with the cam chain pin that is directly above the arrow marked 2 on the exhaust camshaft sprocket, count twenty-four pins along the chain towards the intake side. Install the intake camshaft (identified by IN) **(see illustration 11.23a)** through the cam chain so that the notch in its right-hand end faces the right-hand side of the engine and points forwards, then engage the sprocket with the chain so that the arrow marked 3 on the sprocket aligns with the twenty-fourth pin **(see illustration)**.

25 Before proceeding further, check that everything aligns as described in Steps 2, 23 and 24. If it doesn't, the valve timing will be inaccurate and the valves will contact the pistons when the engine is turned over.

26 Oil the camshaft journal caps. Ensure the camshaft cap dowels are installed then fit the caps **(see illustrations 11.5b and 11.5a)**, making sure they are in their proper positions as noted on removal (Step 4) **(see illustration 11.4b)**. Tighten the cap bolts on one camshaft evenly and a little at a time in a criss-cross sequence, until the specified torque setting is

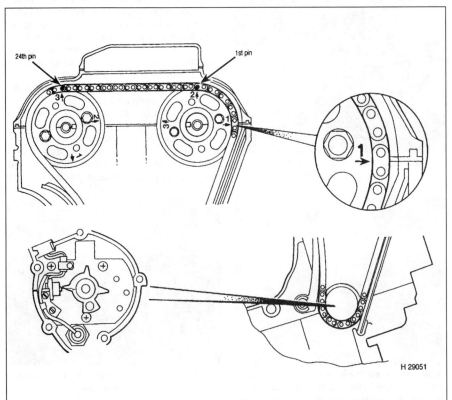

11.24 Valve timing marks

2

11.26 Tighten the journal cap bolts to the specified torque setting

11.33 Remove the rocker shaft plug ...

11.34 ... and the rocker shaft locking bolt

reached **(see illustration)**. Repeat for the other camshaft. **Note:** *The journal cap bolts are of the high tensile type, indicated by a 9 mark on the bolt head. Don't use any other type of bolt..*

27 With all caps tightened down, check that the valve timing marks still align (see Steps 2, 23 and 24). Check that each camshaft is not pinched by turning the crankshaft a few degrees in each direction with a 19 mm spanner on the ignition rotor.

Caution: If the marks are not aligned exactly as described, the valve timing will be incorrect and the valves may strike the pistons, causing extensive damage to the engine.

28 On GSF600 and GSF600S models, install the cam chain top guide (see Section 9).
29 Install the cam chain tensioner (see Section 9).
30 Check the valve clearances and adjust them if necessary (see Chapter 1).
31 The remainder of installation is the reverse of removal.

Rocker arm shafts and rocker arms

Removal

32 Remove the camshafts following the procedure given above.
33 Unscrew one rocker shaft plug from the cylinder head **(see illustration)**. Discard the

plug sealing washer as a new one must be used.
34 Unscrew the rocker shaft locking bolt **(see illustration)**.
35 Thread an M8 bolt into the end of the rocker shaft and use it to pull the shaft out **(see illustrations)**.
36 Remove the rocker arms and springs, noting how they fit **(see illustrations 11.40b and 11.40a)**.
37 Repeat the above Steps to remove the other rocker arm shafts and rocker arms. Keep all of the parts in order so they can be reinstalled in their original locations.

Inspection

38 Clean all of the components with solvent and dry them off. Blow through the oil passages in the rocker arms with compressed air, if available. Inspect the rocker arm faces for pits, spalling, score marks and rough spots **(see illustration)**. Check the rocker arm-to-shaft contact areas and the clearance adjusting screws. Look for cracks in each rocker arm. If the faces of the rocker arms are damaged, the rocker arms and the camshafts should be replaced as a set.
39 Measure the diameter of the rocker arm shafts, in the area where the rocker arms ride, and compare the results with this Chapter's Specifications. Also measure the inside diameter of the rocker arms **(see illustrations)** and compare the results with

11.35a Thread M8 bolt into the end of the rocker shaft ...

11.35b ... then pull on the bolt to withdraw the shaft

11.38 Inspect the rocker arms, especially the faces that contact the cam lobes, for wear

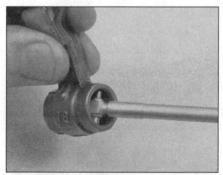

11.39a Measure the inside diameter of the rocker arm - in this case a telescoping gauge is expanded against the bore of the arm, then locked ...

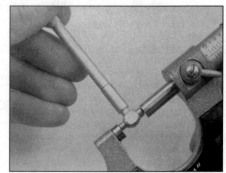

11.39b ... and a micrometer is used to measure the gauge

11.40a Install the spring on the outside . . .

11.40b . . . followed by the rocker arm, then slide the shaft through

11.41 Tighten the rocker shaft locking bolt . . .

this Chapter's Specifications. If either the shaft or the rocker arms are worn beyond the specified limits, replace them as a set.

Installation

40 Lubricate the rocker arm shaft with engine oil. Position the springs and rocker arms in the cylinder head, making sure that each spring is on the outside of its rocker and slide the shaft into the cylinder head and through the rocker arms and springs **(see illustrations)**.

41 Install the rocker shaft locking bolt and tighten it to the torque setting specified at the beginning of the Chapter **(see illustration)**. Remove the 8 mm bolt from the end of the rocker shaft, if not already done.

42 Install the rocker shaft plug with a new sealing washer and tighten it to the specified torque setting **(see illustration)**.

43 Install the other rocker assemblies. Install the camshafts following the procedure described earlier in this Section.

12 Cylinder head - removal and installation

Caution: *The engine must be completely cool before beginning this procedure or the cylinder head may become warped.*

11.42 . . . and plug to the specified torque setting

Note: *The cylinder head can be removed with the engine in the frame. If the engine has already been removed, ignore the steps which don't apply.*

Removal

1 Remove the exhaust system (see Chapter 3).
2 Remove the carburettors (see Chapter 3).
3 Remove the spark plugs (see Chapter 1).
4 Remove the camshafts (see Section 11).
5 On GSF600 and GSF600S models, the cylinder head is secured by eight 10 mm domed nuts with copper washers, four 10 mm plain nuts with steel washers and one 6 mm

12.5a Remove the cylinder head bolt front(arrow)

bolt. Unscrew the bolt on the front of the cylinder head **(see illustration)**. The eight domed nuts and four plain nuts are numbered for identification **(see illustrations)**. Slacken the nuts evenly and a little at a time in a **reverse** of their numerical sequence until they are all slack. Remove all the nuts and their washers, taking great care not to drop any of them into the crankcase. Note which type of nut and washer fits on which stud.

6 On GSF1200 and GSF1200S models, the cylinder head is secured by four 10 mm domed nuts with copper washers, four 10 mm plain nuts with copper washers and a common plate, four 10 mm plain nuts with

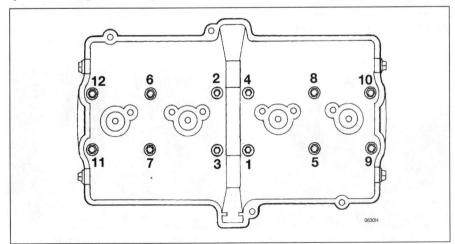

12.5b Cylinder head nut TIGHTENING sequence

12.5c The cylinder head tightening sequence numbers are cast into the head next to the nuts; loosen from the highest number to the lowest, and tighten from the lowest number to the highest

2

12.6 Lift off the cylinder head plate after the nuts have been removed

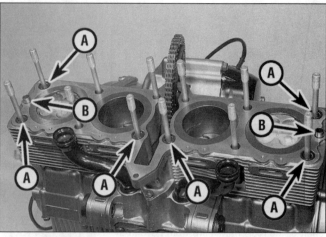

12.8 Remove the stud O-rings (A), and also the dowels (B) if they are loose

steel washers, and one 6 mm bolt. Unscrew the bolt on the front of the cylinder head **(see illustration 12.5a)**. The four domed nuts and eight plain nuts are numbered for identification **(see illustrations 12.5b and c)**. Slacken the nuts evenly and a little at a time in a **reverse** of their numerical sequence until they are all slack. Remove all the nuts and their washers, taking great care not to drop any of them into the crankcase. Note which type of nut and washer fits on which stud. Also remove the plate from the centre of the cylinder head **(see illustration)**.

12.10 Remove the O-ring from each oil drain tube

7 Pull the cylinder head up off the studs. If it is stuck, tap around the joint faces of the cylinder head with a soft-faced mallet to free the head. Do not attempt to free the head by inserting a screwdriver between the head and cylinder block - you'll damage the sealing surfaces.

8 Lift the head off the block, passing the cam chain down through the tunnel as you do. Do not let the chain fall into the block - secure it with a piece of wire or metal bar to prevent it from doing so. Remove the old cylinder head gasket and the O-rings which fit around the four end cylinder head studs and the two centre studs at the front **(see illustration)**. Stuff a clean rag into the cam chain tunnel to prevent any debris falling into the engine. Discard the gasket and O-rings as new ones must be used.

9 If they are loose, remove the dowel from each end of the cylinder block **(see illustration 11.8)**. If either appears to be missing it is probably stuck in the underside of the cylinder head.

10 Remove the O-rings from the top of the oil drain tubes and discard them as new ones must be used **(see illustration)**.

11 Check the cylinder head gasket and the mating surfaces on the cylinder head and

block for signs of leakage, which could indicate warpage. Refer to Section 14 and check the flatness of the cylinder head.

12 Clean all traces of old gasket material from the cylinder head and block. If a scraper is used, take care not to scratch or gouge the soft aluminium. Be careful not to let any of the gasket material fall into the crankcase, the cylinder bores or the oil passages.

Installation

13 If removed, install the two dowels onto the cylinder block **(see illustration 12.8)**. Lubricate the cylinder bores with engine oil.

14 Fit new O-rings onto the four end cylinder head studs and the two centre studs at the front **(see illustration)**. Make sure they are pressed into their recesses and are properly seated.

15 Fit a new O-ring onto the top of each oil drain tube **(see illustration 12.10)**. Apply a smear of grease to the O-rings.

16 Ensure both cylinder head and block mating surfaces are clean, then lay the new head gasket in place on the cylinder block, making sure all the holes are correctly aligned and that the UP letters stamped out of the gasket read the correct way round **(see illustrations)**. Never re-use the old gasket.

12.14 Fit new O-rings around the two front centre studs and all four end studs

12.16a Fit the new cylinder head gasket . . .

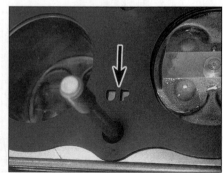

12.16b . . . making sure the UP mark (arrow) reads correctly

12.17a Lower the cylinder head onto the block . . .

12.17b . . . making sure the drain tubes locate correctly into the head

17 Carefully lower the cylinder head over the studs and onto the block **(see illustration)**. It is helpful to have an assistant to pass the cam chain up through the tunnel and slip a piece of wire through it to prevent it falling back into the engine. Keep the chain taut to prevent it becoming disengaged from the crankshaft sprocket. Make sure the oil drain tubes locate correctly into the base of the cylinder head **(see illustration)**.

18 On GSF600 and GSF600S models, install the eight 10 mm domed nuts with their copper washers and the four 10 mm plain nuts with their steel washers onto their correct studs **(see illustration)** and tighten them finger-tight. Now tighten the nuts evenly and a little at a time in their numerical sequence **(see illustration 12.5b)** to the torque setting specified at the beginning of the Chapter **(see illustration)**.

19 On GSF1200 and GSF1200S models, install the cylinder head plate and the four 10 mm plain nuts with their copper washers, the four 10 mm domed nuts with their copper washers and the four 10 mm plain nuts with steel washers onto their correct studs **(see illustration)** and tighten them finger-tight. Now tighten the nuts evenly and a little at a time in their numerical sequence **(see**

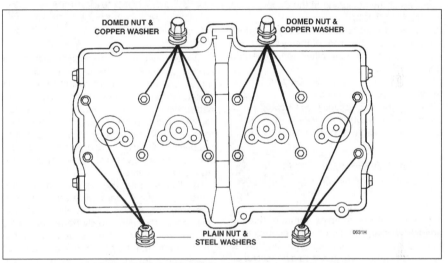

12.18a Cylinder head nuts and washers - 600 models

12.18b Tighten the cylinder head nuts to the specified torque setting

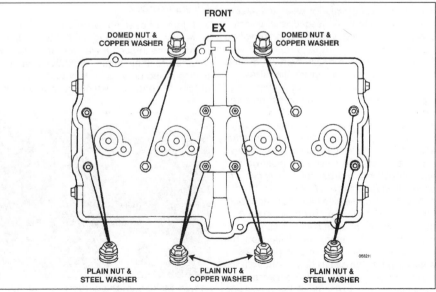

12.19 Cylinder head nuts and washers - 1200 models

2

12.20a Install the front cylinder head bolt . . .

12.20b . . . and tighten it to the specified torque setting

illustration 12.5b) to the torque setting specified at the beginning of the Chapter **(see illustration 12.18b)**.

20 When the nuts are correctly torqued, install the bolt in the front of the cylinder head and tighten it to the specified torque setting **(see illustrations)**.

21 Install the camshafts (see Section 11) and the valve cover (see Section 8).

22 Install the spark plugs (see Chapter 1).

23 Install the carburettors (see Chapter 3).

24 Install the exhaust system (see Chapter 3).

13 Valves/valve seats/valve guides - servicing

1 Because of the complex nature of this job and the special tools and equipment required, most owners leave servicing of the valves, valve seats and valve guides to a professional.

2 The home mechanic can, however, remove the valves from the cylinder head, clean and check the components for wear and assess the extent of the work needed, and, unless a valve service is required, grind in the valves (see Section 14).

3 The dealer service department will remove the valves and springs, replace the valves and guides, recut the valve seats, check and replace the valve springs, spring retainers and collets (as necessary), replace the valve seals with new ones and reassemble the valve components. **Note**: *Suzuki recommends against grinding in the valves after they've been serviced. The valve seat must be soft and unpolished in order for final seating to occur when the engine is first run.*

4 After the valve service has been performed, the head will be in like-new condition. When the head is returned, be sure to clean it again very thoroughly before installation on the engine to remove any metal particles or abrasive grit that may still be present from the valve service operations. Use compressed air, if available, to blow out all the holes and passages.

14 Cylinder head and valves - disassembly, inspection and reassembly

1 As mentioned in the previous section, valve servicing, valve seat re-cutting and valve guide replacement should be left to a Suzuki dealer. However, disassembly, cleaning and inspection of the valves and related components can be done (if the necessary special tools are available) by the home mechanic. This way no expense is incurred if the inspection reveals that overhaul is not required at this time.

2 To disassemble the valve components without the risk of damaging them, a valve spring compressor is absolutely necessary. This special tool can usually be rented, but if it's not available, have a dealer service department handle the entire process of disassembly, inspection, service or repair (if required) and reassembly of the valves.

Disassembly

3 Before proceeding, arrange to label and store the valves along with their related components in such a way that they can be returned to their original locations without getting mixed up. A good way to do this is to obtain a container which is divided into

14.6a Make sure the compressor locates correctly onto the spring . . .

sixteen compartments, and to label each compartment with the identity of the valve which will be stored in it (ie number of cylinder, intake or exhaust valve). Alternatively, labelled plastic bags will do just as well.

4 Remove the rocker arm shafts and rocker arms (see Section 11).

5 If not already done, clean all traces of old gasket material from the cylinder head. If a scraper is used, take care not to scratch or gouge the soft aluminium.

> **HAYNES HINT** *Refer to Tools and Workshop Tips for details of gasket removal methods.*

6 Compress the valve spring with a spring compressor, making sure it is correctly located onto each end of the valve assembly **(see illustrations)**. Remove the collets from the valve groove **(see illustrations)**; do not compress the springs any more than is absolutely necessary. Carefully release the valve spring compressor and remove the retainer (noting which way up it fits), springs and the valve from the head. If the valve binds

14.6b . . . and the valve. The compressor must only contact the valve and not the soft aluminium of the head - use a spacer if the plate on the compressor is too big for the valve

14.6c Remove the collets with needle-nose pliers, tweezers, a magnet or a screwdriver with a dab of grease on it

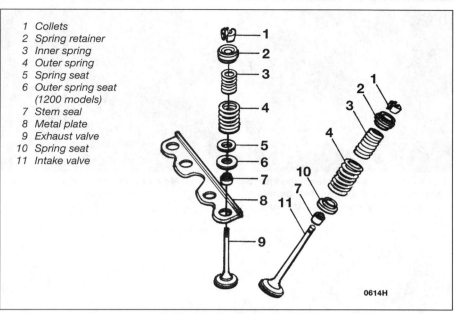

1 Collets
2 Spring retainer
3 Inner spring
4 Outer spring
5 Spring seat
6 Outer spring seat (1200 models)
7 Stem seal
8 Metal plate
9 Exhaust valve
10 Spring seat
11 Intake valve

0614H

14.6d Valve components

in the guide (won't pull through), push it back into the head and deburr the area around the collet groove with a very fine file or whetstone (see illustration).

7 Repeat the procedure for the remaining valves. Remember to keep the parts for each valve together and in order so they can be reinstalled in the same location.

8 Once the valves have been removed and labelled, pull the valve stem seals off the top of the valve guides with pliers and discard them (the old seals should never be reused), then remove the spring seats, noting which way up they fit (see illustrations 14.28b and 14.28a). On GSF1200 and GSF1200S models, also remove the outer spring seats fitted to the exhaust valves only, followed on 600 and 1200 engines by the two metal plates which locate over the exhaust valve guides, one for each side of the engine (see illustration 14.27).

9 Next, clean the cylinder head with solvent and dry it thoroughly. Compressed air will speed the drying process and ensure that all holes and recessed areas are clean.

10 Clean all of the valve springs, collets, retainers and spring seats with solvent and dry them thoroughly. Do the parts from one valve at a time so that no mixing of parts between valves occurs.

11 Scrape off any deposits that may have formed on the valve, then use a motorised wire brush to remove deposits from the valve heads and stems. Again, make sure the valves do not get mixed up.

Inspection

12 Inspect the head very carefully for cracks and other damage. If cracks are found, a new head will be required. Check the cam bearing surfaces for wear and evidence of seizure. Check the camshafts and rocker arms for wear as well (see Section 11).

13 Using a precision straight-edge and a feeler gauge set to the warpage limit listed in the specifications at the beginning of the Chapter, check the head gasket mating surface for warpage. Refer to *Tools and Workshop Tips* in the Reference section for details of how to use the straight-edge.

14 Examine the valve seats in the combustion chamber. If they are pitted, cracked or burned, the head will require work beyond the scope of

the home mechanic. Measure the valve seat width and compare it to this Chapter's Specifications (see illustration). If it exceeds the service limit, or if it varies around its circumference, valve overhaul is required. If available, use Prussian blue to determine the extent of valve seat wear. Uniformly coat the seat with the Prussian blue, then install the valve and rotate it back and forth using a lapping tool. Remove the valve and check whether the ring of blue on the valve is uniform and continuous around the valve, and of the correct width as specified.

15 Clean the valve guides to remove any carbon build-up, then install the valve in its guide so that its face is 10 mm above the seat. Mount a dial gauge against the side of the valve face and measure the amount of side clearance (wobble) between the valve stem and its guide in two perpendicular directions. If the clearance exceeds the limit specified, remove the valve and measure the valve stem diameter (see illustration). Also

2

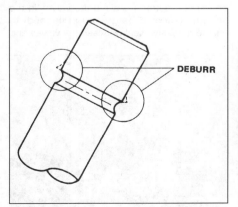

DEBURR

14.6e If the valve stem won't pull through the guide, deburr the area above the collet groove

14.14 Measure the valve seat width with a ruler (or for greater precision use a vernier caliper)

14.15a Measure the valve stem diameter with a micrometer

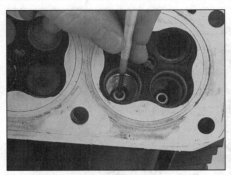

14.15b Insert a small hole gauge into the valve guide and expand it so there's a slight drag when it's pulled out

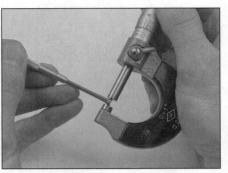

14.15c Measure the small hole gauge with a micrometer

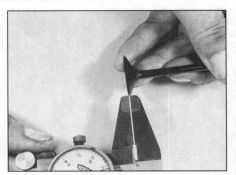

14.16 Measure the valve face thickness as shown

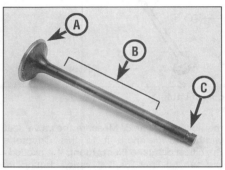

14.17 Check the valve face (A), stem (B) and collet groove (C) for signs of wear and damage

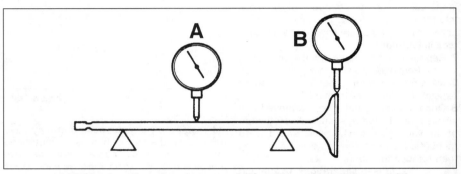

14.18 Measure the valve stem runout (A) and the valve head runout (B)

measure the inside diameters of the guides (at both ends and the centre of the guide) with a small hole gauge and micrometer **(see illustrations)**. The guides are measured at the ends and at the centre to determine if they are worn in a bell-mouth pattern (more wear at the ends). If the valve stem or guide is worn beyond its limit, it must be replaced.

16 Carefully inspect each valve face for cracks, pits and burned spots. Measure the valve face thickness and compare it to this Chapter's Specifications **(see illustration)**. If it exceeds the service limit, or if it varies around its circumference, valve overhaul is required.

17 Check the valve stem and the collet groove area for cracks **(see illustration)**. Rotate the valve and check for any obvious indication that it is bent. Check the end of the stem for pitting and excessive wear. The presence of any of the above conditions indicates the need for valve servicing. The stem end can be ground down, provided that the amount of stem above the collet groove after grinding is not less than the minimum specified. When installing a valve whose end has been ground, check that the stem end protrudes above the collets.

18 Using V-blocks and a dial gauge, measure the valve stem runout and the valve head runout and compare the results to the specifications **(see illustrations)**. If either

measurement exceeds the service limit specified, the valve must be replaced.

19 Check the end of each valve spring for wear and pitting. Measure the spring free length and compare it to that listed in the specifications **(see illustration)**. If any spring is shorter than specified it has sagged and must be replaced. Also place the spring upright on a flat surface and check it for bend by placing a ruler against it **(see illustration)**. If the bend in any spring is excessive, it must be replaced. The spring tension should also be checked by measuring the amount of weight needed to compress each spring to a particular length. If the weight required to compress the spring to the specified length is

greater or less than the weight specified, the spring must be replaced.

20 Check the spring retainers and collets for obvious wear and cracks. Any questionable parts should not be reused, as extensive damage will occur in the event of failure during engine operation.

21 If the inspection indicates that no overhaul work is required, the valve components can be reinstalled in the head.

Reassembly

22 Unless a valve service has been performed, before installing the valves in the head they should be ground in (lapped) to ensure a positive seal between the valves and

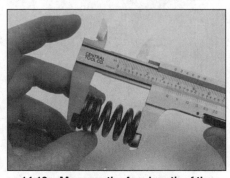

14.19a Measure the free length of the valve springs

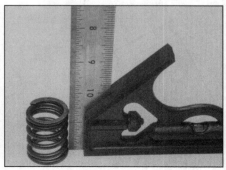

14.19b Check the valve springs for squareness

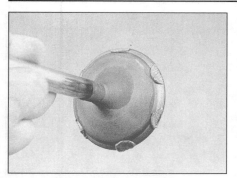

14.23 Apply the lapping compound very sparingly, in small dabs, to the valve face only

14.24a Rotate the valve grinding tool back and forth between the palms of your hands

14.24b The face and seat should be the specified width and have a smooth, unbroken appearance (arrow)

seats. This procedure requires coarse and fine valve grinding compound and a valve grinding tool. If a grinding tool is not available, a piece of rubber or plastic hose can be slipped over the valve stem (after the valve has been installed in the guide) and used to turn the valve. **Note:** *Suzuki advise that the valves should not be ground in immediately after seat recutting; the valve seat must be soft in order for final seating to occur when the engine is first run.*

23 Apply a small amount of coarse grinding compound to the valve face, then slip the valve into the guide **(see illustration)**. **Note:** *Make sure each valve is installed in its correct guide and be careful not to get any grinding compound on the valve stem.*

24 Attach the grinding tool (or hose) to the valve and rotate the tool between the palms of your hands. Use a back-and-forth motion (as though rubbing your hands together) rather than a circular motion (ie so that the valve rotates alternately clockwise and anti-clockwise rather than in one direction only) **(see illustration)**. Lift the valve off the seat and turn it at regular intervals to distribute the grinding compound properly. Continue the grinding procedure until the valve face and seat contact area is of uniform width and unbroken around the entire circumference of the valve face and seat **(see illustration)**.

25 Carefully remove the valve from the guide

and wipe off all traces of grinding compound. Use solvent to clean the valve and wipe the seat area thoroughly with a solvent soaked cloth.

26 Repeat the procedure with fine valve grinding compound, then repeat the entire procedure for the remaining valves.

27 Install the metal plates over the exhaust valve guides on each side of the engine, followed by an outer spring seat on some models **(see illustration)**.

28 Lay the spring seats for all the valves in place in the cylinder head with their shouldered side facing up so that they fit into the base of the springs (the spring seat can be

identified from the spring retainer by its larger internal diameter - be sure not to mix up the two), then install new valve stem seals on each of the guides **(see illustrations)**. Use an appropriate size deep socket to push the seals over the end of the valve guide until they are felt to clip into place. Don't twist or cock them, or they will not seal properly against the valve stems. Also, don't remove them again or they will be damaged.

29 Coat the valve stems with molybdenum disulphide grease, then install one of them into its guide, rotating it slowly to avoid damaging the seal **(see illustration)**. Check that the valve moves up and down freely in

14.27 A metal plate (arrow) fits over the exhaust valve stem seals, followed by an outer spring seat

14.28a Install the spring seat

2

14.28b Fit the oil seal over the valve stem

14.29a Coat the valve stem with molybdenum disulphide grease and install the valve in its guide

14.29b Install the inner spring with its closer-wound coils at the bottom, next to the head

14.29c Install the outer spring with its closer-wound coils at the bottom, next to the head

14.29d Make sure the spring retainer is the correct way round

14.30 A small dab of grease will help to keep the collets in place on the valve while the spring is released

the guide. Next, install the inner and outer springs, with their closer-wound coils facing down into the cylinder head, followed by the spring retainer, with its shouldered side facing down so that it fits into the top of the springs **(see illustrations)**.

30 Apply a small amount of grease to the collets to help hold them in place as the pressure is released from the springs **(see illustration)**. Compress the springs with the valve spring compressor and install the collets **(see illustration 14.6c)**. When compressing the springs, depress them only as far as is absolutely necessary to slip the collets into place. Make certain that the collets are securely locked in their retaining grooves.

31 Support the cylinder head on blocks so the valves can't contact the workbench top,

then very gently tap each of the valve stems with a soft-faced hammer. This will help seat the collets in their grooves.

 HAYNES HiNT *Check for proper sealing of the valves by pouring a small amount of solvent into each of the valve ports. If the solvent leaks past any valve into the combustion chamber area the valve grinding operation on that valve should be repeated.*

15 Cylinder block - removal, inspection and installation

Note: *The cylinder block can be removed with the engine in the frame.*

Removal

1 Remove the cylinder head (see Section 12).
2 Pull the oil drain tubes out of their holes in the crankcase **(see illustration)**. Discard the O-rings as new ones must be used.
3 Unscrew the single nut which secures the front of the block to the crankcase **(see illustration)**.
4 Hold the cam chain up and lift the cylinder block up to remove it from the studs **(see illustration)**, then pass the cam chain down through the tunnel. Do not let the chain fall

into the crankcase - secure it with a piece of wire or metal bar to prevent it from doing so. If the block is stuck, tap around the joint faces of the block with a soft-faced mallet to free it from the crankcase. Don't attempt to free the block by inserting a screwdriver between it and the crankcase - you'll damage the sealing surfaces. When the block is removed, stuff clean rags around the pistons to prevent anything falling into the crankcase.

5 Note the location of the two dowels which will be either on the bottom of the block or in the crankcase **(see illustration)**. Remove them if they are loose.

6 Remove the gasket and clean all traces of old gasket material from the cylinder block and crankcase mating surfaces. If a scraper is used, take care not to scratch or gouge the soft aluminium. Be careful not to let any of the gasket material fall into the crankcase or the oil passages.

Inspection

5 Do not attempt to separate the cylinder liners from the cylinder block.
6 Check the cylinder walls carefully for scratches and score marks. A rebore will be necessary to remove any deep scores.
7 Using a precision straight-edge and a feeler gauge set to the warpage limit listed in the specifications at the beginning of the Chapter, check the block gasket mating surface for warpage. Refer to *Tools and Workshop Tips* in the Reference section for details of how to

15.2 Remove the oil drain tubes from their holes . . .

15.3 . . . and remove the single nut (arrow)

15.4 Hold the cam chain up and lift the block off the crankcase

15.5 Cylinder block locating dowels (arrows)

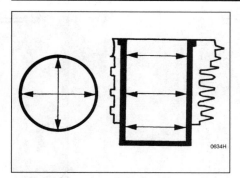

15.8 Measure the cylinder bore in the directions shown with a telescoping gauge, then measure the gauge with a micrometer

use the straight-edge. If warpage is excessive the block must be replaced with a new one.

8 Using telescoping gauges and a micrometer (see *Tools and Workshop Tips*), check the dimensions of each cylinder to assess the amount of wear. Measure near the top (but below the level of the top piston ring at TDC), centre and bottom (but above the level of the oil ring at BDC) of the bore, both parallel to and across the crankshaft axis **(see illustration)**. Compare the results to the specifications at the beginning of the Chapter. If the cylinders are worn beyond the service limit, or badly scratched, scuffed or scored, have them rebored and honed by a Suzuki dealer or specialist motorcycle repair shop. If the cylinders are rebored, they will require oversize pistons and rings.

9 If the precision measuring tools are not available, take the block to a Suzuki dealer or specialist motorcycle repair shop for assessment and advice.

10 If the block and cylinders are in good condition and the piston-to-bore clearance is within specifications (see Section 16), the cylinders should be honed (de-glazed). To perform this operation you will need the proper size flexible hone with fine stones, or a bottle-brush type hone, plenty of light oil or honing oil, some clean rags and an electric drill motor.

11 Hold the block sideways (so that the bores are horizontal rather than vertical) in a vice with soft jaws or cushioned with wooden

blocks. Mount the hone in the drill motor, compress the stones and insert the hone into the cylinder. Thoroughly lubricate the cylinder, then turn on the drill and move the hone up and down in the cylinder at a pace which produces a fine cross-hatch pattern on the cylinder wall with the lines intersecting at an angle of approximately 60°. Be sure to use plenty of lubricant and do not take off any more material than is necessary to produce the desired effect. Do not withdraw the hone from the cylinder while it is still turning. Switch off the drill and continue to move it up and down in the cylinder until it has stopped turning, then compress the stones and withdraw the hone. Wipe the oil from the cylinder and repeat the procedure on the other cylinder. Remember, do not take too much material from the cylinder wall.

12 Wash the cylinders thoroughly with warm soapy water to remove all traces of the abrasive grit produced during the honing operation. Be sure to run a brush through the stud holes and flush them with running water. After rinsing, dry the cylinders thoroughly and apply a thin coat of light, rust-preventative oil to all machined surfaces.

13 If you do not have the equipment or desire to perform the honing operation, take the block to a Suzuki dealer or specialist motorcycle repair shop.

14 Check that all the cylinder studs are tight in the crankcase halves. If any are loose, remove them, noting which fits where as they are of different lengths and colours, then clean their threads. Refer to *Tools and Workshop Tips* in the Reference section for stud removal methods. Apply a suitable non-permanent thread locking compound and, where possible, tighten them to the torque setting specified at the beginning of the Chapter.

Installation

15 Check that the mating surfaces of the cylinder block and crankcase are free from oil or pieces of old gasket.

16 If removed, install the dowels into their correct locations in the crankcase, and push them firmly home **(see illustration 15.5)**.

17 Remove the rags from around the pistons and lay the new base gasket in place on the

crankcase, making sure all the holes are correctly aligned and the UP marking stamped out of the gasket reads the correct way round **(see illustration)**. Never re-use the old gasket.

18 If required, install piston ring clamps onto the pistons to ease their entry into the bores as the block is lowered. This is not essential as each cylinder has a good lead-in enabling the piston rings to be hand-fed into the bore. If possible, have an assistant support the block while this is done.

HAYNES HiNT *Rotate the crankshaft until the inner pistons (2 and 3) are uppermost and feed them into the block first. Access to the lower pistons (1 and 4) is easier since they are on the outside.*

19 Lubricate the cylinder bores, pistons and piston rings, and the connecting rod big- and small-ends, with clean engine oil, then install the block down over the studs until the uppermost piston crowns fit into the bores. At this stage feed the cam chain up through the block and secure it in place with a piece of wire to prevent it from falling back down **(see illustration 15.4)**.

20 Gently push down on the cylinder block, making sure the pistons enter the bores squarely and do not get cocked sideways. If piston ring clamps are not being used, carefully compress and feed each ring into the bore as the block is lowered. If necessary, use a soft mallet to gently tap the block down, but do not use force if the block appears to be stuck as the pistons and/or rings will be damaged. If clamps are used, remove them once the pistons are in the bore.

21 When the pistons are correctly installed in the cylinders, press the block down onto the base gasket. Install the single nut which secures the front of the block to the crankcase and tighten it to the torque setting specified at the beginning of the Chapter **(see illustration)**.

22 Fit a new O-ring onto the bottom of each oil drain tube, then press the tubes into their holes in the crankcase **(see illustration)**.

23 Install the cylinder head (see Section 12).

2

15.17 Make sure the UP letters stamped out of the gasket read correctly

15.21 Install the single nut and tighten it to the specified torque setting

15.22 Use a new O-ring on each oil drain tube

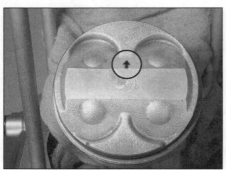

16.2 Note the arrow stamped into each piston crown which must face forward

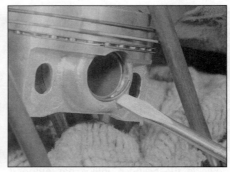

16.3a Remove the circlip using a pair of pliers or screwdriver inserted in the notch . . .

16.3b . . . then push the pin out from the other side and withdraw it from the piston

16 Pistons - removal, inspection and installation

Note: *The pistons can be removed with the engine in the frame.*

Removal

1 Remove the cylinder block (see Section 15).
2 Before removing the piston from the connecting rod, stuff a clean rag into the hole around the rod to prevent the circlips or anything else from falling into the crankcase. Use a sharp scriber or felt marker pen to write the cylinder identity on the crown of each piston (or on the inside of the skirt if the piston is dirty and going to be cleaned). Each piston should also have an arrow marked on its crown which should face forwards **(see illustration)**. If this is not visible, mark the piston accordingly so that it can be installed the correct way round.
3 Carefully prise out the circlip on one side of the piston using needle-nose pliers or a small flat-bladed screwdriver inserted into the notch **(see illustration)**. Push the piston pin out from the other side to free the piston from the connecting rod **(see illustration)**. Remove the

other circlip and discard them as new ones must be used. When the piston has been removed, install its pin back into its bore so that related parts do not get mixed up. Rotate the crankshaft so that the best access is obtained for each piston.

HAYNES HiNT *To prevent the circlip from pinging away or from dropping into the crankcase, pass a rod or screwdriver, whose diameter is greater than the gap between the circlip ends, through the piston pin. This will trap the circlip if it springs out.*

HAYNES HiNT *If a piston pin is a tight fit in the piston bosses, soak a rag in boiling water then wring it out and wrap it around the piston - this will expand the alloy piston sufficiently to release its grip on the pin. If the piston pin is particularly stubborn, extract it using a drawbolt tool, but be careful to protect the piston's working surfaces.*

Inspection

4 Before the inspection process can be carried out, the pistons must be cleaned and the old piston rings removed. Note that if the cylinders are being rebored, piston inspection can be overlooked as new ones will be fitted.
5 Using your thumbs or a piston ring removal and installation tool, carefully remove the rings from the pistons **(see illustration)**. Do not nick or gouge the pistons in the process. Carefully note which way up each ring fits and in which groove as they must be installed in their original positions if being re-used. The upper surface of each ring is marked with a letter at one end **(see illustration)**. On 600 models, the top ring is identified by the letter R, and the second (middle) ring by the letters RN. On 1200 models, the top ring is identified by the letter N, and the second (middle) ring by 2N. On both models, the top face of the top ring is chrome plated. The rings can also be identified by their different cross-section shape **(see illustration 17.12)**.
6 Scrape all traces of carbon from the tops of the pistons. A hand-held wire brush or a piece of fine emery cloth can be used once most of the deposits have been scraped away. Do not, under any circumstances, use a wire

16.5a Removing the piston rings using a ring removal and installation tool

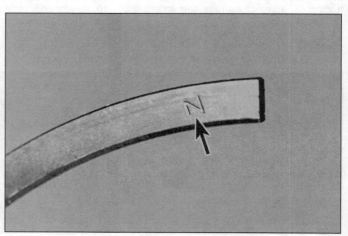

16.5b Note the letter (arrow) which must face up

16.11 Measure the piston ring-to-groove clearance with a feeler gauge

16.12 Measure the piston diameter with a micrometer at the specified distance from the bottom of the skirt

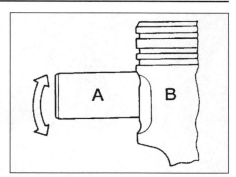

16.13a Slip the pin (A) into the piston (B) and try to rock it back and forth. If it's loose, replace the piston and pin

brush mounted in a drill motor to remove deposits from the pistons; the piston material is soft and will be eroded away by the wire brush.

7 Use a piston ring groove cleaning tool to remove any carbon deposits from the ring grooves. If a tool is not available, a piece broken off an old ring will do the job. Be very careful to remove only the carbon deposits. Do not remove any metal and do not nick or gouge the sides of the ring grooves.

8 Once the deposits have been removed, clean the pistons with solvent and dry them thoroughly. If the identification previously marked on the piston is cleaned off, be sure to re-mark it with the correct identity. Make sure the oil return holes below the oil ring groove are clear.

9 Carefully inspect each piston for cracks around the skirt, at the pin bosses and at the ring lands. Normal piston wear appears as even, vertical wear on the thrust surfaces of the piston and slight looseness of the top ring in its groove. If the skirt is scored or scuffed, the engine may have been suffering from overheating and/or abnormal combustion, which caused excessively high operating temperatures. The oil pump should be checked thoroughly. Also check that the circlip grooves are not damaged.

10 A hole in the piston crown, an extreme to be sure, is an indication that abnormal

combustion (pre-ignition) was occurring. Burned areas at the edge of the piston crown are usually evidence of spark knock (detonation). If any of the above problems exist, the causes must be corrected or the damage will occur again.

11 Measure the piston ring-to-groove clearance by laying each piston ring in its groove and slipping a feeler gauge in beside it **(see illustration)**. Make sure you have the correct ring for the groove (see Step 5). Check the clearance at three or four locations around the groove. If the clearance is greater than specified, replace both the piston and rings as a set. If new rings are being used, measure the clearance using the new rings. If the clearance is greater than that specified, the piston is worn and must be replaced.

12 Check the piston-to-bore clearance by measuring the bore (see Section 15) and the piston diameter. Make sure each piston is matched to its correct cylinder. Measure the piston 15.0 mm up from the bottom of the skirt and at 90° to the piston pin axis **(see illustration)**. Subtract the piston diameter from the bore diameter to obtain the clearance. If it is greater than the specified figure, the piston must be replaced (assuming the bore itself is within limits, otherwise a rebore is necessary).

13 Apply clean engine oil to the piston pin, insert it into the piston and check for any

freeplay between the two **(see illustration)**. Measure the pin external diameter and the pin bore in the piston and compare the measurements to the specifications at the beginning of the Chapter **(see illustrations)**. Repeat the measurements between the pin and the connecting rod small-end **(see illustration)**. Replace components that are worn beyond the specified limits.

14 If the pistons are to be replaced, ensure the correct size of piston is ordered. Suzuki produce two oversize pistons for the 600 engine and one for the 1200 engine, as well as the standard piston. The oversize pistons available are: +0.5 mm (600 and 1200 engines) and +1.00 mm (600 engine only). **Note:** *Oversize pistons usually have their relevant size stamped on top of the piston crown, eg a 0.50 mm oversize piston will be marked 0.50. Be sure to obtain the correct oversize rings for the pistons.*

Installation

15 Inspect and install the piston rings (see Section 17).

16 Lubricate the piston pin, the piston pin bore and the connecting rod small-end bore with clean engine oil.

17 Install a new circlip in one side of the piston (do not re-use old circlips) **(see**

2

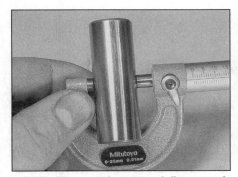

16.13b Measure the external diameter of the pin . . .

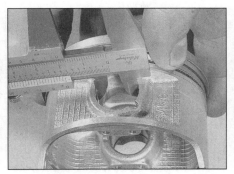

16.13c . . . the internal diameter of the bore in the piston . . .

16.13d . . . and the internal diameter of the connecting rod small-end

16.17 Install the circlip, making sure it is properly seated in its groove, with the open end away from the notch

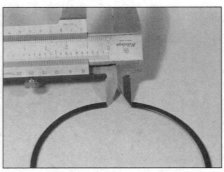

17.3 Measuring piston ring free end gap

17.4 Measuring piston ring installed end gap

illustration). Line up the piston on its correct connecting rod, making sure the arrow on the piston crown faces forwards, and insert the piston pin from the other side **(see illustration 16.3b)**. Secure the pin with the other new circlip. When installing the circlips, compress them only just enough to fit them in the piston, and make sure they are properly seated in their grooves with the open end away from the removal notch.

17 Piston rings -
inspection and installation

1 It is good practice to replace the piston rings when an engine is being overhauled. Before installing the new piston rings, the ring end gaps must be checked, both free and installed.

2 Lay out the pistons and the new ring sets so the rings will be matched with the same piston and cylinder during the end gap measurement procedure and engine assembly.

3 To measure the free end gap of each ring, lay each ring on a flat surface and measure the gap between the ends of the ring using a vernier caliper **(see illustration)**. Compare the results to the specifications at the beginning of the Chapter and replace any ring that is below its service limit.

4 To measure the installed end gap, insert the top ring into the top of the first cylinder and square it up with the cylinder walls by pushing it in with the top of the piston. The ring should be about 20 mm below the top edge of the cylinder. To measure the end gap, slip a feeler gauge between the ends of the ring and compare the measurement to the specifications at the beginning of the Chapter **(see illustration)**.

5 If the gap is larger or smaller than specified, double check to make sure that you have the correct rings before proceeding.

6 If the gap is too small, it must be enlarged or the ring ends may come in contact with each other during engine operation, which can cause serious damage. The end gap can be increased by filing the ring ends very carefully with a fine file. When performing this operation, file only from the outside in **(see illustration)**.

7 Excess end gap is not critical unless it exceeds the service limit. Again, double-check to make sure you have the correct rings for your engine and check that the bore is not worn.

8 Repeat the procedure for each ring that will be installed in the cylinders. Remember to keep the rings, pistons and cylinders matched up.

9 Once the ring end gaps have been checked/corrected, the rings can be installed on the pistons.

10 The oil control ring (lowest on the piston) is installed first. It is composed of three separate components, namely the expander and the upper and lower side rails. Slip the expander into the groove, then install the upper side rail. Do not use a piston ring installation tool on the oil ring side rails as they may be damaged. Instead, place one end of the side rail into the groove between the expander and the ring land. Hold it firmly in place and slide a finger around the piston while pushing the rail into the groove. Next, install the lower side rail in the same manner **(see illustrations)**. Make sure the ends of the expander do not overlap.

11 After the three oil ring components have been installed, check to make sure that both the upper and lower side rails can be turned smoothly in the ring groove.

12 The upper surface of each compression ring is marked with a letter at one end **(see illustration 16.5b)**. On 600 models, the top ring is identified by the letter R, and the second (middle) ring by the letters RN. On 1200 models, the top ring is identified by the letter N, and the second (middle) ring by 2N. On both models, the top face of the top ring is chrome plated. The rings can also be identified by their different cross-section shape **(see illustration)**. Install the second (middle) ring next. Make sure that the identification letter near the end gap is facing up. Fit the ring into the middle groove in the piston. Do not expand

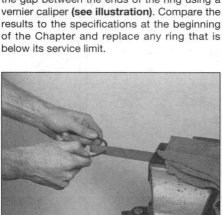

17.6 Ring end gap can be enlarged by clamping a file in a vice and filing the ring ends

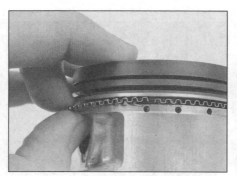

17.10a Install the oil ring expander in its groove . . .

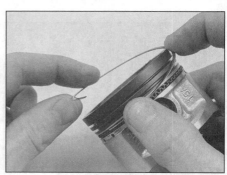

17.10b . . . and fit the side rails each side of it. The oil ring must be installed by hand

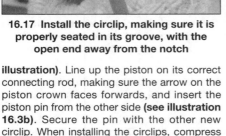

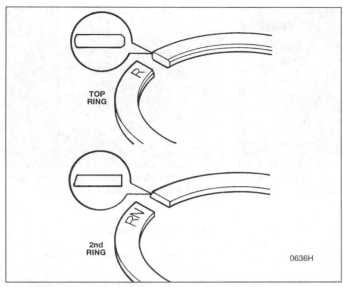

17.12 Don't confuse the top ring with the second ring

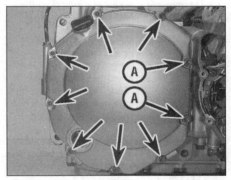

17.14 When installing the rings, stagger the end gaps as shown

the ring any more than is necessary to slide it into place. To avoid breaking the ring, use a piston ring installation tool.

13 Finally, install the top ring in the same manner into the top groove in the piston. Make sure the identification letter near the end gap is facing up.

14 Once the rings are correctly installed, check they move freely without snagging and stagger their end gaps as shown **(see illustration)**.

18 Clutch - removal, inspection and installation

Note: *The clutch can be removed with the engine in the frame.*

Removal

GSF600 and GSF600S

1 Drain the engine oil as described in Chapter 1.
2 Working in a criss-cross pattern, evenly slacken the clutch cover retaining bolts **(see illustration)**. Note which size bolts fit where,

and that the two front bolts are fitted with sealing washers. Discard these washers as new ones must be used. Lift the cover away from the engine, being prepared to catch any residual oil which may be released as the cover is removed. Remove the gasket and discard it. Note the positions of the two locating dowels fitted to the crankcase and remove them for safe-keeping if they are loose.

3 Working in a criss-cross pattern, gradually and evenly slacken the clutch pressure plate bolts until spring pressure is released. Use one of the following methods to stop the clutch from turning while initially loosening the bolts:

  a) *If the engine is in the frame, shift it into gear and have an assistant apply the rear brake.*

  b) *If the cylinder block has been removed, use a con-rod stopper or block of wood under the pistons.*

  c) *Use a holding tool similar to the clutch centre holding tool (see Tool Tip), but with a bolt in each of the ends rather than the ends being bent over (the same*

as the starter clutch holding tool - see Section 24) (see illustration).

Remove the bolts and springs, then withdraw the pressure plate **(see illustration)**. Remove the thrust washer, release bearing and pushrod end piece from either the back of the pressure plate or the end of the input shaft **(see illustration)**. If required, withdraw the

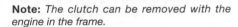

18.2 The clutch cover is secured by nine bolts (arrows), two of which have sealing washers (A)

18.3a A home-made tool can be used to stop the clutch turning while loosening the pressure plate bolts

18.3b Having removed the bolts and springs, remove the pressure plate (arrow)

18.3c Withdraw the pushrod end piece along with the thrust washer and release bearing

18.4 Grasp the clutch plates (arrows) and remove them as a pack

18.8 Remove the needle bearing and spacer from the middle of the clutch housing

18.9 Lift the alternator/oil pump drive gear off the back of the clutch housing

clutch pushrod right-hand half from the input shaft **(see illustration 18.36a)** - it may have to be poked through from the other side using the left-hand half of the pushrod, requiring removal of the front sprocket cover, or the engine will have to be tipped on its side.

4 Grasp the complete set of clutch plates and remove them as a pack **(see illustration)**. Unless the plates are being replaced with new ones, keep them in their original order.

5 If a tabbed lockwasher is fitted under the clutch nut, bend back the tabs. To remove the clutch nut the input shaft must be locked using one of the following methods:

　　a)　*If the engine is in the frame, engage 1st gear and have an assistant hold the rear brake on hard with the rear tyre in firm contact with the ground.*

　　b)　*The Suzuki service tool (Pt. No. 09920-53740), or a home-made equivalent made from two strips of steel bent at the ends and bolted together in the middle (see **Tool Tip**), can be used to stop the clutch centre from turning whilst the nut is slackened (see illustration 18.34f).*

Unscrew the nut and remove the lockwasher (either tabbed or splined - where fitted) and

the dished washer, noting which way round it fits, from the input shaft. If a tabbed lockwasher is fitted, discard it as a new one must be used on installation.

6 Remove the outer thrust washer **(see illustration 18.34c)**.

7 Remove the clutch centre from the shaft, followed by the middle thrust washer **(see illustrations 18.34b and a)**.

8 Withdraw the needle roller bearing and spacer from the centre of the clutch housing **(see illustration)**. It may be necessary to pull the clutch housing part-way out and then push it back in order to expose the bearing and spacer.

9 Remove the clutch housing along with the alternator/oil pump drive gear from the shaft, then remove the inner thrust washer **(see illustrations 18.33a and 18.32)**. If required, the alternator/oil pump drive gear can be separated from the clutch housing by lifting it off the back of the primary driven gear **(see illustration)**.

10 If the engine is being completely disassembled, remove the circlip from the end of the oil pump drive shaft, then remove the outer washer and the oil pump driven gear **(see illustration)**. Also remove the drive pin from the shaft, noting how it fits into the slot in the back of the oil pump driven gear, and the inner washer.

GSF1200 and GSF1200S

Note: *Take care not to operate the clutch lever whilst the clutch is disassembled.*

Note: *It is advisable to order new diaphragm spring holder screws in advance of disassembling the clutch and replace them as a matter of course, as their size means they are easily damaged or stressed, even though it may not be apparent.*

11 Drain the engine oil as described in Chapter 1.

12 Working in a criss-cross pattern, evenly slacken the clutch cover retaining bolts **(see illustration 18.2)**. Note which size bolts fit where, and that the two front bolts are fitted with sealing washers. Discard these washers as new ones must be used. Lift the cover away from the engine, being prepared to catch any residual oil which may be released as the cover is removed. Remove the gasket and discard it. Note the positions of the two locating dowels fitted to the crankcase and remove them for safe-keeping if they are loose.

13 Remove the circlip securing the pressure plate lifter inside the pressure plate and remove the lifter **(see illustration)**.

14 Remove the thrust washer, release bearing and pushrod end piece from either the back of the pressure plate or the end of

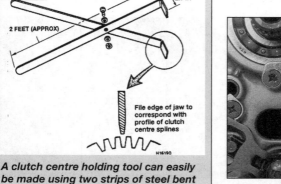

A clutch centre holding tool can easily be made using two strips of steel bent over at the ends and bolted together in the middle.

18.10 The oil pump driven gear is secured by a circlip (arrow)

18.13 Remove the circlip using a pair of internal circlip pliers, then remove the pressure plate lifter (arrow)

18.14 Withdraw the pushrod end piece along with the thrust washer and release bearing

18.15 Remove the clutch nut, noting how it is staked against the shaft (arrow)

18.16 The diaphragm spring holder is secured by three screws (arrows)

the input shaft **(see illustration)**. If required, withdraw the clutch pushrod right-hand half from the input shaft - it may have to be poked through from the other side using the left-hand half of the pushrod, requiring removal of the front sprocket cover, or the engine will have to be tipped on its side.

15 To remove the clutch nut the input shaft must be locked using one of the following two methods:

   a)   *If the engine is in the frame, engage 1st gear and have an assistant hold the rear brake on hard with the rear tyre in firm contact with the ground.*

   b)   *The Suzuki service tool (Pt. No. 09920-34820), or a home-made equivalent made from two strips of steel with a bolt through one end of each strip, and bolted together in the middle (see Tool Tip), can be used (by inserting the bolts into the holes in the pressure plate) to stop the clutch centre from turning whilst the nut is slackened (see illustration 18.51c).*

Unscrew the nut and remove the dished washer from the input shaft, noting which way round it fits **(see illustration)**.

16 Unscrew the three screws securing the diaphragm spring holder and remove the holder, noting how it fits **(see illustration)**. Take care to use the correct size screwdriver

when removing these screws as the heads are easily rounded off. Also make sure that the screws are removed immediately after the clutch nut, as they are not strong enough to hold the pressure of the diaphragm springs without the nut and will stretch. It is advisable to order new screws in advance of disassembling the clutch and replace them as a matter of course, as their size means they are easily damaged or stressed, even though it may not be apparent.

17 Remove the two diaphragm springs, noting how they fit, followed by the pressure plate **(see illustration)**. If required, remove the spring seat from inside the pressure plate **(see illustration)**.

18 Pull the clutch centre and the clutch friction and plain plates off the shaft as an assembly **(see illustration)**. If required, screw two M6 bolts into the threaded holes in the clutch centre and use them to pull the assembly off. Also remove the outer thrust washer from behind the clutch centre **(see illustration 18.46c)**.

19 Withdraw the needle roller bearing and spacer from the centre of the clutch housing **(see illustration 18.8)**. It may be necessary to pull the clutch housing part-way out and then push it back in order to expose the bearing and spacer.

20 Remove the clutch housing along with the

alternator/oil pump drive gear from the shaft, then remove the inner thrust washer **(see illustrations 18.46a and 18.45)**. If required, the alternator/oil pump drive gear can be separated from the clutch housing by lifting it off the back of the primary driven gear **(see illustration 18.9)**.

21 If required for either inspection or replacement, remove the clutch friction and plain plates from the clutch centre, followed by the anti-judder spring and spring seat, noting which way round they fit **(see illustrations 18.47b and 18.47a)**. Keep the friction and plain plates in their original order (there are two types of each plate - keeping them in order will avoid confusion on reassembly).

22 If the engine is being completely disassembled, remove the circlip from the end of the oil pump drive shaft, then remove the outer washer and the oil pump driven gear **(see illustration 18.10)**. Also remove the drive pin from the shaft, noting how it fits into the slot in the back of the oil pump driven gear, and the inner washer.

Inspection - all models

23 After an extended period of service the clutch friction plates will wear and promote clutch slip. Measure the thickness of each friction plate and the width of their tabs using

18.17a Remove the two diaphragm springs (A), followed by the pressure plate (B)

18.17b The spring seat (arrow) fits inside the pressure plate

18.18 Grasp the clutch centre and pull it off with the plates. Two M6 bolts can be threaded into the holes (arrows) to aid removal

2

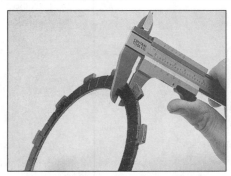

18.23a Measure the thickness of the friction plates . . .

18.23b . . . and the width of their tabs

18.24 Check the plain plates for warpage

a vernier caliper **(see illustrations)**. If any plate has worn to or beyond the service limits given in the Specifications at the beginning of the Chapter, the friction plates must be replaced as a set. Also, if any of the plates smell burnt or are glazed, they must be replaced as a set.

24 The plain plates should not show any signs of excess heating (bluing). Check for warpage using a surface plate and feeler gauges **(see illustration)**. If any plate exceeds the maximum permissible amount of warpage, or shows signs of bluing, all plain plates must be replaced as a set.

25 On GSF600 and GSF600S models, measure the free length of each clutch spring using a vernier caliper **(see illustration)**. If any

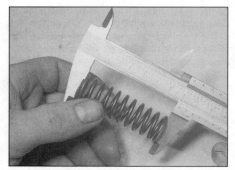

18.25 Measure the free length of the clutch springs

spring is below the service limit specified, replace all the springs as a set.

26 On GSF1200 and GSF1200S models, lay the diaphragm springs on a surface plate (or a piece of plate glass) and measure the height of the inner edge of the spring **(see illustration)**. Replace the springs if the height measured is less than the limit specified at the beginning of the Chapter.

27 Inspect the clutch assembly for burrs and indentations on the edges of the protruding tangs of the friction plates and/or slots in the edge of the housing with which they engage. Similarly check for wear between the inner tongues of the plain plates and the slots in the clutch centre. Wear of this nature will cause clutch drag and slow disengagement during gear changes, since the plates will snag when the pressure plate is lifted. With care, a small amount of wear can be corrected by dressing with a fine file, but if this is excessive the worn components should be replaced.

28 Check the pressure plate, release bearing, pushrod end piece and thrust washer for signs of roughness, wear or damage, and replace any parts as necessary. Check that the pushrod is straight by rolling it on a flat surface.

29 To access the pushrod oil seal, unscrew the gearchange lever linkage arm pinch bolt and remove the arm from the shaft, noting any alignment marks **(see illustration 18.40f)**. If no marks are visible, make your

own before removing the arm so that it can be correctly aligned with the shaft on installation. Unscrew the bolts securing the engine sprocket cover to the crankcase and draw the cover away from the engine **(see illustration 18.40c)**. Note the position of the dowels and remove them if loose. Withdraw the clutch pushrod left-hand half and check it for straightness by rolling it on a surface plate **(see illustration)**. Check the pushrod oil seal for signs of leakage and replace it if necessary. The oil seal can be levered out once the engine sprocket has been removed (see Chapter 5) and the bearing and seal retainer plate detached; bend back the tabs on the retainer plate bolts, then unscrew the bolts and remove the plate **(see illustrations 26.5a and b)**. Drive a new seal squarely into place and install the plate. Bend the tabs up against the bolt flats to lock the bolts in place. Install the engine sprocket as described in Chapter 5.

30 On 600 models inspect the clutch release actuating mechanism whilst the engine sprocket cover is removed. Check the actuating mechanism for smooth operation and any signs of wear or damage. Unscrew the two bolts securing the mechanism to the cover and remove the mechanism for cleaning and re-greasing if required **(see illustration)**. On 1200 models, refer to Section 21 for details of the release cylinder.

18.26 Measure the height of the inner edge of the diaphragm springs

18.29 Remove the cover dowels (A) if loose. Withdraw the pushrod (B) and check it for straightness

18.30 The release actuating mechanism is secured in the cover by two bolts (arrows)

18.31a Install the inner washer (arrow), and the drive pin . . .

18.31b . . . then slide on the gear so that the drive pin locates in the slots in the back of the gear (arrows)

18.31c Fit the outer washer and secure the gear with the circlip

Installation

GSF600 and GSF600S

31 If removed, install the inner washer onto the oil pump drive shaft, then install the drive pin into its hole in the shaft, making sure it is central **(see illustration)**. Locate the oil pump driven gear onto the shaft so that the drive pin locates into the slot in the back of the gear, then install the outer washer and secure the assembly with the circlip, making sure it is properly seated in its groove **(see illustrations)**.

32 Slide the inner thrust washer, with its flat surface facing out, onto the end of the input shaft **(see illustration)**.

33 Lubricate the needle roller bearing and spacer with clean engine oil. Slide the clutch housing onto the shaft, making sure it engages correctly with the teeth on the primary drive gear, the alternator driven gear and the oil pump driven gear, then support it in position and slide the spacer and needle roller bearing onto the shaft and into the middle of the housing **(see illustrations)**.

34 Slide the middle thrust washer onto the shaft, then install the clutch centre, making sure it locates correctly onto the shaft splines **(see illustrations)**. Slide the outer thrust washer onto the shaft, followed by the dished washer, with its raised inner edge facing out **(see illustrations)**. If fitted, install a new lockwasher (either tabbed or splined according to model) onto the shaft splines, then install the clutch nut and, using the

18.32 Fit the inner thrust washer with its flat side facing out

18.33a Engage the clutch housing with the primary drive, alternator driven and oil pump driven gears . . .

18.33b . . . then slide the spacer and needle bearing into the centre of the housing

18.34a Slide the middle thrust washer . . .

2

18.34b . . . the clutch centre . . .

18.34c . . . the outer thrust washer . . .

18.34d . . . and the dished washer, with its raised inner edge facing out, onto the shaft

18.34e Install the clutch nut . . .

18.34f . . . and tighten it to the specified torque setting using the holding tool to stop the clutch from turning

18.35a Install a friction plate first . . .

18.35b . . . followed by a plain plate

18.36a Install the right-hand pushrod . . .

method employed on removal to prevent the input shaft turning, tighten the nut to the torque setting specified at the beginning of the Chapter (see illustrations). Note: *Check that the clutch centre rotates freely after tightening.* Where a tabbed lockwasher is fitted, bend up the tabs to secure the nut.

35 Coat each clutch plate with clean engine oil, then build up the plates in the clutch housing, starting with a friction plate, then a plain plate and alternating friction and plain plates until all are installed (see illustrations).

36 If removed, lubricate the pushrod right-hand half and install it into the end of the input shaft, followed by the pushrod end piece (see illustrations). Lubricate both sides of the release bearing and thrust washer with clean engine oil, then install them onto the pushrod end piece (see illustrations).

37 Install the pressure plate onto the clutch (see illustration). Install the springs, then install the pressure plate bolts, and tighten them evenly in a criss-cross sequence to the specified torque setting, using the method employed on removal (see Step 3) to prevent the clutch from turning (see illustrations).

38 Remove all traces of old gasket from the crankcase and clutch cover surfaces. Apply a smear of sealant (Suzuki Bond 1207B or equivalent) to the area around the crankcase joints as shown (see illustration). If removed, insert the clutch cover dowels into the crankcase, then place a new gasket onto the

18.36b . . . followed by the pushrod end piece . . .

18.36c . . . the release bearing . . .

18.36d . . . and the thrust washer

18.37a Install the pressure plate . . .

18.37b . . . followed by the springs . . .

18.37c . . . and the bolts with their washers

18.37d Hold the pressure plate whilst the bolts are secured

18.38a Apply sealant to the crankcase joints (arrows)

18.38b Make sure the gasket locates correctly over the dowels (arrows)

18.39a Fit the clutch cover . . .

18.39b . . . making sure new sealing washers are installed on the front two bolts

crankcase, making sure it locates correctly over the dowels (see illustration).

39 Install the clutch cover and tighten its bolts evenly in a criss-cross sequence, making sure that two new sealing washers are used on the front two bolts (see illustrations).

40 If disassembled, install the clutch release mechanism in the engine sprocket cover and tighten its bolts securely (see illustration). Lubricate the pushrod left-hand half and insert it through the oil seal and into the input shaft, then install the sprocket cover and tighten its bolts securely (see illustrations). Remove the plug covering the release mechanism in the sprocket cover, then loosen the locknut on the release mechanism adjuster screw (see illustration). Unscrew the

18.40a Clutch release mechanism

18.40b Install the pushrod left-hand half . . .

18.40c . . . followed by the clutch cover

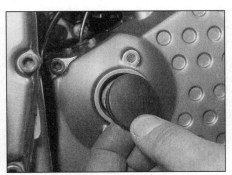

18.40d Remove the rubber plug . . .

18.40e . . . then slacken the locknut and turn the adjuster screw as described. Counter-hold the screw when tightening the locknut

2

18.40f Align the gearchange arm on the shaft and install the pinch bolt

18.45 Fit the inner thrust washer with its flat side facing out

18.46a Engage the clutch housing with the primary drive, alternator driven and oil pump driven gears . . .

adjuster screw a few turns, then tighten it until resistance is met as it contacts the end of the pushrod. From this position, unscrew the adjuster 1/4 to 1/2 a turn, then tighten the locknut securely, making sure the adjuster does not turn (see illustration). Install the release mechanism plug. Install the gearchange linkage arm onto its shaft, aligning the punch marks, and tighten the pinch bolt securely (see illustration).

41 Check and adjust the amount of clutch lever freeplay (see Chapter 1).

42 Refill the engine with oil (see Chapter 1).

GSF1200 and GSF1200S

43 Remove all traces of old gasket from the crankcase and clutch cover surfaces.

44 If removed, install the inner washer onto the oil pump drive shaft, then install the drive pin into its hole in the shaft, making sure it is central (see illustration 18.31a). Locate the oil pump driven gear onto the shaft so that the drive pin locates into the slot in the back of the gear, then install the outer washer and secure the assembly with the circlip, making sure it is properly seated in its groove (see illustrations 18.31b and c).

45 Slide the inner thrust washer, with its flat surface facing out, onto the end of the input shaft (see illustration).

46 Lubricate the needle roller bearing and spacer with clean engine oil. Slide the clutch housing onto the shaft, making sure it engages correctly with the teeth on the

primary drive gear, the alternator driven gear and the oil pump driven gear, then support it in position and slide the spacer and needle roller bearing onto the shaft and into the middle of the housing (see illustrations). Slide the outer thrust washer onto the shaft (see illustration).

47 Install the spring seat and anti-judder spring onto the clutch centre (see illustrations), noting that the anti-judder spring must be fitted the correct way round, with its raised outer edge facing away from the spring seat (see illustration). Install the clutch centre onto the shaft splines (see illustration).

48 Before building up the plates in the clutch housing, identify the single friction plate that

18.46b . . . then slide the spacer and needle bearing into the centre of the housing

18.46c followed by the outer thrust washer

18.47a Install the anti-judder spring seat . . .

18.47b . . . and the anti-judder spring

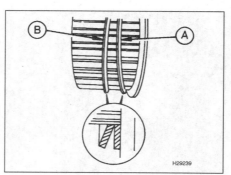

18.47c Correct fitting of spring seat (A) and anti-judder spring (B)

18.47d Slide the clutch centre onto the shaft

18.48a Install the first friction plate . . .

18.48b . . . followed by a plain plate

18.49a Fit the diaphragm spring seat into the clutch centre . . .

has a larger internal diameter than the rest (108 mm instead of 101 mm), and the two plain plates that are slightly thicker than the rest (2.0 mm instead of 1.6 mm). The friction plate with the larger internal diameter is fitted first and locates over the anti-judder spring and seat. The thicker plain plates are the fifth and sixth (out of nine) plain plates to be fitted. Coat each clutch plate with clean engine, then build up the plates in the clutch housing, starting with the friction plate (with the larger internal diameter), then a plain plate and alternating friction and plain plates (not forgetting the order) until all are installed **(see illustration)**.

49 If removed, install the diaphragm spring seat into the pressure plate **(see illustration)**. Install the pressure plate into the clutch centre, then Install the two diaphragm springs, making sure their higher inner edges face out **(see illustration)**.

50 Install the diaphragm spring holder and secure it with the three screws, preferably using new ones **(see illustrations)**. Tighten the screws evenly, taking care not to strip the threads as the screws are very small. Proceed to the next step immediately, as the screws are not strong enough to secure the spring holder against the pressure of the springs without the clutch nut, and consequently will stretch.

51 Fit the dished washer, with its raised inner edge facing out, onto the shaft splines, then install the clutch nut and, using the method employed on dismantling to lock the input shaft, tighten the nut to the torque setting specified at the beginning of the Chapter **(see illustrations)**. Stake the nut against the

18.49b . . . then slide the centre onto the shaft

18.49c Fit the two diaphragm springs with their raised inner edges facing out

18.50a Fit the diaphragm spring holder into the pressure plate . . .

18.50b . . . and secure it with the screws

18.51a Install the dished washer with its raised inner edge facing out

2

18.51b ... then fit the clutch nut ...

18.51c ... and tighten it to the specified torque setting, using the holding tool to stop the clutch turning

18.51d Stake the nut against the shaft using a punch

18.52a Install the pushrod end piece ...

18.52b ... followed by the release bearing ...

18.52c ... and the thrust washer

shaft using a punch to secure it **(see illustration)**.

52 If removed, lubricate the pushrod right-hand half and install it into the end of the input shaft **(see illustrations 18.36a)**. Install the pushrod end piece, then lubricate both sides of the release bearing and thrust washer with clean engine oil, and install them onto the end piece **(see illustrations)**.

53 Install the pressure plate lifter and secure it with the circlip, making sure it is properly seated in its groove and that its sharper edge faces out **(see illustrations)**.

54 Apply a smear of sealant (Suzuki Bond 1207B or equivalent) to the area around the crankcase joints as shown **(see illustration 18.38a)**. If removed, insert the clutch cover dowels into the crankcase, then place a new

gasket onto the crankcase, making sure it locates correctly over the dowels **(see illustration 18.38b)**.

55 Install the clutch cover and tighten its bolts evenly in a criss-cross sequence, making sure that two new sealing washers are used on the front two bolts **(see illustrations 18.39a and b)**.

56 Refill the engine with oil (see Chapter 1).

18.53a Install the pressure plate lifter ...

18.53b ... and secure it with its circlip

19.1a Unscrew the pinch bolt (arrow) and remove the lever

19.1b Remove its five bolts and lift the sprocket cover off the crankcase

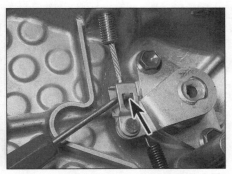

19.2a Bend out the retainer tab (arrow), then lift the release mechanism arm and slip the cable end out of its retainer

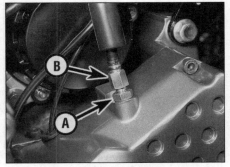

19.2b Slacken the locknut (A) and unscrew the adjuster (B) . . .

19.2c . . . then withdraw the cable from the cover

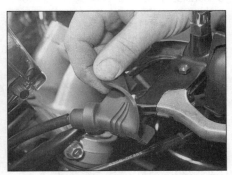

19.3a Pull back the rubber cover . . .

19 Clutch cable (GSF600 and GSF600S) - removal and installation

1 Unscrew the gearchange linkage arm pinch bolt and remove the arm from the shaft, noting any alignment marks (see illustration). If no marks are visible, make your own before removing the arm so that it can be correctly aligned with the shaft on installation. Unscrew the bolts securing the engine sprocket cover to the crankcase and remove the cover (see illustration).

2 Bend out the tab in the cable retainer on the end of the release mechanism arm, then lift the arm and slip the cable end out of the retainer, noting how it fits (see illustration). Pull up the rubber sleeve on the top of the cover to expose the cable adjuster. Slacken the cable adjuster locknut, then unscrew the adjuster and withdraw the cable from the cover (see illustrations).

3 Pull back the rubber cover from the clutch adjuster at the handlebar end of the cable (see illustration). Fully slacken the lockwheel then screw the adjuster fully in (see illustration). This resets it to the beginning of its adjustment span.

4 Align the slots in the adjuster and lockwheel

with that in the lever bracket, then pull the outer cable end from the socket in the adjuster and release the inner cable from the lever (see illustrations). Remove the cable from the machine, noting its routing.

HAYNES HINT *Before removing the cable from the bike, tape the lower end of the new cable to the upper end of the old cable. Slowly pull the lower end of the old cable out, guiding the new cable down into position. Using this method will ensure the cable is routed correctly.*

2

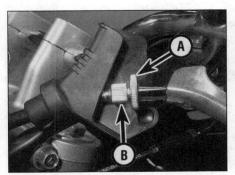

19.3b . . . then slacken the lockwheel (A) and screw in the adjuster (B)

19.4a Align the slots in the adjuster and lockwheel, then remove the cable from the adjuster . . .

19.4b . . . and the lever

19.5 Bend in the retainer tab to secure the cable end

20.4 The reservoir cover is secured by two screws

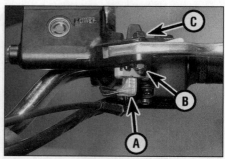

20.5 Disconnect the electrical connectors (A), then unscrew the locknut (B) and remove the pivot bolt (C) and lever

5 Installation is the reverse of removal, making sure the cable is correctly routed. Bend in the retainer to secure the cable end (see illustration). Before installing the cover, check the clutch release actuating mechanism for smooth operation and any signs of wear or damage. Adjust the amount of clutch lever freeplay (see Chapter 1).

20 Clutch master cylinder (GSF1200 and GSF1200S) - removal, overhaul and installation

1 If the master cylinder is leaking fluid, or if the clutch does not work when the lever is applied, and bleeding the system does not help (see Section 22), and the hydraulic hoses are all in good condition, then master cylinder overhaul is recommended.
2 Before disassembling the master cylinder, read through the entire procedure and make sure that you have the correct rebuild kit. Also, you will need some new DOT 4 hydraulic brake and clutch fluid, some clean rags and internal circlip pliers. Note: To prevent damage to the paint from spilled brake fluid, always cover the fuel tank and fairing (where fitted) when working on the master cylinder. Caution: Disassembly, overhaul and reassembly of the master cylinder must be done in a spotlessly clean work area to avoid contamination and possible failure of the hydraulic system components.

Removal

3 If required, remove the rear view mirror (see Chapter 7).
4 Loosen, but do not remove, the screws holding the reservoir cover in place (see illustration).
5 Disconnect the electrical connectors from the clutch switch (see illustration).
6 Remove the locknut from the underside of the brake lever pivot bolt, then unscrew the bolt and remove the brake lever (see illustration 20.5).
7 Unscrew the clutch hose banjo bolt and separate the hose from the master cylinder, noting its alignment. Discard the two sealing washers as new ones must be used. Wrap the end of the hose in a clean rag and suspend it

20.8a Prise out the caps . . .

in an upright position or bend it down carefully and place the open end in a clean container. The objective is to prevent excessive loss of brake fluid, fluid spills and system contamination.
8 Remove the master cylinder clamp mounting bolt caps, then unscrew the bolts, noting how the mating surfaces of the clamp align with the slit in the handlebar spacer and the punch mark on the underside of the handlebar (see

20.8b . . . then remove the clamp bolts (arrows)

illustrations). Lift the master cylinder and reservoir away from the handlebar.
Caution: Do not tip the master cylinder upside down or fluid will run out.

Overhaul

9 Remove the reservoir cover retaining screws and lift off the cover, the diaphragm plate and the rubber diaphragm (see illustration). Drain the fluid from the reservoir

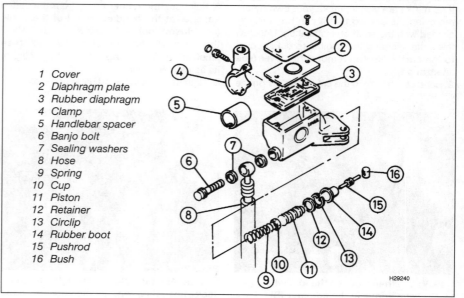

1 Cover
2 Diaphragm plate
3 Rubber diaphragm
4 Clamp
5 Handlebar spacer
6 Banjo bolt
7 Sealing washers
8 Hose
9 Spring
10 Cup
11 Piston
12 Retainer
13 Circlip
14 Rubber boot
15 Pushrod
16 Bush

H29240

20.9 Clutch master cylinder components

into a suitable container. Wipe any remaining fluid out of the reservoir with a clean rag.

10 Remove the screws securing the clutch switch to the bottom of the master cylinder and remove the switch.

11 Remove the bush and pushrod, then remove the dust boot from the end of the piston.

12 Using circlip pliers, remove the circlip and slide out the piston assembly and the spring, noting how they fit. Lay the parts out in the proper order and way round to prevent confusion during reassembly.

13 Clean all parts with clean DOT 4 fluid. If compressed air is available, use it to dry the parts thoroughly (make sure it's filtered and unlubricated).

Caution: Do not, under any circumstances, use a petroleum-based solvent to clean brake parts.

14 Check the master cylinder bore for corrosion, scratches, nicks and score marks. If the necessary measuring equipment is available, compare the dimensions of the piston and bore to those given in the Specifications Section of this Chapter. If damage or wear is evident, the master cylinder must be replaced with a new one. If the master cylinder is in poor condition, then the release cylinder should be checked as well. Check that the fluid inlet and outlet ports in the master cylinder are clear.

15 The dust boot, circlip, piston assembly and spring are included in the rebuild kit. Use all of the new parts, regardless of the apparent condition of the old ones.

16 Install the spring in the master cylinder bore so that its tapered (narrow) end faces out.

17 Lubricate the cup and piston with clean brake fluid and install them into the master cylinder, making sure they are the correct way round. Make sure the lips on the cup seals do not turn inside out when they are slipped into the bore. Depress the piston and install the retainer and a new circlip, making sure that it locates in the master cylinder groove.

18 Install the rubber dust boot, pushrod and bush, making sure the lip of the boot is seated correctly in the pushrod groove.

21.1 Clutch release cylinder

A *Clutch hose banjo bolt*
B *Cylinder mounting bolts*
C *Bleed valve and cap*

20.21 Align the clamp mating surface with the slit in the handlebar spacer (arrow) and the punch mark on the handlebar

19 Install the clutch switch.

20 Inspect the reservoir cover rubber diaphragm and replace if damaged or deteriorated.

Installation

21 Attach the master cylinder to the handlebar and fit the clamp. Align the lower mating surfaces of the clamp with the slit in the handlebar spacer and the punch mark on the underside of the handlebar, then fully tighten the upper bolt first then the lower bolt to the torque setting specified at the beginning of the Chapter **(see illustration)**. There will be a gap at the bottom between the clamp and the master cylinder body.

22 Connect the clutch hose to the master cylinder, using new sealing washers on each side of the union, and aligning the hose as noted on removal. Tighten the banjo bolt to the torque setting specified at the beginning of this Chapter.

23 Install the clutch lever into its bracket and secure it with its pivot bolt. Tighten the bolt then install the pivot bolt locknut **(see illustration 20.5)**.

24 Connect the clutch switch wiring **(see illustration 20.5)** and install the rear view mirror if removed (see Chapter 7).

25 Fill the fluid reservoir with DOT 4 fluid (see *Daily (pre-ride) checks*). Refer to Section 22 of this Chapter and bleed the air from the system.

26 Fit the rubber diaphragm, making sure it is correctly seated, the diaphragm plate and the cover onto the master cylinder reservoir.

21 Clutch release cylinder (GSF1200 and GSF1200S) - removal, overhaul and installation

Removal

1 Remove the clutch hose banjo bolt and separate the hose from the release cylinder, noting its alignment **(see illustration)**. Plug the hose end or wrap a plastic bag around it to minimise fluid loss and prevent dirt entering the system. Discard the sealing washers as new ones must be used on installation. **Note:** *If you're planning to overhaul the release cylinder and don't have a source of compressed air to blow out the piston, just loosen the banjo bolt at this stage and retighten it lightly. The bike's hydraulic system can then be used to force the piston out of the body once the cylinder has been unbolted. Disconnect the hose once the piston has been sufficiently displaced.*

2 Unscrew the two bolts securing the release cylinder to the sprocket cover and withdraw the cylinder from the cover **(see illustration 21.1)**. Retrieve the two dowels if they are a loose fit in the sprocket cover. Do not operate the clutch lever with the release cylinder removed.

> **HAYNES HINT** *If the release cylinder is not being disassembled, the piston can be prevented from creeping out of the release cylinder by restraining it with a couple of cable ties passed through the mounting bolt holes.*

Overhaul

3 The release cylinder has a slot on its underside which allows the escape of hydraulic fluid in the event of the piston seal failing. Hydraulic fluid might otherwise be forced under pressure past the single-lipped pushrod seal and into the transmission.

4 Have a supply of clean rags on hand, then pump the clutch lever to expel the piston under hydraulic pressure. If the hose has already been detached, use a jet of compressed air directed into the fluid inlet to expel the piston **(see illustration)**.

2

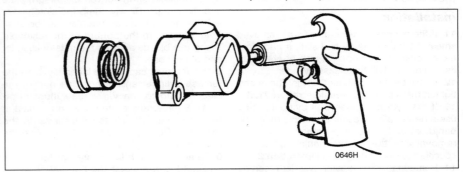

0646H

21.4 A jet of compressed air directed into the fluid inlet will expel the piston

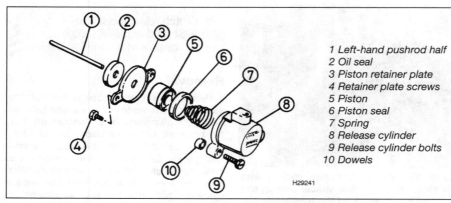

1 Left-hand pushrod half
2 Oil seal
3 Piston retainer plate
4 Retainer plate screws
5 Piston
6 Piston seal
7 Spring
8 Release cylinder
9 Release cylinder bolts
10 Dowels

21.9 Clutch release cylinder components

Warning: Use only low air pressure, otherwise the piston may be forcibly expelled causing injury.

5 Recover the spring from the piston.

6 Using a plastic or wood tool, remove the piston seal from the piston groove.

7 Clean the piston and release cylinder bore with clean hydraulic fluid.

Caution: Do not, under any circumstances, use a petroleum-based solvent to clean hydraulic parts.

8 Inspect the piston and release cylinder bore for signs of corrosion, nicks and burrs and loss of plating. If surface defects are found, the piston and cylinder should be replaced. If the release cylinder is in poor condition the master cylinder should also be overhauled. Measure the piston diameter and release cylinder bore diameter and compare with the specifications at the beginning of this chapter.

9 Lubricate the new piston seal with clean hydraulic fluid and install it on the piston. Install the spring in the release cylinder so that its tapered (narrow) end faces the piston **(see illustration)**. Lubricate the piston and seal with clean hydraulic fluid and insert it in the release cylinder, making sure it is the correct way round. Use your thumbs to press it fully into the cylinder.

10 To access the pushrod oil seal, refer to Section 18, Step 29. If required, the piston retainer plate can be removed from the inside of the engine sprocket cover - it is retained by two screws.

Installation

11 If the pushrod left-hand half was removed smear it with engine oil and slide it back into the sprocket cover. Apply a dab of grease to its end and install the release cylinder.

12 Install the two cylinder retaining bolts and tighten them securely **(see illustration 21.1)**.

13 If the hydraulic hose was disconnected, use a new sealing washer on each side of the banjo union. Position the union as noted on removal and tighten the banjo bolt to the specified torque setting **(see illustration 21.1)**.

14 Remove the two master cylinder reservoir cover screws and lift off the cover, diaphragm

plate and diaphragm. Fill the reservoir with new hydraulic fluid (see *Daily (pre-ride) checks*) and bleed the system as described in the next section.

22 Clutch - bleeding (GSF1200 and GSF1200S)

1 Bleeding the clutch is simply the process of removing all the air bubbles from the clutch fluid reservoir, the hydraulic hose and the release cylinder. Bleeding is necessary whenever a clutch system hydraulic connection is loosened, when a component or hose is replaced, or when the master cylinder or release cylinder is overhauled. Leaks in the system may also allow air to enter, but leaking clutch fluid will reveal their presence and warn you of the need for repair.

2 To bleed the clutch, you will need some new DOT 4 brake and clutch fluid, a length of clear vinyl or plastic tubing, a small container partially filled with clean fluid, a supply of clean rags and a spanner to fit the bleed valve.

3 Cover the fuel tank and other painted components to prevent damage in the event that fluid is spilled.

4 Position the bike on its centrestand (where fitted), or on an auxiliary stand so that the master cylinder is level. Remove the two screws securing the master cylinder reservoir cover, then lift off the cover, diaphragm plate and diaphragm. Slowly pump the clutch lever a few times until no air bubbles can be seen floating up from the bottom of the reservoir. Doing this bleeds air from the master cylinder end of the hose.

5 Pull the dust cap off the bleed valve on the release cylinder and attach one end of the clear tubing to the valve **(see illustration 21.1)**. Submerge the other end in the fluid in the container. Check the fluid level in the reservoir. Do not allow it to drop below the lower mark during the bleeding process.

6 Pump the clutch lever three or four times and hold it in against the handlebar whilst opening the bleed valve. When the valve is

opened, fluid will flow out of the release cylinder into the clear tubing.

7 Tighten the bleed valve, then release the lever gradually. Repeat the process until no air bubbles are visible in the fluid leaving the release cylinder and the clutch action feels smooth and progressive. On completion, tighten the bleed valve to the torque setting specified at the beginning of the Chapter.

8 Ensure that the reservoir is topped up above the lower level mark on the sightglass, install the diaphragm, diaphragm plate and cover and secure them with the two screws. Wipe up any spilled fluid and check that there are no leaks from the system. Refit the dust cap over the bleed valve.

23 Gearchange mechanism (external components) - removal, inspection and installation

Note: *The gearchange mechanism (external components) can be removed with the engine in the frame.*

Removal

1 Remove the clutch (see Section 18).

2 Shift the transmission into neutral. Working on the left-hand side of the engine, unscrew the gearchange linkage arm pinch bolt and remove the arm from the shaft, noting any alignment marks **(see illustration 19.1a)**. If no marks are visible, make your own before removing the arm so that it can be correctly aligned with the shaft on installation.

3 Unscrew the bolts securing the engine sprocket cover to the crankcase and remove the cover **(see illustration 19.1b)**. The cover can be secured out of the way with the clutch cable (600 models) or release cylinder and hose (1200 models) still connected. Remove the clip from the left-hand end of the gearchange shaft and slide off the washer.

4 Working on the right-hand side of the engine, note how the gearchange shaft centralising spring ends fit on each side of the locating pin in the crankcase, and how the teeth of the shaft arm engage with those of the shift cam, then withdraw the gearchange shaft from the right-hand side of the engine **(see illustration)**.

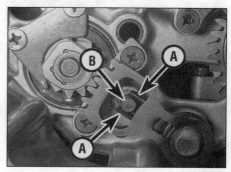

23.4 Note how all the components align before removing them, and how the spring ends (A) locate on either side of the pin (B)

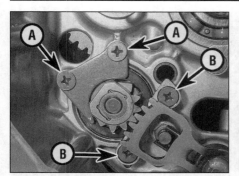

23.5 Remove the screws securing the pawl lifter (A) and the cam guide plate (B)

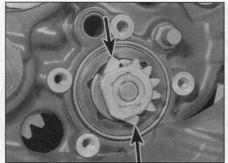

23.6 Hold the pawls (arrows) so they won't fly out when removing the selector cam

23.8a Prise out the old gearchange shaft seal . . .

5 Remove the screws securing the pawl lifter and cam guide plates to the crankcase and remove them (see illustration). A thread locking compound is used on these screws during assembly, which may necessitate the use of an impact driver for removal.
6 The pawls are spring-loaded in the selector cam. Before withdrawing the cam, place a finger over each pawl to prevent them from springing out when the cam is withdrawn (see illustration). Remove the cam along with the pawls. Place the cam on a bench and carefully release the pawls, noting how they and their pins and springs fit in the cam.

Inspection

7 Inspect the shaft centralising spring for fatigue, wear or damage. If any is found, it must be replaced. Also check that the spring locating pin in the crankcase is securely tightened.
8 Check the gearchange shaft for straightness and damage to the splines or arm teeth. If the shaft is bent you can attempt to straighten it, but if the splines or teeth are damaged the shaft must be replaced. Also check the condition of the shaft oil seal in the left-hand side of the crankcase. If it is damaged or deteriorated it must be replaced with a new one. Lever out the old seal and drive the new one squarely into place, with its

lip facing inward, using a seal driver or suitable socket (see illustrations).
9 Check the shift cam, pawls, pins and springs for wear and damage. Replace them if defects are found.

Installation

10 Install the springs, pins and pawls in the selector cam as shown (see illustration). Make sure the rounded end of each pawl fits into the rounded cut-out in the cam, and that the pins locate correctly in the cut-outs in the pawls, with the wider edge of the cut-out facing the cam teeth. It will be necessary to hold each pawl assembly in place while the cam is installed in the end of the selector drum.
11 Install the selector cam with its teeth facing forward and down so that they will align centrally with the teeth on the shaft arm when it is installed. Apply a suitable non-permanent thread locking compound to the pawl lifter and cam guide plate screws, then install the plates and tighten the screws securely (see illustration 23.5).
12 Apply a smear of high melting-point grease to the lip of the gearchange shaft seal in the left-hand side of the crankcase.
13 If removed, slide the centralising spring onto the gearchange shaft and locate the spring ends either side of the pin on the arm. Smear clean engine oil over the gearchange

shaft then carefully guide the gearshift shaft into place, making sure the centralising spring ends locate correctly on each side of the pins on the shaft arm and the crankcase, and engage the shaft arm teeth centrally with the teeth of the shift cam (see illustration 23.4).
14 Install the washer and clip onto the left-hand end of the gearchange shaft, then install the sprocket cover.
15 Install the gearchange lever onto the end of the shaft on the left-hand side of the engine, aligning the punch marks on the arm and shaft, and check that the mechanism works correctly (see illustration 19.1a). Tighten the pinch bolt securely.
16 Install the clutch (see Section 18).

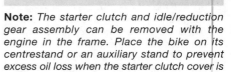

24 Starter clutch and idle/reduction gear assembly - removal, inspection and installation

Note: *The starter clutch and idle/reduction gear assembly can be removed with the engine in the frame. Place the bike on its centrestand or an auxiliary stand to prevent excess oil loss when the starter clutch cover is removed.*

Removal

1 Working in a criss-cross pattern, evenly slacken the starter clutch cover retaining bolts on the left-hand side of the engine, noting the

2

23.8b . . . position a new one in the bore with its lip facing into the engine . . .

23.8c . . . and drive the seal in with a socket the same diameter as the seal

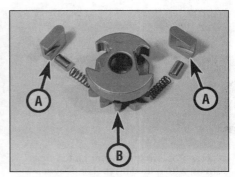

23.10 Wider edge of pawls (A) should be on the side of selector cam teeth (B)

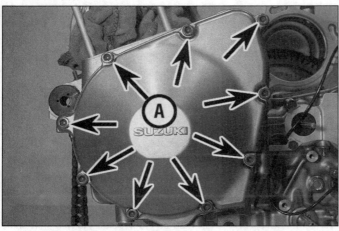

24.1 The starter clutch cover is secured by nine bolts (arrows), one of which (A) has a sealing washer

24.2 Withdraw the shaft (A), then remove the idle/reduction gear (B)

sealing washer on the front top bolt **(see illustration)**. Lift the cover away from the engine, being prepared to catch any residual oil which may be released as the cover is removed. Remove the gasket and discard it. Note the position of the locating dowel fitted to the crankcase and remove it for safe-keeping if it is loose. Note how the idle/reduction gear shaft end locates in the socket in the crankcase cover.

2 Withdraw the starter idle/reduction gear shaft, then remove the gear, noting which way round it fits **(see illustration)**.

3 To remove the starter clutch bolt it is necessary to stop the starter clutch and crankshaft from turning using one of the following methods:

  a)   *If the engine is in the frame, engage 1st gear and have an assistant hold the rear brake on hard with the rear tyre in firm contact with the ground.*

  b)   *If the cylinder block has been removed, use a con-rod stopper or block of wood under the pistons.*

  c)   *The Suzuki service tool (Pt. No. 09920-34810), or a home-made equivalent made from two strips of steel, with a bolt through one end of each strip,*

*and bolted together in the middle (see **Tool Tip** in Section 18), can be used (by inserting the bolts into the holes in the starter clutch) to stop the clutch from turning* **(see illustration)**.

Slacken the bolt by a few turns - **do not** remove the bolt from the crankshaft because it must be used in conjunction with the puller described below.

4 The starter clutch locates on the crankshaft taper and will require pulling off with the Suzuki service tool (Pt. No. 09920-33720). Thread the service tool onto the outer threads of the starter clutch, then counter-hold the tool using a suitable spanner on its large flats, and tighten the centre bolt against the crankshaft bolt head to free the starter clutch from the crankshaft **(see illustration)**. Once dislodged from the taper, remove the tool, then unscrew the crankshaft bolt and remove the starter clutch along with the starter driven gear.

5 Clean all old gasket and sealant from the cover and crankcase.

Inspection

6 Install the starter driven gear into the starter clutch (if removed) and, with the clutch face down on a workbench, check that the gear

rotates freely in an anti-clockwise direction and locks against the rotor in a clockwise direction. If it doesn't, replace the starter clutch.

7 Withdraw the starter driven gear from the starter clutch. If it appears stuck, rotate it anti-clockwise as you withdraw it to free it from the starter clutch.

8 Check the bearing surface of the starter driven gear hub and the condition of the rollers inside the clutch body **(see illustration)**. If the bearing surface shows signs of excessive wear or the rollers are damaged, marked or flattened at any point, they should be replaced.

9 Examine the teeth of the starter idle/reduction gear and the corresponding teeth of the starter driven gear and starter motor drive shaft. Replace the gears and/or starter motor if worn or chipped teeth are discovered on related gears. Also check the idle/reduction gear shaft for damage, and check that the gear is not a loose fit on the shaft. Replace the shaft if necessary.

Installation

10 Lubricate the hub of the starter driven gear with clean engine oil, then install the

24.3 Prevent the starter clutch from turning with a holding tool and loosen the starter clutch bolt

24.4 Thread the service tool onto the starter clutch, then counter-hold the tool and tighten the centre bolt until the clutch is free

24.8 Inspect the friction surface (A) and the rollers (B)

24.12a Position the starter clutch assembly on the crankshaft

24.12b Apply thread locking compound to the threads of the starter clutch bolt . . .

24.12c . . . then prevent the starter clutch from turning and tighten the bolt to the specified torque setting

starter driven gear into the clutch, rotating it anti-clockwise as you do so to spread the rollers and allow the hub of the gear to enter.
11 Thoroughly clean the tapered end of the crankshaft and the corresponding friction surface inside the starter clutch with solvent to remove all traces of oil. Blow them dry.
12 Install the starter clutch assembly onto the end of the crankshaft (see illustration). Apply a suitable non-permanent thread locking compound to the threads of the starter clutch bolt, then install the bolt (see illustration). Using the method employed on removal to

stop the clutch from turning, tighten the bolt to the torque setting specified at the beginning of the Chapter (see illustration).
13 Lubricate the idle/reduction gear shaft with clean engine oil, then install the idle/reduction gear followed by its shaft. Check that the smaller pinion on the idle/reduction gear faces outwards and meshes correctly with the teeth of the starter driven gear, and the teeth of the larger pinion mesh correctly with the teeth of the starter motor shaft (see illustrations).
14 Apply a smear of sealant (Suzuki Bond

1207B or equivalent) to the area around the crankcase joints as shown (see illustration). If removed, insert the dowel in the crankcase, then install the crankcase cover using a new gasket, making sure it locates correctly onto the dowel and the idle/reduction gear shaft (see illustrations). Tighten the cover bolts evenly in a criss-cross sequence, making sure the sealing washer is installed on the front top bolt (see illustration).
15 Check the engine/transmission oil level and top up if necessary (see Daily (pre-ride) checks).

24.13a Position the idle/reduction gear in the casing . . .

24.13b . . . and locate it with the shaft, making sure all the pinions mesh correctly

24.14a Apply the sealant to the crankcase joints (arrows)

24.14b Check that the dowel is installed (arrow), then fit a new gasket . . .

24.14c . . . and the cover . . .

24.14d . . . making sure the sealing washer is fitted with the front top bolt

2

25.3 Unscrew the oil hose banjo bolts (arrows)

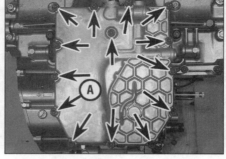

25.4 Sump bolts (arrows). A sealing washer is fitted with the bolt (A)

25.5 The oil pressure regulator threads into the sump

25 Oil sump, oil strainer and oil pressure regulator - removal, inspection and installation

Note: *The oil sump, strainer and pressure regulator can be removed with the engine in the frame. If work is being carried out with the engine removed ignore the preliminary steps.*

Removal

1 Remove the exhaust system (see Chapter 3).
2 Drain the engine oil (see Chapter 1).
3 Unscrew the banjo bolt securing each oil cooler hose to the oil sump just below the oil filter **(see illustration)**. Discard the sealing washers as new ones must be used.

4 Unscrew the sump bolts, slackening them evenly in a criss-cross sequence to prevent distortion, and not forgetting the bolt in the middle **(see illustration)**. Note the position of the bolt with the sealing washer. Remove the sump and its gasket. Discard the gasket as a new one must be used. Also discard the sealing washer on the rear bolt on the right-hand side of the sump.
5 Unscrew the oil pressure regulator from inside the sump and remove it with its washer **(see illustration)**.
6 Unscrew the two bolts securing the oil strainer assembly to the underside of the crankcase **(see illustration)**. Discard the gasket as a new one must be used.

7 Remove the oil outlet shim and its O-ring from the underside of the crankcase just ahead of the oil strainer **(see illustration 25.12b)**. Discard the O-ring as a new one must be fitted whenever the sump is removed.
8 Remove all traces of gasket from the sump and crankcase mating surfaces.

Inspection

9 Clean the sump, making sure all the oil passages are free of any debris.
10 Make sure the oil strainer is clean and remove any debris caught in the mesh. Inspect the strainer for any signs of wear or damage and replace it if necessary; it is secured to the strainer body by three bolts **(see illustration 25.13a)**.
11 Clean the pressure regulator, and check that the plunger moves freely in the body. Inspect it for signs of wear or damage and replace it if necessary.

Installation

12 Fit a new O-ring into the oil outlet in the underside of the crankcase, then install the shim **(see illustrations)**.
13 If removed, install the strainer onto the strainer body, making sure the arrow points to the front of the engine, and tighten its bolts securely **(see illustration)**. Install the oil strainer assembly onto the crankcase using a new gasket and tighten its bolts securely **(see illustration)**.

25.6 The oil strainer assembly is secured by two bolts (arrows)

25.12a Fit a new O-ring . . .

25.12b . . . and the shim to the oil outlet

25.13a The strainer is secured to the body by three bolts (arrows). Make sure the arrow points to the front of the engine

25.13b Install the strainer assembly using a new gasket

25.15 Fit a new gasket . . .

25.16a . . . then install the sump . . .

25.16b . . . not forgetting to position the bolt with the sealing washer correctly

14 Install the oil pressure regulator, using a new washer, and tighten it to the torque setting specified at the beginning of the Chapter **(see illustration 25.5)**.
15 Lay a new gasket onto the sump (if the engine is in the frame) or onto the crankcase (if the engine has been removed and is positioned upside down on the work surface) **(see illustration)**. Make sure the holes in the gasket align correctly with the bolt holes.
16 Position the sump onto the crankcase and install the sump bolts, using a new sealing washer on the rear bolt on the right-hand side of the sump **(see illustrations)**. Tighten the bolts evenly in a criss-cross pattern to the torque setting specified at the beginning of the Chapter **(see illustration 25.4)**.
17 Install the oil cooler hoses onto the sump using new sealing washers, and tighten the banjo bolts to the specified torque setting **(see illustration)**.
18 Install the exhaust system (see Chapter 3).
19 Fill the engine with the correct type and quantity of oil as described in Chapter 1. Start the engine and check for leaks around the sump.

---

26 Crankcase - separation and reassembly

Note: *When the engine is upside down (Steps 8 to 27), referrals to the right and left-hand ends or sides of the transmission shafts or components are made as though the engine is the correct way up. Therefore the right-hand end of a shaft or side of a crankcase will actually be on your left as you look down onto the underside of the crankcase assembly.*

Separation

1 To access the oil pump, crankshaft, cam chain and tensioner blade, connecting rods, bearings and transmission components, the crankcase must be split into two parts.
2 To enable the crankcases to be separated, the engine must be removed from the frame

(see Section 5). Before the crankcases can be separated the following components must be removed:
   a) *Cam chain tensioner (Section 9).*
   b) *Camshafts (Section 11).*
   c) *Cylinder head (Section 12).*
   d) *Cylinder block (Section 15).*
   e) *Ignition pulse generator coil assembly (Chapter 4)*
   f) *Clutch (Section 18).*
   g) *Gearchange mechanism external components (Section 23).*
   h) *Alternator (Chapter 8).*
   i) *Starter motor (Chapter 8).*
   j) *Starter clutch and starter idle/reduction gear (Section 24).*
   k) *Oil sump and oil strainer (Section 25).*
   l) *Oil filter (Chapter 1).*
Note: *If the crankcases are being separated to inspect or access the transmission components, or to inspect the crankshaft without removing it, the engine top-end components (cam chain tensioner, camshafts, cylinder head, cylinder block) can remain in situ. However, if removal of the crankshaft and connecting rod assemblies is intended, full disassembly of the top-end is necessary.*
3 If not already done following removal of the clutch, remove the circlip from the end of the oil pump drive shaft, then remove the outer washer and the oil pump driven gear **(see illustrations 18.31c and 18.31b)**. Also

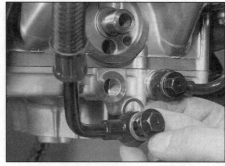

25.17 Use new sealing washers on each side of the banjo fittings

remove the drive pin from the shaft, noting how it fits into the slot in the back of the oil pump driven gear, and the inner washer **(see illustration 18.31a)**.
4 Unscrew the two screws securing the transmission input shaft bearing retainer plate to the right-hand side of the crankcase and remove the plate, noting how it fits **(see illustration)**. A thread locking compound is used on these screws during assembly, which may necessitate the use of an impact driver for removal.
5 Bend back the tabs on the retainer plate for the transmission output shaft bearing and the clutch pushrod oil seal, located on the left-hand side of the crankcase **(see illustration)**.

26.4 Remove the input shaft bearing retainer plate screws

26.5a Bend back the lock tabs on the retainer plate bolts . . .

2

26.5b . . . then remove the bolts and the plate

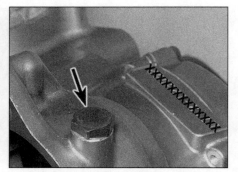

26.6 Remove the plug (arrow) for access to one of the upper crankcase bolts

Unscrew the four bolts and remove the plate (see illustration).

6 Unscrew the plug located next to the alternator mounting flange in the upper crankcase half (see illustration). This provides access to one of the upper crankcase bolts. Discard the plug's sealing washer as a new one must be used.

7 Unscrew the seven 6 mm upper crankcase bolts and the single 6 mm nut which is located inside the alternator mounting flange (see illustrations). Note the position of the earth (ground) cable.

8 Turn the engine upside down so that it rests on the cylinder studs and the back of the upper crankcase half. Support it on wood blocks so that no strain is placed on the cylinder studs.

9 Unscrew the ten 6 mm lower crankcase bolts as shown (see illustration). Also unscrew the 6 mm bolt securing the left-hand oil drain tube, and the single 6 mm nut located just ahead of the transmission output shaft on the left-hand side of the crankcase (see illustrations). Remove the oil drain tube.

10 Unscrew the main oil gallery plug from the right-hand side of the crankcase, below the ignition pulse generator coil assembly housing (see illustration). Discard the plug's O-ring as a new one must be used.

11 Working in a reverse of the tightening

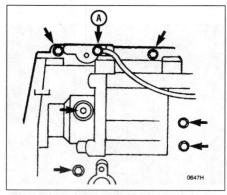

26.7a Remove the upper crankcase bolts (arrows), noting the position of the earth (ground) cable (A)

26.7b One of the bolts (A) is accessed via the plug hole. Also remove the nut (B)

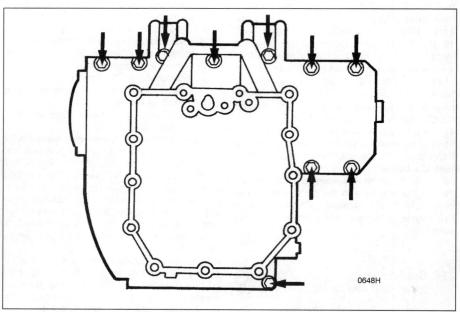

26.9a Remove the 6 mm lower crankcase bolts (arrows) . . .

26.9b . . . the oil drain tube bolt (arrow) . . .

26.9c . . . and the 6 mm nut (arrow)

26.10 Remove the main oil gallery plug for access to the crankcase bolt next to it

sequence shown (see illustrations), and noting that two of the bolts (nos. 2 and 4) are Allen bolts, and that the no. 1 bolt also secures the right-hand oil drain tube (see illustration), slacken each 8 mm lower crankcase bolt a little a time until they are all finger-tight, then remove the bolts. Note: As each bolt is removed, store it in its relative position in a cardboard template of the crankcase halves. This will ensure all bolts are installed in the correct location on reassembly. Note that bolts no. 9 and 11 are fitted with copper sealing washers. Also remove the oil drain tube.

12 Carefully lift the lower crankcase half off the upper half, using a soft-faced hammer to tap around the joint to initially separate the halves if necessary (see illustration). Note: If the halves do not separate easily, make sure all fasteners have been removed. Do not try and separate the halves by levering against the crankcase mating surfaces as they are easily scored and will leak oil. A leverage point is cast into the crankcase in the front of the engine (see illustration). The lower crankcase half will come away with the oil pump, selector drum and selector forks, leaving the crankshaft, cam chain tensioner blade and transmission shafts in the upper crankcase half.

13 Remove the four locating dowels from the crankcase if they are loose (they could be in either crankcase half), noting their locations (see illustration). Also remove the three oil

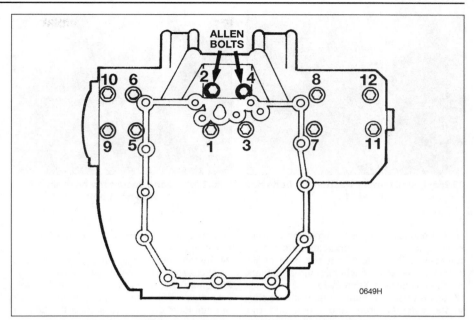

26.11a 8 mm lower crankcase bolt TIGHTENING sequence

passage O-rings from the upper crankcase half (see illustration). Discard these as new ones must be used.

14 Refer to Sections 27 to 34 for the removal and installation of the components housed within the crankcases.

Reassembly

15 Remove all traces of sealant from the crankcase mating surfaces.

16 Ensure that all components and their bearings are in place in the upper and lower crankcase halves. Check that the crankshaft

26.11b The bolt numbers are cast into the casing

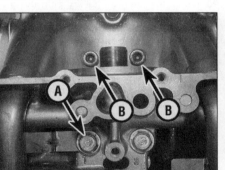

26.11c No. 1 bolt (A) secures the other oil drain tube, and nos. 2 and 4 are Allen bolts (B)

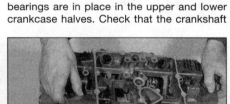

26.12a With all bolts and nuts removed, lift the lower crankcase half off the upper one

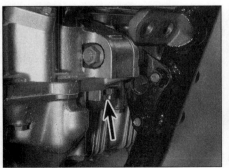

26.12b Insert a screwdriver into the leverage point (arrow) to aid separation

26.13a Remove the four dowels (arrows) if loose

26.13b Remove the O-rings (arrows) and discard them

26.25a Install copper washers on bolts no. 9 and 11 . . .

26.25b . . . and secure the oil drain tube with no. 1 bolt

26.28 Do not forget to install the earth (ground) cable

thrust bearings and the transmission bearing locating pins and half-ring retainers are all correctly located, and that the cam chain tensioner blade, its cushions, and all oil jets have been installed, if removed.

17 Generously lubricate the transmission shafts, selector drum and forks, and the crankshaft, particularly around the bearings, with clean engine oil, then use a rag soaked in high flash-point solvent to wipe over the gasket surfaces of both halves to remove all traces of oil.

18 Install the four locating dowels in the upper crankcase half (see illustration 26.13a). Make sure that the selector drum is in the neutral position.

19 Fit new O-rings into the oil passage holes in the upper crankcase half (see illustration 26.13b).

20 Apply a small amount of suitable sealant to the mating surface of the lower crankcase half.

Caution: Do not apply an excessive amount of sealant as it will ooze out when the case halves are assembled and may obstruct oil passages. Do not apply the sealant on or too close to any of the bearing inserts or surfaces.

21 Check again that all components are in position, particularly that the bearing shells are still correctly located in the lower crankcase half. Carefully install the lower crankcase half down onto the upper crankcase half, making sure that the selector forks locate correctly into their grooves in the gears. Make sure the dowels all locate correctly into the lower crankcase half.

22 Check that the lower crankcase half is correctly seated. **Note:** *The crankcase halves should fit together without being forced. If the casings are not correctly seated, remove the lower crankcase half and investigate the problem. Do not attempt to pull them together using the crankcase bolts as the casing will crack and be ruined.*

23 Check that the transmission shafts rotate freely and independently in neutral, then rotate the selector drum by hand and select each gear in turn whilst rotating the input shaft. Check that all gears can be

selected and that the shafts rotate freely in every gear.

24 Install the oil drain tubes into the lower crankcase, but do not yet install their bolts.

25 Clean the threads of the 8 mm lower crankcase bolts and insert them in their original locations, not forgetting the copper washers with bolts no. 9 and 11 (using new ones if necessary), and that the right-hand oil drain tube is secured by bolt no. 1 (see illustrations). Secure all bolts finger-tight at first, then tighten the bolts a little at a time and in the numerical sequence shown to the torque setting specified at the beginning of the Chapter (see illustrations 26.11a, b and c).

26 Install the main oil gallery plug using a new O-ring and tighten it to the specified torque setting (see illustration 26.10).

27 Clean the threads of the 6 mm lower crankcase bolts and insert them in their original locations (see illustration 26.9a). Also insert the 6 mm bolt securing the left-hand oil drain tube (see illustration 26.9b), and the single 6 mm nut located just ahead of the transmission output shaft on the left-hand side of the crankcase (see illustration 26.9c). Tighten all the bolts and the nut a little at a time to the specified torque setting.

28 Turn the engine over. Install the seven 6 mm upper crankcase bolts and the single nut which is located inside the alternator mounting flange (see illustrations 26.7a and b). Clean the terminal on the earth (ground) cable and secure it with the middle rear bolt (see illustration). Tighten all the bolts and the nut a little at a time to the specified torque setting.

29 With all crankcase fasteners tightened, check that the crankshaft and transmission shafts rotate smoothly and easily. Check the operation of the transmission in each gear (see Step 23). If there are any signs of undue stiffness, tight or rough spots, or of any other problem, the fault must be rectified before proceeding further.

30 Install the plug into its hole next to the alternator mounting flange using a new sealing washer, and tighten it securely (see illustration 26.6).

31 Install the retainer plate for the transmission output shaft bearing and the clutch pushrod oil seal onto the left-hand side of the crankcase (see illustration 26.5b). Tighten the bolts securely, then bend up the tabs on the plate to lock them in place (see illustration 26.5a).

32 Install the transmission input shaft bearing retainer plate onto the right-hand side of the crankcase. Apply a suitable non-permanent thread locking compound to the threads of the screws and tighten them securely (see illustration 26.4).

33 Install the main oil gallery plug with a new sealing washer, and tighten it to the specified torque setting. Install all other removed assemblies in the reverse of the sequence given in Steps 3 and 2.

27 Crankcase - inspection and servicing

1 After the crankcases have been separated, remove the crankshaft, bearings, cam chain tensioner blade, oil pressure switch, neutral switch and transmission components, referring to the relevant Sections of this Chapter and to Chapter 8 for the oil pressure and neutral switches. Remove the oil jets from the outer cylinder holes and from the bearing cut-outs in the top of the upper crankcase half (see illustrations). Check the condition of

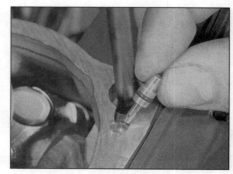

27.1a Remove the cylinder oil jets . . .

27.1b ... and crankshaft oil jets, and check their O-rings

28.2a Unbolt the oil pump and lift it out of the engine

28.2b Remove the O-ring from the pump ...

their O-rings, and replace them if necessary. Also remove the transmission shaft oil jets from the lower crankcase half.

2 The crankcases should be cleaned thoroughly with new solvent and dried with compressed air. All oil passages and oil jets should be blown out with compressed air.

3 All traces of old gasket sealant should be removed from the mating surfaces. Minor damage to the surfaces can be cleaned up with a fine sharpening stone or grindstone..

Caution: Be very careful not to nick or gouge the crankcase mating surfaces or oil leaks will result. Check both crankcase halves very carefully for cracks and other damage.

4 Small cracks or holes in aluminium castings may be repaired with an epoxy resin adhesive as a temporary measure. Permanent repairs can only be effected by argon-arc welding, and only a specialist in this process is in a position to advise on the economy or practical aspect of such a repair. If any damage is found that can't be repaired, replace the crankcase halves as a set.

5 Damaged threads can be economically reclaimed by using a diamond section wire insert, of the Heli-Coil type, which is easily fitted after drilling and re-tapping the affected thread.

6 Sheared studs or screws can usually be removed with screw extractors, which consist of a tapered, left thread screw of very hard steel. These are inserted into a pre-drilled hole in the stud, and usually succeed in dislodging the most stubborn stud or screw.

7 Check that all the cylinder studs are tight in the crankcase halves. If any are loose, remove

 HAYNES HiNT *Refer to Tools and Workshop Tips for details of installing a thread insert and using screw extractors.*

them, noting which fits where as they are of different lengths and colours, then clean their threads. Apply a suitable non-permanent thread locking compound and tighten them to the torque setting specified at the beginning of the Chapter.

8 Apply clean engine oil to the oil jet O-rings and install the jets into their correct locations **(see illustrations 27.1a and b)**. Install all other components and assemblies, referring to the relevant Sections of this Chapter and to Chapter 8, before reassembling the crankcase halves.

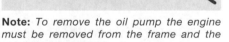

28 Oil pump - removal, inspection and installation

Note: *To remove the oil pump the engine must be removed from the frame and the crankcases separated.*

Removal

1 Separate the crankcase halves (see Section 26). The oil pump is located inside the lower half.

2 Unscrew the three bolts securing the pump to the crankcase, then remove the pump **(see illustration)**. Remove the O-rings from the pump and the oil passage and discard them as new ones must be used **(see illustrations)**. Also remove the two dowels from either the crankcase or the pump if they are loose.

Inspection

3 Inspect the pump body for any obvious damage such as cracks or distortion, and check that the shaft rotates freely and without any side-to-side play or excessive endfloat. Check the relief valve in the pump for clogging and check that the plunger moves freely in the body.

4 The oil pump fitted to this machine is not serviceable and Suzuki provide no inspection procedure or specifications for it. If the pump is suspected of being faulty, it must be replaced as a unit.

Installation

5 Fit the dowels into their holes in the crankcase, making sure they are secure **(see illustration 28.2c)**.

6 Install new O-rings onto the oil passage and the pump, then install the pump, making sure it is correctly located over the dowels **(see illustrations 28.2c and 28.2b)**. Apply a suitable non-permanent thread locking compound to the threads of the pump bolts and tighten them to the torque setting specified at the beginning of the Chapter **(see illustrations)**.

7 Reassemble the crankcase halves (see Section 26).

2

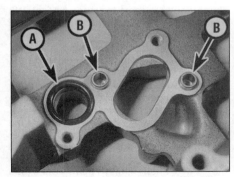

28.2c ... and from the passage (A). Also remove the dowels (B) if loose

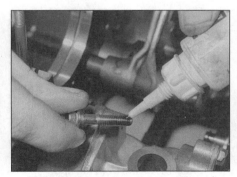

28.6a Apply a non-permanent thread locking compound to the bolt threads ...

28.6b ... and tighten them to the specified torque

29 Main and connecting rod bearings - general information

1 Even though main and connecting rod bearings are generally replaced with new ones during the engine overhaul, the old bearings should be retained for close examination as they may reveal valuable information about the condition of the engine.

2 Bearing failure occurs mainly because of lack of lubrication, the presence of dirt or other foreign particles, overloading the engine and/or corrosion. Regardless of the cause of bearing failure, it must be corrected before the engine is reassembled to prevent it from happening again.

3 When examining the connecting rod bearings, remove them from the connecting rods and caps and lay them out on a clean surface in the same general position as their location on the crankshaft journals. This will enable you to match any noted bearing problems with the corresponding crankshaft journal.

4 Dirt and other foreign particles get into the engine in a variety of ways. It may be left in the engine during assembly or it may pass through filters or breathers. It may get into the oil and from there into the bearings. Metal chips from machining operations and normal engine wear are often present. Abrasives are sometimes

left in engine components after reconditioning operations, especially when parts are not thoroughly cleaned using the proper cleaning methods. Whatever the source, these foreign objects often end up imbedded in the soft bearing material and are easily recognised. Large particles will not imbed in the bearing and will score or gouge the bearing and journal. The best prevention for this cause of bearing failure is to clean all parts thoroughly and keep everything spotlessly clean during engine reassembly. Frequent and regular oil and filter changes are also recommended.

5 Lack of lubrication or lubrication breakdown has a number of interrelated causes. Excessive heat (which thins the oil), overloading (which squeezes the oil from the bearing face) and oil leakage or throw off (from excessive bearing clearances, worn oil pump or high engine speeds) all contribute to lubrication breakdown. Blocked oil passages will also starve a bearing and destroy it. When lack of lubrication is the cause of bearing failure, the bearing material is wiped or extruded from the steel backing of the bearing. Temperatures may increase to the point where the steel backing and the journal turn blue from overheating.

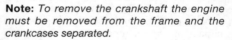
HAYNES HiNT *Refer to Tools and Workshop Tips for bearing fault finding.*

6 Riding habits can have a definite effect on bearing life. Full throttle low speed operation, or labouring the engine, puts very high loads on bearings, which tend to squeeze out the oil film. These loads cause the bearings to flex, which produces fine cracks in the bearing face (fatigue failure). Eventually the bearing material will loosen in pieces and tear away from the steel backing. Short trip riding leads to corrosion of bearings, as insufficient engine heat is produced to drive off the condensed water and corrosive gases produced. These products collect in the engine oil, forming acid and sludge. As the oil is carried to the engine bearings, the acid attacks and corrodes the bearing material.

7 Incorrect bearing installation during engine assembly will lead to bearing failure as well. Tight fitting bearings which leave insufficient bearing oil clearances result in oil starvation. Dirt or foreign particles trapped behind a bearing insert result in high spots on the bearing which lead to failure.

8 To avoid bearing problems, clean all parts thoroughly before reassembly, double check all bearing clearance measurements and lubricate the new bearings with clean engine oil during installation.

30 Crankshaft and main bearings - removal, inspection and installation

Note: *To remove the crankshaft the engine must be removed from the frame and the crankcases separated.*

Removal

1 Separate the crankcase halves (see Section 26).

2 Before removing the crankshaft check the thrust bearing clearance. The thrust bearings are located between the crank webs and the main bearing housing between cylinder nos. 1 and 2. Push the crankshaft as far as it will go toward the starter clutch end (this eliminates play in the inner bearing). Insert a feeler gauge between the crankshaft and the outer thrust bearing and record the clearance **(see illustration)**. Compare the measurement with this Chapter's Specifications. If the clearance is excessive, refer to Steps 10 and 11 for selection of replacement bearings.

3 Lift the crankshaft together with the connecting rods and cam chain out of the upper crankcase half **(see illustration)**. If the crankshaft appears stuck, tap it gently using a soft faced mallet. Remove the thrust bearings, noting how and where they fit - do not get the inner and outer bearing mixed up.

4 The main bearing shells can be removed from their cut-outs by pushing their centres to the side, then lifting them out **(see illustrations)**. Keep the bearing shells in order.

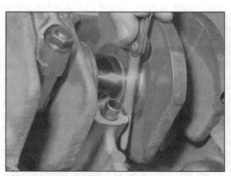
30.2 Measure the clearance between the outer thrust bearing and the crankshaft

30.3 Lift the crankshaft out of the case, together with the connecting rods and cam chain

30.4a Remove the bearing shells from the lower case half - they can be identified by their oil holes ...

30.4b ... and from the upper case half

5 If required, remove the connecting rods from the crankshaft (see Section 31), and disengage the cam chain from its sprocket.

Inspection

6 Clean the crankshaft with solvent, using a rifle-cleaning brush to scrub out the oil passages. If available, blow the crank dry with compressed air, and also blow through the oil passages. Check the cam chain sprocket for wear or damage. If any of the sprocket teeth are excessively worn, chipped or broken, the crankshaft must be replaced. Similarly check the primary drive gear.

7 Refer to Section 29 and examine the main bearing shells. If they are scored, badly scuffed or appear to have been seized, new bearings must be installed. Always replace the main bearings as a set. If they are badly damaged, check the corresponding crankshaft journals. Evidence of extreme heat, such as discoloration, indicates that lubrication failure has occurred. Be sure to thoroughly check the oil pump and pressure regulator as well as all oil holes and passages before reassembling the engine.

8 The crankshaft journals should be given a close visual examination, paying particular attention where damaged bearings have been discovered. If the journals are scored or pitted in any way a new crankshaft will be required. Note that undersizes are not available, precluding the option of re-grinding the crankshaft.

9 Place the crankshaft on V-blocks and check the runout at the main bearing journals using a dial gauge. Compare the reading to the maximum specified at the beginning of the Chapter. If the runout exceeds the limit, the crankshaft must be replaced.

Thrust bearing selection

10 If the thrust bearing clearance was excessive (see Step 2), measure the thickness of the inner thrust bearing, and compare the result to the specifications at the beginning of the Chapter **(see illustration)**. If the thickness measured is below the service limit specified, the inner thrust bearing must be replaced. There is only one size of replacement inner bearing. Install the replacement and check the clearance again (see Step 2). If the clearance is still excessive, or if the inner bearing was within specifications, select a replacement outer bearing as follows:

11 Remove the outer thrust bearing. Install the inner bearing and push the crankshaft as far as it will go toward the starter clutch end to eliminate any clearance. Insert a feeler gauge between the crankshaft and the main bearing housing where the outer bearing fits, and record the clearance. Using the table below, select a replacement outer thrust bearing according to the clearance measured. For example, if the clearance recorded was 2.475 mm, the bearing colour-code required is blue. Re-check the clearance with the new bearings (see Step 2).

GSF600 and GSF600S models

Outer bearing clearance (bearing removed)	Bearing colour-code required
2.415 to 2.440 mm	Red
2.440 to 2.465 mm	Black
2.465 to 2.490 mm	Blue
2.490 to 2.515 mm	Green
2.515 to 2.540 mm	Yellow
2.540 to 2.565 mm	White

GSF1200 and GSF1200S models

Outer bearing clearance (bearing removed)	Bearing colour-code required
2.420 to 2.440 mm	Black
2.440 to 2.460 mm	Orange
2.460 to 2.480 mm	Blue
2.480 to 2.500 mm	Green
2.500 to 2.520 mm	Yellow
2.520 to 2.540 mm	Red
2.540 to 2.560 mm	Brown
2.560 to 2.570 mm	Pink

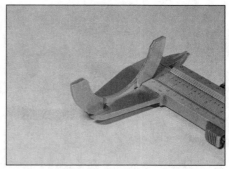

30.10 Measure the thickness of the inner thrust bearing

Main bearing shell selection

12 Replacement bearing shells for the main bearings are supplied on a selected fit basis. Code numbers stamped on various components are used to identify the correct replacement bearings. The crankshaft main bearing journal size letters, one letter for each journal (either an A, a B or a C), are stamped on the outside of the crankshaft left-hand web **(see illustration)**. The corresponding main bearing housing size letters (either an A or a B), are stamped into the rear of the upper crankcase half **(see illustration)**. The first letter of each set of six is for the outer left-hand journal, the second for the middle left-hand, the third for the inner left-hand, the fourth for the inner right-hand, the fifth for the middle right-hand and the sixth for the outer right-hand. **Note:** *Referrals to left- and right-hand are made as though the engine is the correct way up. Do not confuse the two if the engine is upside down.*

13 A range of bearing shells is available. To select the correct bearing for a particular journal, using the table below cross-refer the main bearing journal size letter (stamped on the crank web) with the main bearing housing size letter (stamped on the crankcase) to

30.12a Crankshaft main bearing journal size letters

30.12b Crankshaft main bearing housing size letters

2

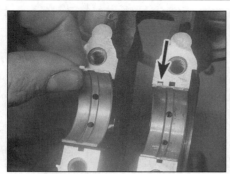

30.16 Make sure the tab on the shell locates in the slot in the housing (arrow)

30.18 Lay a strip of Plastigauge (arrow) on each journal parallel to the crankshaft centreline

30.21 Measure the width of the crushed Plastigauge (be sure to use the correct scale - metric and imperial are included)

determine the colour code of the bearing required. For example, if the journal code is C, and the housing code is B, then the bearing required is Yellow.

Crankcase housing code	Crankshaft journal code		
	A	B	C
A	Green	Black	Brown
B	Black	Brown	Yellow

Oil clearance check

14 Whether new bearing shells are being fitted or the original ones are being re-used, the main bearing oil clearance should be checked before the engine is reassembled. Main bearing oil clearance is measured with a product known as Plastigauge.
15 Clean the backs of the bearing shells and the bearing housings in both crankcase halves.
16 Press the bearing shells into their cut-outs, ensuring that the tab on each shell engages in the notch in the crankcase **(see illustration)**. Make sure the bearings are fitted in the correct locations and take care not to touch any shell's bearing surface with your fingers.
17 Ensure the shells and crankshaft are clean and dry. Lay the crankshaft in position in the upper crankcase.
18 Cut several lengths of the appropriate size Plastigauge (they should be slightly shorter than the width of the crankshaft journals). Place a strand of Plastigauge on each (cleaned) journal **(see illustration)**. Make sure the crankshaft is not rotated.
19 Carefully install the lower crankcase half on to the upper half. Make sure that the selector forks (if fitted) engage with their respective slots in the transmission gears as the halves are joined. Check that the lower crankcase half is correctly seated. **Note:** *Do not tighten the crankcase bolts if the casing is not correctly seated.* Install the lower crankcase 8 mm bolts numbers 1 to 12 **(see illustration 26.11a, b and c)** in their original locations and tighten them a little at a time in

sequence to the torque setting specified at the beginning of the Chapter. Make sure that the crankshaft is not rotated as the bolts are tightened.
20 Slacken each bolt in reverse sequence starting at number 12 and working backwards to number 1. Slacken each bolt a little at a time until they are all finger-tight, then remove the bolts. Carefully lift off the lower crankcase half, making sure the Plastigauge is not disturbed.
21 Compare the width of the crushed Plastigauge on each crankshaft journal to the scale printed on the Plastigauge envelope to obtain the main bearing oil clearance **(see illustration)**. Compare the reading to the specifications at the beginning of the Chapter.
22 On completion carefully scrape away all traces of the Plastigauge material from the crankshaft journal and bearing shells; use a fingernail or other object which is unlikely to score them.
23 If the oil clearance falls into the specified range, no bearing shell replacement is required (provided they are in good condition). If the clearance is more than the standard range, but within the service limit, refer to the marks on the case and the marks on the crankshaft and select new bearing shells (see Steps 12 and 13). Install the new shells and check the oil clearance once again (the new shells may bring bearing clearance within the

30.24 Measure the diameter of each crankshaft journal

specified range). Always replace all of the shells at the same time.
24 If the clearance is greater than the service limit listed in this Chapter's Specifications (even with replacement shells), measure the diameter of the crankshaft journals with a micrometer and compare your findings with this Chapter's Specifications **(see illustration)**. By measuring the diameter at a number of points around each journal's circumference, you'll be able to determine whether or not the journal is out-of-round. Also take a measurement at each end of the journal, near the crank throws, as well as in the middle, to determine if the journal is tapered.

Installation

25 If removed, install the connecting rods onto the crankshaft (see Section 31), and engage the cam chain onto its sprocket.
26 Clean the backs of the bearing shells and the bearing cut-outs in both crankcase halves. If new shells are being fitted, ensure that all traces of the protective grease are cleaned off using paraffin (kerosene). Wipe dry the shells and crankcase halves with a lint-free cloth. Make sure all the oil passages and holes are clear, and blow them through with compressed air if it is available.
27 Lubricate each shell, preferable with molybdenum paste, or if not available then with clean engine oil. Press the bearing shells into their locations. The shells with the oil holes locate in the lower crankcase half **(see illustration 30.4a)**. Make sure the tab on each shell engages in the notch in the casing **(see illustration 30.16)**. Make sure the bearings are fitted in the correct locations and take care not to touch any shell's bearing surface with your fingers.
28 Lower the crankshaft into position in the upper crankcase, feeding the cam chain down through its tunnel **(see illustration 30.3)**.
29 Install the thrust bearings into their correct locations (do not mix up the inner with the outer) between the crank webs and the main bearing housing between cylinder nos. 1 and 2, making sure that the oil grooves

30.29 Install the thrust bearings with their grooves toward the crankshaft

31.2 Slip a feeler gauge between the connecting rod and the crank web to check side clearance

31.3 This number indicates the connecting rod bearing size and faces back - make your own marks to indicate cylinder number

face towards the crankshaft web (see illustration).

30 Reassemble the crankcase halves (see Section 26).

31 Connecting rods - removal, inspection and installation

Note: To remove the connecting rods the engine must be removed from the frame and the crankcases separated.

Removal

1 Remove the crankshaft (see Section 30).
2 Before removing the rods from the crankshaft, measure the side clearance on each rod with a feeler gauge (see illustration). If the clearance on any rod is greater than the service limit listed in this Chapter's Specifications, measure the big-end and crankpin widths as described in Step 7.
3 Using paint or a felt marker pen, mark the relevant cylinder identity on each connecting rod and bearing. Mark across the cap-to-connecting rod join and note which side of the rod faces the front of the engine to ensure that the cap and rod are fitted the correct way around on reassembly. Note that the number already across the rod and cap indicates

bearing size grade, not cylinder number, and that this number faces the rear of the engine (see illustration).
4 Unscrew the big-end cap nuts and separate the connecting rod, cap and both bearing shells from the crankpin (see illustration). Do not remove the bolts from the connecting rods. Keep the rod, cap, nuts and (if they are to be reused) the bearing shells together in their correct positions to ensure correct installation.

Inspection

5 Check the connecting rods for cracks and other obvious damage.
6 If not already done (see Section 16), apply clean engine oil to the piston pin, insert it into the connecting rod small-end and check for any freeplay between the two (see illustration). Measure the pin external diameter and the small-end bore diameter and compare the measurements to the specifications at the beginning of the Chapter (see illustrations 16.13b and 16.13d). Replace components that are worn beyond the specified limits.
7 If the side clearance measured in Step 2 exceeds the service limit specified, measure the width of the connecting rod big-end and the width of the crankpin (see illustrations). Compare the results to the specifications at the beginning of the Chapter, and replace whichever component exceeds those specifications.

31.4 Remove the connecting rod cap nuts and separate the rods from the crankshaft

8 Refer to Section 29 and examine the connecting rod bearing shells. If they are scored, badly scuffed or appear to have seized, new shells must be installed. Always replace the shells in the connecting rods as a set. If they are badly damaged, check the corresponding crankpin. Evidence of extreme heat, such as discoloration, indicates that lubrication failure has occurred. Be sure to thoroughly check the oil pump and pressure regulator as well as all oil holes and passages before reassembling the engine.
9 Have the rods checked for twist and bend by a Suzuki dealer if you are in doubt about their straightness.

2

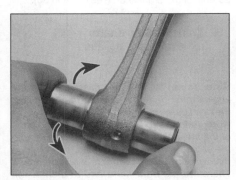

31.6 Check the piston pin and connecting rod small-end bore for wear by rocking the pin back and forth

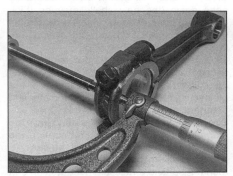

31.7a Measure the width of the connecting rod . . .

31.7b . . . and of the corresponding crankpin

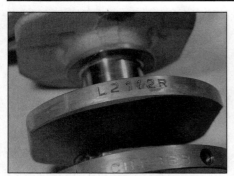

31.10 Crankpin journal size numbers

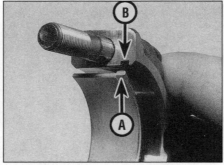

31.14 Make sure the tab (A) locates in the notch (B)

31.23 Tighten the connecting rod cap nuts to the specified torque setting in two stages

Bearing shell selection

10 Replacement bearing shells for the big-end bearings are supplied on a selected fit basis. Codes stamped on various components are used to identify the correct replacement bearings. The crankpin journal size numbers are stamped on the crankshaft inner left web and will be either a 1, a 2 or a 3 (see illustration). The number coming immediately after the L is for the outer left-hand big-end (cyl no. 1), the next number is for the inner left-hand big-end (cyl no. 2), the next for the inner right-hand (cyl no. 3) and the number coming before the R is for the outer right-hand big-end cyl no. 4. The connecting rod size code is marked on the flat face of the connecting rod and cap and will be either a 1 or a 2 (see illustration 31.3).

11 A range of bearing shells is available. To select the correct bearing for a particular big-end, using the table below cross-refer the crankpin journal size number (stamped on the web) with the connecting rod size letter (stamped on the rod) to determine the colour code of the bearing required. For example, if the connecting rod size is 2, and the crankpin size is 3, then the bearing required is Yellow.

Connecting rod code	Crankpin code		
	1	2	3
1	Green	Black	Brown
2	Black	Brown	Yellow

Oil clearance check

12 Whether new bearing shells are being fitted or the original ones are being re-used, the connecting rod bearing oil clearance should be checked prior to reassembly.

13 Clean the backs of the bearing shells and the bearing locations in both the connecting rod and cap.

14 Press the bearing shells into their locations, ensuring that the tab on each shell engages the notch in the connecting rod/cap (see illustration). Make sure the bearings are fitted in the correct locations and take care not to touch any shell's bearing surface with your fingers.

15 Cut a length of the appropriate size Plastigauge (it should be slightly shorter than the width of the crankpin). Place a strand of Plastigauge on the (cleaned) crankpin journal and fit the (clean) connecting rod, shells and cap. Make sure the cap is fitted the correct way around so the previously made markings align, and that the rod is facing the right way, and tighten the bearing cap nuts in two stages, first to the initial torque setting specified at the beginning of the Chapter, and then to the final torque setting specified, whilst ensuring that the connecting rod does not rotate. Slacken the cap nuts and remove the connecting rod, again taking great care not to rotate the crankshaft.

16 Compare the width of the crushed Plastigauge on the crankpin to the scale printed on the Plastigauge envelope to obtain the connecting rod bearing oil clearance (see illustration 30.21). Compare the reading to the specifications at the beginning of the Chapter.

17 On completion carefully scrape away all traces of the Plastigauge material from the crankpin and bearing shells using a fingernail or other object which is unlikely to score the shells.

18 If the clearance is within the range listed in this Chapter's Specifications and the bearings are in perfect condition, they can be reused. If the clearance is beyond the service limit, replace the bearing shells with new ones (see Steps 10 and 11). Check the oil clearance once again (the new shells may be thick enough to bring bearing clearance within the specified range). Always replace all of the inserts at the same time.

19 If the clearance is still greater than the service limit listed in this Chapter's Specifications, measure the diameter of the connecting rod journal with a micrometer and compare your findings with this Chapter's Specifications. Also, by measuring the diameter at a number of points around the journal's circumference, you'll be able to determine whether or not the journal is out-of-round. Also take a measurement at each end of the journal, near the crank throws, as well as in the middle, to determine if the journal is tapered.

20 If any journal has worn down past the service limit, replace the crankshaft.

21 Repeat the bearing selection procedure for the remaining connecting rods.

Installation

22 Install the bearing shells in the connecting rods and caps, aligning the notch in the bearing with the groove in the rod or cap (see illustration 31.14). Lubricate the shells, preferably with molybdenum paste, or if not available with clean engine oil, and assemble each connecting rod on its correct crankpin so that the previously made matchmarks align and the connecting rod size letter is facing the rear of the engine when the crankshaft is installed (see illustrations 31.4 and 31.3). Tighten the nuts finger-tight at this stage. Check to make sure that all components have been returned to their original locations using the marks made on disassembly.

23 Tighten the bearing cap nuts in two stages, first to the initial torque setting specified at the beginning of the Chapter, and then to the final torque setting specified (see illustration).

24 Check that the rods rotate smoothly and freely on the crankpin. If there are any signs of roughness or tightness, remove the rods and re-check the bearing clearance. Sometimes tapping the bottom of the connecting rod cap will relieve tightness, but if in doubt, recheck the clearances.

25 Install the crankshaft (see Section 30).

32 Transmission shafts - removal and installation

Note: To remove the transmission shafts the engine must be removed from the frame and the crankcases separated.

Note: Referrals to the right and left-hand ends of the transmission shafts are made as though the engine is the correct way up, even though throughout this procedure it is upside down. Therefore the right-hand end of a shaft will actually be on your left as you look down onto the underside of the upper crankcase assembly.

32.2a Lift out the input shaft . . .

32.2b . . . and the output shaft

Removal

1 Separate the crankcase halves (see Section 26). Note the positions of the ball bearing locating pins on the right-hand end of the input shaft and the left-hand end of the output shaft.

2 Lift the input shaft and output shaft out of the crankcase, noting their relative positions in the crankcase and how they fit together **(see illustrations)**. If they are stuck, use a soft-faced hammer and gently tap on the ends of the shafts to free them.

3 Remove the ball bearing half-ring retainers and the needle bearing dowel pins from the upper crankcase half, noting how they fit **(see illustrations 32.5a and b)**. If they are not in their slots or hole in the crankcase, remove them from the bearings themselves on the shafts.

4 Remove the spacer and oil seal from the left-hand end of the output shaft, and on 1200 models the O-ring, noting how they fit. Discard the oil seal and O-ring as new ones should be used **(see illustration 32.6)**. Also remove the clutch pushrod oil seal from the left-hand end of the input shaft, which will probably have remained in the crankcase. If necessary, the input shaft and output shaft can be disassembled and inspected for wear or damage (see Section 33).

Installation

5 Install the ball bearing half-ring retainers into their slots in the upper crankcase half, and install the needle bearing dowels into their holes **(see illustrations)**.

6 Slide a new O-ring (1200 models only), the

spacer and a new oil seal onto the left-hand end of the output shaft, having first coated the seal lips with grease **(see illustration)**.

7 Lower the input shaft into position in the upper crankcase, making sure the hole in the needle bearing engages correctly with the dowel, the ball bearing locating pin faces forward and locates in its recess, and the groove in the bearing engages correctly with the bearing half-ring retainer **(see illustrations)**. Install the clutch pushrod oil seal against the left-hand end of the shaft.

8 Lower the output shaft into position in the crankcase half, making sure the hole in the needle bearing engages correctly with the dowel, the ball bearing locating pin faces back and locates in its recess, and the groove in the bearing engages correctly with the bearing half-ring retainer **(see illustrations 32.7a and b)**.

9 Make sure both transmission shafts are correctly seated and their related pinions are correctly engaged.

Caution: If the ball bearing locating pins and half-ring retainers or needle bearing dowel pins are not correctly engaged, the crankcase halves will not seat correctly.

10 Position the gears in the neutral position and check the shafts are free to rotate easily and independently (ie the input shaft can turn whilst the output shaft is held stationary) before proceeding further.

11 Reassembly the crankcase halves (see Section 26).

33 Transmission shafts - disassembly, inspection and reassembly

Note: *References to the right- and left-hand ends of the transmission shafts are made as though they are installed in the engine and the engine is the correct way up.*

1 Remove the transmission shafts from the upper crankcase half (see Section 32). Always disassemble the transmission shafts separately to avoid mixing up the components.

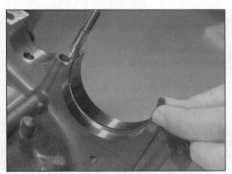

32.5a Install the caged-ball bearing half-ring retainers . . .

32.5b . . . and the needle bearing dowel pins

32.6 Slide a new oil seal onto the output shaft

32.7a Align the hole in the needle bearing at one end of each shaft with the bearing dowel . . .

32.7b . . . and at the other end of each shaft position the bearing pin in the case recess (A) and install the half-ring retainer in the case and bearing grooves (B)

2

H29237

33.2 Six-speed transmission - input shaft components

1 Dowel pin	5 2nd gear pinion	9 3rd/4th gear pinion	12 Input shaft with integral 1st
2 Needle bearing	6 6th gear pinion	10 5th gear pinion bush	gear pinion
3 Oil seal	7 Splined washer	11 5th gear pinion	13 Half-ring retainer
4 Wire circlip	8 Circlip		14 Ball bearing

GSF600 and GSF600S - six-speed transmission

Input shaft disassembly

> **HAYNES HINT**
> *When disassembling the transmission shafts, place the parts on a long rod or thread a wire through them to keep them in order and facing the proper direction.*

2 Remove the needle bearing and oil seal from the left-hand end of the shaft (**see illustration**).

3 Remove the wire circlip securing the 2nd gear pinion, then slide the 2nd gear pinion and the 6th gear pinion and its splined washer off the shaft. If the wire circlip is difficult to access, reach behind the 6th gear pinion with circlip pliers, spread the circlip and slide it toward the 3rd/4th gear pinion. Slide the splined washer and the 6th and 2nd drive gear pinions back to expose the 2nd gear pinion wire circlip, then remove it and slide the 2nd and 6th gear pinions and the splined washer off the shaft.

4 Remove the circlip securing the combined 3rd/4th gear pinion, then slide the pinion off the shaft.

5 Remove the circlip securing the 5th gear pinion, then slide the 5th gear pinion and its bush off the shaft.

6 The 1st gear pinion is integral with the shaft.

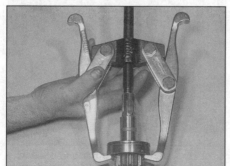

33.13 Use a puller to remove the input shaft ball bearing

Input shaft inspection

7 Wash all of the components in clean solvent and dry them off.

8 Check the gear teeth for cracking chipping, pitting and other obvious wear or damage. Any pinion that is damaged as such must be replaced.

9 Inspect the dogs and the dog holes in the gears for cracks, chips, and excessive wear especially in the form of rounded edges. Make sure mating gears engage properly. Replace the paired gears as a set if necessary.

10 Check for signs of scoring or bluing on the pinions, bushes and shaft. This could be caused by overheating due to inadequate lubrication. Check that all the oil holes and passages are clear. Replace any damaged pinions or bushes.

11 Check that each pinion moves freely on the shaft or bush but without undue freeplay. Check that each bush moves freely on the shaft but without undue freeplay.

12 The shaft is unlikely to sustain damage unless the engine has seized, placing an unusually high loading on the transmission, or the machine has covered a very high mileage. Check the surface of the shaft, especially where a pinion turns on it, and replace the shaft if it has scored or picked up, or if there are any cracks. Damage of any kind can only be cured by replacement.

13 Check the ball bearing for play or roughness, and that it is a tight fit on the shaft. Replace the bearing if it is worn, loose or damaged, using a bearing puller to remove it (**see illustration**). Install the bearing using a press or a length of tubing which bears only on the bearing's inner race. Install the needle roller bearing onto the shaft, and check it for play or roughness. Replace the bearing if it is worn or damaged.

14 Check the washers and replace any that are bent or appear weakened or worn. Discard all the circlips as new ones must be used.

Input shaft reassembly

15 During reassembly, apply molybdenum paste or engine oil to the mating surfaces of the shaft, pinions and bushes. When installing

the circlips, do not expand the ends any further than is necessary. Install the stamped circlips so that their chamfered side faces the pinion it secures, ie so that its sharp edge faces the direction of thrust load (see *correct fitting of a stamped circlip* illustration in Tools and Workshop Tips of the Reference section).

16 Slide the 5th gear pinion, with its dogs facing away from the integral 1st gear, onto the left-hand end of the shaft (**see illustration 33.2**). Slide the 5th gear bush onto the shaft so that it fits into the pinion. Install the circlip, making sure that it locates correctly in the groove in the shaft.

17 Slide the combined 3rd/4th gear pinion onto the shaft, so that the larger (4th gear) pinion faces the 5th gear pinion dogs. Secure it in place with the circlip, making sure it is properly seated in its groove.

18 Slide the splined washer and the 6th gear pinion onto the shaft, so that its dog holes face the dogs on the 3rd gear pinion.

19 Slide the 2nd gear pinion onto the shaft and secure it with the wire circlip, making sure it is properly seated in its groove.

20 Slide the oil seal and the needle bearing onto the shaft end. Check that all components have been correctly installed.

Output shaft disassembly

21 Remove the needle bearing and the thrust washer from the right-hand end of the shaft (**see illustration**).

22 Slide the 1st gear pinion and its bush off the shaft, followed by the thrust washer and the 5th gear pinion.

23 Remove the circlip securing the 4th gear pinion, then slide the splined washer, the pinion and its bush off the shaft.

24 Slide the two lockwashers off the shaft, noting how they fit, followed by the 3rd gear pinion, its bush and the splined washer.

25 Remove the circlip securing the 6th gear pinion, then slide the pinion off the shaft.

26 Remove the circlip securing the 2nd gear pinion, then slide the thrust washer, the 2nd gear pinion and its bush off the shaft.

Output shaft inspection

27 Refer to Steps 7 to 14 above.

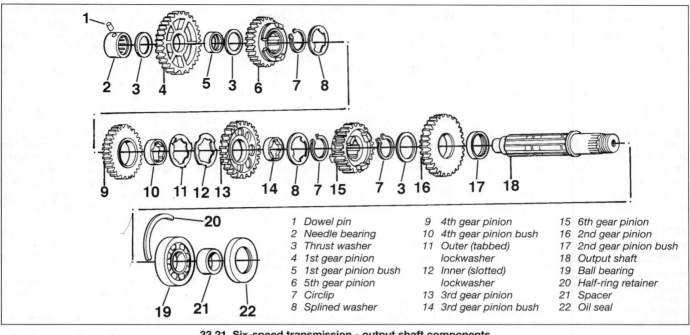

33.21 Six-speed transmission - output shaft components

1	Dowel pin	9	4th gear pinion	15	6th gear pinion
2	Needle bearing	10	4th gear pinion bush	16	2nd gear pinion
3	Thrust washer	11	Outer (tabbed)	17	2nd gear pinion bush
4	1st gear pinion		lockwasher	18	Output shaft
5	1st gear pinion bush	12	Inner (slotted)	19	Ball bearing
6	5th gear pinion		lockwasher	20	Half-ring retainer
7	Circlip	13	3rd gear pinion	21	Spacer
8	Splined washer	14	3rd gear pinion bush	22	Oil seal

Output shaft reassembly

28 During reassembly, apply molybdenum paste or engine oil to the mating surfaces of the shaft, pinions and bushes. When installing the circlips, do not expand the ends any further than is necessary, and install them so that the chamfered side faces the pinion it secures, ie so that its sharp edge faces the direction of thrust load (see *correct fitting of a stamped circlip* illustration in Tools and Workshop Tips of the Reference section).

29 Slide the 2nd gear pinion and its bush onto the shaft, followed by the thrust washer, and secure them in place with the circlip, making sure it is properly seated in its groove **(see illustration 33.21)**.

30 Slide the 6th gear pinion onto the shaft with its selector fork groove facing away from the 2nd gear pinion, and secure it in place with the circlip, making sure it is properly seated in its groove.

31 Slide the splined washer, followed by the 3rd gear pinion and its bush, onto the shaft, making sure the oil hole in the bush aligns with the hole in the shaft. Slide the inner lockwasher onto the shaft until it aligns with its groove, then turn it in the groove so that its splines align with those on the shaft. Slide the outer lockwasher onto the shaft so that its tabs fit into the slots in the inner lockwasher, thus locking it in place.

32 Slide the 4th gear pinion and its bush onto the shaft, making sure the oil hole in the bush aligns with the hole in the shaft, followed by the splined washer, and secure them in place with the circlip, making sure it is properly seated in its groove.

33 Slide the 5th gear pinion onto the shaft with its selector fork groove facing the 4th gear pinion, followed by the thrust washer.

34 Slide the 1st gear pinion and its bush onto the shaft, followed by the thrust washer.

35 Slide the needle bearing onto the shaft end. Check that all components have been correctly installed.

GSF1200 and GSF1200S - five-speed transmission

Input shaft disassembly

 When disassembling the transmission shafts, place the parts on a long rod or thread a wire through them to keep them in order and facing the proper direction.

36 Remove the needle bearing and oil seal from the left-hand end of the shaft **(see illustration)**.

37 Remove the wire circlip securing the 2nd gear pinion, then slide the 2nd gear pinion off the shaft. If the wire circlip is difficult to

2

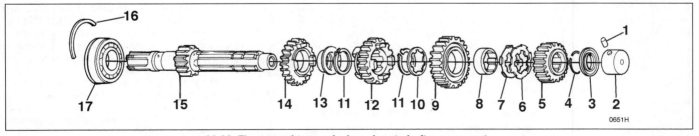

33.36 Five-speed transmission - input shaft components

1	Dowel pin	6	Outer (slotted) lockwasher	11	Circlip	15	Input shaft with integral 1st
2	Needle bearing	7	Inner (tabbed) lockwasher	12	3rd gear pinion		gear pinion
3	Oil seal	8	5th gear pinion bush	13	4th gear pinion bush	16	Half-ring retainer
4	Wire circlip	9	5th gear pinion	14	4th gear pinion	17	Ball bearing
5	2nd gear pinion	10	Splined washer				

0651H

access, reach behind the 5th gear pinion with circlip pliers, spread the circlip and slide it toward the 3rd gear pinion. Slide the 5th gear pinion back to expose the two interlocking splined washers. Slide the inner lockwasher back, then turn the outer lock washer in its groove until it can also slide back. Slide the 2nd gear pinion back to expose the wire circlip, then remove it and slide the 2nd gear pinion off the shaft.

38 Slide the two lockwashers off the shaft, noting how they fit, followed by the 5th gear pinion, its bush and the splined washer.

39 Remove the circlip securing the 3rd gear pinion, then slide the pinion off the shaft.

40 Remove the circlip securing the 4th gear pinion, then slide the pinion and its bush off the shaft.

41 The 1st gear pinion is integral with the shaft.

Input shaft inspection

42 Wash all of the components in clean solvent and dry them off.

43 Check the gear teeth for cracking, chipping, pitting and other obvious wear or damage. Any pinion that is damaged as such must be replaced.

44 Inspect the dogs and the dog holes in the gears for cracks, chips, and excessive wear especially in the form of rounded edges. Make sure mating gears engage properly. Replace the paired gears as a set if necessary.

45 Check for signs of scoring or bluing on the pinions, bushes and shaft. This could be caused by overheating due to inadequate lubrication. Check that all the oil holes and passages are clear. Replace any damaged pinions or bushes.

46 Check that each pinion moves freely on the shaft or bush but without undue freeplay. Check that each bush moves freely on the shaft but without undue free play.

47 The shaft is unlikely to sustain damage unless the engine has seized, placing an unusually high loading on the transmission, or the machine has covered a very high mileage. Check the surface of the shaft, especially where a pinion turns on it, and replace the shaft if it has scored or picked up, or if there are any cracks. Damage of any kind can only be cured by replacement.

48 Check the ball bearing for play or roughness, and that it is a tight fit on the shaft. Replace the bearing if it is worn, loose or damaged, using a bearing puller to remove it **(see illustration 33.13)**. Install the bearing using a press or a length of tubing which bears on the bearing's inner race. Install the needle bearing onto the shaft, and check it for play or roughness. Replace the bearing if it is worn or damaged.

49 Check the washers and replace any that are bent or appear weakened or worn. Discard all the circlips as new ones must be used.

Input shaft reassembly

50 During reassembly, apply molybdenum paste or engine oil to the mating surfaces of the shaft, pinions and bushes. When installing the circlips, do not expand the ends any further than is necessary. Install the stamped circlips so that their chamfered side faces the pinion it secures (see *correct fitting of a stamped circlip* illustration in Tools and Workshop Tips of the Reference section).

51 Slide the 4th gear pinion, with its dogs facing away from the integral 1st gear, onto the left-hand end of the shaft **(see illustration 33.36)**. Slide the 4th gear bush onto the shaft so that it fits into the pinion. Install the circlip, making sure that it locates correctly in the groove in the shaft.

52 Slide the 3rd gear pinion onto the shaft with its selector fork groove facing the 4th gear pinion. Secure it in place with the circlip, making sure it is properly seated in its groove.

53 Slide the splined washer onto the shaft, followed by the 5th gear pinion and its bush, making sure the dog holes in the pinion face the dogs on the 3rd gear pinion, and the oil hole in the bush aligns with the hole in the shaft.

54 Slide the inner lockwasher onto the shaft with its tabs facing out. Slide the outer lockwasher onto the shaft until it aligns with its groove, then turn it in the groove so that its splines align with those on the shaft. Slide the inner lockwasher so that its tabs fit into the slots in the outer lockwasher, thus locking it in place.

55 Slide the 2nd gear pinion onto the shaft and secure it with the wire circlip, making sure it is properly seated in its groove.

56 Slide the oil seal and the needle bearing onto the shaft end. Check that all components have been correctly installed.

Output shaft disassembly

57 Remove the needle bearing and the thrust washer from the right-hand end of the shaft **(see illustration)**.

58 Slide the 1st gear pinion and its bush off the shaft, followed by the thrust washer and the 4th gear pinion.

59 Remove the circlip securing the 3rd gear pinion, then slide the splined washer, the pinion and its bush off the shaft.

60 Slide the splined washer and the 5th gear pinion off the shaft.

61 Remove the circlip securing the 2nd gear pinion, then slide the thrust washer, the 2nd gear pinion and its bush off the shaft.

Output shaft inspection

62 Refer to Steps 42 to 49 above.

Output shaft reassembly

63 During reassembly, apply molybdenum paste or engine oil to the mating surfaces of the shaft, pinions and bushes. When installing the circlips, do not expand the ends any further than is necessary, and install them so that the chamfered side faces the pinion it secures (see *correct fitting of a stamped circlip* illustration in Tools and Workshop Tips of the Reference section).

64 Slide the 2nd gear pinion and its bush onto the shaft, followed by the thrust washer, and secure them in place with the circlip, making sure it is properly seated in its groove **(see illustration 33.57)**.

65 Slide the 5th gear pinion onto the shaft with its selector fork groove facing away from the 2nd gear pinion, followed by the splined washer.

66 Slide the 3rd gear pinion and its bush onto the shaft, making sure the oil hole in the bush

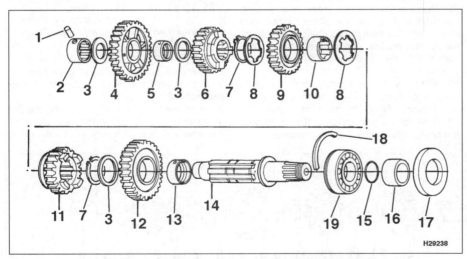

33.57 Five-speed transmission - output shaft components

1 *Dowel pin*	8 *Splined washer*	14 *Output shaft*
2 *Needle bearing*	9 *3rd gear pinion*	15 *O-ring*
3 *Thrust washer*	10 *3rd gear pinion bush*	16 *Spacer*
4 *1st gear pinion*	11 *5th gear pinion*	17 *Oil seal*
5 *1st gear pinion bush*	12 *2nd gear pinion*	18 *Half-ring retainer*
6 *4th gear pinion*	13 *2nd gear pinion bush*	19 *Ball bearing*
7 *Circlip*		

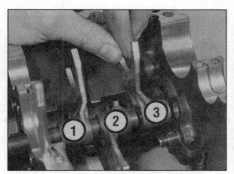

34.2 It's a good idea to number the forks with a felt pen so they can be re-installed in the correct position. Also note which way the fork is offset

34.5a Unhook the stopper arm return spring from the case

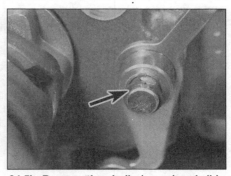

34.5b Remove the circlip (arrow) and slide the arm off the shaft

aligns with the hole in the shaft, followed by the splined washer, and secure them in place with the circlip, making sure it is properly seated in its groove.

67 Slide the 4th gear pinion onto the shaft with its selector fork groove facing the 3rd gear pinion, followed by the thrust washer.

68 Slide the 1st gear pinion and its bush onto the shaft, so that the gear's recessed side faces the 4th gear pinion. Install the thrust washer.

69 Slide the needle roller bearing onto the shaft end. Check that all components have been correctly installed.

34.5c Remove the stopper arm shaft and its washer if required

34.6a Remove the circlip . . .

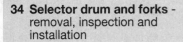

34 Selector drum and forks - removal, inspection and installation

Note: *Access can be gained to the gearchange mechanism (external components) with the engine in the frame and the clutch removed (see Section 23). All other operations require the engine to be removed and the crankcases to be separated.*

Removal

1 Separate the crankcase halves (see Section 26). The selector drum and forks are housed inside the lower half.

2 Before removing the selector forks, note that each fork is numbered for identification. The left-hand fork is number 3, the middle fork is number 2, and the right-hand fork is number 1 **(see illustration)**. If no numbers are visible, number them yourself using a felt pen. Also note which way round they fit as an aid to installation.

3 Supporting the selector forks, withdraw the fork shaft from the right-hand side of the crankcase, then remove the forks. Once removed from the crankcase, slide the forks back onto the shaft in their correct order and way round.

4 Remove the neutral switch (see Chapter 8).

5 Unhook the stopper arm return spring from

its lug in the crankcase **(see illustration)**. Remove the circlip securing the stopper arm on its shaft, then slide the arm off the shaft, noting how it fits **(see illustration)**. If required, unscrew the stopper arm shaft from the outside of the crankcase and remove it **(see illustration)**.

6 Remove the circlip from the left-hand end of the selector drum, then slide the drum out of the right-hand side of the case **(see illustrations)**.

7 If required, slide the stopper plate off the end of the drum, noting how the slot in the plate locates over the pin in the drum **(see illustration)**. Take care not to lose the pin - remove it from the drum if it is loose.

2

34.6b . . . and slide the drum out of the crankcase

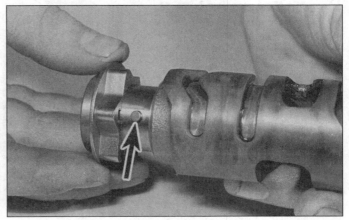

34.7 Note how the stopper plate locates over the pin (arrow)

34.9a Measure the fork-to-groove clearance using a feeler gauge

34.9b Measure the thickness of the fork end . . .

34.9c . . . and the width of the groove

34.13a Remove the circlip from the crankcase . . .

Inspection

8 Inspect the selector forks for any signs of wear or damage, especially around the fork ends where they engage with the groove in the pinion. Check that each fork fits correctly in its pinion groove. Check closely to see if the forks are bent. If the forks are in any way damaged they must be replaced.

9 With the fork engaged with its pinion groove, measure the fork-to-groove clearance using a feeler gauge, and compare the result to the specifications at the beginning of the

Chapter **(see illustration)**. If the clearance exceeds the service limit specified, measure the thickness of the fork ends and the width of the groove and compare the readings to the specifications **(see illustrations)**. Replace whichever components are worn beyond their specifications.

10 Check that the forks fit correctly on their shaft. They should move freely with a light fit but no appreciable freeplay. Check that the fork shaft holes in the crankcases are not worn or damaged.

11 The selector fork shaft can be checked for trueness by rolling it along a flat surface. A bent rod will cause difficulty in selecting gears and make the gearshift action heavy. Replace the shaft if it is bent.

12 Inspect the selector drum grooves and selector fork guide pins for signs of wear or damage. If either component shows signs of wear or damage the selector(s) and drum must be replaced.

13 Check that the selector drum bearings rotate freely and have no sign of freeplay between them and the crankcase. Replace the bearings if necessary. To replace the ball bearing, remove the circlip and drift the bearing out of the crankcase **(see**

illustration)**. To replace the needle bearing, drift it out of the crankcase, noting that once it has been removed it cannot be re-used. Draw or drive the new bearings onto place, making sure they enter squarely. Secure the ball bearing with its circlip.

14 Check the stopper arm roller and the stopper plate for signs of wear or damage and replace them if necessary. Check that the arm is a light fit on the shaft with no appreciable freeplay between them.

Installation

15 If removed, install the pin into the drum **(see illustration)**. Slide the stopper plate onto the selector drum, making sure the slot in the plate locates over the pin in the drum **(see illustration 34.7)**.

16 Slide the drum into position in the crankcase **(see illustration 34.6b)**. Secure the left-hand end of the drum with the circlip, making sure it fits properly in its groove **(see illustration 34.6a)**.

17 If removed, apply a suitable non-permanent thread locking compound to the stopper arm shaft threads, then install it in the crankcase and tighten it securely **(see illustration 34.5c)**. Slide the arm onto the

34.13b . . . then remove the bearing

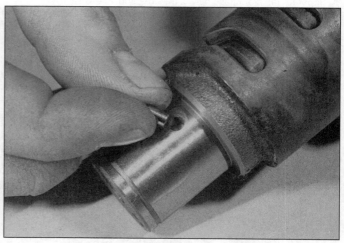

34.15 Fit the pin into the drum if removed

shaft and secure it with the circlip **(see illustration)**. Locate the arm roller onto the stopper plate, then hook the return spring onto its lug, making sure it is secure in the cut-out **(see illustration 34.5a)**. Rotate the drum into the neutral position, so that the stopper arm locates in the neutral detent, identifiable by its shallower depth, in the stopper plate.

18 Lubricate the selector fork shaft with clean engine oil and slide it into its bore in the crankcase. As the shaft is installed, fit each selector fork in turn, making sure it is in its correct location and the right way round (see Step 2), and that its guide pin locates in its track in the selector drum **(see illustration)**.

19 Install the neutral switch (see Chapter 8).

20 Reassemble the crankcase halves (see Section 26).

35 Initial start-up after overhaul

1 Make sure the engine oil level is correct (see *Daily (pre-ride) checks*).

2 Pull the plug caps off the spark plugs and insert a spare spark plug into each cap. Position the spare plugs so that their bodies are earthed (grounded) against the engine. Turn on the ignition switch and crank the engine over with the starter until the oil pressure indicator light goes off (which indicates that oil pressure exists). Turn off the ignition. Remove the spare spark plugs and reconnect the plug caps.

3 Make sure there is fuel in the tank, then turn the fuel tap to the ON position and operate the choke.

4 Start the engine and allow it to run at a moderately fast idle until it reaches operating temperature.

 Warning: If the oil pressure indicator light doesn't go off, or it comes on while the engine is running, stop the engine immediately.

5 Check carefully for oil leaks and make sure the transmission and controls, especially the brakes, function properly before road testing

34.17 Slide the arm onto the shaft

34.18 Install the forks on the shaft as you slide it in

the machine. Refer to Section 36 for the recommended running-in procedure.

6 Upon completion of the road test, and after the engine has cooled down completely, recheck the valve clearances (Chapter 1) and check the engine oil level (Daily (pre-ride) checks).

36 Recommended running-in procedure

1 Treat the machine gently for the first few miles to make sure oil has circulated throughout the engine and any new parts installed have started to seat.

2 Even greater care is necessary if the engine has been rebored or a new crankshaft has been installed. In the case of a rebore, the

bike will have to be run in as when new. This means greater use of the transmission and a restraining hand on the throttle until at least 500 miles (800 km) have been covered. There's no point in keeping to any set speed limit - the main idea is to keep from labouring the engine and to gradually increase performance up to the 500 mile (800 km) mark. These recommendations can be lessened to an extent when only a new crankshaft is installed. Experience is the best guide, since it's easy to tell when an engine is running freely. The following maximum engine speed limitations, which Suzuki provide for new motorcycles, can be used as a guide.

3 If a lubrication failure is suspected, stop the engine immediately and try to find the cause. If an engine is run without oil, even for a short period of time, severe damage will occur.

GSF600 and GSF600S

Up to 500 miles (800 km)	6000 rpm max	Vary throttle position/speed
500 to 1000 miles (800 to 1600 km)	9000 rpm max	Vary throttle position/speed. Use full throttle for short bursts
Over 1000 miles (1600 km)	12,000 rpm max	Do not exceed tachometer red line

GSF1200 and GSF1200S

Up to 500 miles (800 km)	5000 rpm max	Vary throttle position/speed
500 to 1000 miles (800 to 1600 km)	7500 rpm max	Vary throttle position/speed. Use full throttle for short bursts
Over 1000 miles (1600 km)	10,000 rpm max	Do not exceed tachometer red line

2

Notes

Chapter 3
Fuel and exhaust systems

Contents

Degrees of difficulty

Easy, suitable for novice with little experience		Fairly easy, suitable for beginner with some experience		Fairly difficult, suitable for competent DIY mechanic		Difficult, suitable for experienced DIY mechanic		Very difficult, suitable for expert DIY or professional	

Specifications

Fuel

Grade	Unleaded, minimum 91 RON (Research Octane Number)
Fuel tank capacity	19 litres
Fuel tank reserve capacity	4.5 litres

Carburettors

	GSF600 and GSF600S	GSF1200 and GSF1200S
Type	Keihin CVK32	Mikuni BST36SS
Bore	32 mm	36 mm
I.D. no.		
UK	26E0	27E1
US	26E1	27E5
California	26E5	27E6
Pilot screw setting (turns out)		
UK	1 7/8 turns out	1 3/4 turns out
US and California	Pre-set	Pre-set
Float height	17.0 ± 1.0 mm	14.6 ± 1.0 mm
Idle speed	see Chapter 1	see Chapter 1

Carburettor jet sizes – GSF600 and GSF600S

Pilot jet	35
Pilot air jet	
UK	150
US and California	155
Needle jet	Not available
Jet needle	
UK	N1QJ
US and California	N1QA
Main jet	
Cylinders 1 and 4	98
Cylinders 2 and 3	100
Main air jet	90

3

Carburettor jet sizes – GSF1200 and GSF1200S

Pilot jet	37.5
Needle jet	
UK	O-8
US and California	O-8M
Jet needle	
UK	5D76 - 4th groove from top
US and California	5D80
Main jet	102.5

Torque settings

Exhaust system	
Downpipe clamp bolts	23 Nm
Front silencer bolt	23 Nm
Rear silencer bolt	
GSF600 and GSF600S	23 Nm
GSF1200 and GSF1200S	29 Nm

1 General information and precautions

General information

The fuel system consists of the fuel tank, the fuel tap and filter, the carburettors, fuel hoses and control cables.

The fuel tap incorporates a filter which sits inside the tank.

The carburettors used on all models are CV types. On all models there is a carburettor for each cylinder. For cold starting, a choke lever mounted on the left-handlebar and connected by a cable controls an enrichment circuit in the carburettor.

The 1200 models have a throttle position sensor incorporated into the electronic ignition system, and a fuel gauge operated by a level sender inside the tank.

Air is drawn into the carburettors via an air filter which is housed under the fuel tank.

The exhaust system is a two piece four-into-one design.

Many of the fuel system service procedures are considered routine maintenance items and for that reason are included in Chapter 1.

Precautions

 Warning: Petrol (gasoline) is extremely flammable, so take extra precautions when you work on any part of the fuel system. Don't smoke or allow open flames or bare light bulbs near the work area, and don't work in a garage where a natural gas-type appliance is present. If you spill any fuel on your skin, rinse it off immediately with soap and water. When you perform any kind of work on the fuel system, wear safety glasses and have a fire extinguisher suitable for a class B type fire (flammable liquids) on hand.

Always perform service procedures in a well-ventilated area to prevent a build-up of fumes.

Never work in a building containing a gas appliance with a pilot light, or any other form of naked flame. Ensure that there are no naked light bulbs or any sources of flame or sparks nearby.

Do not smoke (or allow anyone else to smoke) while in the vicinity of petrol (gasoline) or of components containing it. Remember the possible presence of vapour from these sources and move well clear before smoking.

Check all electrical equipment belonging to the house, garage or workshop where work is being undertaken (see the Safety first! section of this manual). Remember that certain electrical appliances such as drills, cutters etc create sparks in the normal course of operation and must not be used near petrol (gasoline) or any component containing it. Again, remember the possible presence of fumes before using electrical equipment.

Always mop up any spilt fuel and safely dispose of the rag used.

Any stored fuel that is drained off during servicing work must be kept in sealed containers that are suitable for holding petrol (gasoline), and clearly marked as such; the containers themselves should be kept in a safe place. Note that this last point applies equally to the fuel tank if it is removed from the machine; also remember to keep its filler cap closed at all times.

Read the Safety first! section of this manual carefully before starting work.

Owners of machines used in the US, particularly California, should note that their machines must comply at all times with Federal or State legislation governing the permissible levels of noise and of pollutants such as unburnt hydrocarbons, carbon monoxide etc. that can be emitted by those machines. All vehicles offered for sale must comply with legislation in force at the date of manufacture and must not subsequently be altered in any way which will affect their emission of noise or of pollutants.

In practice, this means that adjustments may not be made to any part of the fuel, ignition or exhaust systems by anyone who is not authorised or mechanically qualified to do so, or who does not have the tools, equipment and data necessary to properly carry out the task. Also if any part of these systems is to be replaced it must be replaced with only genuine Suzuki components or by components which are approved under the relevant legislation. The machine must never be used with any part of these systems removed, modified or damaged.

2 Fuel tank and fuel tap - removal and installation

 Warning: Refer to the precautions given in Section 1 before starting work.

Fuel tank

Removal

1 Make sure the fuel tap is turned to the ON position and the fuel cap is secure.
2 Remove the seat and the side panels (see Chapter 7), then disconnect the battery, negative (-ve) terminal first.
3 Remove the screw from the centre of the fuel tap knob, then pull the knob off the tap (see illustration).

2.3 Remove the screw from the centre of the tap knob (arrow) and remove the knob

2.4 The tank is secured by two bolts (arrows)

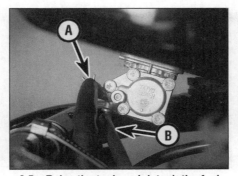

2.5a Raise the tank and detach the fuel hose (A) and the vacuum hose (B) from the tap . . .

2.5b . . . and the water drain hose from its union

4 Unscrew the bolts securing the rear of the tank to the tank bracket on the frame **(see illustration)**.

5 Draw the tank back slightly and raise it up at the rear, then release the clamp securing the fuel hose to the tap and detach the hose **(see illustration)**. Also detach the vacuum hose from the tap and the water drain hose from its union on the underside of the tank **(see illustration)**.

6 Remove the tank by carefully drawing it back and away from the bike. Take care not to lose the mounting rubbers from the front of the tank and from between the sides of the tank and the frame, noting how they fit.

7 Inspect the tank mounting rubbers for signs of damage or deterioration and replace them if necessary. Also inspect the rubbers on the fuel tank mounting bracket. If necessary, unscrew the four bolts securing the bracket to the frame and remove the bracket, noting how the rubbers and the spacer fit **(see illustration)**. Replace the rubbers if necessary.

Installation

8 If removed, install the tank mounting bracket, making sure the rubbers and spacers are correctly positioned, and tighten the bracket bolts securely. Check that the front

and side tank rubbers are fitted, then carefully lower the fuel tank into position, making sure the rubbers remain in place **(see illustration)**.

9 With the tank raised at the rear, attach the water drain hose, the fuel hose and the vacuum hose to their unions **(see illustrations)**. Secure the fuel hose with its clamp. Lower the tank and check that it is properly seated and is not pinching any control cables or wires, and that the bracket at the front is correctly located under the rubber. Check that there is no sign of fuel leakage.

10 Install the tank mounting bolts and tighten them securely **(see illustration)**.

2.7 The tank bracket is secured on each side by two bolts (arrows)

2.8 Carefully position the tank on the frame. The bracket at the front (A) locates under the rubber pad on the frame (B)

2.9a Attach the water drain hose . . .

3

2.9b . . . the fuel hose . . .

2.9c . . . and the vacuum hose, making sure they are secure

2.10 Install the tank mounting bolts . . .

2.11 . . . and fit the knob onto the tap

2.16a The tap is secured by two bolts (arrows)

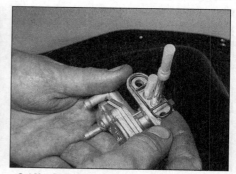

2.16b Check the condition of the O-ring and replace it if necessary

2.18a If the tap is leaking, tighten the front . . .

2.18b . . . and rear assembly screws (arrows)

2.19 Install the tap and secure it with its bolts

11 Fit the fuel tap knob onto the tap, making sure it is correctly set to the ON position (or as it was on removal), and secure it with the screw **(see illustration)**.

12 Connect the battery, fitting the negative (-ve) terminal last. Start the engine and check that there is no sign of fuel leakage, then shut if off.

13 Install the seat and the side panels (see Chapter 7).

Fuel tap

Removal

14 Only remove the tap from the fuel tank for filter cleaning or tap replacement. Apart from the tap-to-tank O-ring, no internal parts are available for the tap.

15 Remove the fuel tank as described above. Connect a drain hose to the fuel hose union and insert its end in a container suitable for holding petrol (gasoline). Turn the fuel tap to the PRI position, and allow the tank to fully drain.

16 Unscrew the two bolts securing the tap to the tank and withdraw the tap assembly **(see illustration)**. Check the condition of the O-ring **(see illustration)**. If it is in good condition it can be re-used. If it is in any way deteriorated or damaged it must be replaced.

17 Clean the gauze filters to remove all traces of dirt and fuel sediment. Check the gauze for holes. If any are found, a new tap should be fitted as the filters are not available individually.

18 If the fuel tap is leaking, tightening the assembly screws on the front and back of the

tap may help **(see illustrations)**. If leakage persists, the tap should be replaced, however nothing is lost by dismantling the tap for further inspection. Remove the screws and disassemble the tap, noting how the components fit. Inspect all components for wear or damage, and replace them as necessary, if available. If any of the components are worn or damaged beyond repair and are not available individually, a new tap must be fitted.

Installation

19 Install the fuel tap into the tank, using a new O-ring if necessary. Make sure the sealing washers are in place on the bolts and tighten the bolts securely **(see illustration)**.

20 Install the fuel tank (see above).

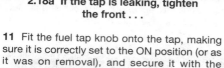

3 Fuel tank - cleaning and repair

1 All repairs to the fuel tank should be carried out by a professional who has experience in this critical and potentially dangerous work. Even after cleaning and flushing of the fuel system, explosive fumes can remain and ignite during repair of the tank.

2 If the fuel tank is removed from the bike, it should not be placed in an area where sparks or open flames could ignite the fumes coming out of the tank. Be especially careful inside garages where a natural gas-type appliance is

located, because the pilot light could cause an explosion.

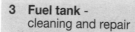

4 Idle fuel/air mixture adjustment - general information

1 Due to the increased emphasis on controlling motorcycle exhaust emissions, certain governmental regulations have been formulated which directly affect the carburation of this machine. In order to comply with the regulations, the carburettors on US models are sealed so they can't be tampered with. The pilot screws on other models are accessible, but the use of an exhaust gas analyser is the only accurate way to adjust the idle fuel/air mixture and be sure the machine doesn't exceed the emissions regulations.

2 The pilot screws are set to their correct position by the manufacturer and should not be adjusted unless it is necessary to do so for a carburettor overhaul. If the screws are adjusted they should be reset to the settings specified at the beginning of the Chapter.

3 If the engine runs extremely rough at idle or continually stalls, and if a carburettor overhaul does not cure the problem, take the motorcycle to a Suzuki dealer equipped with an exhaust gas analyser. They will be able to properly adjust the idle fuel/air mixture to achieve a smooth idle and restore low speed performance.

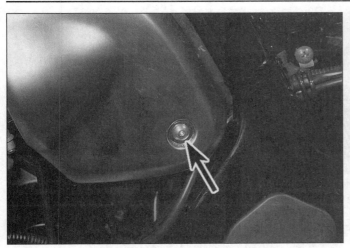

6.2a Remove the screw (arrow) . . .

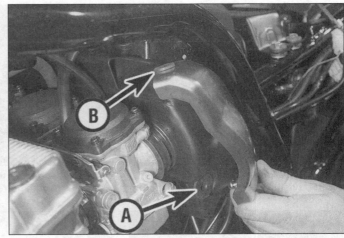

6.2b . . . then release the front peg (A) and lift the cover off its top mount (B)

5 Carburettor overhaul - general information

1 Poor engine performance, hesitation, hard starting, stalling, flooding and backfiring are all signs that major carburettor maintenance may be required.

2 Keep in mind that many so-called carburettor problems are really not carburettor problems at all, but mechanical problems within the engine or ignition system malfunctions. Try to establish for certain that the carburettors are in need of maintenance before beginning a major overhaul.

3 Check the fuel filter, the fuel hoses, the intake manifold joint clamps, the air filter, the ignition system, the spark plugs and carburettor synchronisation before assuming that a carburettor overhaul is required.

4 Most carburettor problems are caused by dirt particles, varnish and other deposits which build up in and block the fuel and air passages. Also, in time, gaskets and O-rings shrink or deteriorate and cause fuel and air leaks which lead to poor performance.

5 When overhauling the carburettors, disassemble them completely and clean the parts thoroughly with a carburettor cleaning solvent and dry them with filtered, unlubricated compressed air. Blow through the fuel and air passages with compressed air to force out any dirt that may have been loosened but not removed by the solvent. Once the cleaning process is complete, reassemble the carburettor using new gaskets and O-rings.

6 Before disassembling the carburettors, make sure you have all necessary O-rings and other parts, some carburettor cleaner, a supply of clean rags, some means of blowing out the carburettor passages and a clean place to work. It is recommended that only one carburettor be overhauled at a time to avoid mixing up parts.

6 Carburettors - removal and installation

> **Warning: Refer to the precautions given in Section 1 before starting work.**

Removal

1 Remove the fuel tank (see Section 2).

2 Unscrew the bolt securing each air filter housing end cover **(see illustration)**. Pull each cover away at the front to release the lug from its rubber mount, then lift the cover off its top mounting peg **(see illustration)**.

3 Unscrew the two screws at the back of the air filter housing, one on each side, which secure the housing to the frame **(see illustration)**. Release the clamp securing the breather hose to the front of the air filter housing and detach the hose **(see illustration)**.

4 Slacken the clamps securing the air filter housing rubbers to the carburettor air intakes **(see illustration)**. Manoeuvre the air filter housing backwards so that the rubbers

detach from the carburettor intakes and provide clearance for the carburettors to be removed. Remove the air filter cover from the housing to provide extra clearance, if required - it is secured by two screws **(see illustration 12.4a)**. Note how the lugs on the bottom of the cover locate in the slots in the housing **(see illustration 12.4b)**.

5 On GSF1200 and GSF1200S, lift up the cover on the throttle position sensor mounted on the outside of the right-hand (no. 4)

6.3a Note the wiring clamp fitted to the left-side housing screw (arrow)

6.3b Release the clamp and detach the hose (arrow)

6.4 Slacken the carburettor intake clamp screws (arrow)

3

6.5 Lift the cover and disconnect the throttle position sensor wiring connector

6.6 Disconnect the heater wiring connectors (arrows)

6.8a Slacken the clamps securing the carburettors to the cylinder head . . .

6.8b . . . and ease them out of the adapters

6.10 Carburettor drain screw (arrow)

carburettor and disconnect the wiring connector **(see illustration)**.

6 On UK GSF600V and GSF600SV models (or earlier models, if fitted), disconnect the carburettor heater wiring connectors from the carburettors **(see illustration)**.

7 On California models disconnect the two EVAP system purge hoses from their T-piece unions on the bottom of the carburettors. Also on California models, disconnect the PAIR system hose from the vacuum take-off point of no. 2 or no. 3 carburettor (whichever it is connected to).

8 Slacken the clamps securing the carburettors to the cylinder head adapters and ease the carburettors off the adapters, noting how they fit **(see illustrations)**. Manoeuvre the carburettors out of the right-hand side of the frame, noting the routing of the various hoses, and support them on the frame or engine for removal of the cables. **Note:** *Keep the carburettors upright to prevent fuel spillage from the float chambers and the possibility of the piston diaphragms being damaged.*

9 Detach the throttle cables from the

carburettors (see Section 10). Detach the choke cable from the carburettors (see Section 11).

10 Place a suitable container below the float chambers then slacken the drain screws and drain all the fuel from the carburettors **(see illustration)**. Once all the fuel has been drained, tighten the drain screws securely.

11 If necessary, remove the screws securing the intake adapters to the cylinder head and remove the adapters and O-rings, noting how they fit **(see illustrations)**. Discard the O-rings as new ones must be used. Note the cylinder number for each adapter as the left-hand and right-hand adapters are not interchangeable - an I.D. code is stamped onto each adapter. Also note the UP mark which must be at the top.

Installation

12 Installation is the reverse of removal, noting the following.

a) *Check for cracks or splits in the cylinder head intake adapters and the air filter housing rubbers, and replace them if necessary.*

b) *If removed, make sure the intake adapters are installed correctly using new O-rings (see Step 11).*

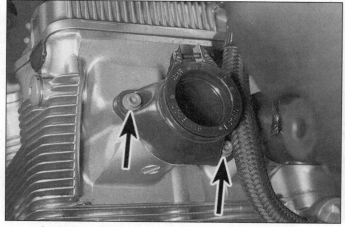

6.11a Each adapter is secured by two bolts (arrows)

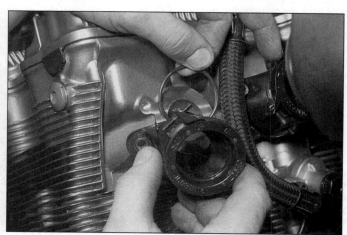

6.11b Remove the adapters and discard their O-rings

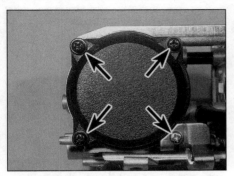

7.2a Remove the screws (arrows) and lift off the cover . . .

7.2b . . . then remove the spring

7.3 Carefully remove the diaphragm and piston assembly

c) *Make sure the air filter housing and the cylinder head intake adapters are fully engaged with the carburettors and their retaining clamps are securely tightened.*
d) *Make sure all hoses are correctly routed and secured and not trapped or kinked.*
e) *On GSF1200 and GSF1200S, do not forget to connect the throttle position sensor wiring connector.*
f) *On UK GSF600V and GSF600SV models (or earlier models, if fitted), do not forget to connect the carburettor heater wiring connectors.*
g) *Check the operation of the choke and throttle cables and adjust them as necessary (see Chapter 1).*
h) *Check idle speed and carburettor synchronisation and adjust as necessary (see Chapter 1).*

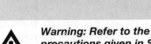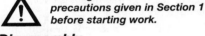

7 Carburettors - disassembly, cleaning and inspection

⚠ **Warning: Refer to the precautions given in Section 1 before starting work.**

Disassembly

GSF600 and GSF600S

1 Remove the carburettors from the machine as described in the previous Section. **Note:** *Do not separate the carburettors unless*

absolutely necessary; each carburettor can be dismantled sufficiently for all normal cleaning and adjustments while in place on the mounting brackets. Dismantle the carburettors separately to avoid interchanging parts.
2 Unscrew and remove the top cover retaining screws **(see illustration)**. Lift off the cover and remove the spring from inside the piston **(see illustration)**. The spring seat may come out with the spring - if not, it will come out with the jet needle (Step 4).
3 Carefully peel the diaphragm away from its sealing groove in the carburettor and withdraw the diaphragm and piston assembly, noting which way round it fits **(see illustration)**.
Caution: Do not use a sharp instrument to displace the diaphragm as it is easily damaged.

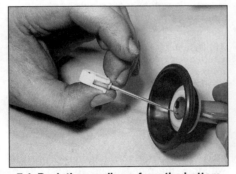

7.4 Push the needle up from the bottom and remove it along with the spring seat if not already removed

4 Push the jet needle up from the bottom of the piston and withdraw it from the top **(see illustration)**. Take care not to lose the spring seat, if not already removed.
5 On UK models (or earlier models, if fitted), unscrew the carburettor heater from its adapter, and the adapter from the carburettor body **(see illustrations)**.
6 Remove the screws securing the float chamber to the base of the carburettor and remove the float chamber, noting how it fits **(see illustration)**. Remove the rubber gasket and discard it as a new one must be used.
7 Using a pair of thin-nose pliers, carefully withdraw the float pivot pin **(see illustration)**. If necessary, carefully displace the pin using a small punch or a nail. Remove the float

7.5a The heater screws into the adapter . . .

3

7.5b . . . and the adapter screws into the carburettor

7.6 The float chamber is secured by four screws (arrows)

7.7 Withdraw the float pivot pin and remove the float assembly

7.8 Unscrew and remove the main jet (arrow)

7.9 Unscrew and remove the needle jet holder (arrow)

7.10 Unscrew and remove the pilot jet (arrow)

assembly, noting how it fits (see illustration 9.6b). Unhook the needle valve from the tab on the float, noting how it fits (see illustration 9.6a).

8 Unscrew and remove the main jet from the base of the needle jet holder (see illustration).

9 Unscrew and remove the needle jet holder (see illustration). With the holder removed the needle jet may come out if it is loose - if it does, note which way round it fits (see illustration 9.4a).

10 Unscrew and remove the pilot jet (see illustration).

11 The pilot screw can be removed if

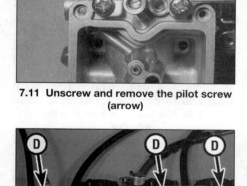

7.11 Unscrew and remove the pilot screw (arrow)

required, but note that its setting will be disturbed (see *Haynes Hint*). On UK models unscrew and remove the pilot screw along with its spring, washer and O-ring (see illustration). Discard the O-ring as a new one must be used. Pilot screw removal is the same for US models, except that the screw head is sealed off with a blanking plug. Carefully punch a hole in the plug and prise it out using a hooked tool.

> **HAYNES HINT** *To record the pilot screw's current setting, turn the screw in until it seats lightly, counting the number of turns necessary to achieve this, then fully unscrew it. On installation, the screw is simply backed out the number of turns you've recorded.*

12 Detach the vacuum hose and remove the vacuum blanking caps, then unhook the choke linkage bar return spring from the vacuum take-off adapter (see illustration). Remove the three screws securing the linkage bar to the carburettors, then remove the outer plastic washers. Lift off the bar, noting how it fits, and remove the inner plastic washers.

13 Unscrew the choke plunger nut and withdraw the plunger and spring from the

carburettor body, noting how they fit. Take care not to lose the spring when removing the nut.

GSF1200 and GSF1200S

14 Remove the carburettors from the machine as described in the previous Section. **Note:** *Do not separate the carburettors unless absolutely necessary; each carburettor can be dismantled sufficiently for all normal cleaning and adjustments while in place on the mounting brackets. Dismantle the carburettors separately to avoid interchanging parts.*

15 Unscrew and remove the top cover retaining screws. Lift off the cover and remove the spring and its seat from inside the piston (see illustration).

16 Carefully peel the diaphragm away from its sealing groove in the carburettor and withdraw the diaphragm and piston assembly (see illustration).

Caution: Do not use a sharp instrument to displace the diaphragm as it is easily damaged.

17 Remove the vacuum take-off pipe O-ring and discard it as a new one must be fitted.

18 Push the jet needle up from the bottom of the piston and withdraw it from the top (see

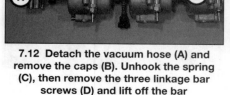

7.12 Detach the vacuum hose (A) and remove the caps (B). Unhook the spring (C), then remove the three linkage bar screws (D) and lift off the bar

7.15 Remove the cover screws, then lift off the cover and remove the spring

7.16 Carefully separate the diaphragm from the body and lift it and the piston out. Also remove the O-ring (arrow)

7.18a Push the jet needle up from the bottom and withdraw it from the piston

7.18b Note which notch the clip is in before removing it from the needle

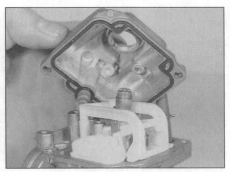

7.19 Remove the float chamber screws and remove the chamber

illustration). Take care not to lose the E-clip and washer. If they are removed from the needle, note which notch the E-clip is fitted into **(see illustration)**.

19 Remove the screws securing the float chamber to the base of the carburettor and remove the float chamber, noting how it fits **(see illustration)**. Remove the rubber gasket and discard it as a new one must be used.

20 Carefully prise the float assembly out of the carburettor body, noting how it fits **(see illustration)**. Remove the O-ring and discard it as a new one must be used. Unhook the needle valve from the tab on the float, noting how it fits **(see illustration)**. Withdraw the needle valve seat and its O-ring **(see illustration)**. Discard the O-ring as a new one must be used.

21 Unscrew and remove the main jet **(see illustration)**. It screws into the bottom of the needle jet.

22 With the main jet removed the needle jet can now be pushed up from the bottom and withdrawn from the top of the carburettor **(see illustration)**.

23 Unscrew and remove the pilot jet **(see illustration)**.

24 The pilot screw can be removed if required, but note that its setting will be disturbed (see **Haynes Hint**). On UK models unscrew and remove the pilot screw along with its spring, washer and O-ring **(see illustration)**. Discard the O-ring as a new one must be used. Pilot screw removal is the

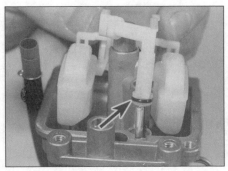

7.20a Lift out the float assembly, noting how it fits, and discard the O-ring (arrow)

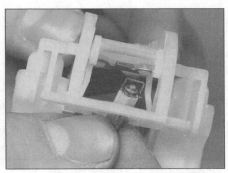

7.20b Unhook the needle valve from its seat

7.20c Remove the needle valve seat and discard the O-ring (arrow)

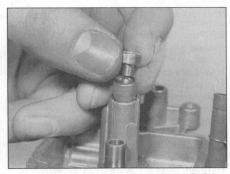

7.21 Unscrew and remove the main jet

7.22 Push the needle jet up and remove it from the top

7.23 Unscrew and remove the pilot jet

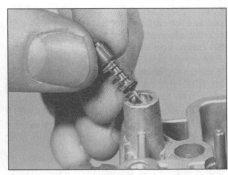

7.24 Unscrew and remove the pilot screw

3

7.25a Slide the clips out . . .

7.25b . . . then remove the choke linkage bar

7.25c Remove the choke plunger retainer . . .

7.25d . . . the spring . . .

7.25e . . . and the plunger

same for US models, except that the screw head is sealed off with a blanking plug. Carefully punch a hole in the plug and prise it out using a hooked tool.

25 Push out the clips securing the choke linkage bar to the carburettors, then remove the choke linkage bar from the plungers, noting how it fits **(see illustrations)**. Compress the clip ends on the retainer securing the choke plunger to the carburettor body and remove the retainer, then withdraw the spring and the plunger, noting how they fit **(see illustrations)**.

26 If required, remove the throttle position sensor from the right-hand (no. 4) carburettor (see Chapter 4).

Caution: Suzuki advise against removing the sensor from the carburettors unless absolutely necessary.

Cleaning

Caution: Use only a petroleum based solvent for carburettor cleaning. Don't use caustic cleaners.

27 Submerge the metal components in the solvent for approximately thirty minutes (or longer, if the directions recommend it).

28 After the carburettor has soaked long enough for the cleaner to loosen and dissolve most of the varnish and other deposits, use a nylon-bristled brush to remove the stubborn deposits. Rinse it again, then dry it with compressed air.

29 Use a jet of compressed air to blow out all of the fuel and air passages in the main and upper body, not forgetting the air jets in the carburettor inlet **(see illustration)**.

Caution: Never clean the jets or passages with a piece of wire or a drill bit, as they will be enlarged, causing the fuel and air metering rates to be upset.

Inspection

30 Check the operation of the choke plunger. If it doesn't move smoothly, inspect the needle on the end of the choke plunger, the spring and the plunger linkage bar. Replace any component that is worn, damaged or bent **(see illustration)**.

31 If removed from the carburettor, check the tapered portion of the pilot screw and the spring and O-ring for wear or damage. Replace them if necessary.

32 Check the carburettor body, float chamber and top cover for cracks, distorted sealing surfaces and other damage. If any

defects are found, replace the faulty component, although replacement of the entire carburettor will probably be necessary (check with a Suzuki dealer on the availability of separate components).

33 Check the piston diaphragm for splits, holes and general deterioration. Holding it up to a light will help to reveal problems of this nature.

34 Insert the piston guide and piston in the carburettor body and check that the piston moves up-and-down smoothly. Check the surface of the piston for wear. If it's worn excessively or doesn't move smoothly in the guide, replace the components as necessary.

35 Check the jet needle for straightness by rolling it on a flat surface such as a piece of glass (having first removed the E-clip and washer, noting which notch the E-clip fits into) **(see illustration 7.18b)**. Replace it if it's bent or if the tip is worn.

36 Check the tip of the float needle valve and the valve seat. If either has grooves or scratches in it, or is in any way worn, they must be replaced as a set.

37 Operate the throttle shaft to make sure the throttle butterfly valve opens and closes smoothly. If it doesn't, cleaning the throttle linkage may help. Otherwise, replace the carburettor.

38 Check the floats for damage. This will usually be apparent by the presence of fuel inside one of the floats. If the floats are damaged, they must be replaced.

7.29 Do not forget the air passages in the inlets (arrows)

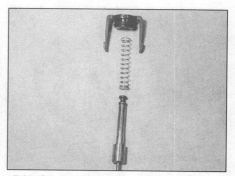

7.30 Choke plunger assembly (1200 type shown)

8.5 Note the arrangement of the various linkage and synchronisation springs (arrows) before separation

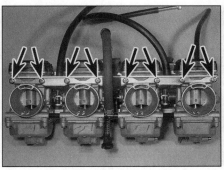

8.6a Unscrew the upper mounting bracket screws (arrows) . . .

8.6b . . . and the lower mounting bracket screws (arrows) - 600 type shown

8 Carburettors - separation and joining

Warning: Refer to the precautions given in Section 1 before proceeding

Separation

1 The carburettors do not need to be separated for normal overhaul. If you need to separate them (to replace a carburettor body, for example), refer to the following procedure.
2 Remove the carburettors from the machine (see Section 6). Mark the body of each carburettor with its cylinder location to ensure that it is positioned correctly on reassembly.
3 On GSF600 and GSF600S models, detach the vacuum hose and remove the vacuum blanking caps, then unhook the choke linkage bar return spring (see illustrations 7.12 and 9.1e). Remove the three screws securing the linkage bar to the carburettors, then remove the outer plastic washers (see illustrations 9.1d). Lift off the bar, noting how it fits, and remove the inner plastic washers (see illustrations 9.1a).
4 On GSF1200 and GSF1200S models, push out the clips securing the choke linkage bar to the carburettors, then remove the choke linkage bar from the plungers, noting how it fits (see illustrations 7.25a and b).

5 Make a note of how the throttle return springs, linkage assembly and carburettor synchronisation springs are arranged to ensure that they are fitted correctly on reassembly (see illustration). Also note the arrangement of the various hoses and their unions.
6 Remove the screws securing the carburettors to the two mounting brackets and remove the brackets (see illustrations). The carburettors are assembled using a thread locking compound which may make the bracket screws difficult to remove.
7 Carefully separate the carburettors. Retrieve the synchronisation springs and note the fitting of the various fuel hose T-pieces and O-rings or seals, and the vent hose T-pieces as they are separated. Discard the O-rings or seals as new ones must be used.

Joining

8 Assembly is the reverse of the disassembly procedure, noting the following.
a) Make sure the fuel hose T-pieces and O-rings or seals and the air vent hose T-pieces are correctly and securely inserted into the carburettors.
b) Install the synchronisation springs after the carburettors are joined together. Make sure they are correctly and squarely seated (see illustration 8.5).
c) Apply a suitable non-permanent thread

locking compound to the carburettor bracket screws and tighten them securely.
d) Check the operation of both the choke and throttle linkages ensuring that both operate smoothly and return quickly under spring pressure before installing the carburettors on the machine.
e) Install the carburettors (see Section 6) and check carburettor synchronisation and idle speed (see Chapter 1).

9 Carburettors - reassembly and float height check

Warning: Refer to the precautions given in Section 1 before proceeding.

GSF600 and GSF600S

Note: When reassembling the carburettors, be sure to use new O-rings and seals. Do not overtighten the carburettor jets and screws as they are easily damaged.
1 Install the choke plunger and spring into the carburettor body and tighten the nut to secure it. Install the inner plastic washers, then fit the choke linkage bar onto the plungers, making sure the slots locate correctly behind the nipple on the end of each choke plunger (see illustrations). Install the outer plastic washers

3

9.1a Fit the inner plastic washers . . .

9.1b . . . and the linkage bar . . .

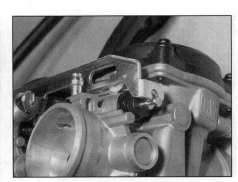

9.1c . . . making sure it locates correctly onto each plunger

9.1d Install the screws with the outer plastic washers

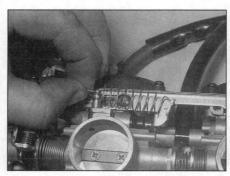

9.1e Hook the spring around the take-off adapter . . .

9.1f . . . then fit the caps and vacuum hose

9.3 Install the pilot jet . . .

9.4a . . . the needle jet (if removed) . . .

and secure the linkage bar in place with the screws **(see illustration)**. Hook the return spring to the vacuum take-off adapter, then fit the caps **(see illustration)**.

2 Install the pilot screw (if removed) along with its spring, washer and O-ring, turning it in until it seats lightly **(see illustration 7.11)**. Now, turn the screw out the number of turns previously recorded, or as specified at the beginning of the Chapter. If the pilot screw was disturbed on US models, read the notes in Sections 1 and 4 concerning maladjustment and emissions; the pilot screw housing should be sealed by fitting a new blanking plug.

3 Install the pilot jet **(see illustration)**.

4 If removed, fit the needle jet into the carburettor, tapered end first **(see illustration)**. Screw the needle jet holder into the carburettor **(see illustration)**.

5 Install the main jet into the needle jet holder **(see illustration)**.

6 Hook the float needle valve onto the tab on the float assembly, then position the float assembly in the carburettor and install the pin, making sure it is secure **(see illustrations)**.

7 To check the float height, hold the carburettor so the float hangs down, then tilt it back until the needle valve is just seated, but not so far that the needle's spring-loaded tip is compressed. Measure the height from the top of the float to the gasket face (with the gasket removed) with an accurate ruler

9.4b . . . the needle jet holder . . .

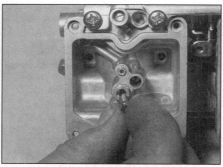

9.5 . . . and the main jet

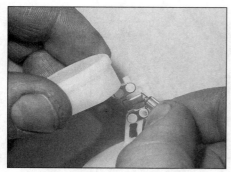

9.6a Fit the needle valve onto its tab on the float . . .

9.6b . . . making sure the needle valve fits into the seat (arrow) . . .

9.6c . . . then install the float and fit the pivot pin

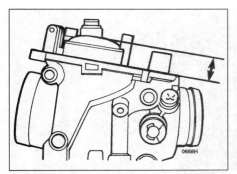

9.7 Measure the height of the top of the float above the gasket surface

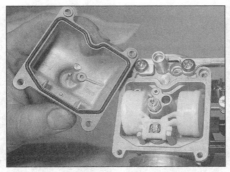

9.8 Install the float chamber using a new gasket

9.11 Install the diaphragm/piston assembly with the indent in the piston (arrow) facing the air intake side

(see illustration). The correct setting should be as given in the Specifications at the beginning of the Chapter. If it is incorrect, adjust the float height by carefully bending the float tab a little at a time until the correct height is obtained. Repeat the procedure for both carburettors.

8 With the float height checked, fit a new gasket to the float chamber, making sure it is seated properly in its groove, then install the chamber on the carburettor and tighten its screws securely (see illustration).

9 If removed, install the carburettor heater adapter in the carburettor body, then install the heater (see illustrations 7.5b and 7.5a).

10 Install the jet needle and the spring seat into the diaphragm assembly (see illustration 7.4).

11 Insert the diaphragm assembly into the piston guide with the indent in the piston facing the air intake side of the carburettor (see illustration). Lightly push the piston down, ensuring the needle is correctly aligned with the needle jet. Press the diaphragm outer edge into its groove, making sure it is correctly seated. Check the diaphragm is not creased, and that the piston moves smoothly up and down in the guide.

12 Install the spring into the diaphragm assembly, making sure it locates correctly onto the spring seat, then fit the top cover, making sure the top of the spring fits over the

lug in the middle of the cover, and tighten its screws securely (see illustration).

13 Install the carburettors (see Section 6).

GSF1200 and GSF1200S

Note: When reassembling the carburettors, be sure to use new O-rings and seals. Do not overtighten the carburettor jets and screws as they are easily damaged.

14 Install the choke plunger and spring into the carburettor body, then fit the retainer, making sure the clips locate correctly in their holes (see illustrations 7.25e, d and c). Fit the choke linkage bar onto the plungers, making sure the slots in the arms locate correctly behind the nipple on the end of each choke plunger (see illustration 7.25b). Secure the linkage bar in place with the clips, making sure their ends locate over the ends of the slide guide (see illustration 7.25a).

15 If removed, install the throttle position sensor (see Chapter 4).

16 Install the pilot screw (if removed) along with its spring, washer and O-ring, turning it in until it seats lightly (see illustration 7.24). Now, turn the screw out the number of turns previously recorded, or as specified at the beginning of the Chapter. If the pilot screw was disturbed on US models, read the notes in Sections 1 and 4 concerning maladjustment and emissions; the pilot screw housing should be sealed by fitting a new blanking plug.

17 Fit the jet needle down into the carburettor (see illustration 7.22), noting the flat on the bottom of the jet which must align with the pin in the carburettor (see illustration). Screw the main jet into the end of the needle jet (see illustration 7.21).

18 Install the pilot jet (see illustration 7.23).

19 Install a new O-ring around the float needle valve seat and press the seat into the carburettor body (see illustration 7.20c).

20 Hook the float needle valve onto the tab on the float assembly (see illustration 7.20b). Fit a new O-ring to the base of the float assembly (see illustration 7.20a), then carefully press the assembly into the carburettor body, making sure the needle valve enters the seat (see illustration).

21 To check the float height, hold the carburettor so the float hangs down, then tilt it back until the needle valve is just seated, but not so far that the needle's spring-loaded tip is compressed. Measure the height from the top of the float to the gasket face (with the gasket removed) with an accurate ruler (see illustration 9.7). The correct setting should be as given in the Specifications at the beginning of the Chapter. If it is incorrect, adjust the float height by carefully bending the float tab a little at a time until the correct height is obtained. Repeat the procedure for both carburettors.

22 With the float height checked, fit a new gasket to the float chamber, making sure it is

3

9.12 Install the top cover, making sure the spring is correctly located top and bottom

9.17 Align the slot in the needle jet with the pin in the passage (arrow)

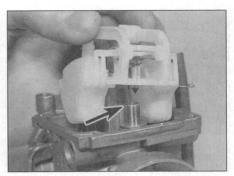

9.20 Make sure the needle valve fits into the seat (arrow)

9.24 Fit the diaphragm assembly into the carburettor

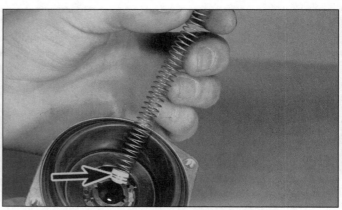

9.25 Make sure the spring seat (arrow) is in the bottom
of the spring

seated properly in its groove, then install the chamber on the carburettor and tighten its screws securely (see illustration 7.19).
23 If removed, install the E-clip into the specified notch in the jet needle, then slide the washer underneath it (see illustration 7.18b). Install the jet needle into the diaphragm assembly (see illustration 7.18a).
24 Insert the diaphragm assembly into the piston guide and lightly push the piston down, ensuring the needle is correctly aligned with the needle jet (see illustration). Press the diaphragm outer edge into its groove, making sure it is correctly seated (see illustration

7.16). Check the diaphragm is not creased, and that the piston moves smoothly up and down in the guide.
25 Fit a new O-ring onto the vacuum take-off passage (see illustration 7.16). Install the spring into the diaphragm assembly, making sure the spring seat is fitted into the bottom of the spring and that it locates correctly onto the needle (see illustration). Fit the top cover onto the carburettor, making sure the top of the spring fits over the lug in the middle of the cover, and tighten its screws securely (see illustration 7.15).
26 Install the carburettors (see Section 6).

10 Throttle cables -
removal and installation

 Warning: Refer to the precautions given in Section 1 before proceeding.

Removal

1 Detach the carburettors from the cylinder head intake adapters (see Section 6, Steps 1 to 8) - this is necessary to access the lower ends of the throttle cables.
2 Slacken the top locknut on one of the cables, then unscrew the adjuster until the bottom locknut is clear of the bracket (see illustration). Free the adjuster from its mounting bracket and detach the inner cable from the throttle cam (see illustrations). Repeat for the other cable. Keep the carburettors upright to prevent fuel spillage.
3 Remove the screw securing the front (accelerator) cable retaining plate to the handlebar switch/throttle pulley housing, and unscrew the rear (decelerator) cable retaining ring (see illustration). Remove the handlebar switch/throttle pulley housing screws and separate the halves (see illustration). Hook the cable ends out of the pulley and remove the cable elbows from the housing. Mark each

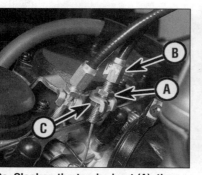

10.2a Slacken the top locknut (A), then unscrew the adjuster (B) until the bottom locknut (C) is clear ...

10.2b ... then remove the adjuster from the bracket ...

10.2c ... and detach the cable end from the throttle cam

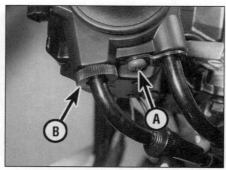

10.3a Remove the retainer plate screw (A) and unscrew the retainer ring (B)

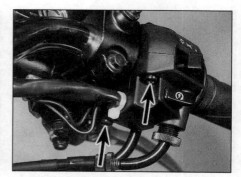

10.3b Remove the housing screws (arrows) and separate the halves

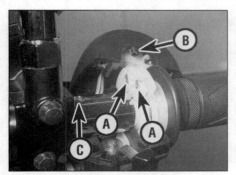

10.6 Fit the cable ends (A) into the pulley. The pin (B) locates in the hole (C) in the handlebar

10.7 Install the cable retainer plate and ring

11.2a Pull the outer cable out of its bracket . . .

cable to ensure it is connected correctly on installation.

4 Remove the cables from the machine noting the correct routing of each cable.

Installation

5 Install the cables making sure they are correctly routed. The cables must not interfere with any other component and should not be kinked or bent sharply.

6 Install the cables into the throttle pulley housing, making sure the accelerator cable is at the front and the decelerator is at the back. Lubricate the end of each inner cable with multi-purpose grease and attach them to the pulley **(see illustration)**. Assemble the housing, aligning its locating pin with the hole in the handlebar. Install the retaining screws, and tighten them securely.

7 Secure the accelerator cable elbow with the retainer plate, and thread the decelerator cable retaining ring into the housing **(see illustration)**.

8 Lubricate the lower end of each inner cable with multi-purpose grease and attach them to the carburettor throttle cam **(see illustration 10.2c)**.

9 Make sure the cables are correctly

connected and locate the outer cable adjusters in the mounting brackets **(see illustration 10.2b)**. Set the adjuster locknuts so that the slack in the inner cable is taken up, but not so that it is tight **(see illustration 10.2a)**. Tighten the top locknut securely.

10 Install the carburettors (see Section 6).

11 Adjust the cables as described in Chapter 1. Turn the handlebars back and forth to make sure the cables don't cause the steering to bind.

12 Install the fuel tank (see Section 2).

13 Start the engine and check that the idle speed does not rise as the handlebars are turned. If it does, correct the problem before riding the motorcycle.

11.2b . . . and detach the inner cable

11 Choke cable - removal and installation

Removal

1 Remove the fuel tank (see Section 2).

2 Free the choke outer cable from its bracket on the carburettor and detach the inner cable from the choke linkage bar **(see illustrations)**.

Note how the spring ends locate on the bracket and the linkage bar.

3 Unscrew the two left-hand side handlebar switch/choke lever housing screws, one of which secures the choke cable elbow via a retainer plate, and separate the two halves, noting how the lever fits into the housing **(see illustration)**. Detach the cable nipple from the choke lever), then withdraw the cable and elbow from the housing **(see illustration)**.

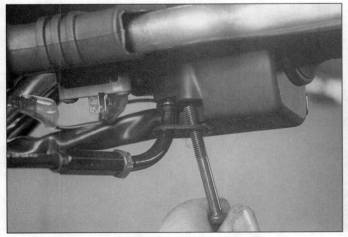

11.3a The front housing screw secures the cable retainer plate

11.3b Detach the cable end from the lever and remove the cable

3

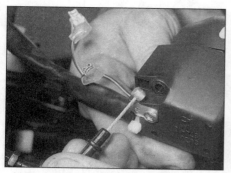

11.6a Install the cable in the housing . . .

11.6b . . . and attach the end to the lever

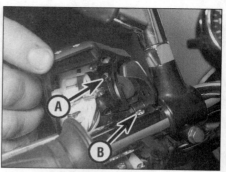

11.6c The pin (A) locates in the hole (B) in the handlebar

4 Remove the cable from the machine noting its correct routing.

Installation

5 Install the cable making sure it is correctly routed. The cable must not interfere with any other component and should not be kinked or bent sharply.
6 Lubricate the upper cable nipple with multi-purpose grease. Install the cable in the switch/choke lever housing and attach the nipple to the choke lever **(see illustrations)**. Fit the two halves of the housing onto the handlebar, making sure the lever fits correctly into the lower half, and the pin in the upper half locates in the hole in the top of the handlebar **(see illustration)**. Install the screws, making sure the elbow retainer is correctly positioned, and tighten them securely **(see illustration 11.3a)**.
7 Lubricate the lower cable nipple with multi-purpose grease and attach it to the choke linkage bar on the carburettor **(see illustration 11.2b)**. Fit the outer cable into its bracket **(see illustration 11.2a)**.
8 Check the operation of the choke cable (see Chapter 1).
9 Install the fuel tank (see Section 2).

12 Air filter housing -
removed and installation

Removal

1 Remove the fuel tank (see Section 2).
2 Remove the carburettors (see Section 6).
3 Release the clamp securing the air filter drain hose to the base of the air filter housing and detach the hose from its union **(see illustration)**.
4 If not already done, remove the two screws securing the air filter cover to the filter housing **(see illustration)**. Remove the cover, noting how the lugs on the bottom of the cover locate in the slots in the housing **(see illustration)**. Withdraw the filter from the housing.

5 Remove the screws securing the two left-hand intake adapters (cyl nos. 1 and 2) to the cylinder head and remove the adapters and O-rings, noting how they fit **(see illustrations 6.11a and b)**. Discard the O-rings as new ones must be used. Note the cylinder number for each adapter as the left-hand and right-hand adapters are not interchangeable - an I.D. code is stamped onto each adapter. Also note the UP mark which must be at the top.
6 Manoeuvre the air filter housing forwards and out of the left-hand side of the frame **(see illustration)**.

Installation

7 Installation is the reverse of removal. Install the intake adapters using new O-rings.

13 Exhaust system -
removal and installation

⚠️ **Warning: If the engine has been running the exhaust system will be very hot. Allow the system to cool before carrying out any work.**

Silencer
Removal

1 Slacken the clamp around the joint between the silencer and the downpipe assembly **(see illustration)**.

12.3 Release the clamp (arrow) and detach the drain hose

12.4a The air filter cover is secured by two screws (arrows)

12.4b Note how the lugs locate in the slot in the housing

12.6 Remove the housing from the left-hand side

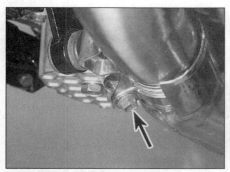

13.1 Slacken the clamp bolt (arrow) . . .

13.2 . . . then remove the front mounting bolt (arrow) . . .

13.3 . . . and the rear mounting nut and bolt

2 Unscrew the front silencer mounting bolt, located under the bike just behind the joint between the silencer and the downpipe assembly (see illustration).

3 Unscrew and remove the rear silencer mounting nut and bolt, then release the silencer from the exhaust downpipe assembly using a twisting motion (see illustration).

4 Inspect the bushes for signs of damage and replace them if necessary. Remove the sealing ring from either the end of the silencer or inside the downpipe assembly and discard it as a new one should be used.

Installation

5 Clean all traces of old sealant from the mating surfaces of the silencer and downpipe assembly. Apply an exhaust gas sealer (Suzuki recommend Permatex 1372) to the inside and outside of the new sealing ring, then install the ring into the end of the downpipe assembly.

6 Install the silencer into the downpipe assembly, making sure it is pushed fully home (see illustration). Align the silencer mounting bracket at the rear and install the bolt, but do not yet tighten the nut (see illustration).

7 Install the front silencer mounting bolt and tighten it to the torque setting specified at the beginning of the Chapter, then tighten the rear silencer mounting bolt to the specified torque (see illustrations). Tighten the clamp bolt securely (see illustration).

8 Run the engine and check the system for leaks.

Downpipe assembly

Removal

9 Remove the silencer (see above).

10 Unscrew the eight downpipe clamp bolts from the cylinder head, then remove the assembly from the machine (see illustration 13.13b).

11 Remove the gasket from each port in the cylinder head and discard them as new ones must be fitted (see illustration 13.12). Note how the gasket retainers fit on the outer pipes of 1200 models.

Installation

12 Fit a new gasket into each of the cylinder head ports with the tabs on each gasket

13.6a Fit the silencer into the downpipe assembly . . .

13.6b . . . and install the rear mounting bolt

13.7a Install the front mounting bolt . . .

13.7b . . . and tighten it . . .

13.7c . . . and the rear mounting bolt to the specified torque setting

13.7d Also tighten the clamp bolt

3

13.12 Fit the gaskets with the tabs on the inside

13.13a Manoeuvre the downpipe assembly into position . . .

13.13b . . . then install the clamp bolts . . .

13.13c . . . and tighten them to the specified torque setting

inwards **(see illustration)**. Apply a smear of grease to the gaskets to keep them in place whilst fitting the downpipe if necessary.

13 Manoeuvre the assembly into position so that the head of each downpipe is located in its port in the cylinder head **(see illustration)**. Make sure the gasket retainers are correctly fitted on the outer pipes (cyl nos. 1 and 4) of 1200 models, then install the clamp bolts and tighten them to the torque setting specified at the beginning of the Chapter **(see illustrations)**.

14 Install the silencer (see above).

Complete system

Removal

15 Unscrew the eight downpipe clamp retaining bolts from the cylinder head **(see illustration 13.13b)**.

16 Unscrew the front silencer mounting bolt, located under the bike just behind the joint between the silencer and the downpipe assembly **(see illustration 13.2)**.

17 Supporting the system, unscrew and remove the rear silencer mounting nut and

bolt, then remove the system from the machine **(see illustration 13.3)**.

18 Remove the gasket from each port in the cylinder head and discard them as new ones must be fitted **(see illustration 13.12)**. Note how the gasket retainers fit on the outer pipes (cyl nos. 1 and 4) of 1200 models. Inspect the bushes for signs of damage and replace them if necessary.

Installation

19 Fit a new gasket into each of the cylinder head ports with the tabs on each gasket facing inwards **(see illustration 13.12)**. Apply a smear of grease to the gaskets to keep them in place whilst fitting the downpipe if necessary.

20 Manoeuvre the system into position so that the head of each downpipe is located in its port in the cylinder head **(see illustration 13.13a)**. Make sure the gasket retainers are correctly fitted on the outer pipes (cyl nos. 1 and 4) of 1200 models, then install the clamp bolts finger-tight to hold the system in place **(see illustration 13.13b)**. Supporting the system, align the silencer mounting bracket at the rear

and install the bolt with its washer but do not yet tighten the nut **(see illustration 13.6)**. Now tighten the downpipe clamp bolts to the torque setting specified at the beginning of the Chapter **(see illustration 13.3c)**.

21 Install the front silencer mounting bolt and tighten it to the torque setting specified at the beginning of the Chapter, then tighten the rear silencer mounting bolt to the specified torque **(see illustrations 13.7a, b and c)**.

22 Run the engine and check the system for leaks.

14 EVAP and PAIR systems - general (California models)

Evaporative emission control system (EVAP)

General information

1 This system prevents the escape of fuel vapour into the atmosphere by storing it in a charcoal-filled canister located on the frame right-hand side at the rear.

2 When the engine is stopped, fuel vapour from the tank is directed into the canister where it is absorbed and stored whilst the motorcycle is standing. When the engine is started, intake manifold depression opens the purge control valves, thus drawing vapours which are stored in the canister into the carburettors to be burned during the normal combustion process.

3 The tank vent pipe also incorporates a roll-over valve which closes and prevents any fuel from escaping through it in the event of the bike falling over. The tank filler cap has a one way valve which allows air into the tank as the volume of fuel decreases, but prevents any fuel vapour from escaping.

4 The system is not adjustable and can be tested only by a Suzuki dealer. Checks which can be performed by the owner are given in Chapter 1.

Removal and installation

5 To access the canister remove the side panels (see Chapter 7). Label and disconnect the hoses, remove the clamp screw and take the canister out. Make sure the hoses are correctly reconnected on installation.

6 The two purge control valves are mounted on bracket on the right-hand side of the frame. If in doubt about hose connections, refer to the emissions label on the bike.

Pulse secondary air injection system (PAIR)
General information

7 When the engine is running, the depression present in the intake manifold of no. 2 or no. 3 carburettor (whichever carburettor the hose connects to) acts on a diaphragm in the purge control valve, opening the valve. With the purge control valve open, whenever there is a negative pulse in the exhaust system, filtered fresh air is drawn from the PAIR air cleaner, through the reed valves and into the exhaust ports in the front of the cylinder head.

8 This fresh air promotes the burning of any excess fuel present in the exhaust gases, so reducing the amount of harmful hydrocarbons emitted into the atmosphere via the exhaust gases. Exhaust gases are prevented from passing back into the PAIR system by the reed valves.

Removal and installation

9 Remove the fuel tank for access the PAIR air cleaner, purge control valve and reed valves (see Section 2).

10 Before disconnecting any of the components from their mountings, label the hoses to ensure correct reconnection. It is not possible to dismantle or repair any of the PAIR components. If the metal pipes from the reed valve hoses to the cylinder head are removed, always use new gaskets at the cylinder joint on installation.

3

Notes

Chapter 4
Ignition system

Contents

Degrees of difficulty

Easy, suitable for novice with little experience		**Fairly easy,** suitable for beginner with some experience		**Fairly difficult,** suitable for competent DIY mechanic		**Difficult,** suitable for experienced DIY mechanic		**Very difficult,** suitable for expert DIY or professional	

Specifications

General information

Firing order	1 - 2 - 4 - 3
Cylinder identification	1 - 2 - 3 - 4, from left to right
Spark plugs	See Chapter 1

Ignition timing

At idle
GSF600 and GSF600S	13° BTDC
GSF1200 and GSF1200S	7° BTDC
Full advance	40° BTDC @ 4000 rpm

Ignition rev limiter
GSF600 and GSF600S	12,000 rpm
GSF1200 and GSF1200S	10,900 rpm

Pulse generator coils

Resistance	135 to 200 ohms

Ignition HT coils

Primary winding resistance	2.0 to 4.0 ohms
Secondary winding resistance (with plug lead and cap)	30 to 40 K ohms

Throttle position sensor - GSF1200 and GSF1200S

Resistance	3.5 to 6.5 K ohms

Torque settings

Ignition rotor Allen bolt	25 Nm

4

1 General information

All models are fitted with a fully transistorised electronic ignition system, which due to its lack of mechanical parts is totally maintenance free. The system comprises a rotor, pulse generator coil, ignition control unit and ignition HT coils (refer to the wiring diagrams at the end of Chapter 8 for details).

The trigger on the rotor, which is fitted to the right-hand end of the crankshaft, magnetically operates the pulse generator coil as the crankshaft rotates. The pulse generator coil sends a signal to the ignition control unit which then supplies the ignition HT coils with the power necessary to produce a spark at the plugs.

The system uses two coils mounted across the frame behind the steering head. The right-hand coil supplies nos. 1 and 4 cylinder spark plugs and the left-hand coil supplies nos. 2 and 3 cylinder plugs.

The system incorporates an electronic advance system controlled by signals generated by the rotor and the pick-up coil, and a limiter to prevent the engine exceeding its maximum rpm. On GSF1200 and GSF1200S models, the ignition control unit is supplied with throttle position information from a sensor mounted on no. 4 carburettor.

The system incorporates a safety interlock circuit which will cut the ignition if the sidestand is put down whilst the engine is running and in gear, or if a gear is selected whilst the engine is running and the sidestand is down.

Because of their nature, the individual ignition system components can be checked but not repaired. If ignition system troubles occur, and the faulty component can be isolated, the only cure for the problem is to replace the part with a new one. Keep in mind that most electrical parts, once purchased, cannot be returned. To avoid unnecessary expense, make very sure the faulty component has been positively identified before buying a replacement part.

Note that there is no provision for checking or adjusting the ignition timing on these models.

2 Ignition system - check

⚠️ **Warning: The energy levels in electronic systems can be very high. On no account should the ignition be switched on whilst the plugs or plug caps are being held. Shocks from the HT circuit can be most unpleasant. Secondly, it is vital that the engine is not turned over or run with any** *of the plug caps removed, and that the plugs are soundly earthed (grounded) when the system is checked for sparking. The ignition system components can be seriously damaged if the HT circuit becomes isolated.*

1 As no means of adjustment is available, any failure of the system can be traced to failure of a system component or a simple wiring fault. Of the two possibilities, the latter is by far the most likely. In the event of failure, check the system in a logical fashion, as described below.

2 Disconnect the HT leads from the spark plugs. Connect each lead to a spare spark plug and lay each plug on the engine with the threads contacting the engine. If necessary, hold each spark plug with an insulated tool.

⚠️ **Warning: Do not remove any of the spark plugs from the engine to perform this check - atomised fuel being pumped out of the open spark plug hole could ignite, causing severe injury!**

3 Having observed the above precautions, check that the kill switch is in the RUN position, turn the ignition switch ON and turn the engine over on the starter motor. If the system is in good condition a regular, fat blue spark should be evident at each plug electrode. If the spark appears thin or yellowish, or is non-existent, further investigation will be necessary. Before proceeding further, turn the ignition off and remove the key as a safety measure.

4 The ignition system must be able to produce a spark which is capable of jumping a particular size gap. Suzuki specify that a healthy system should produce a spark capable of jumping 8 mm. A simple testing tool can be made to test the minimum gap across which the spark will jump (see **Tool Tip**).

A simple spark gap testing tool can be made from a block of wood, a large alligator clip and two nails, one of which is fashioned so that a spark plug cap or bare HT lead end can be connected to its end. Make sure the gap between the two nail ends is the same as specified.

5 Connect one of the spark plug HT leads from one coil to the protruding electrode on the test tool, and clip the tool to a good earth (ground) on the engine or frame. Check that the kill switch is in the RUN position, turn the ignition switch ON and turn the engine over on the starter motor. If the system is in good condition a regular, fat blue spark should be seen to jump the gap between the nail ends. Repeat the test for the other coil. If the test results are good the entire ignition system can be considered good. If the spark appears thin or yellowish, or is non-existent, further investigation will be necessary.

6 Ignition faults can be divided into two categories, namely those where the ignition system has failed completely, and those which are due to a partial failure. The likely faults are listed below, starting with the most probable source of failure. Work through the list systematically, referring to the subsequent sections for full details of the necessary checks and tests. **Note:** *Before checking the following items ensure that the battery is fully charged and that all fuses are in good condition.*

a) *Loose, corroded or damaged wiring connections, broken or shorted wiring between any of the component parts of the ignition system (see Chapter 8).*
b) *Faulty HT lead or spark plug cap, faulty spark plug, dirty, worn or corroded plug electrodes, or incorrect gap between electrodes.*
c) *Faulty ignition (main) switch or engine kill switch (see Chapter 8).*
d) *Faulty neutral or sidestand switch (see Chapter 8).*
e) *Faulty pulse generator coil or damaged rotor.*
f) *Faulty ignition HT coil(s).*
g) *Faulty ignition control unit.*

7 If the above checks don't reveal the cause of the problem, have the ignition system tested by a Suzuki dealer. Suzuki produce a tester which can perform a complete diagnostic analysis of the ignition system.

3 Ignition HT coils - check, removal and installation

Check

1 In order to determine conclusively that the ignition coils are defective, they should be tested by a Suzuki dealer equipped with the special diagnostic tester.

2 However, the coils can be checked visually (for cracks and other damage) and the primary and secondary coil resistances can be measured with a multimeter. If the coils are undamaged, and if the resistance readings are as specified at the beginning of the Chapter, they are probably capable of proper operation.

3.3 The coils are mounted across the frame behind the steering head

3.4 Disconnect the primary circuit connectors

3.5 Ignition coil primary circuit test connections

3 Remove the seat (see Chapter 7) and disconnect the battery negative (-ve) lead. To gain access to the coils, remove the fuel tank (see Chapter 3). The coils are mounted across the frame behind the steering head **(see illustration)**.

4 Disconnect the primary circuit electrical connectors from the coil being tested and the HT leads from the spark plugs **(see illustration)**. Mark the locations of all wires and leads before disconnecting them.

5 Set the meter to the ohms x 1 scale and measure the resistance between the primary circuit terminals **(see illustration)**. This will give a resistance reading of the primary windings and should be consistent with the value given in the Specifications at the beginning of the Chapter.

3.6 Ignition coil secondary circuit test connections

6 To check the condition of the secondary windings, set the meter to the K ohm scale. Connect one meter probe to one spark plug cap and the other probe to the other spark plug cap **(see illustration)**. If the reading obtained is not within the range shown in the Specifications, it is likely that the coil is defective.

7 Should any of the above checks not produce the expected result, have your findings confirmed on the diagnostic tester (see Step 1). If the coil is confirmed to be faulty, it must be replaced; the coil is a sealed unit and cannot therefore be repaired.

Removal

8 Remove the seat (see Chapter 7) and disconnect the battery negative (-ve) lead, then remove the fuel tank (see Chapter 3).

9 The coils are mounted across the frame behind the steering stem **(see illustration 3.3)**. Disconnect the primary circuit electrical connectors from the coils **(see illustration 3.4)** and disconnect the HT leads from the spark plugs. Mark the locations of all wires and leads before disconnecting them.

10 Unscrew the two bolts securing each coil, noting the position of the spacers, and remove the coils **(see illustration)**. Note the routing of the HT leads.

Installation

11 Installation is the reverse of removal. Install the coils with the primary circuit connectors on the inside, and with the

spacers fitted with the longer bolts on the outside **(see illustration)**. Make sure the wiring connectors and HT leads are securely connected.

4 Pulse generator coil assembly - check, removal and installation

Check

1 Remove the seat and the side panels (see Chapter 7) and disconnect the battery negative (-ve) lead.

2 Trace the pulse generator coil and oil pressure switch wiring back from its exit hole in the crankcase behind the cylinder block and disconnect it at the 2-pin and bullet connectors **(see illustration)**. Using a multimeter set to the ohms x 100 scale, measure the resistance between the terminals on the pulse generator coil side of the connector.

3 Compare the reading obtained with that given in the Specifications at the beginning of this Chapter. The pulse generator coil must be replaced if the reading obtained differs greatly from that given, particularly if the meter indicates a short circuit (no measurable resistance) or an open circuit (infinite, or very high resistance).

4 If the pulse generator coil is thought to be faulty, first check that this is not due to a damaged or broken wire from the coil to the

3.10 Each coil is secured by two bolts (arrows)

3.11 Fit the spacer (arrow) with the longer bolt on the outer mounting

4.2 Disconnect the oil pressure switch (A) and pulse generator (B) wiring connectors

4

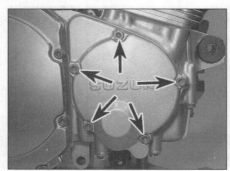

4.7 The pulse generator assembly cover is secured by five bolts (arrows)

4.8 Counter-hold the rotor and remove the bolt from its centre

4.9 Remove the screw (arrow) and disconnect the oil pressure switch wire

4.10a The assembly mounting plate is secured by three screws (arrows)

4.10b Feed the wiring and connector through the hole in the crankcase

9 Remove the screw securing the wire to the terminal on the oil pressure switch and detach the wire **(see illustration)**.

10 Remove the three screws securing the pulse generator coil assembly mounting plate to the crankcase cover **(see illustration)**. Remove the rubber wiring grommet from its recess in the crankcase cover and carefully pull the wiring through the hole in the crankcase, then remove the coil assembly, noting how it fits **(see illustration)**.

11 Examine the rotor for signs of damage and replace it if necessary.

Installation

12 Install the pulse generator coil assembly onto the crankcase and tighten the assembly mounting screws securely **(see illustration 4.10a)**.

13 Apply a smear of sealant to the rubber wiring seal and fit the grommet in its recess in the crankcase **(see illustration)**. Feed the wiring connector through the hole in the crankcase **(see illustration)**.

14 Connect the oil pressure switch wire to its terminal on the switch and tighten the screw securely **(see illustration 4.9)**.

15 Install the timing rotor onto the end of the crankshaft, making sure the slot in the rotor locates correctly over the pin in the end of the

connector; pinched or broken wires can usually be repaired. Note that the coil is not available individually but comes as an assembly with the mounting plate and wiring.

Removal

5 Remove the seat and side panels (see Chapter 7) and disconnect the battery negative (-ve) lead.

6 Trace the pulse generator coil and oil pressure switch wiring back from the right-hand side crankcase cover and disconnect it at the 2-pin and bullet connectors **(see illustration 4.2)**. Free the wiring from any clips

or ties and feed it through to its exit hole in the crankcase behind the cylinder block.

7 Unscrew the five bolts securing the pulse generator assembly cover to the right-hand side of the crankcase **(see illustration)**. Remove the cover. Discard the gasket as a new one must be used. Note the sealing washer fitted with the top cover bolt.

8 Using a 19 mm spanner to counter-hold the timing rotor, unscrew the bolt in the centre of the rotor which secures it to the end of the crankshaft **(see illustration)**. Remove the rotor, noting how the pin in the end of the crankshaft locates in the slot in the rotor.

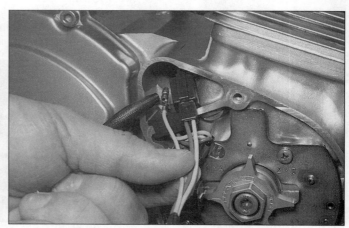

4.13a Fit the grommet into its cut-out . . .

4.13b . . . and feed the wiring through the hole

4.16a Install the cover using a new gasket

4.16b A sealing washer is fitted on the top bolt

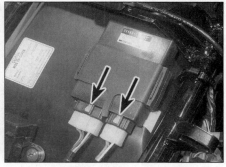

5.3 Disconnect the two wiring connectors (arrow) . . .

crankshaft. Using a 19 mm spanner to counter-hold the rotor, install the rotor bolt and tighten it to the torque setting specified at the beginning of the Chapter **(see illustration 4.8)**.

16 Install the pulse generator assembly cover using a new gasket and tighten its bolts securely, making sure the sealing washer is fitted with the top bolt **(see illustrations)**.

17 Route the wiring up to the connectors and reconnect it **(see illustration 4.2)**. Secure the wiring in its clips or ties.

18 Reconnect the battery negative (-ve) lead and install the seat and side panels (see Chapter 7).

5 Ignition control unit - check, removal and installation

Check

1 If the tests shown in the preceding Sections have failed to isolate the cause of an ignition fault, it is likely that the ignition control unit itself is faulty. No test details are available with which the unit can be tested on home workshop equipment. Take the machine to a Suzuki dealer for testing on the diagnostic tester.

Removal

2 Remove the seat (see Chapter 7) and disconnect the battery negative (-ve) lead.

3 Disconnect the two wiring connectors from the ignition control unit **(see illustration)**.

4 Remove the ignition control unit from its rubber sleeve, or lift the sleeve and unit together off the sleeve's mounting lugs, and remove the unit **(see illustration)**.

Installation

5 Installation is the reverse of removal. Make sure the wiring connectors are correctly and securely connected.

6 Throttle position sensor (GSF1200 and GSF1200S) - check and replacement

Check

1 The throttle sensor is mounted on the outside of the right-hand (no. 4) carburettor.

2 Lift the rubber cover and disconnect the wiring connector from the top of the sensor **(see illustration)**. Using a multimeter set to the K ohm scale, connect the probes to the two outer terminals on the sensor. If the resistance reading obtained is not within the range specified at the beginning of the Chapter for testing. If it is confirmed to be faulty, it must be replaced; the sensor is a sealed unit and cannot therefore be repaired.

3 Also check the sensor visually (for cracks and other damage) and check the wiring

between the sensor and the ignition control module for continuity.

4 Using a multimeter set to resistance or a continuity tester, check for continuity between the terminals of the sensor wiring connector and the corresponding terminals on the ignition control module connector. There should be continuity between each terminal. If not, this is probably due to a damaged or broken wire between the connectors; pinched or broken wires can usually be repaired.

Replacement

Caution: Suzuki advise against removing the sensor from the carburettors unless absolutely necessary.

5 The throttle sensor is mounted on the outside of the right-hand (no. 4) carburettor. Lift the rubber cover and disconnect the wiring connector from the top of the sensor **(see illustration 7.2)**.

6 Before removing the screws, mark or scribe lines on the mounting plate to indicate the exact position of the sensor mounting screws in relation to the plate **(see illustration)**. Unscrew the sensor mounting screws and remove the sensor, noting how it fits.

7 Install the sensor, aligning the screws with the marks made on the plate, and tighten its screws securely.

8 Connect the wiring connector to the top of the sensor and slip the rubber cover into place.

4

5.4 . . . and remove the ignition control unit

6.2 Lift the cover and disconnect the TPS wiring connector

6.6 The sensor is secured by two screws (arrows)

Notes

Chapter 5
Frame, suspension and final drive

Contents

Degrees of difficulty

Easy, suitable for novice with little experience	Fairly easy, suitable for beginner with some experience	Fairly difficult, suitable for competent DIY mechanic	Difficult, suitable for experienced DIY mechanic	Very difficult, suitable for expert DIY or professional

Specifications

Front forks

Fork oil type . . . . SAE 10W fork oil
Fork oil capacity
  GSF600 and GSF600S
    UK models . . . . 521 cc
    US models . . . . 522 cc
  GSF1200 and GSF1200S
    UK models . . . . 516 cc
    US models . . . . 514 cc
Fork oil level*
  GSF600 and GSF600S
    UK models . . . . 97 mm
    US models . . . . 96 mm
  GSF1200 and GSF1200S
    UK models . . . . 99 mm
    US models . . . . 101 mm
Fork spring free length (min)
  GSF600 and GSF600S . . . . 281 mm
  GSF1200 and GSF1200S
    UK models . . . . 362 mm
    US models . . . . 360 mm
Fork tube runout limit . . . . 0.2 mm
Oil level is measured from the top of the tube with the fork spring removed and the leg fully compressed.

Rear suspension
Swingarm pivot bolt runout (max) . . . . 0.3 mm

5

Torque settings

Brake pedal and gearchange lever pivot bolts . . . .   39 Nm
Front footrest bracket bolts . . . .   23 Nm
Rear brake master cylinder bolts . . . .   23 Nm
Handlebar clamp bolts . . . .   23 Nm
Handlebar clamp base nuts (GSF1200 and GSF1200S) . . . .   45 Nm
Front brake master cylinder bolts . . . .   10 Nm
Clutch master cylinder bolts (GSF1200 and GSF1200S) . . . .   10 Nm
Fork top bolts . . . .   23 Nm
Fork clamp bolts (top yoke) . . . .   23 Nm
Fork clamp bolts (bottom yoke) . . . .   23 Nm
Damper rod bolt
    GSF600 and GSF600S . . . .   30 Nm
    GSF1200 and GSF1200S . . . .   20 Nm
Steering head bearing adjuster nut . . . .   45 Nm
Steering stem nut . . . .   65 Nm
Shock absorber mounting bolts . . . .   50 Nm
Suspension linkage rod nuts
    GSF600 and GSF600S . . . .   76 Nm
    GSF1200 and GSF1200S . . . .   78 Nm
Suspension linkage arm nut
    GSF600 and GSF600S . . . .   76 Nm
    GSF1200 and GSF1200S . . . .   78 Nm
Swingarm pivot nut . . . .   100 Nm
Brake torque arm nuts . . . .   35 Nm
Front sprocket nut . . . .   115 Nm
Front sprocket lockbolt (GSF600 and GSF600S) . . . .   11 Nm
Rear sprocket nuts . . . .   60 Nm

1 General information

All models use a full cradle twin spar steel frame. The right-hand side frame downtube is detachable to ease engine removal.

Front suspension is by a pair of conventional oil-damped telescopic forks. On GSF1200 and GSF1200S models, the forks are adjustable for pre-load.

At the rear, a box-section steel swingarm acts on a single shock absorber via a linkage which provides a rising rate system. The shock absorber is adjustable for pre-load on all models, and on GSF1200 and GSF1200S, for rebound damping.

The drive to the rear wheel is by chain. A rubber damper system (often called a 'cush drive') is fitted between the rear wheel coupling and the wheel.

2 Frame - inspection and repair

1 The frame should not require attention unless accident damage has occurred. In most cases, frame replacement is the only satisfactory remedy for such damage. A few frame specialists have the jigs and other equipment necessary for straightening the frame to the required standard of accuracy, but even then there is no simple way of assessing to what extent the frame may have been over stressed.

2 After the machine has accumulated a lot of miles, the frame should be examined closely for signs of cracking or splitting at the welded joints. Loose engine mount bolts can cause ovaling or fracturing of the mounting tabs. Minor damage can often be repaired by welding, depending on the extent and nature of the damage.

3 Remember that a frame which is out of alignment will cause handling problems. If misalignment is suspected as the result of an accident, it will be necessary to strip the machine completely so the frame can be thoroughly checked.

3 Footrests, brake pedal and gearchange lever - removal and installation

Footrests

Removal

1 Remove the E-clip from the bottom of the footrest pivot pin, then withdraw the pivot pin and remove the footrest (see illustrations). On the front footrests, note the fitting of the return spring, spacer and rubber damper. On the rear footrests, note the fitting of the detent ball and spring, and take care that they do not spring out when removing the footrest.

2 If necessary, on all except the rear footrests on 600 models, the footrest rubber can be separated from the footrest by removing the two screws or bolts on the underside of the footrest.

Installation

3 Installation is the reverse of removal.

3.1a Remove the E-clip (arrow) . . .

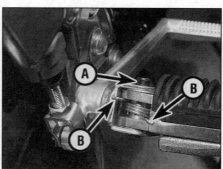

3.1b . . . and withdraw the pin (A) from the top. Note how the return spring ends (B) are located

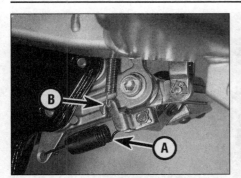

3.4 Unhook the brake pedal return spring (A) and the brake light switch spring (B)

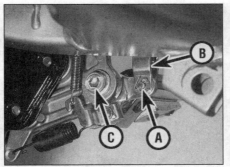

3.5 Remove the split pin (A) and withdraw the clevis pin. Separate the clevis (B) from the pedal, then remove the pivot bolt (C)

3.8 Remove the pinch bolt (arrow) and slide the gearchange arm off the shaft

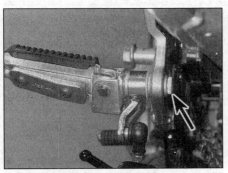

3.9 Remove the pivot bolt (arrow) and separate the footrest and lever

3.10 Slacken the locknut (arrow) and unscrew the rod if required

3.11 Align the previously made marks (arrows) and install the pinch bolt

Brake pedal

Removal

4 Unhook the brake pedal return spring from the bracket and the brake light switch spring from the brake pedal **(see illustration)**.
5 Remove the split pin from the clevis pin securing the brake pedal to the master cylinder pushrod. Remove the clevis pin and separate the pedal from the pushrod **(see illustration)**.
6 Unscrew the pivot bolt securing the brake pedal and footrest carrier to the footrest bracket **(see illustration 3.5)**. Separate the footrest assembly and remove the pedal.

Installation

7 Installation is the reverse of removal. Check the operation of the rear brake light switch and the height of the brake pedal (see Chapter 1).

Gearchange lever

Removal

8 Unscrew the gearchange lever linkage arm pinch bolt and remove the arm from the shaft, noting any alignment marks **(see illustration)**. If no marks are visible, make your own before removing the arm so that it can be correctly aligned with the shaft on installation.
9 Unscrew the pivot bolt securing the gearchange lever and footrest carrier

assembly to the footrest bracket **(see illustration)**. Separate the footrest assembly and remove the lever and linkage arm.
10 If required, slacken the linkage rod locknut and unscrew the rod from the lever **(see illustration)**. Note the how far the rod is threaded into the lever as this determines the height of the lever relative to the footrest.

Installation

11 Installation is the reverse of removal. Align the marks made on the gearchange lever linkage arm and shaft when installing the arm onto the shaft, and tighten the pinch bolt securely **(see illustration)**. Adjust the gear lever height as required by screwing the rod in or out of the lever and arm. Tighten the locknuts securely.

---

4 Stands -
  removal and installation

Centrestand (where fitted)

1 The centrestand is secured in the frame by two pivot bolts which fit inside spacers in the stand pivots. Support the bike on its sidestand and unhook the centre stand springs, then unscrew the bolts and remove the stand **(see illustration)**. Withdraw the spacer from each pivot.

2 Inspect the stand, spacers and bolts for signs of wear and replace them if necessary. Apply a smear of grease to the outside of the spacers and the bolts and fit the stand back on the bike, tightening the bolts securely. Reconnect the return springs.
3 Make sure the springs are in good condition and capable of holding the stand up when not in use. A broken or weak spring is an obvious safety hazard.

Sidestand

4 The sidestand is attached to a bracket on the frame. Springs anchored to the bracket ensure that the stand is held in the retracted or extended position.

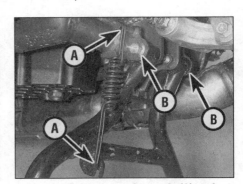

4.1 Unhook the spring ends (A) and remove the pivot bolts (B)

5

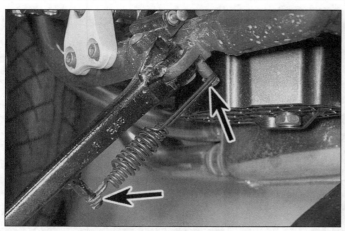

4.6a Unhook the spring ends (arrows) . . .

4.6b . . . then remove the nut (arrow) and withdraw the bolt from the back

5 Support the bike on its centrestand (if fitted), or support it using an auxiliary stand.

6 Unhook the stand springs and unscrew the nut from the pivot bolt **(see illustrations)**. Withdraw the pivot bolt to free the stand from its bracket. On installation apply grease to the pivot bolt shank and tighten the bolt securely. Reconnect the sidestand springs and check that the return spring holds the stand securely up when not in use - an accident is almost certain to occur if the stand extends while the machine is in motion.

7 For check and replacement of the sidestand switch see Chapter 8.

5 Handlebars and levers - removal and installation

Handlebars

Removal

Note: *If required, the handlebars can be displaced for access to the fork top bolts or the steering stem nut without removing the*
switch housings and the front brake master cylinder assembly and the clutch lever/master cylinder assembly.

1 Disconnect the brake light switch wiring connectors from the underside of the master cylinder and the clutch switch connectors from the underside of the master cylinder (1200 models) or lever bracket (600 models) **(see illustrations)**. Remove the screws securing both the left- and right-hand switch housings to the handlebar, then separate the switch halves and remove them from the handlebar, noting how they fit (see Chapter 8 if required). There is no need to disconnect the switch housing wiring at its connector blocks.

2 Unscrew the two clamp bolts securing the front brake master cylinder assembly to the handlebar, noting how the mating surfaces of the clamp align with the punch mark on the underside of the handlebar, and lift the assembly away (see Chapter 6 if required). There is no need to disconnect the hose from the master cylinder. Support the assembly in an upright position and so that no strain is placed on the hose.

3 On GSF600 and GSF600S, pull back the rubber cover from the clutch lever assembly.
Fully slacken the cable lockwheel then screw the adjuster fully in. Align the slots in the adjuster and lockwheel with that in the lever bracket, then pull the outer cable end from the socket in the adjuster and release the inner cable from the lever (see Chapter 2 if required). If it is to be removed from the handlebar, slacken the clutch lever assembly bracket pinch bolt **(see illustration)**. It can only be slid off the handlebar after removal of the grip. Note how the mating surfaces of the bracket align with the punch mark on the underside of the handlebar.

4 On GSF1200 and GSF1200S, unscrew the two clamp bolts securing the clutch master cylinder assembly to the handlebar, noting how the mating surfaces of the clamp align with the slit in the handlebar spacer and the punch mark on the underside of the handlebar, and lift the assembly away (see Chapter 2 if required). There is no need to disconnect the hose from the master cylinder. Support the assembly in an upright position and so that no strain is placed on the hose.

5 Prise out the caps from the bolts securing the handlebar clamp tops, then unscrew the bolts and remove the clamp tops and the

5.1a Disconnect the front brake switch . . .

5.1b . . . and the clutch switch wiring connectors

5.3 Slacken the clutch lever clamp bolt (arrow)

5.5a Prise out the caps . . .

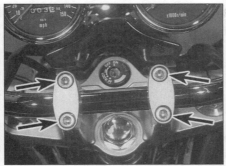

5.5b . . . and remove the four handlebar clamp bolts (arrows)

5.6 Remove the screw from the end of the grip to separate the end-weight components

handlebars **(see illustrations)**. Note the punch mark on the front of the handlebar which aligns with the mating surfaces of the left-hand clamp.

6 If necessary, unscrew the handlebar end-weight retaining screws, then remove the weights from the end of the handlebars **(see illustration)**. If replacing the grips, it may be necessary to slit them using a sharp knife as they are adhered to the throttle twist (right-hand) and the handlebar (left-hand).

7 On GSF1200 and GSF1200S, the handlebar clamp bases are rubber mounted on the top yoke. If required, unscrew the two nuts on the underside of the top yoke, then withdraw the bolts from the top and remove the clamp bases. Inspect the rubber dampers for wear and deterioration and replace them if necessary.

Installation

8 Installation is the reverse of removal, noting the following.

a) Align the handlebars so that the punch mark on the front of the handlebar aligns with the front mating surfaces of the left-hand clamp **(see illustration)**. Tighten the handlebar mounting bolts to the torque setting specified at the beginning of the Chapter, making sure that the gap between the mating surfaces of the clamps are equal front and rear.

b) Make sure the front brake and clutch

master cylinder or lever assembly clamps are installed with the lower clamp mating surfaces aligned with the punch mark on the underside of the handlebar **(see illustrations)**. Tighten the upper master cylinder clamp bolt first, then the lower bolt, to the torque setting specified at the beginning of the Chapter.

c) If removed, apply a suitable non-permanent locking compound to the handlebar end-weight retaining screws. If new grips are being fitted, secure them using a suitable adhesive.

d) On GSF1200 and GSF1200S, if removed, tighten the clamp base nuts to the specified torque setting.

5.8a Align the clamp mating surfaces with the punch mark on the handlebar (arrow)

5.8b Align the lower clamp mating surfaces on the brake master cylinder . . .

Levers

Removal

9 To remove the complete front brake lever assembly from the master cylinder, unscrew the main inner pivot bolt locknut, then withdraw the bolt and remove the lever assembly **(see illustrations)**.

10 To remove the lever blade from the pivot assembly, unscrew the span adjuster pivot bolt locknut, then withdraw the bolt and remove the lever blade **(see illustrations 5.9a and b)**.

11 To remove the clutch lever, unscrew the pivot bolt locknut, then withdraw the pivot bolt and remove the lever. On 600 models,

5.8c . . . and the clutch lever bracket or master cylinder with the punch marks on the handlebars (arrows)

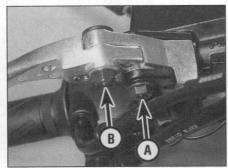

5.9a Main pivot bolt locknut (A), span adjuster pivot bolt locknut (B)

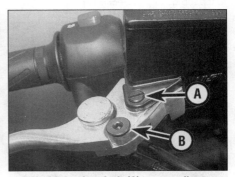

5.9b Main pivot bolt (A), span adjuster pivot bolt (B)

5.11 Clutch lever pivot bolt (arrow)

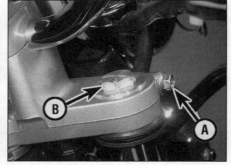

6.5 Top yoke fork clamp bolt (A), fork top
bolt (B)

6.6a Note the alignment of the fork with
the top yoke as an aid to installation
(arrow)

detach the clutch cable end from the lever as
you remove it **(see illustration)**.

Installation

12 Installation is the reverse of removal.
Apply grease to the pivot bolt shafts and to
the contact areas between the lever and its
bracket. On 600 models, grease the clutch
cable end and fit it into the lever before
installing the lever in its bracket.

6 Forks -
removal and installation

Removal

1 On S models, remove the fairing (see
Chapter 7).
2 Remove the front wheel (see Chapter 6).
3 Remove the front mudguard and brace (see
Chapter 7).
4 Unscrew the bolts securing the brake hose
clamps and the speedometer cable guides to
the forks.
5 Slacken, but do not remove, the fork clamp
bolts in the top yoke **(see illustration)**. If the
forks are to be disassembled, or if the fork oil
is being changed, it is advisable to slacken the
fork top bolts at this stage. On GSF1200 and
GSF1200S models set the pre-load adjuster to
its minimum setting (see Section 12). Displace
the handlebars if required for improved access
to the top bolts (see Section 5).

HAYNES HiNT
*Slackening the fork clamp
bolts in the top yoke before
slackening the fork top bolts
releases pressure on the top
bolt. This makes it much easier to
remove and helps to preserve the
threads.*

6 Note the position of the top of the fork
tubes relative to the top yoke so that they can
be installed in the same position **(see
illustration)**. Slacken but do not remove the
fork clamp bolts in the bottom yoke, and
remove the forks by twisting them and pulling
them downwards **(see illustration)**. Note how
the forks pass through the headlight brackets.

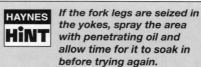

HAYNES HiNT
*If the fork legs are seized in
the yokes, spray the area
with penetrating oil and
allow time for it to soak in
before trying again.*

Installation

7 Remove all traces of corrosion from the fork
tubes and the yokes and slide the forks up
through the bottom yoke, the headlight
brackets and the top yoke **(see illustration)**.
Align the forks with the top yoke as noted on
removal **(see illustration 6.6a)**.
8 Tighten the fork clamp bolts in the bottom
yoke to the torque setting specified at the
beginning of the Chapter **(see illustration)**. If

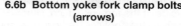

6.6b Bottom yoke fork clamp bolts
(arrows)

the fork legs have been dismantled or if the
fork oil has been changed, the fork top bolts
should now be tightened to the specified
torque setting. Now tighten the fork clamp
bolts in the top yoke to the specified torque
setting **(see illustration)**. Install the
handlebars if displaced.
9 Install the front brace and mudguard (see
Chapter 7) and the front wheel (see Chapter 6). Install the brake hose and speedometer
cable clamps onto the forks and tighten their
bolts securely.
10 Check the operation of the front forks and
brakes before taking the machine out on the
road. On GSF1200 and GSF1200S, adjust the
fork pre-load as required (see Section 12).
11 On S models, install the fairing (see
Chapter 7).

6.7 Install the fork up through the yokes
and headlight bracket

6.8a Tighten the bottom yoke clamp
bolts . . .

6.8b . . . and the top yoke clamp bolts to
the specified torque setting

7 Forks - disassembly, inspection and reassembly

GSF600 and GSF600S

Disassembly

1 Always dismantle the fork legs separately to avoid interchanging parts and thus causing an accelerated rate of wear. Store all components in separate, clearly marked containers (see illustration).

2 Before dismantling the fork, it is advised that the damper rod bolt be slackened at this stage. Compress the fork tube in the slider so that the spring exerts maximum pressure on the damper rod head, then have an assistant slacken the damper rod bolt in the base of the fork slider.

3 If the fork top bolt was not slackened with the fork in situ, carefully clamp the fork tube in a vice equipped with soft jaws, taking care not to overtighten or score its surface, and slacken the top bolt.

4 Unscrew the fork top bolt from the top of the fork tube.

Warning: The fork spring is pressing on the fork top bolt with considerable pressure. Unscrew the bolt very carefully, keeping a downward pressure on it and release it slowly as it is likely to spring clear. It is advisable to wear some form of eye and face protection when carrying out this operation.

5 Slide the fork tube down into the slider and withdraw the spacer, spring seat and the spring from the tube. Take note of which way up the spring is fitted - the closer-wound coils should be uppermost.

6 Invert the fork leg over a suitable container and pump the fork vigorously to expel as much fork oil as possible.

7 Remove the previously slackened damper rod bolt and its copper sealing washer from the bottom of the slider. Discard the sealing washer as a new one must be used on reassembly. If the damper rod bolt was not slackened before dismantling the fork, it may be necessary to re-install the spring, spring seat, spacer and top bolt to prevent the damper rod from turning. Alternatively, a long metal bar or length of wood doweling passed down through the fork tube and pressed hard into the damper rod head quite often suffices.

8 Invert the fork and withdraw the damper rod from inside the fork tube. Remove the rebound spring from the damper rod (see illustration).

9 Carefully prise out the dust seal from the top of the slider to gain access to the oil seal retaining clip (see illustration). Discard the dust seal as a new one must be used.

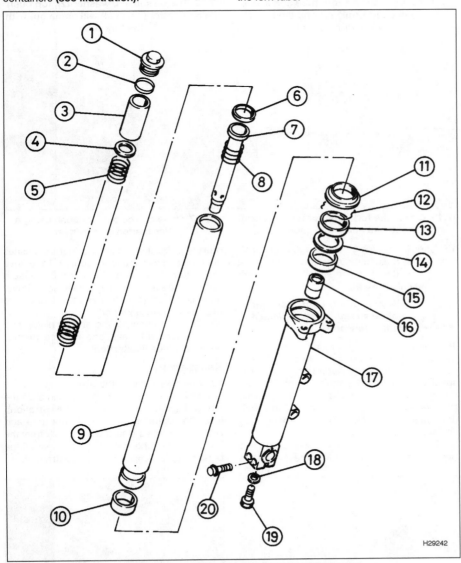

7.1 Front fork components - GSF600 and GSF600S

1 Top bolt
2 O-ring
3 Spacer
4 Spring seat
5 Spring
6 Piston ring
7 Damper rod
8 Rebound spring
9 Fork tube
10 Bottom bush
11 Dust seal
12 Retaining clip
13 Oil seal
14 Washer
15 Top bush
16 Damper rod seat
17 Fork slider
18 Sealing washer
19 Damper rod bolt
20 Axle clamp bolt

7.8 Withdraw the damper rod and rebound spring from the tube

7.9 Prise out the dust seal using a flat-bladed screwdriver

5

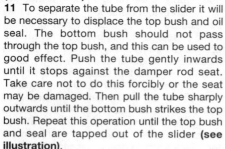

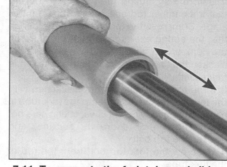

7.10 Prise out the retaining clip using a flat-bladed screwdriver

7.11 To separate the fork tube and slider, pull them apart firmly several times in a slide-hammer action

7.12 The oil seal (1), washer (2), top bush (3) and bottom bush (4) will come out with the fork tube

10 Carefully remove the retaining clip, taking care not to scratch the surface of the tube **(see illustration)**.

11 To separate the tube from the slider it will be necessary to displace the top bush and oil seal. The bottom bush should not pass through the top bush, and this can be used to good effect. Push the tube gently inwards until it stops against the damper rod seat. Take care not to do this forcibly or the seat may be damaged. Then pull the tube sharply outwards until the bottom bush strikes the top bush. Repeat this operation until the top bush and seal are tapped out of the slider **(see illustration)**.

12 With the tube removed, slide off the oil seal, washer and top bush, noting which way up they fit **(see illustration)**. Discard the oil seal as a new one must be used.

Caution: Do not remove the bottom bush from the tube unless it is to be replaced.

13 Tip the damper rod seat out of the slider, noting which way up it fits.

Inspection

14 Clean all parts in solvent and blow them dry with compressed air, if available. Check the fork tube for score marks, scratches, flaking of the chrome finish and excessive or abnormal wear. Look for dents in the tube and replace the tube in both forks if any are found. Check the fork seal seat for nicks, gouges and scratches. If damage is evident, leaks will occur.

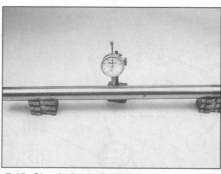

7.15 Check the fork tube for runout using V-blocks and a dial gauge

15 Check the fork tube for runout using V-blocks and a dial gauge, or have it done at a dealer service department or other repair shop **(see illustration)**.

 Warning: If it is bent, it should not be straightened; replace it with a new one.

16 Check the spring for cracks and other damage. Measure the spring free length and compare the measurement to the specifications at the beginning of the Chapter. If it is defective or sagged below the service limit, replace the springs in both forks with new ones. Never replace only one spring. Also check the rebound spring.

17 Examine the working surfaces of the two bushes; if worn or scuffed they must be

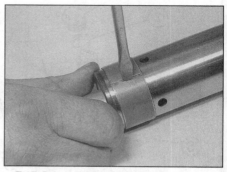

7.17 Prise off the bottom bush using a flat-bladed screwdriver

replaced. Suzuki recommend that the bushes are replaced as a matter of course. To remove the bottom bush from the fork tube, prise it apart at the slit using a flat-bladed screwdriver and slide it off **(see illustration)**. Make sure the new one seats properly.

18 Check the damper rod and its piston ring for damage and wear, and replace them if necessary **(see illustration)**.

Reassembly

19 If removed, install the piston ring into the groove in the damper rod head, then slide the rebound spring onto the rod **(see illustration)**. Insert the damper rod into the fork tube and slide it into place so that it projects fully from the bottom of the tube, then install the seat on the bottom of the damper rod **(see illustration)**.

7.18 Replace the damper rod piston ring if it is worn or damaged

7.19a Slide the rebound spring onto the damper rod

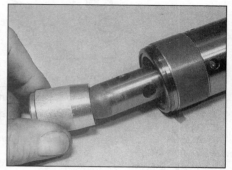

7.19b Fit the seat to the bottom of the rod

7.20a Slide the tube into the slider

7.20b Apply a thread locking compound to the damper rod bolt and use a new sealing washer

7.21a Install the top bush . . .

20 Oil the fork tube and bottom bush with the specified fork oil and insert the assembly into the slider **(see illustration)**. Fit a new copper sealing washer to the damper rod bolt and apply a few drops of a suitable non-permanent thread locking compound, then install the bolt into the bottom of the slider **(see illustration)**. Tighten the bolt to the specified torque setting. If the damper rod rotates inside the tube, temporarily install the fork spring and top bolt (see Steps 26 and 27) and compress the fork to hold the damper rod. Alternatively, pass a metal bar or length of wood dowel down the fork tube and press it into the damper rod head. Otherwise, wait until the fork is fully reassembled before tightening the bolt.

21 Push the fork tube fully into the slider, then oil the top bush and slide it down over

the tube **(see illustration)**. Press the bush squarely into its recess in the slider as far as possible, then install the oil seal washer **(see illustration)**. Either use the service tool (Pt. No. 09940-52860) or a suitable piece of tubing to tap the bush fully into place; the tubing must be slightly larger in diameter than the fork tube and slightly smaller in diameter than the bush recess in the slider. Take care not to scratch the fork tube during this operation; it is best to make sure that the fork tube is pushed fully into the slider so that any accidental scratching is confined to the area above the oil seal.

22 When the bush is seated fully and squarely in its recess in the slider, (remove the washer to check, wipe the recess clean, then reinstall the washer), install the new oil seal. Smear the seal's lips with fork oil and slide it

over the tube so that its markings face upwards and drive the seal into place as described in Step 21 until the retaining clip groove is visible above the seal.**(see illustration)**.

23 Once the seal is correctly seated, fit the retaining clip, making sure it is correctly located in its groove **(see illustration)**.

24 Lubricate the lips of the new dust seal then slide it down the fork tube and press it into position **(see illustration)**.

25 Slowly pour in the specified quantity of the specified grade of fork oil and pump the fork to distribute it evenly **(see illustration)**; the oil level should also be measured and adjustment made by adding or subtracting oil. Fully compress the fork tube into the slider and measure the fork oil level from the top of the tube **(see illustration)**. Add or subtract

7.21b . . . followed by the washer

7.22 Make sure the oil seal is the correct way up

7.23 Install the retaining clip . . .

7.24 . . . followed by the dust seal

7.25a Pour the oil into the top of the tube

7.25b Measure the oil level with the fork held vertical

5

7.26a Install the spring . . .

7.26b . . . followed by the spring seat . . .

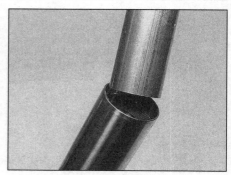

7.26c . . . and the spacer

fork oil until the oil is at the level specified in the Specifications Section of this Chapter.

26 Clamp the slider in a vice via the brake caliper mounting lugs, taking care not to overtighten and damage them. Pull the fork tube out of the slider as far as possible then install the spring with its closer-wound coils at the top, followed by the spring seat and the spacer **(see illustrations)**.

27 Fit a new O-ring to the fork top bolt and thread the bolt into the top of the fork tube **(see illustration)**.

> ⚠ **Warning: It will be necessary to compress the spring by pressing it down using the top bolt to engage the threads of the top bolt with the fork tube. This is a potentially dangerous operation and should be performed with care, using an assistant if necessary. Wipe off any excess oil before starting to prevent the possibility of slipping.**

Keep the fork tube fully extended whilst pressing on the spring. Screw the top bolt carefully into the fork tube making sure it is not cross-threaded. **Note:** *The top bolt can be tightened to the specified torque setting at this stage if the tube is held between the padded jaws of a vice, but do not risk distorting the tube by doing so. A better method is to tighten the top bolt when the fork has been installed in the bike and is securely held in the bottom yoke.*

7.27 Fit a new O-ring onto the top bolt and thread the bolt into the fork tube

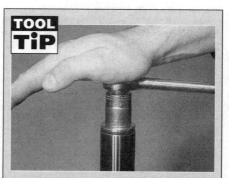

Use a ratchet-type tool when installing the fork top bolt. This makes it unnecessary to remove the tool from the bolt whilst threading it in, thus making it easier to maintain a downward pressure on the spring.

28 Install the forks (see Section 6).

GSF1200 and GSF1200S

Disassembly

29 Always dismantle the fork legs separately to avoid interchanging parts and thus causing an accelerated rate of wear. Store all components in separate, clearly marked containers **(see illustration)**.

30 Before dismantling the fork, it is advised that the damper rod bolt be slackened at this stage. Compress the fork tube in the slider so that the spring exerts maximum pressure on the damper rod head, then have an assistant slacken the damper rod bolt in the base of the fork slider.

31 If the fork top bolt was not slackened with the fork in situ, carefully clamp the fork tube in a vice, taking care not to overtighten or score its surface. Set the pre-load adjuster to its minimum setting (see Section 12), then slacken the top bolt.

32 Unscrew the fork top bolt from the top of the fork tube.

33 Slide the fork tube down into the slider. Whilst counter-holding the base of the spring pre-load adjuster, slacken the locknut immediately below it. Unscrew the fork top

bolt and pre-load adjuster from the top of the damper rod.

34 Remove the slotted spring collar by compressing the fork spring using the spring spacer as a grip. With the spring compressed, and keeping the damper rod fully extended, slip the collar out to the side. Slowly release the spring until all pressure has been relieved, then remove the spacer and the spring seat. Withdraw the spring from the tube, noting which way up it fits.

> ⚠ **Warning: The fork spring may be exerting considerable pressure, making this a potentially dangerous operation. Wipe off as much oil as possible to minimise the risk of your hands slipping on oily components and enlist the help of an assistant.**

35 Invert the fork leg over a suitable container and pump the fork vigorously to expel as much fork oil as possible.

36 Unscrew the damper rod bolt and its copper sealing washer from the bottom of the slider. Discard the sealing washer as a new one must be used on reassembly.

37 Invert the fork and withdraw the damper rod from inside the fork tube.

38 Carefully prise out the dust seal from the top of the slider to gain access to the oil seal retaining clip. Discard the dust seal as a new one must be used.

39 Carefully remove the retaining clip, taking care not to scratch the surface of the tube.

40 To separate the tube from the slider it will be necessary to displace the top bush and oil seal. The bottom bush should not pass through the top bush, and this can be used to good effect. Push the tube gently inwards until it stops against the damper rod seat. Take care not to do this forcibly or the seat may be damaged. Then pull the tube sharply outwards until the bottom bush strikes the top bush. Repeat this operation until the top bush and seal are tapped out of the slider **(see illustration 7.11)**.

41 With the tube removed, slide off the oil seal, washer and top bush **(see illustration 7.12)**. Discard the oil seal as a new one must be used.

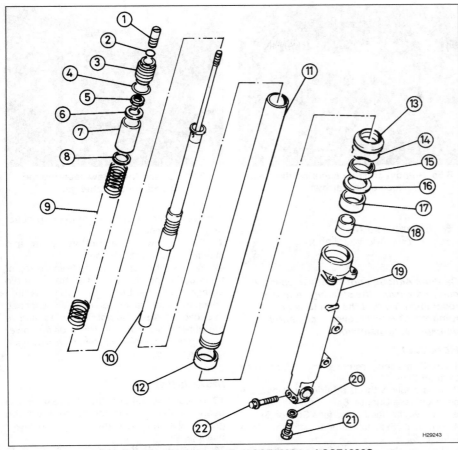

7.29 Front fork components - GSF1200 and GSF1200S

1 Pre-load adjuster	6 Slotted spring	11 Fork tube	17 Top bush
2 O-ring	collar	12 Bottom bush	18 Damper rod seat
3 Top bolt	7 Spacer	13 Dust seal	19 Fork slider
4 O-ring	8 Spring seat	14 Retaining clip	20 Sealing washer
5 Locknut	9 Spring	15 Oil seal	21 Damper rod bolt
	10 Damper rod	16 Washer	22 Axle clamp bolt

Caution: Do not remove the bottom bush from the tube unless it is to be replaced.

42 Tip the damper rod seat out of the slider, noting which way up it fits.

Inspection

43 Clean all parts in solvent and blow them dry with compressed air, if available. Check the fork tube for score marks, scratches, flaking of the chrome finish and excessive or abnormal wear. Look for dents in the tube and replace the tube in both forks if any are found. Check the fork seal seat for nicks, gouges and scratches. If damage is evident, leaks will occur.

44 Check the fork tube for runout using V-blocks and a dial gauge, or have it done at a dealer service department or other repair shop **(see illustration 7.15)**.

 Warning: If it is bent, it should not be straightened; replace it with a new one.

45 Check the spring for cracks and other damage. Measure the spring free length and

compare the measurement to the specifications at the beginning of the Chapter. If it is defective or sagged below the service limit, replace the springs in both forks with new ones. Never replace only one spring. Also check the rebound spring.

46 Examine the working surfaces of the two bushes; if worn or scuffed they must be replaced. Suzuki recommend that the bushes are replaced as a matter of course. To remove the bottom bush from the fork tube, prise it apart at the slit using a flat-bladed screwdriver and slide it off **(see illustration 7.17)**. Make sure the new one seats properly.

47 Check the damper rod assembly for damage and wear, and replace it if necessary. Holding the outside of the damper, pump the rod in and out of the damper. If the rod does not move smoothly in the damper it must be replaced.

Reassembly

48 Insert the damper rod into the fork tube and slide it into place so that it projects fully

from the bottom of the tube, then install the seat on the bottom of the damper rod **(see illustration 7.19b)**.

49 Oil the fork tube and bottom bush with the specified fork oil and insert the assembly into the slider **(see illustration 7.20a)**. Fit a new copper sealing washer to the damper rod bolt and apply a few drops of a suitable non-permanent thread locking compound, then install the bolt into the bottom of the slider **(see illustration 7.20b)**. Tighten the bolt to the specified torque setting. If the damper rod rotates inside the tube, preventing tightening of the bolt, wait until the fork is fully reassembled so that spring pressure holds the damper in place.

50 Push the fork tube fully into the slider, then oil the top bush and slide it down over the tube **(see illustration 7.21a)**. Press the bush squarely into its recess in the slider as far as possible, then install the oil seal washer **(see illustration 7.21b)**. Either use the service tool (Pt. No. 09940-52860) or a suitable piece of tubing to tap the bush fully into place; the tubing must be slightly larger in diameter than the fork tube and slightly smaller in diameter than the bush recess in the slider. Take care not to scratch the fork tube during this operation; it is best to make sure that the fork tube is pushed fully into the slider so that any accidental scratching is confined to the area above the oil seal.

51 When the bush is seated fully and squarely in its recess in the slider (remove the washer to check, wipe the recess clean, then reinstall the washer), install the new oil seal **(see illustration 7.22)**. Smear the seal's lips with fork oil and slide it over the tube so that its markings face upwards and drive the seal into place as described in Step 50 until the retaining clip groove is visible above the seal.

52 Once the seal is correctly seated, fit the retaining clip, making sure it is correctly located in its groove **(see illustration 7.23)**.

53 Lubricate the lips of the new dust seal then slide it down the fork tube and press it into position **(see illustration 7.24)**.

54 Slowly pour in the specified quantity of the specified grade of fork oil and pump the damper rod to distribute it evenly **(see illustration 7.25a)**; the oil level should also be measured and adjustment made by adding or subtracting oil. Fully compress the fork tube into the slider and measure the fork oil level from the top of the tube **(see illustration 7.25b)**. Add or subtract fork oil until the oil is at the level specified in the Specifications Section of this Chapter.

55 Clamp the slider in a vice via the brake caliper mounting lugs, taking care not to overtighten and damage them. Pull the damper rod out of the slider as far as possible and keep it extended either by tying a piece of wire around the rod and having an assistant hold it tight, or by using service tool (Pt. No. 09940-52840) or an equivalent which threads onto the top of the damper rod. Thread the locknut down as far as possible down the

5

damper rod. Install the spring, with its tapered end downwards, followed by the spring seat and the spacer. Using the spacer as a grip, compress the spring far enough so that the slotted collar can be inserted, shouldered side down, in the top of the spacer below the damper rod locknut. Slowly release the spring, making sure the spring seat, spacer and slotted collar are correctly seated against each other.

56 Fit a new O-ring onto the fork top bolt and thread the bolt onto the damper rod as far as possible by hand. Counter-holding the base of the pre-load adjuster, tighten the locknut on the damper rod securely against the fork top bolt.

57 Extend the fork tube and screw the top bolt carefully into the tube making sure it is not cross-threaded. **Note:** *The top bolt can be tightened to the specified torque setting at this stage if the tube is held between the padded jaws of a vice, but do not risk distorting the tube by doing so. A better method is to tighten the top bolt when the fork has been installed in the bike and is securely held in the bottom yoke.*

58 Install the forks (see Section 6). Adjust the fork pre-load (see Section 12).

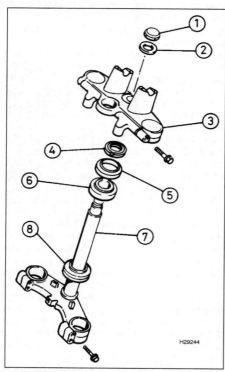

8.8a Steering stem components

1 *Steering stem nut*
2 *Washer*
3 *Top yoke*
4 *Adjuster nut*
5 *Bearing cover*
6 *Upper bearing*
7 *Bottom yoke and steering stem*
8 *Lower bearing*

8.5a Remove the bolt securing the brake hose union (arrow) . . .

8 Steering stem - removal and installation

Caution: Although not strictly necessary, before removing the steering stem it is recommended that the fuel tank be removed. This will prevent accidental damage to the paintwork.

Removal

1 On S models, remove the fairing (see Chapter 7).
2 On models without a fairing, remove the headlight (see Chapter 8).
3 Remove the handlebars (see Section 5).
4 Remove the instrument cluster (see Chapter 8).
5 Unscrew the bolt securing the brake hose union and the screw securing the speedometer cable guide to the bottom yoke **(see illustrations)**.
6 Remove the front forks (see Section 6).
7 On S models, trace the ignition switch wiring and disconnect it at the connector.
8 On models without a fairing, remove the headlight brackets (with the turn signals attached), noting how they fit.
9 Remove the steering stem nut and washer **(see illustrations)**. Lift the top yoke off the steering stem.
10 Supporting the bottom yoke, unscrew the adjuster nut using a suitable C-spanner, then

8.8b Steering stem nut (arrow)

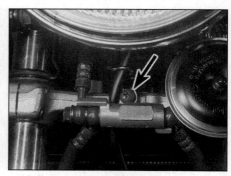

8.5b . . . and the screw securing the speedometer cable guide

remove the adjuster and the bearing cover from the steering stem.
11 Gently lower the bottom yoke and steering stem out of the frame.
12 Remove the upper bearing from the top of the steering head. Remove all traces of old grease from the bearings and races and check them for wear or damage as described in Section 9. **Note:** *Do not attempt to remove the outer races from the frame or the lower bearing from the steering stem unless they are to be replaced.*

Installation

13 Smear a liberal quantity of grease on the bearing outer races in the frame. Work the grease well into both the upper and lower bearings.
14 Carefully lift the steering stem/bottom yoke up through the frame. Install the upper bearing in the top of the steering head. Install the bearing cover and thread the adjuster nut on the steering stem. Tighten the adjuster nut to the torque setting specified at the beginning of the Chapter, then turn the steering stem through its full lock five or six times, and then slacken the adjuster nut by 1/4 to 1/2 turn. If it is not possible to apply a torque wrench to the adjuster nut, tighten the nut to settle the bearings, then slacken it off 1/2 a turn and adjust the bearings as described in Chapter 1 after the installation procedure is complete.

Caution: Take great care not to apply excessive pressure because this will cause premature failure of the bearings.

15 Install the top yoke onto the steering stem. Install the steering stem nut and its washer and tighten it finger-tight at this stage. Temporarily install one of the forks to align the top and bottom yokes, and secure it by tightening the bottom yoke clamp bolt only.
16 Tighten the steering stem nut to the specified torque setting.
17 On models without a fairing, install the headlight brackets (with the turn signals attached) between the yokes, making sure the rubbers are in place and the holes of the

8.17 Make sure the headlight brackets and their dampers are correctly installed

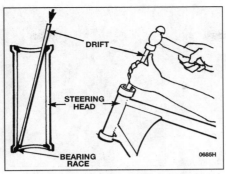

9.4 Drive the bearing outer races out with a drift as shown

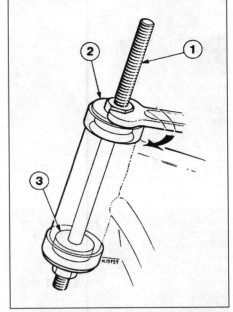

9.6 Drawbolt arrangement for fitting steering stem bearing outer races

1 Long bolt or threaded bar
2 Thick washer
3 Guide for lower race

headlight brackets align with the holes in the yokes **(see illustration)**.

18 On S models, reconnect the ignition switch wiring connector.

19 Install the front forks (see Section 6).

20 Install the brake hose union and the speedometer cable guide onto the bottom yoke **(see illustrations 8.5a and b)**. Make sure the pin on the hose union bracket locates in the hole in the underside of the yoke.

21 Install the instrument cluster (see Chapter 8).

22 Install the handlebars (see Section 5).

23 On models without a fairing, install the headlight (see Chapter 8).

24 On S models, install the fairing (see Chapter 8).

25 Carry out a check of the steering head bearing freeplay as described in Chapter 1, and if necessary re-adjust.

9 Steering head bearings - inspection and replacement

Inspection

1 Remove the steering stem (see Section 8).

2 Remove all traces of old grease from the bearings and races and check them for wear or damage.

3 The outer races should be polished and free from indentations. Inspect the bearing rollers for signs of wear, damage or discoloration, and examine the bearing roller retainer cage for signs of cracks or splits. Spin the bearings by hand. They should spin freely and smoothly. If there are any signs of wear on any of the above components both upper and lower bearing assemblies must be replaced as a set. Only remove the races if they need to be replaced - do not re-use them once they have been removed.

Replacement

4 The outer races are an interference fit in the steering head and can be tapped from position with a suitable drift **(see illustration)**.

Tap firmly and evenly around each race to ensure that it is driven out squarely. It may prove advantageous to curve the end of the drift slightly to improve access.

5 Alternatively, the races can be removed using a slide-hammer type bearing extractor; these can often be hired from tool shops.

6 The new outer races can be pressed into the head using a drawbolt arrangement **(see illustration)**, or by using a large diameter tubular drift which bears only on the outer edge of the race. Ensure that the drawbolt washer or drift (as applicable) bears only on the outer edge of the race and does not contact the working surface. Alternatively, have the races installed by a Suzuki dealer equipped with the bearing race installing tools.

HAYNES HINT *Installation of new bearing outer races is made much easier if the races are left overnight in the freezer. This causes them to contract slightly making them a looser fit.*

7 To remove the lower bearing from the steering stem, use two screwdrivers placed on opposite sides of the race to work it free. If

the bearing is firmly in place it will be necessary to use a bearing puller, or in extreme circumstances to split the bearing's inner section **(see illustration)**. Take the steering stem to a Suzuki dealer if required.

8 Fit the new lower bearing onto the steering stem. A length of tubing with an internal diameter slightly larger than the steering stem will be needed to tap the new bearing into position **(see illustration)**. Ensure that the drift bears only on the inner edge of the bearing and does not contact the rollers.

9 Install the steering stem (see Section 8).

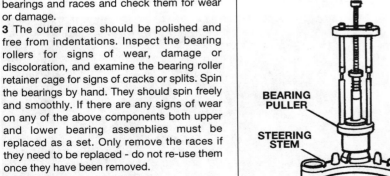

9.7 It is best to remove the lower bearing using a puller

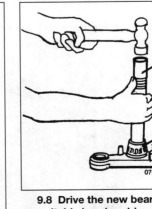

9.8 Drive the new bearing on using a suitable bearing driver or a length of tubing that bears only against the inner race and not against the rollers or cage

5

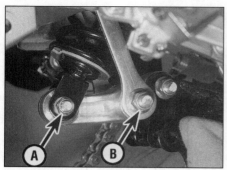

10.2 Shock absorber lower mounting bolt (A), suspension linkage rod bolt (B)

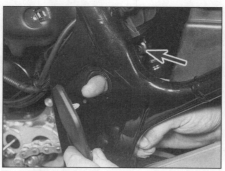

10.4a Remove the cover by poking it from the inside for access to the shock absorber upper mounting bolt (arrow) . . .

10.4b . . . then unscrew the bolt using a socket extension inserted through the hole . . .

10.4c . . . and manoeuvre the shock absorber downwards

10.6 Inspect the damper rod for pitting and leakage (arrow) . . .

10 Rear shock absorber - removal, inspection and installation

Removal

1 Place the machine on its centrestand or support it upright using an auxiliary stand. Position a support under the rear wheel so that it does not drop when the shock absorber is removed, but also making sure that the weight of the machine is off the rear suspension so that the shock is not compressed.

2 Unscrew the nut and withdraw the bolt securing the bottom of the shock absorber to the suspension linkage arm (see illustration).
3 Unscrew the nut and withdraw the bolt securing the suspension linkage rods to the linkage arm, then swing the linkage arm down to provide clearance for removal of the shock absorber (see illustration 10.2).
4 Access to the shock absorber upper mounting bolt is best achieved via the hole in the left-hand side of the frame. Remove the blanking cover, then counter-hold the nut and unscrew the bolt, using a socket extension inserted through the hole (see illustrations). Support the shock absorber and withdraw the bolt, then manoeuvre the shock absorber out

through the bottom of the swingarm (see illustration).

Inspection

5 Inspect the shock absorber for obvious physical damage and the coil spring for looseness, cracks or signs of fatigue.
6 Inspect the damper rod for signs of bending, pitting and oil leakage (see illustration).
7 Inspect the pivot hardware at the top and bottom of the shock for wear or damage (see illustration).
8 If the shock absorber is in any way damaged or worn it must be replaced. Individual replacement components are not available.

Installation

9 Installation is the reverse of removal, noting the following.
a) Apply general purpose grease to the pivot points and to the bearings in the linkage arm.
b) Install the upper mounting bolt first, but do not tighten it until the lower mounting bolt and linkage rod bolt are installed.
c) Tighten all the bolts to the torque settings specified at the beginning of the Chapter (see illustration).
d) Adjust the suspension as required (see Section 12).

10.7 . . . and the top bush for wear and deterioration

10.9 Tighten the bolts to the specified torque setting

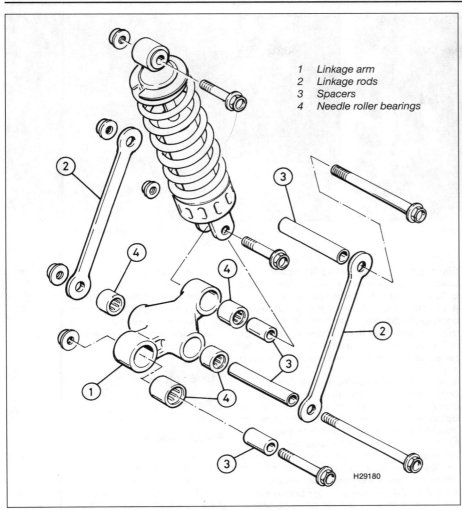

1 Linkage arm
2 Linkage rods
3 Spacers
4 Needle roller bearings

H29180

11.2a Suspension linkage components

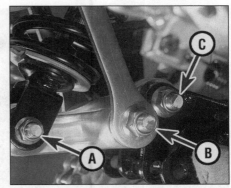

11.2b Shock absorber lower mounting bolt (A), linkage rod bolt (B), linkage arm bolt (C)

11.2c Remove the shock absorber lower mounting bolt . . .

11 Rear suspension linkage - removal, inspection and installation

Removal

1 Place the machine on its centrestand or support it upright using an auxiliary stand.

Position a support under the rear wheel so that it does not drop when the shock absorber is removed, but also making sure that the weight of the machine is off the rear suspension so that the shock is not compressed.

2 Unscrew the nut and withdraw the bolt securing the linkage arm to the bottom of the shock absorber (see illustrations).

3 Unscrew the nut and withdraw the bolt securing the linkage arm to the linkage rods (see illustration).

4 Unscrew the nut and withdraw the bolt securing the linkage arm to the frame, then remove the arm from the frame, noting how it fits (see illustration).

5 Unscrew the nut from the bolt securing the linkage rods to the swingarm and remove the right-hand rod (see illustration). To allow room for the bolt to be withdrawn, push the spacer through from the left, then withdraw the bolt at an angle so that it clears the

11.3 . . . the linkage rods bolt . . .

11.4 . . . and the linkage arm bolt, then remove the arm from the frame

11.5a Unscrew the nut . . .

5

11.5b ... and remove the right-hand rod

11.5c Push the spacer through (arrow) and remove the bolt at an angle

11.6 Linkage arm bearing spacers

footrest bracket, and remove the other linkage rod (see illustrations).

Inspection

6 Withdraw the spacers from the linkage arm, noting their different sizes (see illustration). Thoroughly clean all components, removing all traces of dirt, corrosion and grease.
7 Inspect all components closely, looking for obvious signs of wear such as heavy scoring, or for damage such as cracks or distortion.

Slip each spacer back into its bearing and check that there is not an excessive amount of freeplay between the two components.
8 Check the condition of the needle roller bearings in the linkage arm and in the top of the swingarm (see illustration). If the linkage rod bearings in the swingarm need to be replaced, remove the swingarm (see Section 13).
9 Worn bearings can be drifted out of their bores, but note that removal will destroy them; new bearings should be obtained before work commences. The new bearings should be pressed or drawn into their bores rather than driven into position. In the absence of a press, a suitable drawbolt tool can be made up as described in *Tools and Workshop Tips* in the Reference section.
10 Lubricate the needle roller bearings and the pivot bolts with general purpose grease and install the spacers (see illustration).

Installation

11 Installation is the reverse of removal, noting the following.
a) *Apply general purpose grease to the pivot points and pivot bolts.*

b) *Do not fully tighten any of the bolts until they have all been installed.*
c) *Tighten the bolts to the torque setting specified at the beginning of the Chapter.*
d) *Check the operation of the rear suspension before taking the machine on the road.*

12 Suspension - adjustments

Front forks

1 On GSF600 and GSF600S models, the front forks are not adjustable.
2 On GSF1200 and GSF1200S models, the front forks are adjustable for pre-load. Place the machine on its centrestand or an auxiliary stand and take the weight off the front forks, either by placing a support under the engine or by having an assistant press down on the rear of the machine, when making adjustments.
3 Adjustment is made by turning the adjuster in the centre of the fork top bolt using a large

11.8 Check the needle roller bearings for wear and damage

11.10 Lubricate all the bearings with grease and install the spacers

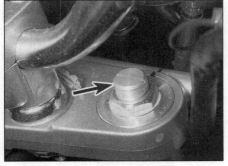

12.3a Turn the adjuster (arrow) using a large flat-bladed screwdriver

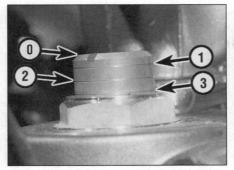

12.3b Standard pre-load setting (no.3)

12.6 Use the C-spanner provided in the toolkit to adjust the rear shock pre-load

flat-bladed screwdriver **(see illustration)**. There are six positions (0, 1, 2, 3, 4, 5), indicated by lines on the adjuster. Position 5 (ie with all 4 lines fully showing above the bolt hex) is the softest setting, position 0 (ie adjuster head level with top bolt hex surface) is the hardest. Align the setting line required with the top of the bolt hex. Position 3 is the standard setting **(see illustration)**.

4 To increase the pre-load, turn the adjuster clockwise. To decrease the pre-load, turn the adjuster anti-clockwise.

Rear shock absorber

5 On all models the rear shock absorber is adjustable for spring pre-load. On GSF1200 and GSF1200S, the rear shock absorber is also adjustable for rebound damping. Place the machine on its sidestand when making adjustments.

6 Pre-load adjustment is made using a suitable C-spanner (one is provided in the toolkit) to turn the spring seat on the top of the shock absorber **(see illustration)**. There are seven positions. Position 1 is the softest setting, position 7 is the hardest. Align the setting number required with the adjustment stopper. Position 4 is the standard setting.

7 To increase the pre-load, turn the spring seat clockwise. To decrease the pre-load, turn the spring seat anti-clockwise.

8 On GSF1200 and GSF1200S, rebound damping adjustment is made by turning the adjuster on the bottom of the shock absorber **(see illustration)**. There are four positions. Position 1 is the softest setting, position 4 the hardest. Turn the adjuster until it aligns with the setting number required. An audible click will be heard and a detent in the adjuster felt when it is correctly aligned with a position. Do not set the adjuster in between any of the positions. Position 2 is the standard setting.

9 To increase the damping, turn the adjuster clockwise. To decrease the damping, turn the adjuster anti-clockwise.

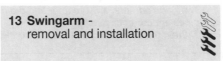

13 Swingarm -
removal and installation

Removal

Note: *Before removing the swingarm, it is advisable to perform the rear suspension checks described in Chapter 1.*

1 Remove the rear brake caliper, but do not disconnect its hydraulic hose (see Chapter 6). Remove the rear wheel (see Chapter 6).

2 Remove the rear shock absorber (see Section 10).

3 Release the brake hose from its clamps and

12.8 Turn the adjuster (arrow) to set rebound damping

withdraw it from the guide on the swingarm. Position the hose clear of the swingarm so that it doesn't impede removal.

4 If required, remove the bolt securing the brake torque arm to the swingarm **(see illustration)**.

5 Prise off the swingarm pivot caps on both sides of the swingarm **(see illustration)**.

6 Before removing the swingarm it is advisable to re-check for play in the bearings. Any problems which may have been overlooked with the wheel and shock absorber in place (see Chapter 1) are highlighted with these components removed.

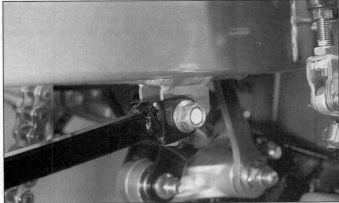

13.4 Brake torque arm front mounting bolt

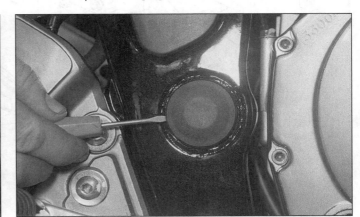

13.5 Remove the swingarm pivot caps

5

13.7a Remove the nut and washer (arrow) . . .

13.7b . . . and withdraw the bolt from the left

13.11 Tighten the swingarm pivot bolt nut to the specified torque setting

7 Unscrew the nut and remove the washer on the right-hand end of the swingarm pivot bolt **(see illustration)**. With the aid of an assistant to support the swingarm if required, drift the pivot bolt out and withdraw it from the left-hand side of the frame **(see illustration)**. Note the positions of any breather and drain pipes and move them aside if necessary, then manoeuvre the swingarm out of the back of the machine.
8 Unscrew the nut and remove the bolt securing the suspension linkage rods to the swingarm.
9 Check the condition of the chain slider on the front of the swingarm and replace it if it is worn or damaged.
10 Inspect all components for wear or damage (see Section 14).

Installation

11 Installation is the reverse of removal, noting the following.

a) *Remove the inner sleeve from each swingarm bearing, then lubricate the bearings and inner sleeves with general purpose grease (see illustration 14.1). Fit the inner sleeves back into the bearings. Also lubricate the pivot bolt and the shock absorber pivot and suspension linkage bearings with grease.*
b) *Loop the drive chain over the swingarm as it is offered up to the frame. Make sure that the chain slider is fitted to the swingarm and that any breather and drain pipes are correctly positioned.*
c) *Tighten the swingarm pivot bolt nut to the*

torque setting specified at the beginning of the Chapter **(see illustration)**.
d) *Secure the brake hose in its clamps and pass it through its guide. Tighten the brake torque arm nuts to the specified torque setting.*
e) *Tighten the shock absorber and linkage bolts to the specified torque settings.*
f) *Check the operation of the rear suspension before taking the machine on the road.*

14 Swingarm - inspection and bearing replacement

Inspection

1 Thoroughly clean all components, removing all traces of dirt, corrosion and grease **(see illustration)**.
2 Inspect all components closely, looking for obvious signs of wear such as heavy scoring, and cracks or distortion due to accident damage. Any damaged or worn component must be replaced.
3 Check the swingarm pivot bolt for straightness by rolling it on a flat surface such as a piece of plate glass (first wipe off all old grease and remove any corrosion using fine emery cloth). If the equipment is available, place the axle in V-blocks and measure the runout using a dial indicator. If the axle is bent or the runout exceeds the limit specified, replace it.

Bearing replacement

4 Remove the bearing inner sleeves. Inspect them and the bearings for signs of wear or damage and replace them if necessary.
5 Worn bearings can be drifted out of their bores, but note that removal will destroy them; new bearings should be obtained before work commences. Pass a long drift through the swingarm and push the centre space aside so that the drift can bear on the inner edge of the bearing. Tap the drift around the bearing's inner edge to ensure that it leaves its bore squarely. Once removed, withdraw the centre spacer and use the same

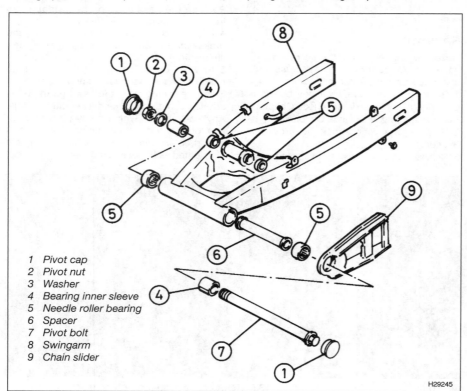

1 Pivot cap
2 Pivot nut
3 Washer
4 Bearing inner sleeve
5 Needle roller bearing
6 Spacer
7 Pivot bolt
8 Swingarm
9 Chain slider

H29245

14.1 Swingarm components

method to extract the other bearing. If available, a slide-hammer with knife-edged bearing puller can be used to extract the bearings.

6 The new bearings should be pressed or drawn into their bores rather than driven into position. In the absence of a press, a suitable drawbolt arrangement can be made up as described in *Tools and Workshop Tips* in the Reference section. Do not forget to install the centre spacer between the two bearings, and fit the bearings with their marked side facing out.

15 Drive chain - removal, cleaning and installation

Removal

Note: *The original equipment drive chain fitted to all models is an endless chain. Removal requires the removal of the swingarm as detailed below, or if the necessary chain breaking and joining tool is available, the chain can be separated and rejoined (see Tools and Workshop Tips in the Reference section).*

> ⚠ **Warning: NEVER install a drive chain which uses a clip-type master (split) link.**

1 Remove the swingarm (see Section 13).
2 Unscrew the gearchange linkage arm pinch bolt and remove the arm from the shaft, noting any alignment marks **(see illustration)**. If no marks are visible, make your own before removing the arm so that it can be correctly aligned with the shaft on installation. Unscrew the bolts securing the engine sprocket cover to the crankcase and move it aside **(see illustration)**. There is no need to detach the clutch cable or release cylinder from the cover. On GSF1200 and GSF1200S, do not operate the clutch lever with the sprocket cover removed.
3 Slip the chain off the front sprocket and remove it from the bike.

Cleaning

4 Soak the chain in paraffin (kerosene) for approximately five or six minutes.

15.2a Make some alignment marks (arrows) then remove the pinch bolt

Caution: Don't use gasoline (petrol), solvent or other cleaning fluids. Don't use high-pressure water. Remove the chain, wipe it off, then blow dry it with compressed air immediately. The entire process shouldn't take longer than ten minutes - if it does, the O-rings in the chain rollers could be damaged.

Installation

5 Installation is the reverse of removal. On completion adjust and lubricate the chain following the procedures described in Chapter 1.
Caution: Use only the recommended lubricant.

16 Sprockets - check and replacement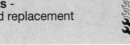

Check

1 Unscrew the gearchange linkage arm pinch bolt and remove the arm from the shaft, noting any alignment marks **(see illustration 15.2a)**. If no marks are visible, make your own before removing the arm so that it can be correctly aligned with the shaft on installation. Unscrew the bolts securing the engine sprocket cover to the crankcase and move the cover aside **(see illustration 15.2b)**. There is no need to detach the clutch cable or release cylinder from the cover. On GSF1200

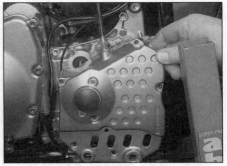

15.2b Remove the sprocket cover

and GSF1200S, do not operate the clutch lever with the sprocket cover removed.
2 Check the wear pattern on both sprockets **(see illustration)**. If the sprocket teeth are worn excessively, replace the chain and both sprockets as a set. Whenever the sprockets are inspected, the drive chain should be inspected also (see Chapter 1). If you are replacing the chain, replace the sprockets as well.
3 Adjust and lubricate the chain following the procedures described in Chapter 1.
Caution: Use only the recommended lubricant.

Replacement

Front sprocket

4 Unscrew the gearchange linkage arm pinch bolt and remove the arm from the shaft, noting any alignment marks **(see illustration 15.2a)**. If no marks are visible, make your own before removing the arm so that it can be correctly aligned with the shaft on installation. Unscrew the bolts securing the engine sprocket cover to the crankcase and move the cover aside **(see illustration 15.2b)**. There is no need to detach the clutch cable or release cylinder from the cover. On GSF1200 and GSF1200S, do not operate the clutch lever with the sprocket cover removed.
5 On GSF600 and GSF600S, install the gearchange linkage arm onto the shaft and shift the transmission into gear, then have an assistant sit on the seat and apply the rear

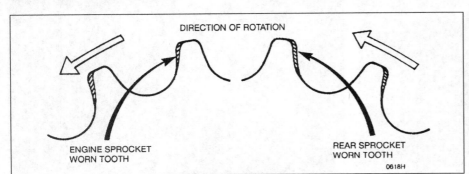

16.2 Check the sprocket teeth for wear

16.5 Front sprocket lockbolt (A) and nut (B)

16.7 Slide the sprocket off the shaft and slip it out of the chain

16.9a Install the washer . . .

16.9b . . . and the nut . . .

brake hard. This will lock the transmission and enable you to slacken and remove the engine sprocket lockbolt and nut. Unscrew the lockbolt in the centre of the sprocket nut and remove it with its washer (see illustration). Now unscrew the sprocket nut and remove it with its washer.

6 On GSF1200 and GSF1200S, install the gearchange linkage arm onto the shaft and shift the transmission into gear, then have an assistant sit on the seat and apply the rear brake hard. This will lock the transmission and enable you to slacken and remove the engine sprocket nut. Bend back the tabs on the sprocket nut lockwasher, then unscrew the

sprocket nut and remove it with the lockwasher. Check the condition of the lockwasher as a new one should be used if it is weakened or damaged.

7 Slide the sprocket and chain off the shaft, then slip the sprocket out of the chain (see illustration). If the chain is too tight to allow the sprocket to be slid off the shaft, slacken the chain adjusters to provide some freeplay (see Chapter 1), or, if the rear sprocket is being replaced as well, remove the rear wheel.

8 Engage the new sprocket with the chain and slide it on the shaft.

9 On GSF600 and GSF600S install the sprocket nut with its washer and tighten it to

the torque setting specified at the beginning of the Chapter, using the method employed on removal to prevent the transmission from turning (see illustrations). Now install the lockbolt with its washer, and tighten it to the specified torque setting (see illustration).

10 On GSF1200 and GSF1200S install the sprocket nut with its lockwasher and tighten it to the torque setting specified at the beginning of the Chapter, using the method employed on removal to prevent the transmission from turning (see illustration). Bend up the tabs on the lockwasher to secure the nut (see illustration).

11 Install the sprocket cover and the

16.9c . . . and tighten it to the specified torque setting

16.9d Then install the lockbolt and its washer . . .

16.9e . . . and tighten it to the specified torque setting

16.10a Install the lockwasher . . .

16.10b . . . and bend up its tabs after the nut is tightened

16.13 The rear sprocket is secured by five nuts (arrows)

17.2 Lift the sprocket coupling out of the wheel . . .

17.3 . . . and check the damper segments for wear and deterioration

gearchange linkage arm, aligning the punch marks **(see illustrations 15.2b and 15.2a)**. Adjust and lubricate the chain following the procedures described in Chapter 1.

Rear sprocket

12 Remove the rear wheel (see Chapter 6).
13 Unscrew the nuts securing the sprocket to the wheel coupling, then remove the sprocket, noting which way round it fits **(see illustration)**.
14 Before installing the new rear sprocket, check the wheel coupling and damper assembly components (see Section 17).
15 Install the sprocket onto the coupling with the stamped mark facing out, then tighten the sprocket nuts to the torque setting specified at the beginning of the Chapter.

16 Install the rear wheel (see Chapter 6).
17 Adjust and lubricate the chain following the procedures described in Chapter 1.

17 Rear wheel coupling/rubber dampers - check and replacement

1 Remove the rear wheel (see Chapter 6).
Caution: Do not lay the wheel down on the disc as it could become warped. Lay the wheel on wooden blocks so that the disc is off the ground.
2 Lift the sprocket coupling away from the wheel leaving the rubber dampers in position

in the wheel **(see illustration)**. Note the spacer inside the coupling. Check the coupling for cracks or any obvious signs of damage. Also check the sprocket studs for wear or damage.
3 Lift the rubber damper segments from the wheel and check them for cracks, hardening and general deterioration **(see illustration)**. Replace the rubber dampers as a set if necessary.
4 Checking and replacement procedures for the sprocket coupling bearing are described in Section 16 of Chapter 6.
5 Installation is the reverse of removal. Make sure the spacer is correctly installed in the coupling.
6 Install the rear wheel (see Chapter 6).

5

Notes

Chapter 6
Brakes, wheels and tyres

Contents

Degrees of difficulty

Easy, suitable for novice with little experience	Fairly easy, suitable for beginner with some experience	Fairly difficult, suitable for competent DIY mechanic	Difficult, suitable for experienced DIY mechanic	Very difficult, suitable for expert DIY or professional 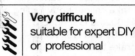

Specifications

Brakes

Brake fluid type	DOT 4
Disc minimum thickness	
Front	
Standard	4.3 to 4.7 mm
Service limit	4.0 mm
Rear	
Standard	4.8 to 5.2 mm
Service limit	4.5 mm
Disc maximum runout (front and rear, all models)	0.3 mm
Caliper bore ID	
Front	
GSF600 and GSF600S	25.400 to 25.450 mm
GSF1200 and GSF1200S	
Piston A	30.230 to 30.280 mm
Piston B	33.960 to 34.010 mm
Rear	38.180 to 38.256 mm
Caliper piston OD	
GSF600 and GSF600S	25.335 to 25.368 mm
GSF1200 and GSF1200S	
Piston A	30.160 to 30.180 mm
Piston B	33.878 to 33.928 mm
Rear	38.098 to 38.148 mm
Master cylinder bore ID	
Front	
GSF600 and GSF600S	14.000 to 14.043 mm
GSF1200 and GSF1200S	15.870 to 15.913 mm
Rear	12.700 to 12.743 mm
Master cylinder piston OD	
Front	
GSF600 and GSF600S	13.957 to 13.984 mm
GSF1200 and GSF1200S	15.827 to 15.854 mm
Rear	12.657 to 12.684 mm

Wheels

Maximum wheel runout (front and rear)
Axial (side-to-side) . . . . 2.0 mm
Radial (out-of-round) . . . . 2.0 mm
Maximum axle runout (front and rear) . . . . 0.25 mm

Tyres

Tyre pressures . . . . see Daily (pre-ride) checks
Tyre sizes*
GSF600 and GSF600S
Front 110/70-17 54H
Rear 150/70-17 69H
GSF1200 and GSF1200S
Front 120/70-ZR17
Rear 180/55-ZR17
*Refer to the owners handbook or the tyre information label on the swingarm for approved tyre brands.

Torque settings

Front brake pad retaining pin . . . . 18 Nm
Front brake caliper body joining bolts (GSF1200 and GSF1200S) . . . . . 23 Nm
Front brake caliper mounting bolts
GSF600 and GSF600S . . . . 25 Nm
GSF1200 and GSF1200S . . . . 39 Nm
Front brake disc retaining bolts . . . . 23 Nm
Front brake master cylinder clamp bolts . . . . 10 Nm
Rear brake caliper mounting bolts . . . . 25 Nm
Rear brake caliper body joining bolts
GSF600 and GSF600S . . . . 33 Nm
GSF1200 and GSF1200S . . . . 30 Nm
Rear brake torque arm nuts . . . . 35 Nm
Rear brake disc retaining bolts . . . . 23 Nm
Rear brake master cylinder mounting bolts . . . . 23 Nm
Brake caliper bleed valves . . . . 8 Nm
Brake hose banjo union bolts . . . . 23 Nm
Front axle
GSF600 and GSF600S . . . . 65 Nm
GSF1200 and GSF1200S . . . . 100 Nm
Front axle clamp bolts . . . . 23 Nm
Rear axle nut . . . . 100 Nm

1 General information

All models covered in this manual are fitted with cast alloy wheels designed for tubeless tyres only. Both front and rear brakes are hydraulically operated disc brakes. On GSF600 and GSF600S, the front has dual sliding calipers with twin pistons, the rear has a single caliper with single opposed pistons. On GSF1200 and GSF1200S, the front has dual calipers with twin opposed pistons, the rear has a single caliper with single opposed pistons.
Caution: Disc brake components rarely require disassembly. Do not disassemble components unless absolutely necessary. If a hydraulic brake line is loosened, the entire system must be disassembled, drained, cleaned and then properly filled and bled upon reassembly. Do not use solvents on internal brake components. Solvents will cause the seals to swell and distort. Use only clean brake fluid or denatured alcohol for cleaning. Use care when working with brake fluid as it can

injure your eyes and it will damage painted surfaces and plastic parts.

2 Front brake pads - replacement

⚠️ **Warning: The dust created by the brake system may contain asbestos, which is harmful to**

your health. Never blow it out with compressed air and don't inhale any of it. An approved filtering mask should be worn when working on the brakes.

1 On GSF600 and GSF600S, unscrew the pad retaining pin plug followed by the pad retaining pin, then remove the pads, noting how they locate against the guide (see illustrations). Also note how the pad spring is fitted and remove it if required.

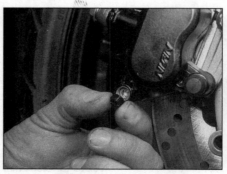

2.1a Remove the pad pin plug . . .

2.1b . . . followed by the pad pin. Note how the pads fit against the spring (arrow)

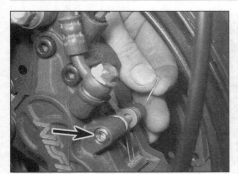

2.2a Remove the split pin, then unscrew the pad pin (arrow) . . .

2.2b . . . and remove the pad spring . . .

2.2c . . . and the pads

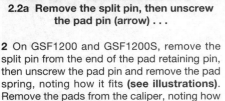

2 On GSF1200 and GSF1200S, remove the split pin from the end of the pad retaining pin, then unscrew the pad pin and remove the pad spring, noting how it fits (see illustrations). Remove the pads from the caliper, noting how they fit (see illustration).

3 Inspect the surface of each pad for contamination and check that the friction material has not worn beyond its service limit (see Chapter 1, Section 13). If either pad is worn down to, or beyond, the service limit wear groove (ie the grooves are no longer visible), fouled with oil or grease, or heavily scored or damaged by dirt and debris, both pads must be replaced as a set. Note that it is not possible to degrease the friction material; if the pads are contaminated in any way they must be replaced.

4 If the pads are in good condition clean them carefully, using a fine wire brush which is completely free of oil and grease to remove all traces of road dirt and corrosion. Using a pointed instrument, clean out the grooves in the friction material and dig out any embedded particles of foreign matter. Any areas of glazing may be removed using emery cloth.

5 Check the condition of the brake disc (see Section 4).

6 Remove all traces of corrosion from the pad pin. Inspect the pin for signs of damage and replace if necessary.

7 Push the pistons as far back into the caliper as possible using hand pressure only. Due to

the increased friction material thickness of new pads, it may be necessary to remove the master cylinder reservoir cover and diaphragm and siphon out some fluid.

8 Smear the backs of the pads and the shank of the pad pin with copper-based grease, making sure that none gets on the front or sides of the pads.

9 On GSF600 and GSF600S, installation of the pads is the reverse of removal. Make sure the pad spring and guide plate are correctly positioned in the caliper. Insert the pads into the caliper so that the friction material of each pad faces the disc (see illustration). Make sure the pads locate correctly against the guide plate (see illustration). Install the pad

retaining pin, making sure it passes through the hole in each pad, and tighten it to the torque setting specified at the beginning of the Chapter (see illustration 2.1b). Install the pad pin plug (see illustration 2.1a).

10 On GSF1200 and GSF1200S, installation of the pads and pad pin is the reverse of removal. Insert the pads into the caliper so that the friction material of each pad faces the disc (see illustration). Fit the pad spring, making sure it is correctly positioned, then install the pad pin so that it passes through each pad and locates on top of the spring (see illustration). Tighten the pin to the specified torque setting and secure it with the split pin (see illustration).

2.9a Install the pads . . .

2.9b . . . making sure the ends locate correctly against the guide plate (arrow)

2.10a Install the pads . . .

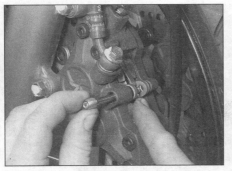

2.10b . . . the pad spring, and the pad pin. Press down on the spring when installing the pin so that the pin locates on top of the spring

2.10c Tighten the pad pin to the specified torque setting

6

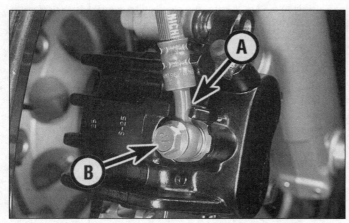

3.1 Note the alignment of the brake hose (A) before unscrewing the banjo bolt (B) - 600 model shown

3.2 Remove the speedometer cable guide bolt (arrow)

11 Top up the master cylinder reservoir if necessary (see *Daily (pre-ride) checks*), and replace the reservoir cover and diaphragm.
12 Operate the brake lever several times to bring the pads into contact with the disc. Check the operation of the brake before riding the motorcycle.

 3 Front brake calipers -
removal, overhaul and installation

 Warning: If a caliper indicates the need for an overhaul (usually due to leaking fluid or sticky operation), all old brake fluid should be flushed from the system. Also, the dust created by the brake system may contain asbestos, which is harmful to your health. Never blow it out with compressed air and don't inhale any of it. An approved filtering mask should be worn when working on the brakes. Do not, under any circumstances, use petroleum-based solvents to clean brake parts. Use clean

brake fluid, brake cleaner or denatured alcohol only.
Note: *Before overhauling the caliper check the availability of the caliper seals with a Suzuki dealer - on certain models it may only be possible to purchase new seals complete with the pistons.*

Removal

1 Remove the brake hose banjo bolt, noting its alignment on the caliper and separate the hose from the caliper **(see illustration)**. Plug the hose end or wrap a plastic bag tightly around it to minimise fluid loss and prevent dirt entering the system. Discard the sealing washers as new ones must be used on installation. **Note:** *If you are planning to overhaul the caliper and don't have a source of compressed air to blow out the pistons, just loosen the banjo bolt at this stage and retighten it lightly. The bike's hydraulic system can then be used to force the pistons out of the body once the pads have been removed. Disconnect the hose once the pistons have been sufficiently displaced.*
2 On GSF600 and GSF600S models, unscrew the bolt securing the speedometer

3.3 Caliper body joining bolts (arrows)

cable guide to the left-hand side caliper and remove the guide **(see illustration)**.
3 On GSF1200 and GSF1200S models, if the caliper body is to be split into its halves for seal replacement, it is advisable to slacken the caliper body joining bolts at this stage and retighten them lightly **(see illustration)**.
4 Unscrew the caliper mounting bolts, and slide the caliper away from the disc **(see illustrations)**. Remove the brake pads (see Section 2).

3.4a Caliper mounting bolts (arrows) - 600 models

3.4b Caliper mounting bolts (arrows) - 1200 models

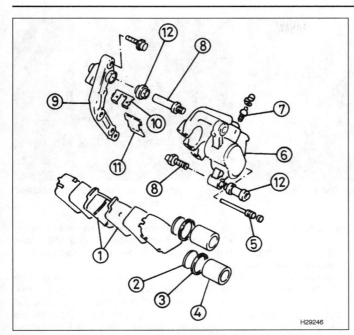

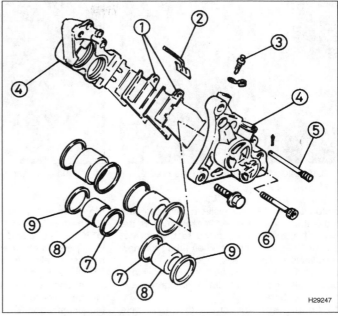

3.5a Front brake caliper components - 600 models

1 Brake pads	5 Pad pin	9 Mounting bracket
2 Dust seal	6 Caliper body	10 Guide plate
3 Piston seal	7 Bleed valve	11 Pad spring
4 Piston	8 Slider pin	12 Rubber boot

3.5b Front brake caliper components - 1200 models

1 Brake pads	4 Caliper body	7 Dust seal
2 Pad spring	5 Pad pin	8 Piston
3 Bleed valve	6 Caliper joining bolt	9 Piston seal

Overhaul

5 Clean the exterior of the caliper with denatured alcohol or brake system cleaner **(see illustrations)**.

6 On GSF600 and GSF600S models, remove the pistons from the caliper body, either by pumping them out by operating the front brake lever until the pistons are displaced, or by forcing them out using compressed air. Mark each piston head and caliper body with a felt marker to ensure that the pistons can be matched to their original bores on reassembly. If the compressed air method is used, place a wad of rag between the pistons and the caliper to act as a cushion, then use compressed air directed into the fluid inlet to force the pistons out of the body. Use only low pressure to ease the pistons out and make sure both pistons are displaced at the same time. If the air pressure is too high and the pistons are forced out, the caliper and/or pistons may be damaged.

 Warning: Never place your fingers in front of the pistons in an attempt to catch or protect them when applying compressed air, as serious injury could result.

7 On GSF1200 and GSF1200S models, displace the pistons as far as possible from the caliper body, either by pumping them out by operating the front brake lever, or by forcing them out using compressed air - do not allow opposing piston heads to touch. If the compressed air method is used, place a

wad of rag between the pistons to act as a cushion, then use compressed air directed into the fluid inlet to force the pistons out of the body. Use only low pressure to ease the pistons out. If the air pressure is too high and the pistons are forced out, the caliper and/or pistons may be damaged. Unscrew the caliper body joining bolts and separate the body halves. Remove the piston from each half. Extract the caliper seals from whichever body half it is in and discard them as new ones must be used. Note that two sizes of piston are used (see Specifications), and that different size seals are used accordingly.

8 Using a wooden or plastic tool, remove the dust seals from the caliper bores. Discard them as new ones must be used on installation. If a metal tool is being used, take great care not to damage the caliper bores.

9 Remove and discard the piston seals in the same way.

10 Clean the pistons and bores with denatured alcohol, clean brake fluid or brake system cleaner. If compressed air is available, use it to dry the parts thoroughly (make sure it's filtered and unlubricated).

Caution: Do not, under any circumstances, use a petroleum-based solvent to clean brake parts.

11 Inspect the caliper bores and pistons for signs of corrosion, nicks and burrs and loss of plating. If surface defects are present, the caliper assembly must be replaced. If the necessary measuring equipment is available, compare the dimensions of the pistons and

bores to those given in the Specifications Section of this Chapter, replacing any component that is worn beyond the service limit. If the caliper is in bad shape the master cylinder should also be checked.

12 On GSF600 and GSF600S models, check that the caliper body is able to slide freely on the slider pins. If seized due to corrosion, separate the two components and clean off all traces of corrosion and hardened grease **(see illustration)**. Apply a smear of copper or silicone based grease to the slider pins and reassemble the two components. Replace the rubber boots if they are damaged or deteriorated.

13 Lubricate the new piston seals with clean brake fluid and install them in their grooves in the caliper bores. Note that on GSF1200 and GSF1200S models, two sizes of bore and

3.12 Slide the caliper off the bracket and clean the pins

6

3.18 Slide the caliper onto the disc . . .

3.19a . . . then install the mounting bolts . . .

3.19b . . . and tighten them to the specified torque setting

piston are used (see Specifications), and care must therefore be taken to ensure that the correct size seals are fitted to the correct bores. The same applies when fitting the new dust seals and pistons.

14 Lubricate the new dust seals with clean brake fluid and install them in their grooves in the caliper bores.

15 Lubricate the pistons with clean brake fluid and install them closed-end first into the caliper bores. Using your thumbs, push the pistons all the way in, making sure they enter the bore squarely.

16 On GSF1200 and GSF1200S models, lubricate the new caliper seals with clean brake fluid and install them into one half of the caliper body. Join the two halves of the caliper body together, making sure that the caliper seals are correctly seated in their recess. Install the caliper body joining bolts and tighten them to the torque setting specified at the beginning of the Chapter. If it is not possible to tighten the bolts fully at this stage, tighten them as much as possible, then tighten them fully once the caliper has been installed on the machine.

Installation

17 Install the brake pads (see Section 2).
18 Install the caliper on the brake disc making sure the pads sit squarely either side of the disc **(see illustration)**.
19 Install the caliper mounting bolts, and tighten them to the torque setting specified at

the beginning of this Chapter **(see illustrations)**.
20 On GSF600 and GSF600S models, install the speedometer cable guide onto the left-hand side caliper **(see illustration 3.2)**.
21 On GSF1200 and GSF1200S models, if not already done, tighten the caliper body joining bolts to the specified torque setting **(see illustration 3.3)**.
22 Connect the brake hose to the caliper, using new sealing washers on each side of the fitting. Align the hose as noted on removal **(see illustration 3.1)**. Tighten the banjo bolt to the torque setting specified at the beginning of the Chapter.
23 Fill the master cylinder reservoir with DOT 4 brake fluid (see *Daily (pre-ride) checks*) and bleed the hydraulic system as described in Section 11.
24 Check for leaks and thoroughly test the operation of the brake before riding the motorcycle.

4 Front brake disc - inspection, removal and installation

Inspection

1 Visually inspect the surface of the disc for score marks and other damage. Light scratches are normal after use and won't affect brake operation, but deep grooves and

heavy score marks will reduce braking efficiency and accelerate pad wear. If a disc is badly grooved it must be machined or replaced.
2 To check disc runout, position the bike on its centrestand and support it so that the front wheel is raised off the ground. Mount a dial gauge to a fork leg, with the plunger on the gauge touching the surface of the disc about 10 mm (1/2 in) from the outer edge **(see illustration)**. Rotate the wheel and watch the indicator needle, comparing the reading with the limit listed in the Specifications at the beginning of the Chapter. If the runout is greater than the service limit, check the wheel bearings for play (see Chapter 1). If the bearings are worn, replace them (see Section 16) and repeat this check. If the disc runout is still excessive, it will have to be replaced, although machining by an engineer may be possible.
3 The disc must not be machined or allowed to wear down to a thickness less than the service limit as listed in this Chapter's Specifications and as marked on the disc itself **(see illustration)**. The thickness of the disc can be checked with a micrometer **(see illustration)**. If the thickness of the disc is less than the service limit, it must be replaced.

Removal

4 Remove the wheel (see Section 14).
Caution: Do not lay the wheel down and allow it to rest on the disc - the disc could

4.2 Set up a dial gauge to contact the brake disc, then rotate the wheel to check for runout

4.3a The minimum disc thickness is marked on the disc

4.3b Using a micrometer to measure disc thickness

4.5 The disc is secured by five bolts (arrows)

become warped. Set the wheel on wood blocks so the disc doesn't support the weight of the wheel.

5 Mark the relationship of the disc to the wheel, so it can be installed in the same position. Unscrew the disc retaining bolts, loosening them a little at a time in a criss-cross pattern to avoid distorting the disc, then remove the disc from the wheel **(see illustration)**.

Installation

6 Install the disc on the wheel, aligning the previously applied matchmarks (if you're reinstalling the original disc).
7 Apply a suitable non-permanent thread locking compound to the disc mounting bolt threads, then install the bolts and tighten them in a criss-cross pattern evenly and

5.5 Disconnect the brake light switch electrical connectors

5.7 Remove the brake hose banjo bolt (arrow)

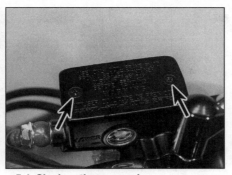

5.4 Slacken the reservoir cover screws (arrows)

progressively to the torque setting specified at the beginning of the Chapter. Clean off all grease from the brake disc(s) using acetone or brake system cleaner. If a new brake disc has been installed, remove any protective coating from its working surfaces.
8 Install the front wheel (see Section 14).
9 Operate the brake lever several times to bring the pads into contact with the disc. Check the operation of the brakes carefully before riding the bike.

5 Front brake master cylinder - removal, overhaul and installation

1 If the master cylinder is leaking fluid, or if the lever does not produce a firm feel when the brake is applied, and bleeding the brakes does not help (see Section 11), and the hydraulic hoses are all in good condition, then master cylinder overhaul is recommended.
2 Before disassembling the master cylinder, read through the entire procedure and make sure that you have the correct rebuild kit. Also, you will need some new DOT 4 brake fluid, some clean rags and internal circlip pliers. **Note:** *To prevent damage to the paint from spilled brake fluid, always cover the fuel tank when working on the master cylinder.*
Caution: Disassembly, overhaul and reassembly of the brake master cylinder must be done in a spotlessly clean work area to avoid contamination and possible

5.8 Front brake master cylinder clamp bolts (arrows)

failure of the brake hydraulic system components.

Removal

3 If required, remove the rear view mirror (see Chapter 7).
4 Loosen, but do not remove, the screws holding the reservoir cover in place **(see illustration)**.
5 Disconnect the electrical connectors from the brake light switch **(see illustration)**.
6 Remove the front brake lever (see Chapter 5).
7 Unscrew the brake hose banjo bolt and separate the hose from the master cylinder, noting its alignment **(see illustration)**. Discard the two sealing washers as they must be replaced with new ones. Wrap the end of the hose in a clean rag and suspend it in an upright position or bend it down carefully and place the open end in a clean container. The objective is to prevent excessive loss of brake fluid, fluid spills and system contamination.
8 Unscrew the master cylinder clamp bolts, then lift the master cylinder and reservoir away from the handlebar, noting how the mating surfaces of the clamp align with the punch mark on the underside of the handlebar **(see illustration)**.
Caution: Do not tip the master cylinder upside down or brake fluid will run out.

Overhaul

9 Remove the reservoir cover retaining screws and lift off the cover, the diaphragm plate and the rubber diaphragm **(see illustration)**. Drain the brake fluid from the reservoir into a suitable container. Wipe any remaining fluid out of the reservoir with a clean rag.

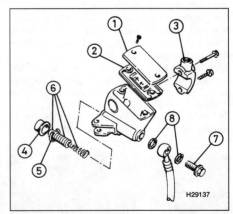

5.9 Front brake master cylinder components

1 Reservoir cover and diaphragm plate
2 Rubber diaphragm
3 Clamp
4 Rubber dust boot
5 Circlip
6 Piston assembly and spring
7 Banjo bolt
8 Sealing washer

6

5.21a Align the mating surfaces of the clamp with the punch mark (arrow) . . .

5.21b . . . and tighten the bolts to the specified torque setting

10 Remove the screw securing the brake light switch to the bottom of the master cylinder and remove the switch.

11 Carefully remove the dust boot from the end of the piston.

12 Using circlip pliers, remove the circlip and slide out the piston assembly and the spring, noting how they fit. Lay the parts out in the proper order to prevent confusion during reassembly.

13 Clean all parts with clean brake fluid or denatured alcohol. If compressed air is available, use it to dry the parts thoroughly (make sure it's filtered and unlubricated).

Caution: Do not, under any circumstances, use a petroleum-based solvent to clean brake parts.

14 Check the master cylinder bore for corrosion, scratches, nicks and score marks. If the necessary measuring equipment is available, compare the dimensions of the piston and bore to those given in the Specifications Section of this Chapter. If damage or wear is evident, the master cylinder must be replaced with a new one. If the master cylinder is in poor condition, then the caliper(s) should be checked as well. Check that the fluid inlet and outlet ports in the master cylinder are clear.

15 The dust boot, circlip, piston assembly and spring are included in the rebuild kit. Use all of the new parts, regardless of the apparent condition of the old ones.

16 Install the spring in the master cylinder so that its tapered end faces the piston.

17 Lubricate the piston assembly components with clean brake fluid and install the assembly into the master cylinder, making sure all the components are the correct way round. Make sure the lips on the cup seals do not turn inside out when they are slipped into the bore. Depress the piston and install the new circlip, making sure that it locates in the master cylinder groove.

18 Install the rubber dust boot, making sure the lip is seated correctly in the piston groove.

19 Install the brake light switch.

20 Inspect the reservoir cover rubber diaphragm and replace if damaged or deteriorated.

Installation

21 Attach the master cylinder to the handlebar and fit the clamp. Align the mating surfaces of the clamp with the punch mark on the underside of the handlebar, then fully tighten the upper bolt first then the lower bolt to the torque setting specified at the beginning of the Chapter **(see illustrations)**.

22 Connect the brake hose to the master cylinder, using new sealing washers on each side of the union, and aligning the hose as noted on removal **(see illustration 5.7)**. Tighten the banjo bolt to the torque setting specified at the beginning of this Chapter.

23 Install the brake lever (see Chapter 5).

24 Connect the brake light switch wiring **(see illustration 5.5)** and install the rear view mirror if removed (see Chapter 7).

25 Fill the fluid reservoir with new DOT 4

brake fluid as described in Daily (pre-ride) checks. Refer to Section 11 of this Chapter and bleed the air from the system.

26 Fit the rubber diaphragm, making sure it is correctly seated, the diaphragm plate and the cover onto the master cylinder reservoir.

27 Check the operation of the front brake before riding the motorcycle.

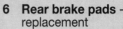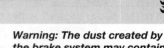

6 Rear brake pads - replacement

⚠️ *Warning: The dust created by the brake system may contain asbestos, which is harmful to your health. Never blow it out with compressed air and don't inhale any of it. An approved filtering mask should be worn when working on the brakes.*

1 Prise off the brake pad cover using a flat-bladed screwdriver **(see illustration)**.

2 Remove the pad pin retaining clip, noting how its ends fit through the holes in the pad pins **(see illustration)**.

3 Withdraw the pad pins from the caliper using a suitable pair of pliers and remove the pad springs, noting how they fit **(see illustration)**.

4 Withdraw the pads from the caliper body and remove the anti-chatter shim from the back of each pad, noting how it fits **(see illustration)**.

6.1 Prise off the cover . . .

6.2 . . . then remove the pad pin retaining clip

6.3 Withdraw the pins (arrows) and springs . . .

6.4 . . . then remove the pads and shims

6.11a Make sure the anti-chatter shims are the right way round

6.11b Install one pin through both pads . . .

6.11c . . . and the other pin through one pad only, then install the springs . . .

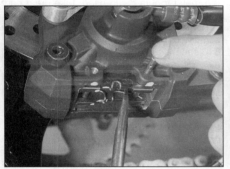

6.11d . . . and push up on the spring end to locate it under the second pin as you slide it through

6.11e Install the retaining clip and cover

5 Inspect the surface of each pad for contamination and check that the friction material has not worn beyond its service limit (see Chapter 1, Section 13). If either pad is worn down to, or beyond, the service limit wear groove (ie the groove is no longer visible), fouled with oil or grease, or heavily scored or damaged by dirt and debris, both pads must be replaced as a set. Note that it is not possible to degrease the friction material; if the pads are contaminated in any way they must be replaced.

6 If the pads are in good condition clean them carefully, using a fine wire brush which is completely free of oil and grease to remove all traces of road dirt and corrosion. Using a pointed instrument, clean out the groove in the friction material and dig out any embedded particles of foreign matter. Any areas of glazing may be removed using emery cloth.

7 Check the condition of the brake disc (see Section 8).

8 Remove all traces of corrosion from the pad pins. Inspect them for signs of damage, and replace them if necessary.

9 Push the pistons as far back into the caliper as possible using hand pressure only. Due to the increased friction material thickness of new pads, it may be necessary to remove the master cylinder reservoir cover and diaphragm and siphon out some fluid.

10 Smear the backs of the pads and the shank of each pad pin with copper-based grease, making sure that none gets on the front or sides of the pads.

11 Installation of the pads, anti-chatter shims, pad pins, springs and retaining clip is the reverse of removal. Install the anti-chatter shim on the back of each pad with its open end facing forward (see illustration). Insert the pads up into the caliper so that the friction material of each pad is facing the disc. Make sure the pad springs are correctly positioned, and the pins fit correctly through the holes in the pads (see illustrations). Secure the pins with the clip, making sure that its ends fit through the holes in the pad pins - if necessary rotate the pad pins to align their holes correctly (see illustration 6.2). Do not forget to install the pad cover (see illustration).

12 Top up the master cylinder reservoir if necessary (see Daily (pre-ride) checks).

13 Operate the brake pedal several times to bring the pads into contact with the disc. Check the operation of the brake before riding the motorcycle.

7 Rear brake caliper - removal, overhaul and installation

⚠️ Warning: If a caliper indicates the need for an overhaul (usually due to leaking fluid or sticky operation), all old brake fluid should be flushed from the system. Also, the dust created by the brake system may contain asbestos, which is harmful to your health. Never blow it out with compressed air and don't inhale any of it. An approved filtering mask should be worn when working on the brakes. Do not, under any circumstances, use petroleum-based solvents to clean brake parts. Use clean brake fluid, brake cleaner or denatured alcohol only.

Note: Before overhauling the caliper check the availability of the caliper seals with a Suzuki dealer - it may only be possible to purchase new seals complete with the pistons.

Removal

1 Remove the brake hose banjo bolt, noting its alignment on the caliper, and separate the hose from the caliper (see illustration). Plug the hose end or wrap a plastic bag tightly around it to minimise fluid loss and prevent dirt entering the system. Discard the sealing washers as new ones must be used on installation. Note: If you are planning to overhaul the caliper and don't have a source of compressed air to blow out the pistons, just loosen the banjo bolt at this stage and retighten it lightly. The bike's hydraulic system can then be used to force the pistons out of the body once the pads have been removed. Disconnect the hose once the pistons have been sufficiently displaced.

7.1 Note the alignment of the hose against the lug (A), then remove the banjo bolt (B)

6

7.2 Remove the torque arm nut and bolt and separate it from the caliper

7.3 Caliper body joining bolts (arrows)

7.4 Caliper mounting bolts (arrows)

2 Unscrew the nut securing the brake torque arm to the caliper, then withdraw the bolt and drop the arm off the caliper **(see illustration)**.
3 If the caliper body is to be split into its halves for seal replacement, it is advisable to slacken the caliper body joining bolts at this stage and retighten them lightly **(see illustration)**.
4 Unscrew the caliper mounting bolts, and slide the caliper away from the disc **(see illustration)**. Remove the brake pads (see Section 6).

Overhaul

5 Clean the exterior of the caliper with denatured alcohol or brake system cleaner **(see illustration)**.
6 Displace the pistons as far as possible from the caliper body, either by pumping them out by operating the rear brake pedal, or by forcing them out using compressed air - do not allow the piston heads to touch. Mark each piston head and caliper body with a felt

marker to ensure that the pistons can be matched to their original bores on reassembly. If the compressed air method is used, place a wad of rag between the pistons to act as a cushion, then use compressed air directed into the fluid inlet to force the pistons out of the body. Use only low pressure to ease the pistons out. If the air pressure is too high and the pistons are forced out, the caliper and/or pistons may be damaged.

 Warning: Never place your fingers in front of the piston in an attempt to catch or protect it when applying compressed air, as serious injury could result.

7 Unscrew the caliper body joining bolts and separate the body halves. Remove the piston from each half. Extract the caliper seal from whichever body half it is in and discard it as a new one must be used
6 Using a wooden or plastic tool, remove the dust seal from each caliper bore and discard them. New seals must be used on installation.

If a metal tool is being used, take great care not to damage the caliper bore.
7 Remove and discard the piston seals in the same way.
8 Clean the pistons and bores with denatured alcohol, clean brake fluid or brake system cleaner. If compressed air is available, use it to dry the parts thoroughly (make sure it's filtered and unlubricated).
Caution: Do not, under any circumstances, use a petroleum-based solvent to clean brake parts.
9 Inspect the caliper bores and pistons for signs of corrosion, nicks and burrs and loss of plating. If surface defects are present, the caliper assembly must be replaced. If the necessary measuring equipment is available, compare the dimensions of the pistons and bores to those given in the Specifications Section of this Chapter, replacing any component that is worn beyond the service limit. If the caliper is in bad shape the master cylinder should also be checked.

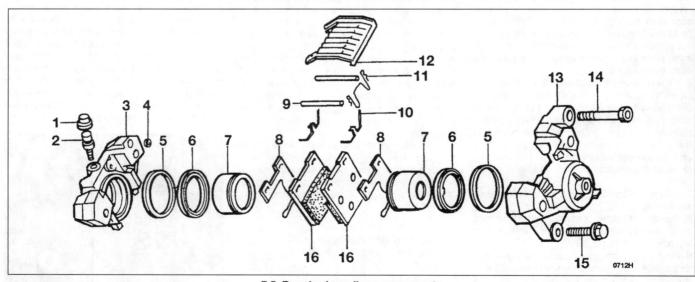

7.5 Rear brake caliper components

1 Bleed valve cap	5 Piston seals	9 Pad pins	13 Caliper body half
2 Bleed valve	6 Dust seals	10 Pad springs	14 Caliper joining bolt
3 Caliper body half	7 Pistons	11 Pad pin clip	15 Caliper mounting bolt
4 Caliper seal	8 Anti-chatter shims	12 Brake pad cover	16 Brake pads

7.17 Slide the caliper into position . . .

7.18 . . . and tighten the mounting bolts to the specified torque setting

10 Lubricate the new piston seals with clean brake fluid and install each one in its groove in the caliper bore.

11 Lubricate the new dust seals with clean brake fluid and install each one in its groove in the caliper bore.

12 Lubricate the pistons with clean brake fluid and install each one closed-end first into its caliper bore. Using your thumbs, push the pistons all the way in, making sure they enter the bores squarely.

13 Lubricate the new caliper seal and install it into one half of the caliper body.

14 Join the two halves of the caliper body together, making sure that the caliper seal is correctly seated in its recess.

15 Install the caliper body joining bolts and tighten them to the torque setting specified at the beginning of the Chapter. If it is not possible to tighten the bolts fully at this stage, tighten them as much as possible, then tighten them fully once the caliper has been installed on the machine.

Installation

16 Install the brake pads as described in Section 6.

17 Install the caliper on the brake disc making sure the pads sit squarely either side of the disc (see illustration).

18 Install the caliper mounting bolts and tighten them to the torque setting specified at the beginning of the Chapter (see illustration).

19 Install the brake torque arm onto the caliper and secure it with its bolt. Tighten the nut to the specified torque setting (see illustration).

20 Connect the brake hose to the caliper, making sure it is routed through its guides on the swingarm, using new sealing washers on each side of the fitting. Align the hose as noted on removal (see illustration 7.1). Tighten the banjo bolt to the torque setting specified at the beginning of the Chapter.

21 Fill the master cylinder with new DOT 4 brake fluid (see Daily (pre-ride) checks) and bleed the hydraulic system as described in Section 11.

22 Check for leaks and thoroughly test the operation of the brake before riding the motorcycle.

8 Rear brake disc - inspection, removal and installation

Inspection

1 Refer to Section 4 of this Chapter, noting that the dial gauge should be attached to the swingarm.

Removal

2 Remove the rear wheel (see Section 15).

3 Mark the relationship of the disc to the wheel so it can be installed in the same position. Unscrew the disc retaining bolts, loosening them a little at a time in a criss-cross pattern to avoid distorting the disc, and remove the disc (see illustration).

Installation

4 Position the disc on the wheel, aligning the previously applied matchmarks (if you're reinstalling the original disc).

5 Apply a suitable non-permanent thread locking compound to the disc mounting bolts, then install the bolts and tighten them in a

7.19 Counter-hold the torque arm bolt and tighten the nut to the specified torque setting

8.3 The disc is secured by five bolts (arrows)

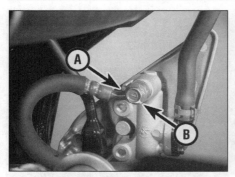

9.4 Note the alignment of the hose against the lug (A), then unscrew the banjo bolt (B)

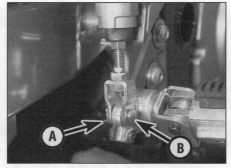

9.5 Remove the split pin (A) and withdraw the clevis pin (B)

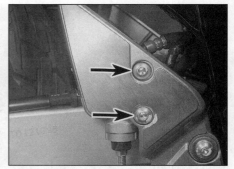

9.6 The master cylinder is secured by two bolts (arrows)

criss-cross pattern evenly and progressively to the torque setting specified at the beginning of this Chapter. Clean off all grease from the brake disc using acetone or brake system cleaner. If a new brake disc has been installed, remove any protective coating from its working surfaces.

6 Install the rear wheel (see Section 15).

7 Operate the brake pedal several times to bring the pads into contact with the disc. Check the operation of the brake carefully before riding the motorcycle.

9 Rear brake master cylinder - removal, overhaul and installation

1 If the master cylinder is leaking fluid, or if the lever does not produce a firm feel when the brake is applied, and bleeding the brakes does not help (see Section 11), and the hydraulic hoses are all in good condition, then master cylinder overhaul is recommended.

2 Before disassembling the master cylinder, read through the entire procedure and make sure that you have the correct rebuild kit. Also, you will need some new DOT 4 brake fluid, some clean rags and internal circlip pliers. **Note:** *To prevent damage to the paint from spilled brake fluid, always cover the surrounding components when working on the master cylinder.*

Caution: Disassembly, overhaul and reassembly of the brake master cylinder must be done in a spotlessly clean work area to avoid contamination and possible failure of the brake hydraulic system components.

Removal

3 Remove the side panels (see Chapter 7).

4 Unscrew the brake hose banjo bolt and separate the brake hose from the master cylinder, noting its alignment **(see illustration)**. Discard the two sealing washers as they must be replaced with new ones. Wrap the end of the hose in a clean rag and suspend the hose in an upright position or bend it down carefully and place the open end in a clean container. The objective is to prevent excessive loss of brake fluid, fluid spills and system contamination.

5 Remove the split pin from the clevis pin securing the brake pedal to the master cylinder pushrod **(see illustration)**. Withdraw the clevis pin and separate the pedal from the pushrod. Discard the split pin as a new one must be used.

6 Unscrew the two bolts securing the master cylinder to the bracket **(see illustration)**.

7 Slacken the master cylinder fluid reservoir cover screws **(see illustration)**. Unscrew the bolt securing the reservoir to the frame, then remove the reservoir cover and pour the fluid into a container.

8 Separate the fluid reservoir hose from the elbow on the master cylinder by releasing the hose clamp **(see illustration)**.

Overhaul

9 If necessary, slacken the clevis locknut, then unscrew the clevis with its nut and locknut and remove them from the pushrod **(see illustration)**.

10 Dislodge the rubber dust boot from the base of the master cylinder to reveal the pushrod retaining circlip.

11 Depress the pushrod and, using circlip pliers, remove the circlip. Slide out the piston assembly and spring. If they are difficult to remove, apply low pressure compressed air to the fluid outlet. Lay the parts out in the proper order to prevent confusion during reassembly.

12 Clean all of the parts with clean brake fluid or denatured alcohol.

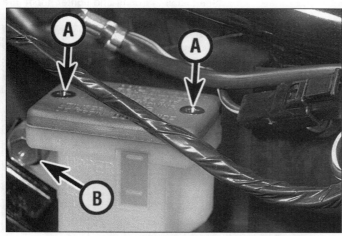

9.7 Reservoir cover screws (A) and mounting bolt (B)

9.8 Release the clamp (arrow) and pull the hose off its union

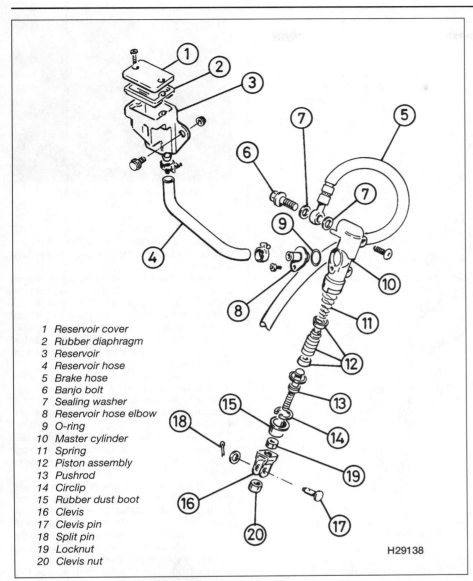

1 Reservoir cover
2 Rubber diaphragm
3 Reservoir
4 Reservoir hose
5 Brake hose
6 Banjo bolt
7 Sealing washer
8 Reservoir hose elbow
9 O-ring
10 Master cylinder
11 Spring
12 Piston assembly
13 Pushrod
14 Circlip
15 Rubber dust boot
16 Clevis
17 Clevis pin
18 Split pin
19 Locknut
20 Clevis nut

H29138

9.9 Rear brake master cylinder components

Caution: Do not, under any circumstances, use a petroleum-based solvent to clean brake parts. If compressed air is available, use it to dry the parts thoroughly (make sure it's filtered and unlubricated).

13 Check the master cylinder bore for corrosion, scratches, nicks and score marks. If the necessary measuring equipment is available, compare the dimensions of the piston and bore to those given in the Specifications Section of this Chapter. If damage is evident, the master cylinder must be replaced with a new one. If the master cylinder is in poor condition, then the caliper should be checked as well.
14 If required, unscrew the fluid reservoir hose union screw and detach the elbow from the master cylinder. Discard the O-ring as a new one must be used. Inspect the reservoir

hose for cracks or splits and replace if necessary.
15 The dust boot, circlip, piston assembly and spring are included in the rebuild kit. Use all of the new parts, regardless of the apparent condition of the old ones.
16 Install the spring in the master cylinder so that its tapered end faces the piston.
17 Lubricate the piston assembly components with clean hydraulic fluid and install the assembly into the master cylinder, making sure all the components are the correct way round. Make sure the lips on the cup seals do not turn inside out when they are slipped into the bore.
18 Install and depress the pushrod, then install a new circlip, making sure it is properly seated in the groove.
19 Install the rubber dust boot, making sure the lip is seated properly in the groove.

20 If removed, fit a new O-ring to the fluid reservoir hose union, then install the union onto the master cylinder and secure it with its screw.

Installation

21 Install the master cylinder onto the footrest bracket and tighten its mounting bolts to the torque setting specified at the beginning of the Chapter **(see illustration 9.6)**.
22 Secure the fluid reservoir to the frame with its retaining bolt **(see illustration 9.7)**. Ensure that the hose is correctly routed behind the frame tube, then connect it to the union on the master cylinder and secure it with the clamp **(see illustration 9.8)**. Check that the hose is secure and clamped at the reservoir end as well. If the clamps have weakened, use new ones.
23 Connect the brake hose banjo bolt to the master cylinder, using a new sealing washer on each side of the banjo union. Ensure that the hose is positioned so that it butts against the lug **(see illustration 9.4)** and tighten the banjo bolt to the specified torque setting.
24 If removed, install the clevis locknut, the clevis and its nut onto the master cylinder pushrod end, but do not yet tighten the locknut.
25 Align the brake pedal with the master cylinder pushrod clevis, then slide in the clevis pin and secure it using a new split pin **(see illustration 9.5)**. If the clevis position on the pushrod was disturbed during overhaul, re-set the brake pedal to its specified height (see Chapter 1, Section 14).
26 Tighten the clevis locknut securely.
27 Fill the fluid reservoir with new DOT 4 brake fluid (see *Daily (pre-ride) checks*) and bleed the system following the procedure in Section 11.
28 Check the operation of the brake carefully before riding the motorcycle.

10 Brake hoses and unions - inspection and replacement

Inspection

1 Brake hose condition should be checked regularly and the hoses replaced at the specified interval (see Chapter 1).
2 Twist and flex the rubber hoses while looking for cracks, bulges and seeping fluid. Check extra carefully around the areas where the hoses connect with the banjo fittings, as these are common areas for hose failure.
3 Inspect the metal banjo union fittings connected to the brake hoses. If the fittings are rusted, scratched or cracked, replace them.

6

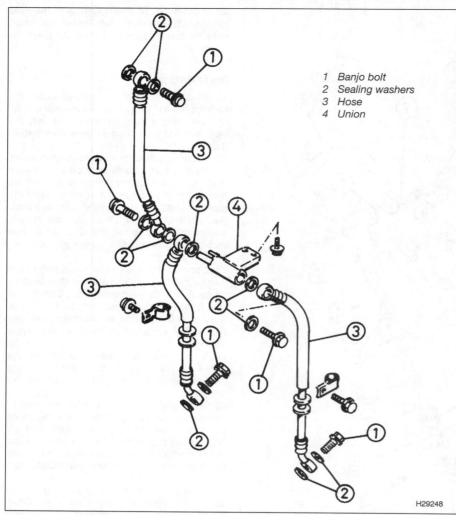

1 Banjo bolt
2 Sealing washers
3 Hose
4 Union

H29248

10.4 Front brake hose arrangement

11.6 Brake caliper bleed valve (arrow)

Replacement

4 The brake hoses have banjo union fittings on each end **(see illustration)**. Cover the surrounding area with plenty of rags and unscrew the banjo bolt at each end of the hose, noting its alignment. Free the hose from any clips or guides and remove the hose. Discard the sealing washers.

5 Position the new hose, making sure it isn't twisted or otherwise strained, and abut the tab on the hose union with the lug on the component casting, where present. Otherwise align the hose as noted on removal. Install the banjo bolts, using new sealing washers on both sides of the unions, and tighten them to the torque setting specified at the beginning of this Chapter. Make sure they are correctly aligned and routed clear of all moving components.

6 Flush the old brake fluid from the system, refill with new DOT 4 brake fluid (see *Daily (pre-ride) checks*) and bleed the air from the system (see Section 11). Check the operation of the brakes carefully before riding the motorcycle.

11 Brake system bleeding

1 Bleeding the brakes is simply the process of removing all the air bubbles from the brake fluid reservoirs, the hoses and the brake calipers. Bleeding is necessary whenever a brake system hydraulic connection is loosened, when a component or hose is replaced, or when the master cylinder or caliper is overhauled. Leaks in the system may also allow air to enter, but leaking brake fluid will reveal their presence and warn you of the need for repair.

2 To bleed the brakes, you will need some new DOT 4 brake fluid, a length of clear vinyl or plastic tubing, a small container partially filled with clean brake fluid, some rags and a spanner to fit the brake caliper bleed valves.

3 Cover the fuel tank and other painted components to prevent damage in the event that brake fluid is spilled.

4 If bleeding the rear brake, remove the side panels (see Chapter 7) for access to the fluid reservoir.

5 Remove the reservoir cover, diaphragm plate (where fitted) and diaphragm and slowly pump the brake lever or pedal a few times, until no air bubbles can be seen floating up from the holes in the bottom of the reservoir. Doing this bleeds the air from the master cylinder end of the line. Loosely refit the reservoir cover.

6 Pull the dust cap off the bleed valve **(see illustration)**. Attach one end of the clear vinyl or plastic tubing to the bleed valve and submerge the other end in the brake fluid in the container.

7 Remove the reservoir cover and check the fluid level. Do not allow the fluid level to drop below the lower mark during the bleeding process.

8 Carefully pump the brake lever or pedal three or four times and hold it in (front) or down (rear) while opening the caliper bleed valve. When the valve is opened, brake fluid will flow out of the caliper into the clear tubing and the lever will move toward the handlebar or the pedal will move down.

9 Retighten the bleed valve, then release the brake lever or pedal gradually. Repeat the process until no air bubbles are visible in the brake fluid leaving the caliper and the lever or pedal is firm when applied. On completion, disconnect the bleeding equipment, then tighten the bleed valve to the torque setting specified at the beginning of the chapter and install the dust cap.

10 Install the diaphragm and cover assembly, wipe up any spilled brake fluid and check the entire system for leaks.

HAYNES HiNT *If it's not possible to produce a firm feel to the lever or pedal the fluid my be aerated. Let the brake fluid in the system stabilise for a few hours and then repeat the procedure when the tiny bubbles in the system have settled out.*

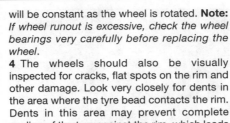

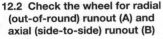

12.2 Check the wheel for radial (out-of-round) runout (A) and axial (side-to-side) runout (B)

12 Wheels - inspection and repair

1 In order to carry out a proper inspection of the wheels, it is necessary to support the bike upright so that the wheel being inspected is raised off the ground. Position the motorcycle on its centrestand or an auxiliary stand. Clean the wheels thoroughly to remove mud and dirt that may interfere with the inspection procedure or mask defects. Make a general check of the wheels (see Chapter 1) and tyres (see *Daily (pre-ride) checks*).

2 Attach a dial gauge to the fork slider or the swingarm and position its stem against the side of the rim **(see illustration)**. Spin the wheel slowly and check the axial (side-to-side) runout of the rim. In order to accurately check radial (out of round) runout with the dial gauge, the wheel would have to be removed from the machine, and the tyre from the wheel. With the axle clamped in a vice and the dial gauge positioned on the top of the rim, the wheel can be rotated to check the runout.

3 An easier, though slightly less accurate, method is to attach a stiff wire pointer to the fork slider or the swingarm and position the end a fraction of an inch from the wheel (where the wheel and tyre join). If the wheel is true, the distance from the pointer to the rim

will be constant as the wheel is rotated. **Note:** *If wheel runout is excessive, check the wheel bearings very carefully before replacing the wheel.*

4 The wheels should also be visually inspected for cracks, flat spots on the rim and other damage. Look very closely for dents in the area where the tyre bead contacts the rim. Dents in this area may prevent complete sealing of the tyre against the rim, which leads to deflation of the tyre over a period of time. If damage is evident, or if runout in either direction is excessive, the wheel will have to be replaced with a new one. Never attempt to repair a damaged cast alloy wheel.

13 Wheels - alignment check

1 Misalignment of the wheels, which may be due to a cocked rear wheel or a bent frame or fork yokes, can cause strange and possibly serious handling problems. If the frame or yokes are at fault, repair by a frame specialist or replacement with new parts are the only alternatives.

2 To check the alignment you will need an assistant, a length of string or a perfectly straight piece of wood and a ruler. A plumb bob or other suitable weight will also be required.

3 In order to make a proper check of the wheels it is necessary to support the bike in an upright position, either on its centrestand or on an auxiliary stand. Measure the width of both tyres at their widest points. Subtract the smaller measurement from the larger measurement, then divide the difference by two. The result is the amount of offset that should exist between the front and rear tyres on both sides.

4 If a string is used, have your assistant hold one end of it about halfway between the floor and the rear axle, touching the rear sidewall of the tyre.

5 Run the other end of the string forward and pull it tight so that it is roughly parallel to the floor. Slowly bring the string into contact with

the front sidewall of the rear tyre, then turn the front wheel until it is parallel with the string. Measure the distance from the front tyre sidewall to the string.

6 Repeat the procedure on the other side of the motorcycle. The distance from the front tyre sidewall to the string should be equal on both sides.

7 As was previously pointed out, a perfectly straight length of wood may be substituted for the string. The procedure is the same.

8 If the distance between the string and tyre is greater on one side, or if the rear wheel appears to be cocked, refer to Chapter 1, Section 2 and check that the chain adjuster markings coincide on each side of the swingarm.

9 If the front-to-back alignment is correct, the wheels still may be out of alignment vertically.

10 Using the plumb bob, or other suitable weight, and a length of string, check the rear wheel to make sure it is vertical. To do this, hold the string against the tyre upper sidewall and allow the weight to settle just off the floor. When the string touches both the upper and lower tyre sidewalls and is perfectly straight, the wheel is vertical. If it is not, place thin spacers under one leg of the stand.

11 Once the rear wheel is vertical, check the front wheel in the same manner. If both wheels are not perfectly vertical, the frame and/or major suspension components are bent.

14 Front wheel - removal and installation

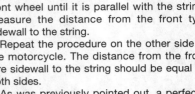
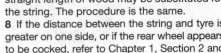

Removal

1 Position the motorcycle on its centre stand or on an auxiliary stand and support it under the crankcase so that the front wheel is off the ground. Always make sure the motorcycle is properly supported.

2 On 600 models unscrew the knurled ring, and on 1200 models remove the screw, securing the speedometer cable to its drive housing on the left-hand side of the wheel hub, and detach the cable **(see illustrations)**.

14.2a On 600 models unscrew the cable retaining ring (arrow)

14.2b On 1200 models unscrew the cable retaining screw (arrow)

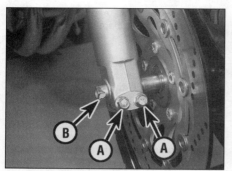

14.4 Slacken the axle clamp bolts (A), then unscrew the axle (B)

14.5 Withdraw the axle and remove the wheel

14.8 Check the condition of the seal (arrow)

3 Remove the brake caliper mounting bolts and slide the caliper off the disc **(see illustration 3.4a or b)**. Support the caliper with a piece of wire or a bungee cord so that no strain is placed on its hydraulic hose. There is no need to disconnect the hose from the caliper.

4 Slacken the axle clamp bolts on the bottom of the right-hand side fork, then unscrew the axle **(see illustration)**.

5 Support the wheel, then withdraw the axle from the right-hand side and carefully lower the wheel **(see illustration)**.

6 Remove the wheel spacer from the right-hand side of the wheel, noting which way round it fits, and the speedometer drive housing from the left-hand side. **Note:** *Do not operate the front brake lever with the wheel removed.*

Caution: Don't lay the wheel down and allow it to rest on the disc - the disc could become warped. Set the wheel on wood blocks so the disc doesn't support the weight of the wheel.

7 Check the axle for straightness by rolling it on a flat surface such as a piece of plate glass (first wipe off all old grease and remove any corrosion using fine emery cloth). If the equipment is available, place the axle in V-blocks and measure the runout using a dial gauge. If the axle is bent or the runout exceeds the limit specified, replace it.

8 Check the condition of the wheel bearings (see Section 16), and of the seal in the speedometer drive housing **(see illustration)**. If the seal is damaged or deteriorated the entire housing must be replaced as the seal is not available by itself, though it is worth trying a specialist bearing shop for one.

Installation

9 Apply a smear of grease to the speedometer drive components. Fit the speedometer drive to the wheel's left-hand side, aligning its drive gear tabs with the slots in the wheel hub **(see illustration)**.

10 Apply a smear of grease to the inside of the wheel spacer, and also to the inner area where it fits into the wheel **(see illustration)**.

11 Manoeuvre the wheel into position. Apply a thin coat of grease to the axle. Fit the wheel spacer in between the wheel and the fork, making sure it is the right way round **(see illustration)**.

12 Lift the wheel into place between the fork slider and making sure the spacer remains in position. Slide the axle into position from the right-hand side **(see illustration 14.5)**. Align the speedometer drive housing so that it butts against the back of the lug on the fork and the cable socket faces to the rear **(see illustration)**.

13 Tighten the axle to the torque setting specified at the beginning of the Chapter **(see illustration)**.

14.9 Make sure the drive gear tabs fit into the slots

14.10 Smear the spacer contact surfaces with grease (600 model spacer shown)

14.11 On 600 models, fit the flat end of the spacer into the wheel

14.12 Butt the speedometer drive housing against the back of the lug on the fork (arrow)

14.13 Tighten the axle . . .

14.14 . . . and then the clamp bolts to the specified torque settings

14.16 Align the notch in the cable end with the drive tab

14 Tighten the axle clamp bolts on the right-hand side fork to the specified torque setting (see illustration).

15 Install the brake caliper, making sure the pads sit squarely on either side of the disc. Tighten the caliper mounting bolts to the torque setting specified at the beginning of the Chapter (see illustrations 3.18, 3.19a and b).

16 Pass the speedometer cable through its guides (if withdrawn), then connect the cable to the drive housing, aligning the slot in the cable end with the drive tab, and securely tighten its knurled ring or screw (see illustration).

17 Apply the front brake a few times to bring the pads back into contact with the discs. Move the motorcycle off its stand, apply the front brake and pump the front forks a few times to settle all components in position.

18 Check for correct operation of the front brake before riding the motorcycle.

15 Rear wheel -
removal and installation

Removal

1 Position the motorcycle on its centrestand or an auxiliary stand. Remove the chain guard (see Chapter 7).

2 Unscrew the nut securing the brake torque arm to the caliper, then withdraw the bolt and drop the arm off the caliper (see illustration 7.2). Remove the brake caliper mounting bolts and slide the caliper off the disc (see illustration 7.4). Support the caliper with a piece of wire or a bungee cord so that no strain is placed on its hydraulic hose. There is no need to disconnect the hose from the caliper.

3 On US models, remove the split pin from the axle nut (see illustration 16.11a). On all models, unscrew the axle nut and remove the washer (GSF1200 and GSF1200S) and the chain adjuster plate or block, noting how it fits (see illustration).

4 Support the wheel then withdraw the axle from the right-hand side along with the adjuster plate or block, then lower the wheel to the ground. Note how the axle passes through the caliper mounting bracket.

5 Disengage the chain from the sprocket and remove the wheel from the swingarm. Remove the spacers from both sides of the wheel, noting which way round they fit (see illustrations 15.9a and b).
Caution: Do not lay the wheel down and allow it to rest on the disc or the sprocket - they could become warped. Set the wheel on wood blocks so the disc or the sprocket doesn't support the weight of the wheel. Do not operate the brake pedal with the wheel removed.

6 Check the axle for straightness by rolling it on a flat surface such as a piece of plate glass (if the axle is corroded, first remove the corrosion with fine emery cloth). If the equipment is available, place the axle in V-blocks and measure the runout using a dial gauge. If the axle is bent or the runout exceeds the limit specified at the beginning of the Chapter, replace it.

7 Check the condition of the wheel bearings (see Section 16).

Installation

8 Apply a thin coat of grease to the lips of each bearing seal, and also to the inside and the inner faces of the spacers where they contact the seals. On 600 models, if removed, install the chain adjusters into the ends of the swingarm (see illustration).

9 Manoeuvre the wheel so that it is in between the ends of the swingarm and apply a thin coat of grease to the axle. Install the spacers into the wheel (see illustrations).

15.3 Unscrew the axle nut (arrow) and remove the adjuster plate or block

15.8 On 600 models install the chain adjusters into the swingarm

15.9a Install the spacer into the left side . . .

6

15.9b . . . and the shouldered spacer into the right side of the wheel

15.10 Engage the chain around the sprocket

15.11a Install the axle from the right, making sure it passes through all components . . .

15.11b . . . then fit the left-hand adjuster plate . . .

15.11c . . . and the axle washer (1200 models) and nut

15.13 Tighten the axle nut to the specified torque setting

10 Engage the drive chain with the sprocket and lift the wheel into position **(see illustration)**. Make sure the spacers remain correctly in place.

11 Slide the right-hand side adjuster plate or block onto the axle, making sure it is the right way round. Install the axle from the right, through the chain adjuster and swingarm, the caliper mounting bracket and the spacer and through the wheel **(see illustration)**. Check

that everything is correctly aligned, then fit the left-hand side adjuster plate or block, washer (GSF1200 and GSF1200S) and the axle nut, but do not tighten it yet **(see illustrations)**. If it is difficult to insert the axle due to the tension of the drive chain, slacken the chain adjusters (see Chapter 1).

12 Adjust the chain slack as described in Chapter 1.

13 Tighten the axle nut to the torque setting

specified at the beginning of the Chapter, counter-holding the axle head on the other side of the wheel if necessary **(see illustration)**. On US models, fit a new split pin into the nut.

14 Install the caliper mounting bolts and tighten them to the torque setting specified at the beginning of the Chapter **(see illustration 7.18)**. Install the brake torque arm onto the caliper and secure it with its bolt. Tighten the nut to the specified torque setting **(see illustration 7.19)**.

15 Operate the brake pedal several times to bring the pads into contact with the disc. Check the operation of the rear brake carefully before riding the bike.

16 Wheel bearings - removal, inspection and installation

Front wheel bearings

Note: *Always replace the wheel bearings in pairs. Never replace the bearings individually. Avoid using a high pressure cleaner on the wheel bearing area.*

1 Remove the wheel (see Section 14) **(see illustration)**.

2 Set the wheel on blocks so as not to allow the weight of the wheel to rest on the brake disc.

3 Using a metal rod (preferably a brass drift punch) inserted through the centre of the

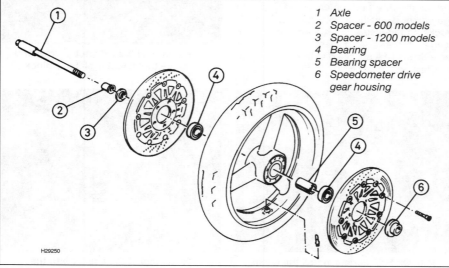

1 Axle
2 Spacer - 600 models
3 Spacer - 1200 models
4 Bearing
5 Bearing spacer
6 Speedometer drive gear housing

16.1 Front wheel components

16.3a Using a drift to knock out the bearings

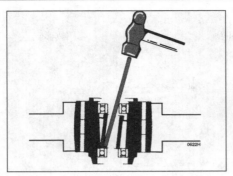

16.3b Locate the drift as shown when driving out the bearing

16.8 Using a socket to drive in the bearings

upper bearing, tap evenly around the inner race of the lower bearing to drive it from the hub (see illustrations). The bearing spacer will also come out.

4 Lay the wheel on its other side so that the remaining bearing faces down. Drive the bearing out of the wheel using the same technique as above.

5 If the bearings are of the unsealed type or are only sealed on one side, clean them with a high flash-point solvent (one which won't leave any residue) and blow them dry with compressed air (don't let the bearings spin as you dry them). Apply a few drops of oil to the bearing. Note: If the bearing is sealed on both sides don't attempt to clean it.

6 Hold the outer race of the bearing and rotate the inner race - if the bearing doesn't turn smoothly, has rough spots or is noisy, replace it with a new one.

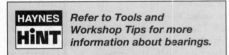

HAYNES HiNT Refer to Tools and Workshop Tips for more information about bearings.

7 If the bearing is good and can be re-used, wash it in solvent once again and dry it, then pack the bearing with grease. Suzuki recommend that the bearings should be renewed if they are removed.

8 Thoroughly clean the hub area of the wheel. First install the left-hand side bearing into its recess in the hub, with the marked or sealed side facing outwards. Using the old bearing (if new ones are being fitted), a bearing driver or a socket large enough to contact the outer race of the bearing, drive it in until it's completely seated (see illustration).

9 Turn the wheel over and install the bearing spacer. Drive the right-hand side bearing into place as described above.

10 Clean off all grease from the brake discs using acetone or brake system cleaner then install the wheel (see Section 14).

Rear wheel bearings

11 Remove the rear wheel (see Section 15). Lift the rear sprocket and sprocket coupling assembly out of the wheel, noting how it fits (see illustrations).

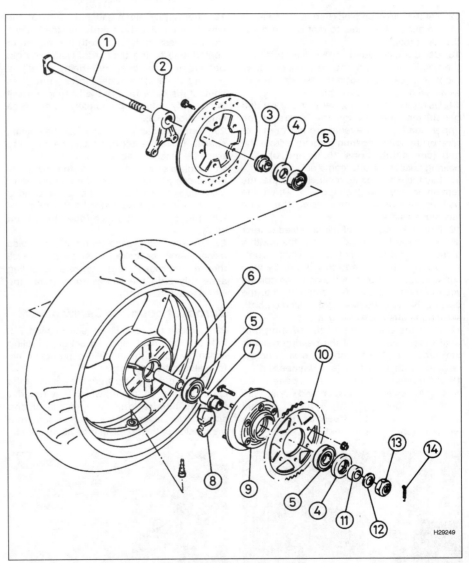

16.11a Rear wheel components

1 Axle
2 Caliper bracket
3 Right-hand spacer
4 Bearing seal
5 Bearing
6 Bearing spacer
7 Sprocket coupling spacer
8 Damper segments
9 Sprocket coupling
10 Sprocket
11 Left-hand spacer
12 Washer (1200 models)
13 Axle nut
14 Split pin (US models)

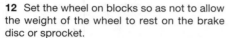

16.11b Lift the sprocket coupling out of the wheel

16.13 Lever out the seal using a screwdriver

16.24a Remove the spacer from inside the sprocket coupling . . .

12 Set the wheel on blocks so as not to allow the weight of the wheel to rest on the brake disc or sprocket.

13 Using a flat-bladed screwdriver, prise out the bearing seal from the right-hand side of the wheel (see illustration). Discard the seal as a new one should be used.

14 Using a metal rod (preferably a brass drift punch) inserted through the centre of the upper bearing, tap evenly around the inner race of the lower bearing to drive it from the hub (see illustrations 16.3a and b). The bearing spacer will also come out.

15 Lay the wheel on its other side so that the remaining bearing faces down. Drive the bearing out of the wheel using the same technique as above.

16 If the bearings are of the unsealed type or are only sealed on one side, clean them with a high flash-point solvent (one which won't leave any residue) and blow them dry with compressed air (don't let the bearings spin as you dry them). Apply a few drops of oil to the bearing. **Note:** *If the bearing is sealed on both sides don't attempt to clean it.*

17 Hold the outer race of the bearing and rotate the inner race - if the bearing doesn't turn smoothly, has rough spots or is noisy, replace it with a new one (see **Haynes Hint**).

18 If the bearing is good and can be re-used, wash it in solvent once again and dry it, then pack the bearing with grease. Suzuki recommend that the bearings should be renewed if they are removed.

19 Thoroughly clean the hub area of the wheel. First install the right-hand side bearing into its recess in the hub, with the marked or sealed side facing outwards. Using the old bearing (if new ones are being fitted), a bearing driver or a socket large enough to contact the outer race of the bearing, drive it in squarely until it's completely seated (see illustration 16.8).

20 Turn the wheel over and install the bearing spacer. Drive the left-hand side bearing into place as described above.

21 Apply a smear of grease to the lips of the new bearing seal, and install it into the right-hand side of the wheel using a seal or bearing driver, a suitable socket or a flat piece of wood to drive it into place (see illustration 16.8).

22 Clean off all grease from the brake disc using acetone or brake system cleaner. Install the rear sprocket and sprocket coupling assembly onto the wheel, then install the wheel (see Section 15).

Sprocket coupling bearing

23 Remove the rear wheel (see Section 15). Lift the sprocket and sprocket coupling assembly out of the wheel, noting how it fits (see illustration 16.11b).

24 Remove the spacer from the inside of the coupling bearing, noting which way round it fits (see illustration). Using a flat-bladed screwdriver, lever out the bearing seal from the outside of the coupling (see illustration).

25 Support the coupling on blocks of wood and drive the bearing out from the inside using a metal rod (preferably a brass drift punch).

26 If the bearings are of the unsealed type or are only sealed on one side, clean them with a high flash-point solvent (one which won't leave any residue) and blow them dry with compressed air (don't let the bearings spin as you dry them). Apply a few drops of oil to the bearing. **Note:** *If the bearing is sealed on both sides don't attempt to clean it.*

27 Hold the outer race of the bearing and rotate the inner race - if the bearing doesn't turn smoothly, has rough spots or is noisy, replace it with a new one (see **Haynes Hint**).

28 If the bearing is good and can be re-used, wash it in solvent once again and dry it, then pack the bearing with grease. Suzuki recommend that the bearing should be renewed if it is removed.

29 Thoroughly clean the bearing recess then install the bearing into the recess in the coupling, with the marked or sealed side facing out. Using the old bearing (if a new one is being fitted), a bearing driver or a socket large enough to contact the outer race of the bearing, drive it in until it is completely seated.

30 Apply a smear of grease to the lips of the new bearing seal, and install it using a seal or bearing driver, a suitable socket or a flat piece of wood to drive it into place (see illustration). Install the spacer into the inside

16.24b . . . then lever out the bearing seal using a screwdriver

16.25 Drive out the sprocket bearing with a drift

16.30 A piece of wood can be used to drive the bearing seal onto the bearing

of the coupling, making sure it is the correct way round **(see illustration 16.24a)**.
31 Clean off all grease from the brake disc using acetone or brake system cleaner. Install the sprocket coupling assembly onto the wheel **(see illustration 16.11b)**, then install the wheel (see Section 15).

17 Tyres - general information and fitting

General information

1 The wheels fitted to all models are designed to take tubeless tyres only. Tyre sizes are given in the Specifications at the beginning of this chapter.
2 Refer to the Daily (pre-ride) checks listed at the beginning of this manual for tyre maintenance.

Fitting new tyres

3 When selecting new tyres, refer to the tyre information label on the swingarm and the tyre options listed in the owners handbook. Ensure that front and rear tyre types are compatible, the correct size and correct speed rating; if necessary seek advice from a Suzuki dealer or tyre fitting specialist **(see illustration)**.

4 It is recommended that tyres are fitted by a motorcycle tyre specialist rather than attempted in the home workshop. This is particularly relevant in the case of tubeless tyres because the force required to break the seal between the wheel rim and tyre bead is substantial, and is usually beyond the capabilities of an individual working with normal tyre levers. Additionally, the specialist will be able to balance the wheels after tyre fitting.
5 Note that punctured tubeless tyres can in some cases be repaired. Suzuki recommend that such repairs are carried out only by an authorised dealer.

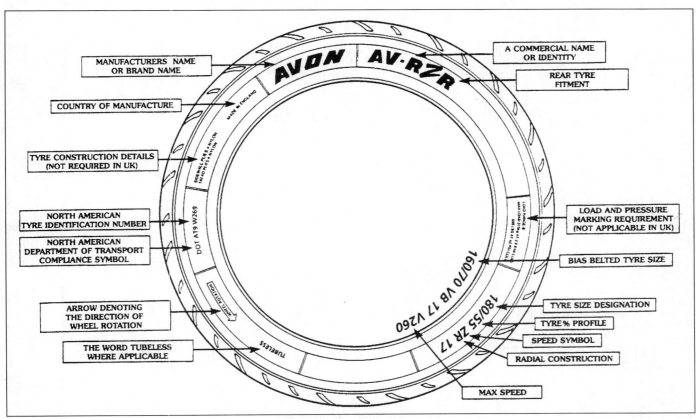

17.3 Common tyre sidewall markings

Notes

Chapter 7
Bodywork

Contents

Degrees of difficulty

Easy, suitable for novice with little experience	**Fairly easy,** suitable for beginner with some experience	**Fairly difficult,** suitable for competent DIY mechanic
Difficult, suitable for experienced DIY mechanic	**Very difficult,** suitable for expert DIY or professional	

1 General information

This Chapter covers the procedures necessary to remove and install the body parts. Since many service and repair operations on these motorcycles require the removal of the body parts, the procedures are grouped here and referred to from other Chapters.

In the case of damage to the body parts, it is usually necessary to remove the broken component and replace it with a new (or used) one. The material that the body panels are composed of doesn't lend itself to conventional repair techniques. There are however some shops that specialise in 'plastic welding', so it may be worthwhile seeking the advice of one of these specialists before consigning an expensive component to the bin.

When attempting to remove any body panel, first study it closely, noting any fasteners and associated fittings, to be sure of returning everything to its correct place on installation. In some cases the aid of an assistant will be required when removing panels, to help avoid the risk of damage to paintwork. Once the evident fasteners have been removed, try to withdraw the panel as described but DO NOT FORCE IT - if it will not release, check that all fasteners have been removed and try again. Where a panel engages another by means of tabs, be careful not to break the tab or its mating slot or to damage the paintwork. Remember that a few moments of patience at this stage will save you a lot of money in replacing broken fairing panels!

When installing a body panel, first study it closely, noting any fasteners and associated fittings removed with it, to be sure of returning everything to its correct place. Check that all fasteners are in good condition, including all trim nuts or clips and damping/rubber mounts; any of these must be replaced if faulty before the panel is reassembled. Check also that all mounting brackets are straight and repair or replace them if necessary before attempting to install the panel. Where assistance was required to remove a panel, make sure your assistant is on hand to install it.

Tighten the fasteners securely, but be careful not to overtighten any of them or the panel may break (not always immediately) due to the uneven stress.

 Note that a small amount of lubricant (liquid soap or similar) applied to the mounting rubbers of the side panels will assist the panel retaining pegs to engage without the need for undue pressure.

2 Rear view mirrors - removal and installation

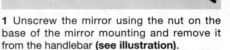

1 Unscrew the mirror using the nut on the base of the mirror mounting and remove it from the handlebar **(see illustration)**.
2 Install the mirror into its mounting and screw it in until it is fully home. Adjust the position of the mirror as required and tighten its nut.

2.1 Unscrew the mirror using a spanner on the nut (arrow)

7

3.1 Turn the key clockwise to unlock the seat

3.3 Locate the tab (arrow) under the tank

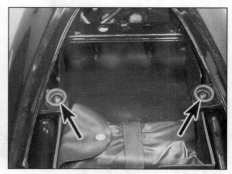

4.3a The side panels are secured by two screws in the middle (arrows) . . .

4.3b . . . a screw on each side at the back (arrow) . . .

4.3c . . . and by two clip fasteners at the front (arrows)

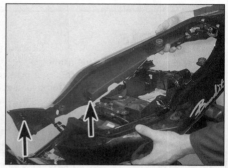

4.3d Carefully release the pegs (arrows) then remove the side panel assembly

3 Seat - removal and installation

Removal

1 Insert the ignition key into the seat lock located under the left-hand side panel, and turn it clockwise to unlock the seat (see illustration).
2 Lift the rear of the seat and draw it back and away from the bike. Note how the tab at the front of the seat locates under the tank mounting bracket, and how the seat locates onto the frame rail.

Installation

3 Locate the tab at the front of the seat under the fuel tank mounting bracket (see illustration). Align the seat at the rear and push down on it to engage the latches.

4 Side panels - removal and installation

Removal

1 Remove the seat (see Section 3). The side panels can only be removed as an assembly, and come away with the tail light assembly

attached. Do not remove the side panels individually.
2 Trace the tail light assembly wiring and disconnect it at the connector. Where fitted, remove the caps from the two bolts securing each passenger grab handle, then unscrew the bolts and remove the handles.
3 The side panels are secured by four screws, two clip-type fasteners and two pegs which fit into rubber grommets (see illustrations). The pegs are located at and near the front of each panel. Remove the four screws securing and the two clip fasteners, then gently pull each panel away from the frame to release the pegs (see illustration). Do not force or bend the panel while removing it.

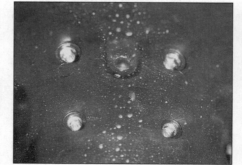

5.2a Counter-hold the nuts . . .

Installation

4 Installation is the reverse of removal.

5 Front mudguard and fork brace - removal and installation

Removal

1 Remove the front wheel (see Chapter 6).
2 Counter-hold the nuts on the underside of the mudguard and unscrew the four screws securing the mudguard to its brace (see illustrations). Take care not to lose the collars and remove them with the nuts (see

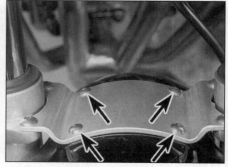

5.2b . . . then unscrew the four screws (arrows)

5.2c Remove the collars with the nuts . . .

5.2d . . . then remove the mudguard

illustration). Lower the mudguard and carefully remove it from between the forks, noting how it fits (see illustration).
3 Unscrew the four screws securing the brace to the forks and remove the brace (see illustration).

Installation

4 Installation is the reverse of removal. Install the brace with the triangle on its underside pointing forwards (see illustration).

6 Chain guard - removal and installation

1 Remove the two screws securing the chain guard to the swingarm and remove the guard, noting how it fits (see illustration).
2 Installation is the reverse of removal.

7 Fairing (GSF600S and GSF1200S) - removal and installation

Removal

1 Remove the front turn signal assemblies (see Chapter 8).
2 Unscrew the four screws securing the windshield to the fairing and remove them with the threaded rubber mounts (see illustrations).

5.3 The brace is secured by four screws (arrows)

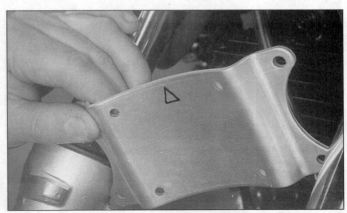

5.4 Install the brace with the arrow pointing forwards

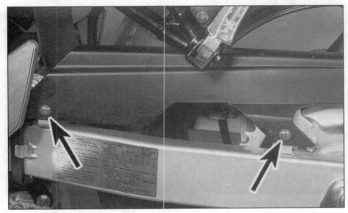

6.1 The chain guard is secured by two screws (arrows)

7.2a The windshield is secured by four screws (arrows)

7

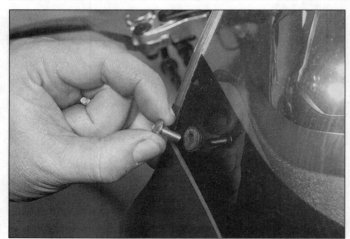

7.2b Remove the screws . . .

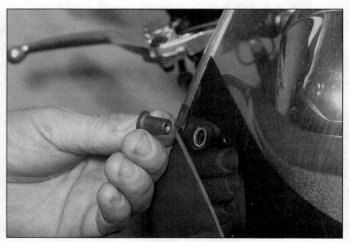

7.2c . . . along with the rubber mounts

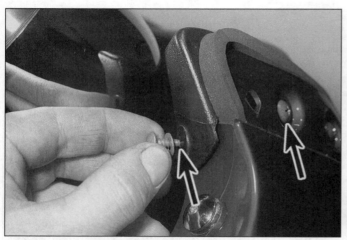

7.3a Remove the two screws (arrows) from each side . . .

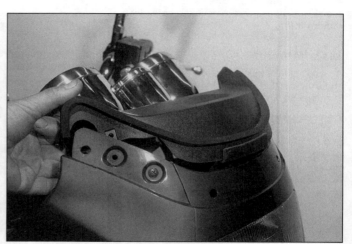

7.3b . . . and remove the trim panel

7.4a Remove the three screws (arrows) securing the fairing side panel . . .

7.4b . . . then carefully remove the panel, noting how its tabs fit into the front panel

Carefully remove the windshield, noting how it fits.

3 Remove the two screws securing each side of the inner trim panel, and remove the panel **(see illustrations)**.

4 Remove the three screws securing one of the fairing side panels, then carefully remove the panel, noting how its tabs locate into the slots in the edge of the front panel **(see illustrations)**. Now remove the other panel.

5 Remove the two screws securing the front panel and draw it off the headlight **(see illustration)**.

Installation

6 Installation is the reverse of removal. Make sure all the fasteners and their washers and rubber dampers are correctly fitted. Replace any of the rubber dampers that are damaged or deteriorated. Make sure all wiring is correctly routed and securely connected.

7 Check the headlight aim before taking the machine on the road.

7.5 The front panel is secured by two screws (arrows)

7

Notes

Chapter 8
Electrical system

Contents

Degrees of difficulty

Easy, suitable for novice with little experience		**Fairly easy,** suitable for beginner with some experience		**Fairly difficult,** suitable for competent DIY mechanic		**Difficult,** suitable for experienced DIY mechanic		**Very difficult,** suitable for expert DIY or professional	

Specifications

Battery

Capacity
GSF600 and GSF600S	12 V, 8 Ah
GSF1200 and GSF1200S	12 V, 10 Ah
Electrolyte specific gravity	1.320 at 20°C

Alternator

Output (max)	405 W at 5000 rpm
Slip ring diameter (min)	14.0 mm
Brush length (min)	4.5 mm

Regulator/rectifier

Regulated voltage (min)	13.5 V at 5000 rpm

Starter motor

Brush length (min)	9.0 mm
Starter relay resistance	3.0 to 5.0 ohms

Fuel level sender (GSF1200 and GSF1200S)

Resistance
Fuel tank full	1 to 5 ohms
Fuel tank empty	103 to 117 ohms

Fuses

Main	30 A
Headlight (high beam)	15 A
Headlight (low beam)	15 A
Turn signal	15 A
Ignition	10 A
Tail light	10 A

Bulbs

Headlight	60/55 W H4 halogen
Sidelight (UK only)	4.0 W
Brake/tail light	21/5 W
Licence plate light	5.0 W
Turn signal lights	21 W
Tachometer light	1.7 W
Speedometer light	1.7 W
Turn signal indicator light	
GSF600 and GSF600S	3.4 W
GSF1200 and GSF1200S	3.0 W
Neutral indicator light	3.0 W
Oil pressure indicator light	
GSF600 and GSF600S	3.4 W
GSF1200 and GSF1200S	3.0 W
High beam indicator light	
GSF600 and GSF600S	1.7 W
GSF1200 and GSF1200S	3.0 W
Fuel gauge light (GSF1200 and GSF1200S)	1.7 W

Torque settings

Alternator mounting bolts	25 Nm
Alternator driven gear nut	60 Nm

1 General information

All models have a 12-volt electrical system. A three-phase alternator unit is fitted which has an integral regulator/rectifier unit.

The regulator maintains the charging system output within the specified range to prevent overcharging, and the rectifier converts the ac (alternating current) output of the alternator to dc (direct current) to power the lights and other components and to charge the battery. The alternator rotor is driven by a drive gear mounted on the back of the primary driven gear.

The starter motor is mounted on the crankcase behind the cylinders. The starting system includes the motor, the battery, the relay and the various wires and switches. If the engine kill switch in the RUN position and the ignition (main) switch is ON, the starter relay allows the starter motor to operate only if the transmission is in neutral (neutral switch on) or, if the transmission is in gear, if the clutch lever is pulled into the handlebar (clutch switch on, where fitted) and the sidestand is up.

Note: *Keep in mind that electrical parts, once purchased, cannot be returned. To avoid unnecessary expense, make very sure the faulty component has been positively identified before buying a replacement part.*

2 Electrical system - fault finding

 Warning: To prevent the risk of short circuits, the ignition (main) switch must always be OFF and the battery negative (-ve) terminal should be disconnected before any of the bike's other electrical components are disturbed. Don't forget to reconnect the terminal securely once work is finished or if battery power is needed for circuit testing.

1 A typical electrical circuit consists of an electrical component, the switches, relays, etc. related to that component and the wiring and connectors that hook the component to both the battery and the frame. To aid in locating a problem in any electrical circuit, refer to the wiring diagrams at the end of this Chapter.

2 Before tackling any troublesome electrical circuit, first study the wiring diagram (see end of Chapter) thoroughly to get a complete picture of what makes up that individual circuit. Trouble spots, for instance, can often be narrowed down by noting if other components related to that circuit are operating properly or not. If several components or circuits fail at one time, chances are the fault lies in the fuse or earth (ground) connection, as several circuits often are routed through the same fuse and earth (ground) connections.

3 Electrical problems often stem from simple causes, such as loose or corroded connections or a blown fuse. Prior to any electrical fault finding, always visually check the condition of the fuse, wires and connections in the problem circuit. Intermittent failures can be especially frustrating, since you can't always duplicate the failure when it's convenient to test. In such situations, a good practice is to clean all connections in the affected circuit, whether or not they appear to be good. All of the connections and wires should also be wiggled to check for looseness which can cause intermittent failure.

4 If testing instruments are going to be utilised, use the wiring diagram to plan where you will make the necessary connections in order to accurately pinpoint the trouble spot.

5 The basic tools needed for electrical fault finding include a battery and bulb test circuit, a continuity tester, a test light, and a jumper wire. A multimeter capable of reading volts, ohms and amps is also very useful as an alternative to the above, and is necessary for performing more extensive tests and checks.

 Refer to Fault Finding Equipment in the Reference section for details of how to use electrical test equipment.

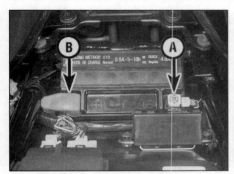

3.1a Disconnect the negative (-ve) terminal (A), then pull back the insulating cover (B) and disconnect the positive (+ve) terminal . . .

3.1b . . . then remove the battery

3.2 Fit the insulating cover over the positive (+ve) terminal

3 Battery - removal, installation, inspection and maintenance

Caution: Be extremely careful when handling or working around the battery. The electrolyte is very caustic and an explosive gas (hydrogen) is given off when the battery is charging.

Removal and installation

1 Remove the seat (see Chapter 7). Unscrew the terminal screws and disconnect the leads from the battery, disconnecting the negative (-ve) terminal first, and noting that the positive (+ve) terminal has an insulating cover which must be pulled back **(see illustration)**. Lift the battery out of its box **(see illustration)**.
2 On installation, clean the battery terminals and lead ends with a wire brush or knife and emery paper. Reconnect the leads, connecting the positive (+ve) terminal first, then fit the insulating cover over the positive (+ve) terminal **(see illustration)**. Install the seat (see Chapter 7).

> **HAYNES HINT**
>
> *Battery corrosion can be kept to a minimum by applying a layer of petroleum jelly to the terminals after the cables have been connected.*

Inspection and maintenance

3 The battery fitted to the models covered in this manual is of the maintenance free (sealed) type, therefore requiring no regular maintenance. However, the following checks should still be regularly performed.
4 Check the battery terminals and leads for tightness and corrosion. If corrosion is evident, unscrew the terminal screws and disconnect the leads from the battery, disconnecting the negative (-ve) terminal first, and clean the terminals and lead ends with a wire brush or knife and emery paper. Reconnect the leads, connecting the negative

(-ve) terminal last, and apply a thin coat of petroleum jelly to the connections to slow further corrosion.
5 The battery case should be kept clean to prevent current leakage, which can discharge the battery over a period of time (especially when it sits unused). Wash the outside of the case with a solution of baking soda and water. Rinse the battery thoroughly, then dry it.
6 Look for cracks in the case and replace the battery if any are found. If acid has been spilled on the frame or battery box, neutralise it with a baking soda and water solution, dry it thoroughly, then touch up any damaged paint.
7 If the motorcycle sits unused for long periods of time, disconnect the cables from the battery terminals, negative (-ve) terminal first. Refer to Section 4 and charge the battery once every month to six weeks.
8 The condition of the battery can be assessed by measuring the voltage present at the battery terminals. Connect the voltmeter positive (+ve) probe to the battery positive (+ve) terminal and the negative (-ve) probe to the battery negative (-ve) terminal. When fully charged there should be more than 12.5 volts present. If the voltage falls below 12.0 volts the battery must be removed, disconnecting the negative (-ve) terminal first, and recharged as described below in Section 4.

4 Battery - charging

Caution: Be extremely careful when handling or working around the battery. The electrolyte is very caustic and an explosive gas (hydrogen) is given off when the battery is charging.

1 Remove the battery (see Section 3). Connect the charger to the battery, making sure that the positive (+ve) lead on the charger is connected to the positive (+ve) terminal on the battery, and the negative (-ve) lead is connected to the negative (-ve) terminal.

2 Suzuki recommend that the battery is charged at a maximum rate of 0.9 amps (GSF600 and GSF600S), or 1.2 amps (GSF1200 and GSF1200S) for 5 hours. Exceeding this figure can cause the battery to overheat, buckling the plates and rendering it useless. Few owners will have access to an expensive current controlled charger, so if a normal domestic charger is used check that after a possible initial peak, the charge rate falls to a safe level **(see illustration)**. If the battery becomes hot during charging **stop**. Further charging will cause damage. **Note:** *In emergencies the battery can be charged at a higher rate of around 4.0 amps (GSF600 and GSF600S), or 5.0 amps (GSF1200 and GSF1200S) for a period of 1 hour. However, this is not recommended and the low amp charge is by far the safer method of charging the battery.*
3 If the recharged battery discharges rapidly if left disconnected it is likely that an internal short caused by physical damage or sulphation has occurred. A new battery will be required. A sound item will tend to lose its charge at about 1% per day.
4 Install the battery (see Section 3).
5 If the motorcycle sits unused for long periods of time, charge the battery once every month to six weeks and leave it disconnected.

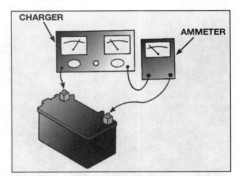

4.2 If the charger doesn't have ammeter built in, connect one in series as shown. DO NOT connect the ammeter between the battery terminals or it will be ruined

5.1 The fusebox is under the seat

5.2a Unclip the fusebox lid to access the fuses

5.2b Remove the starter relay cover . . .

5.2c . . . to access the main fuse (arrow)

5 Fuses - check and replacement

1 The electrical system is protected by fuses of different ratings. All except the main fuse are housed in the fusebox, which is located under the seat **(see illustration)**. The main fuse is integral with the starter relay, which is located behind the left-hand side panel **(see illustration 5.2c)**.
2 To access the fusebox fuses, remove the seat (see Chapter 7) and unclip the fusebox lid **(see illustration)**. To access the main fuse, remove the side panels (see Chapter 7) and the starter relay cover **(see illustrations)**.
3 The fuses can be removed and checked

visually. If you can't pull the fuse out with your fingertips, use a pair of needle-nose pliers **(see illustration)**. A blown fuse is easily identified by a break in the element **(see illustration)**. Each fuse is clearly marked with its rating and must only be replaced by a fuse of the correct rating. A spare fuse of each rating is housed in the fusebox, and a spare main fuse is housed in the bottom of the starter relay **(see illustration)**. If a spare fuse is used, always replace it so that a spare of each rating is carried on the bike at all times.

> ⚠ **Warning: Never put in a fuse of a higher rating or bridge the terminals with any other substitute, however temporary it may be. Serious damage may be done to the circuit, or a fire may start.**

4 If a fuse blows, be sure to check the wiring circuit very carefully for evidence of a short-circuit. Look for bare wires and chafed, melted or burned insulation. If the fuse is replaced before the cause is located, the new fuse will blow immediately.
5 Occasionally a fuse will blow or cause an open-circuit for no obvious reason. Corrosion of the fuse ends and fusebox terminals may occur and cause poor fuse contact. If this happens, remove the corrosion with a wire brush or emery paper, then spray the fuse end and terminals with electrical contact cleaner.

6 Lighting system - check

1 The battery provides power for operation of the headlight, tail light, brake light and instrument cluster lights. If none of the lights operate, always check battery voltage before proceeding. Low battery voltage indicates either a faulty battery or a defective charging system. Refer to Section 3 for battery checks and Sections 32 and 33 for charging system tests. Also, check the condition of the fuses.

Headlight

2 If the headlight fails to work, first check the fuse with the key ON (see Section 5), and then the bulb (see Section 7). If they are both good, use jumper wires to connect the bulb directly to the battery terminals. If the light comes on, the problem lies in the wiring or one of the switches in the circuit. Refer to Section 20 for the switch testing procedures, and also the wiring diagrams at the end of this Chapter.

Tail light

3 If the tail light fails to work, check the bulb and the bulb terminals first, then the fuse, then check for battery voltage on the supply side of the tail light wiring connector. If voltage is present, check the earth (ground) circuit for an open or poor connection.
4 If no voltage is indicated, check the wiring between the tail light and the ignition switch, then check the switch. Also check the lighting switch.

5.3a Pull the fuse out of its socket

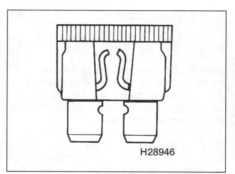

5.3b A blown fuse can be identified by a break in its element

H28946

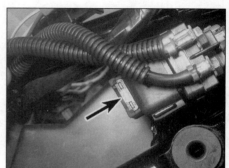

5.3c A spare main fuse (arrow) is housed under the relay

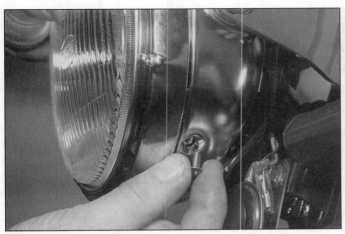

7.1a The headlight rim is secured by two screws, one on each side

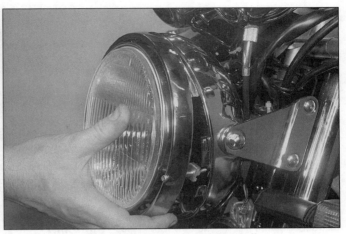

7.1b Ease the rim out of the shell

Brake light

5 See Section 14 for the brake light switch checking procedure.

Neutral light

6 If the neutral light fails to operate when the transmission is in neutral, check the fuse and the bulb (see Sections 5 and 17). If they are in good condition, trace the neutral switch wiring back from the engine sprocket cover and disconnect it at the connector behind the left-hand side panel. Check for battery voltage on the supply side of the connector. If battery voltage is present, refer to Section 22 for the neutral switch check and replacement procedures.

7 If no voltage is indicated, check the wiring between the switch and the bulb for open-circuits and poor connections.

Oil pressure light

8 See Section 18 for the oil pressure switch check.

Instrument lights

9 See Section 17 for instrument light bulb replacement.

7.2 Disconnect the wiring connector and remove the rubber cover

7.3a Release the bulb retaining clip . . .

7.3b . . . and remove the bulb

7.5 Fit the rubber cover with the TOP mark facing upwards

7 Headlight bulb and sidelight bulb - replacement

Note: *The headlight bulb is of the quartz-halogen type. Do not touch the bulb glass as skin acids will shorten the bulb's service life. If the bulb is accidentally touched, it should be wiped carefully when cold with a rag soaked in methylated spirit and dried before fitting.*

⚠️ **Warning: Allow the bulb time to cool before removing it if the headlight has just been on.**

Headlight

GSF600 and GSF1200

1 Unscrew the two screws securing the headlight rim to the headlight shell, and ease the rim out of the shell, noting how it fits **(see illustrations)**.

2 Disconnect the wiring connector and remove the rubber dust cover, noting how it fits **(see illustration)**.

3 Release the bulb retaining clip, noting how it fits, then remove the bulb **(see illustrations)**.

4 Fit the new bulb, bearing in mind the information in the **Note** above. Make sure the tabs on the bulb fit correctly in the slots in the bulb housing, and secure it in position with the retaining clip.

5 Install the dust cover, making sure it is correctly seated and with the TOP mark facing up, and connect the wiring connector **(see illustration)**.

6 Check the operation of the headlight, then install the rim into the shell and secure it with the screws **(see illustrations 7.1a and b)**.

GSF600S and GSF1200S

7 Disconnect the wiring connector from the back of the headlight assembly and remove

8

7.7 Disconnect the wiring connector and remove the rubber cover

7.8a Release the bulb retaining clip . . .

7.8b . . . and remove the bulb

the rubber dust cover, noting how it fits **(see illustration)**.

8 Release the bulb retaining clip, noting how it fits, then remove the bulb **(see illustrations)**.

9 Fit the new bulb, bearing in mind the information in the **Note** above. Make sure the tabs on the bulb fit correctly in the slots in the bulb housing, and secure it in position with the retaining clip.

10 Install the dust cover, making sure it is correctly seated and with the tab at the bottom, and connect the wiring connector **(see illustration 7.7)**.

11 Check the operation of the headlight.

Sidelight

GSF600 and GSF1200

12 Unscrew the two screws securing the headlight rim to the headlight shell, and ease the rim out of the shell, noting how it fits **(see illustrations 7.1a and b)**.

13 Pull up the rubber cover, then push the bulbholder in and twist it anti-clockwise to release it from its socket in the headlight **(see illustration)**. Push the bulb in and twist it anti-clockwise to release it from the bulbholder **(see illustration)**.

14 Install the new bulb in the bulbholder, then install the bulbholder by pressing it in and twisting it clockwise.

15 Check the operation of the sidelight, then install the headlight rim into the shell and secure it with the screws **(see illustrations 7.1a and b)**.

GSF600S and GSF1200S

16 Pull the bulbholder out of its socket in the base of the headlight **(see illustration)**. Push the bulb in and twist it anti-clockwise to release it from the bulbholder **(see illustration)**.

17 Install the new bulb in the bulbholder, then install the bulbholder by pressing it in. Make sure the rubber cover is correctly seated.

18 Check the operation of the sidelight.

7.13a Remove the sidelight bulbholder from the headlight . . .

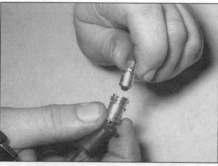

7.13b . . . and remove the bulb from the holder

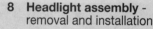

8 Headlight assembly - removal and installation

GSF600 and GSF1200

Removal

1 Remove the two screws securing the headlight rim to the headlight shell, and ease the rim out of the shell, noting how it fits **(see illustrations 7.1a and b)**.

2 Disconnect the wiring connector from the headlight bulb and the sidelight bulb **(see illustration)**.

7.16a The sidelight bulb is in the base of the headlight (arrow)

7.16b To release the bulb gently push it in and twist it anti-clockwise

8.2 Disconnect the wiring connectors (arrows) from the headlight and sidelight bulbs

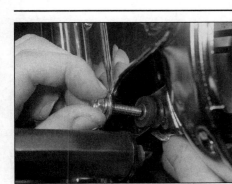

8.3a Remove the guide bolt

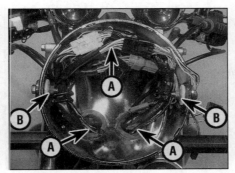

8.3b Feed the wiring through the holes (A), then unscrew the nuts (B) and remove the bolts

8.6 Disconnect the wiring connectors (arrows) from the headlight and sidelight bulbs

3 To remove the headlight shell, first unscrew the nut and withdraw the bolt on the guide on the right-hand side of the headlight (see illustration). Free the wiring inside the shell from any clamps, then disconnect any wiring connectors necessary and ease the wiring out the back of the shell. Unscrew the nuts on the inside of the shell and remove the bolts securing the shell to the brackets and remove the shell (see illustration). If necessary, unscrew the bolts securing the brackets to the support frames and remove the brackets.

 HAYNES HiNT **When disconnecting wiring, label the connectors to avoid confusion on reconnection.**

Installation

4 Installation is the reverse of removal. Make sure all the wiring is correctly connected and secured. Check the operation of the headlight and sidelight. Check the headlight aim (see Chapter 1).

GSF600S and GSF1200S

Removal

5 Remove the fairing (see Chapter 7).
6 Disconnect the wiring connector from the headlight bulb and the sidelight bulb (see illustration).

7 Unscrew the four screws securing the headlight unit to the fairing stay and remove the headlight, noting how it fits (see illustration).

Installation

8 Installation is the reverse of removal. Make sure all the wiring is correctly connected and secured. Check the operation of the headlight and sidelight. Check the headlight aim (see Chapter 1).

9 Tail light bulb and licence plate bulb - replacement

Tail light bulb

1 Remove the seat (see Chapter 7).
2 Remove the two screws securing the top cover to the side panels and remove the cover, noting how it locates (see illustrations 10.2a and b).
3 Turn the bulbholder anti-clockwise and withdraw it from the tail light (see illustration).
4 Push the bulb into the holder and twist it anti-clockwise to remove it (see illustration). Check the socket terminals for corrosion and clean them if necessary. Line up the pins of the new bulb with the slots in the socket, then push the bulb in and turn it clockwise until it

8.7 The headlight assembly is secured by four screws (arrows)

locks into place. **Note:** *The pins on the bulb are offset so it can only be installed one way. It is a good idea to use a paper towel or dry cloth when handling the new bulb to prevent injury if the bulb should break and to increase bulb life.*
5 Install the bulbholder into the tail light and turn it clockwise to secure it.
6 Install the seat (see Chapter 7).

Licence plate bulb

7 Remove the seat and the side panels (see Chapter 7).
8 Unscrew the two nuts securing the licence plate light assembly cover and remove the cover (see illustration).

9.3 Twist the bulbholder anti-clockwise to release it from the tail light

9.4 To release the bulb gently push it in and twist it anti-clockwise. Note that the pins on the bulb are offset

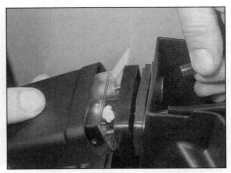

9.8 The licence plate light assembly is secured by two nuts

9.9 To release the bulb gently push it in and twist it anti-clockwise

10.2a Remove the two screws (arrows) . . .

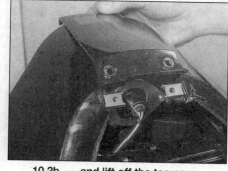

10.2b . . . and lift off the top cover

9 Push the bulb into the holder and twist it anti-clockwise to remove it **(see illustration)**. Check the socket terminals for corrosion and clean them if necessary. Line up the pins of the new bulb with the slots in the socket, then push the bulb in and turn it clockwise until it locks into place. **Note:** *It is a good idea to use a paper towel or dry cloth when handling the new bulb to prevent injury if the bulb should break and to increase bulb life.*
10 Install the cover and tighten the nuts.
11 Install the side panels and seat (see Chapter 7).

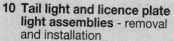
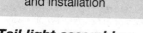

10 Tail light and licence plate light assemblies - removal and installation

Tail light assembly

Removal

1 Remove the seat (see Chapter 7).
2 Remove the two screws securing the top cover to the side panels and remove the cover, noting how it locates **(see illustrations)**.
3 Trace the tail light wiring back from the bulbholder and disconnect it at the connector **(see illustration)**.
4 Remove the three screws securing the tail light and carefully withdraw it from the bike **(see illustration)**. If required, turn the bulbholder anti-clockwise and withdraw it from the tail light.

10.3 Disconnect the tail light wiring connector

Installation

5 Installation is the reverse of removal. Check the operation of the tail light and the brake light.

Licence plate light assembly

Removal

6 Remove the seat and side panels (see Chapter 7).
7 Trace the licence plate light wiring back from the bulbholder and disconnect it at the connector.
8 Unscrew the two nuts securing the licence plate light assembly and remove the assembly, taking care not to snag the wiring connector as you draw it through the hole **(see illustration 9.8)**. If required, push the

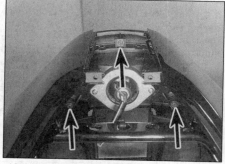

10.4 The tail light assembly is secured by three screws (arrows)

bulb into the holder and twist it anti-clockwise to remove it.

Installation

9 Installation is the reverse of removal. Check the operation of the light.

11 Turn signal bulbs - replacement

1 Remove the three screws securing the lens to the turn signal assembly and remove the lens, noting which way round it fits **(see illustrations)**. Remove the rubber gasket and check it for damage or deterioration **(see illustration)**. Replace it if necessary.

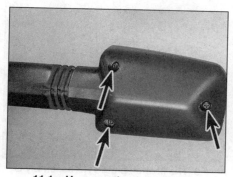

11.1a Unscrew the three screws (arrows) . . .

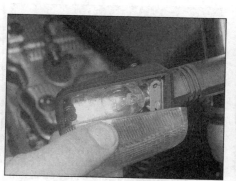

11.1b . . . and remove the turn signal lens

11.1c Replace the gasket if necessary

11.2 To release the bulb gently push it in and twist it anti-clockwise

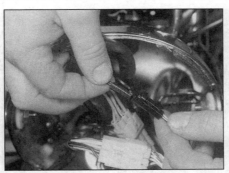

12.2 The front turn signal wire connectors are inside the headlight

12.3 Front turn signal mounting nut

2 Push the bulb into the holder and twist it anti-clockwise to remove it **(see illustration)**. Check the socket terminals for corrosion and clean them if necessary. Line up the pins of the new bulb with the slots in the socket, then push the bulb in and turn it clockwise until it locks into place. **Note:** *It is a good idea to use a paper towel or dry cloth when handling the new bulb to prevent injury if the bulb should break and to increase bulb life.*
3 Install the lens back onto the cover, using a new gasket if required, and tighten the cover retaining screws. Take care not to overtighten the screws as the assembly is easily cracked.

> **HAYNES HiNT**
> *If the socket contacts are dirty or corroded, scrape them clean and spray with electrical contact cleaner before a new bulb is installed.*

12 Turn signal assemblies - removal and installation

Front - GSF600 and GSF1200

Removal

1 Remove the two screws securing the headlight rim to the headlight shell, and ease the rim out of the shell, noting how it fits **(see illustrations 7.1a and b)**.

2 Trace the turn signal wiring back from the turn signal and disconnect it at the connectors inside the headlight shell **(see illustration)**. Pull the wiring through to the turn signal mounting, noting its routing.
3 Unscrew the nut securing the turn signal assembly to the support frame and carefully remove the assembly, taking care not to snag the wiring connectors as you draw them through the mounting hole **(see illustration)**.

Installation

4 Installation is the reverse of removal. Make sure the wiring is correctly routed and securely connected. Check the operation of the turn signals.

Front - GSF600S and GSF1200S

Removal

5 Trace the turn signal wiring back from the turn signal and disconnect it at the connector inside the fairing. Pull the wiring through to the turn signal mounting, noting its routing.
6 Unscrew the nut securing the turn signal assembly to the support frame and carefully withdraw the turn signal from the fairing, taking care not to snag the wiring connectors as you draw them through the mounting hole **(see illustrations)**.

Installation

7 Installation is the reverse of removal. Make sure the wiring is correctly routed and securely connected. Check the operation of the turn signals.

Rear - all models

Removal

8 Remove the seat (see Chapter 7). Trace the turn signal wiring back from the turn signal and disconnect it at the connector **(see illustration)**. Pull the wiring through to the turn signal mounting, releasing it from any clips and noting its routing.
9 Unscrew the nut securing the turn signal assembly to the mudguard and carefully remove the assembly, taking care not to snag the wiring connectors as you draw them through the mounting hole **(see illustration)**.

Installation

10 Installation is the reverse of removal. Make sure the wiring is correctly routed and securely connected. Check the operation of the turn signals.

12.6a Unscrew the nut (arrow) . . .

12.6b and remove the turn signal

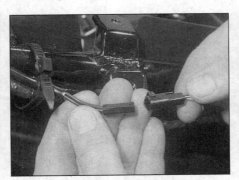

12.8 Disconnect the turn signal wiring connector

12.9 The rear turn signal assembly is secured to the mudguard by a single nut (arrow)

13.3 Disconnect the turn signal relay wiring connector (arrow) and check for power at the orange/green terminal

14.5 Disconnect the wiring connectors (A), then remove the switch screw (B)

13 Turn signal circuit - check

1 The battery provides power for operation of the turn signal lights, so if they do not operate, always check the battery voltage first. Low battery voltage indicates either a faulty battery or a defective charging system. Refer to Section 3 for battery checks and Sections 32 and 33 for charging system tests. Also, check the fuse (see Section 5) and the switch (see Section 20).

2 Most turn signal problems are the result of a burned out bulb or corroded socket. This is especially true when the turn signals function properly in one direction, but fail to flash in the other direction. Check the bulbs and the sockets (see Section 11).

3 If the bulbs and sockets are good, check for power at the turn signal relay orange/green wire with the ignition ON. The relay is mounted behind the left-hand side panel (see illustration). Remove the side panels for access (see Chapter 7). Turn the ignition OFF when the check is complete.

4 If no power was present at the relay, check the wiring from the relay to the ignition (main) switch for continuity.

5 If power was present at the relay, using the appropriate wiring diagram at the end of this Chapter, check the wiring between the relay, turn signal switch and turn signal lights for continuity. If the wiring and switch are sound, replace the relay with a new one.

14 Brake light switches - check and replacement

Circuit check

1 Before checking any electrical circuit, check the bulb (see Section 9) and fuse (see Section 5).

2 Using a multimeter or test light connected to a good earth (ground), check for voltage at the brake light switch wiring connector (see illustration 14.5 or 14.8). If there's no voltage present, check the wire between the switch and the ignition switch (see the wiring diagrams at the end of this Chapter).

3 If voltage is available, touch the probe of the test light to the other terminal of the switch, then pull the brake lever in or depress the brake pedal. If no reading is obtained or the test light doesn't light up, replace the switch.

4 If a reading is obtained or the test light does light up, check the wiring between the switch and the brake light bulb (see the wiring diagrams at the end of this Chapter).

Switch replacement

Front brake lever switch

5 Disconnect the wiring connectors from the switch (see illustration).

6 Remove the single screw securing the switch to the bottom of the front brake master cylinder and remove the switch (see illustration 14.5).

7 Installation is the reverse of removal. The switch isn't adjustable.

Rear brake pedal switch

8 The switch is mounted to the back of the right-hand footrest bracket. Pull the terminal cover off the top of the switch and disconnect the wiring connector (see illustration).

9 Detach the lower end of the switch spring from the brake pedal, then unscrew the switch (see illustration).

14.8 Rear brake light switch wiring connector (arrow)

14.9 Unhook the spring from the pedal (arrow)

15.1a Instrument cluster wiring connector - GSF600 and GSF1200

15.1b On GSF600S and GSF1200S models, the connectors are housed inside a cover that sits on top of the headlight

15.2 Unscrew its knurled ring (arrow) and detach the speedometer cable

10 Installation is the reverse of removal. Make sure the brake light is activated just before the rear brake pedal takes effect. If adjustment is necessary, hold the switch and turn the adjusting nut on the switch body until the brake light is activated when required.

15 Instrument cluster and speedometer cable - removal and installation

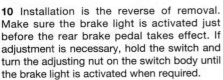

Instrument cluster

Removal

1 Trace the wiring back from the instrument cluster and disconnect it at the connector (blue). On models without a fairing, the connector is located inside the top of the headlight shell (**see illustration**). Remove the two screws securing the headlight rim to the headlight shell, and ease the rim out of the shell, noting how it fits (**see illustrations 7.1a and b**). Release the wiring from any clips or ties. On S models, the connector is in a cover which sits on top of the headlight inside the fairing (**see illustration**).
2 Unscrew the speedometer cable retaining ring from the back of the speedometer and detach the cable (**see illustration**).
3 Unscrew the bolts (four on 600 models, two on 1200 models) which secure the instrument

cluster bracket to the underside of the top yoke and carefully remove the assembly from the yoke, taking care not to snag the wiring and noting its routing.

Installation

4 Installation is the reverse of removal. Make sure that the speedometer cable and wiring connector are correctly routed and secured.

Speedometer cable

Removal

5 Unscrew the speedometer cable retaining ring from the rear of the instrument cluster and detach the cable (**see illustration 15.2**).
6 Unscrew the retaining ring (600 models) or screw (1200 models) securing the lower end of the cable to the drive housing on the left-hand side of the front wheel.
7 Withdraw the cable from its guides and remove it from the bike, noting its correct routing.

Installation

8 Route the cable correctly and install it in its retaining guides.
9 Connect the cable upper end to the instrument cluster and tighten the retaining ring securely (**see illustration**).
10 Connect the cable lower end to the drive housing, aligning the slot in the cable end with the drive tab, and tighten the retaining ring

(600 models) or screw (1200 models) securely (**see illustration**).
11 Check that the cable doesn't restrict steering movement or interfere with any other components.

16 Instruments - check and replacement

Speedometer

Check

1 Special instruments are required to properly check the operation of this meter. If it is believed to be faulty, take the motorcycle to a Suzuki dealer for assessment.

Replacement

2 Unscrew the speedometer cable retaining ring from the rear of the instrument cluster and detach the cable (**see illustration 15.2**).
3 On 600 models, unscrew the two bolts securing the speedometer and lift it off the bracket (**see illustration**). Note how the holes in the mounting plate locate over the lugs on the bracket. Remove the single screw securing the casing and withdraw the speedometer from the casing, then remove the bulbholders.

15.9 Install the upper end . . .

15.10 . . . and the lower end of the speedometer cable

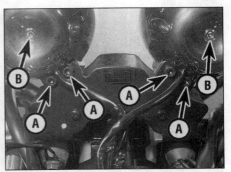

16.3 Remove the relevant instrument mounting bolts (A), then remove the casing screw (B) and withdraw the instrument

16.4a Remove the screw (arrow) . . .

16.4b . . . and remove the speedometer casing

16.4c The speedometer is secured by two nuts (arrows)

4 On 1200 models, remove the single screw securing the speedometer casing and remove the casing, noting how it fits **(see illustrations)**. Remove the bulbholders from the back of the speedometer. Unscrew the two nuts securing the speedometer to the bracket and remove the speedometer **(see illustration)**.

5 Installation is the reverse of removal. Make sure the cable is correctly and securely connected.

Tachometer

Check

6 Trace the wiring back from the instrument cluster and disconnect it at the connector (blue). On models without a fairing, the connector is located inside the top of the headlight shell **(see illustration 15.1a)**. Remove the two screws securing the headlight rim to the headlight shell, and ease the rim out of the shell, noting how it fits **(see illustrations 7.1a and b)**. On S models, the connector is in a cover which sits on top of the headlight inside the fairing **(see illustration 15.1b)**.

7 Using a multimeter or continuity tester, check for continuity first between the black/red and black/white terminals on the

instrument side of the wiring connector, then between the orange/green and black/white terminals. There should be continuity in both cases. If not, check the wiring between the connector and the tachometer for breakage. If the wiring is good, check for voltage at the orange/green wire connector on the wiring loom side of the connector. If voltage is present, check the black/red wire between the connector and the ignition control module for continuity (see the *wiring diagrams* at the end of this Chapter). If the wiring is good, then a faulty tachometer is indicated; take the tachometer to a Suzuki dealer for assessment.

Replacement

8 On 600 models, unscrew the two bolts securing the tachometer and lift it off the bracket **(see illustration 16.3)**. Note how the holes in the mounting plate locate over the lugs on the bracket. Remove the single screw securing the casing and withdraw the tachometer from the casing, then remove the bulbholders. Remove the screws securing the three tachometer wires, noting their positions **(see illustration)**.

9 On 1200 models, unscrew the single screw securing the tachometer casing and remove

the casing **(see illustrations 16.4a and b)**. Remove the bulbholders from the back of the tachometer followed by the screws securing the three wires, noting their positions **(see illustration)**. Unscrew the two nuts securing the tachometer to the bracket and remove the tachometer.

10 Installation is the reverse of removal. Make sure the wires are correctly and securely connected.

Fuel gauge (GSF1200 and GSF1200S)

Check

11 Remove the seat (see Chapter 7). Trace the fuel level sender wiring from the underside of the fuel tank and disconnect it at the connector.

12 Connect a jumper wire between the black/white and yellow/black terminals on the wiring loom side of the connector. With the ignition switched ON, the fuel gauge should read FULL. If it doesn't, check the wiring between the connector and the gauge, and check for voltage at the orange/green wire on the back of the fuel gauge. If the wiring is good, then the gauge is faulty.

13 If the gauge reads FULL, check the fuel level sender inside the fuel tank (see Section 27).

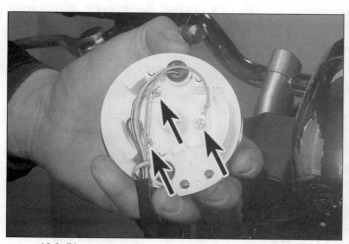

16.8 Disconnect the three tachometer wires (arrows)

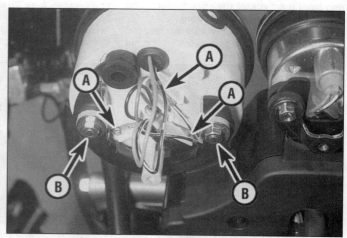

16.9 Disconnect the three tachometer wires (A), then remove the two nuts (B)

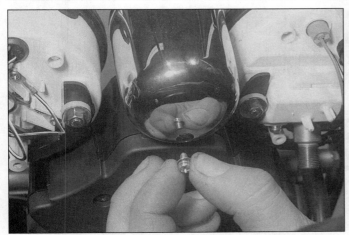

16.14a Remove the screw to free the fuel gauge casing

16.14b The fuel gauge is secured by two nuts (arrows)

Replacement

14 Remove the single screw securing the fuel gauge casing and remove the casing **(see illustration)**. Unscrew the two nuts securing the gauge to the bracket and slip the gauge of the bracket **(see illustration)**. Pull the bulbholder out of the gauge and remove the three screws securing the gauge wires; make a note of the wire locations as a guide to installation.

15 Installation is the reverse of removal. Make sure the wires are correctly and securely connected.

---

17 Instrument and warning light bulbs - replacement

Instrument light bulbs

1 Remove the relevant instrument from the casing (GSF600 and GSF600S) or the casing from the instrument (GSF1200 and GSF1200S) (see Section 16).
2 Gently pull the bulbholder out of the instrument, then pull the bulb out of the bulbholder **(see illustrations)**. If the socket contacts are dirty or corroded, scrape them

clean and spray with electrical contact cleaner before a new bulb is installed. Carefully push the new bulb into the holder and install the instrument (see Section 16).

Warning light bulbs

3 On 600 models, remove the two screws on the back of the instrument cluster, then snip the cable tie and lift the warning light panel off the cluster **(see illustrations)**. Pull the relevant bulbholder out of the back of the panel. Gently pull the bulb out of the

bulbholder. If the socket contacts are dirty or corroded, scrape them clean and spray with electrical contact cleaner before a new bulb is installed. Carefully push the new bulb into position, then push the bulbholder back into the rear of the panel.
4 On 1200 models, remove the screw securing each instrument casing and remove the casings **(see illustration 16.4a and b)**. Release the instrument wiring from any ties, then remove the two screws securing the rear cover and remove the cover **(see illustration)**.

17.2a Pull the bulbholder out of the instrument . . .

17.2b . . . and the bulb out of the holder

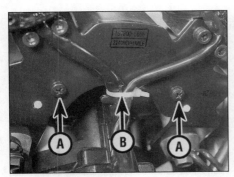

17.3a Remove the two screws (A) and snip the cable tie (B) . . .

17.3b . . . and lift the panel off the cluster

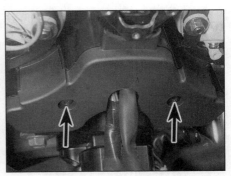

17.4a Unscrew the screws (arrows) and remove the cover

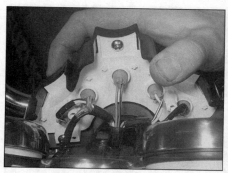

17.4b Lift up the panel . . .

17.4c . . . then remove the bulbholder . . .

17.4d . . . and replace the bulb

Lift the warning light panel up, noting how it fits **(see illustration)**. Pull the relevant bulbholder out of the back of the panel, then gently pull the bulb out of the bulbholder **(see illustrations)**. If the socket contacts are dirty or corroded, scrape them clean and spray with electrical contact cleaner before a new bulb is installed. Carefully push the new bulb into position, then push the bulbholder back into the rear of the panel.

18 Oil pressure switch - check, removal and installation

Check

1 The oil pressure warning light should come on when the ignition (main) switch is turned ON and extinguish a few seconds after the engine is started. If the oil pressure warning light comes on whilst the engine is running, stop the engine immediately and carry out an oil pressure check as described in Chapter 1.
2 If the oil pressure warning light does not come on when the ignition is turned on, check the bulb (see Section 17) and fuse (see Section 5).
3 The oil pressure switch is screwed into the right-hand side of the crankcase and is accessed by unscrewing the bolts securing the pulse generator assembly cover **(see illustration 18.7)**. Remove the cover and its

gasket (a new one must be used) and detach the wiring connector from the switch **(see illustration)**. With the ignition switched ON, earth (ground) the wire on the crankcase and check that the warning light comes on. If the light comes on, the switch is defective and must be replaced.
4 If the light still does not come on, check for voltage at the wire terminal. If there is no voltage present, check the wire between the switch, the instrument cluster and fusebox for continuity (see the *wiring diagrams* at the end of this Chapter).
5 If the warning light comes on whilst the engine is running, yet the oil pressure is satisfactory, remove the wire from the oil pressure switch **(see illustration 18.3)**. With the wire detached and the ignition switched ON the light should be out. If it is illuminated, the wire between the switch and instrument cluster must be earthed (grounded) at some point. If the wiring is good, the switch must be assumed faulty and replaced.

Removal

6 Drain the engine oil (see Chapter 1).
7 Unscrew the five bolts securing the pulse generator assembly cover to the right-hand side of the crankcase **(see illustration)**. Remove the cover and discard the gasket as a new one must be used. Note the sealing washer fitted on the top bolt.
8 Detach the wiring connector from the switch **(see illustration 18.3)**.

9 Unscrew the oil pressure switch and withdraw it from the crankcase.

Installation

10 Apply a suitable sealant (Suzuki-Bond 1207B or equivalent) to the threads of the switch, then install it in the crankcase and tighten it securely.
11 Install the pulse generator assembly cover using a new gasket and tighten the bolts securely. Do not forget to fit the sealing washer on the top cover bolt **(see illustration)**.
12 Fill the engine with the correct type and quantity of oil as described in Chapter 1.

19 Ignition (main) switch - check, removal and installation

> **Warning: To prevent the risk of short circuits, disconnect the battery negative (-ve) lead before making any ignition (main) switch checks.**

Check

1 Trace the ignition (main) switch wiring back from the base of the switch and disconnect it at the connector (green). On models without a fairing, the connector is in the headlight

18.3 Oil pressure switch wiring connector (arrow)

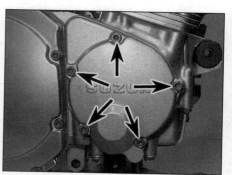

18.7 The pulse generator assembly cover is secured by five bolts

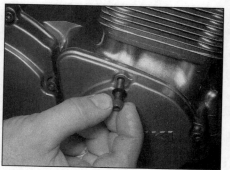

18.11 A sealing washer is fitted on the top bolt

19.1 Ignition switch wiring connector

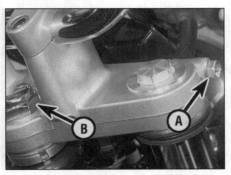

19.9 Slacken the clamp bolts (A), then remove the steering stem nut (B)

housing **(see illustration)**. Remove the two screws securing the headlight rim to the headlight shell, and ease the rim out of the shell **(see illustrations 7.1a and b)**.

2 Using an ohmmeter or a continuity tester, check the continuity of the connector terminal pairs (see the *wiring diagrams* at the end of this Chapter). Continuity should exist between the terminals connected by a solid line on the diagram when the switch is in the indicated position.

3 If the switch fails any of the tests, replace it.

Removal

Note: *Support the bike on its centrestand or an auxiliary stand and tie the back end down so that all weight is off the front end of the bike.*

4 On S models, remove the fairing (see Chapter 7).

5 On models without a fairing, remove the headlight (see Section 8).

6 Displace the handlebars from the top yoke (see Chapter 5).

7 Remove the instrument cluster (see Section 15).

8 Trace the ignition switch wiring and disconnect it at the connector (see Step 1).

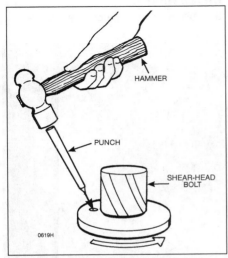

19.10 The shear-head bolts must be carefully unscrewed using a hammer and punch

9 Slacken the fork clamp bolts in the top yoke, then remove the steering stem nut and washer **(see illustration)**. Lift the top yoke off the steering stem.

10 Special security bolts are used to mount the ignition switch to the underside of the top yoke. Remove the two special Torx bolts using a centre punch and hammer to initially slacken them **(see illustration)**. Alternatively, drill the bolt heads off. New bolts must be used on installation.

Installation

11 Install the switch onto the top yoke. Using new special Torx bolts, tighten them until either the tool slips round on the bolt head, or until the bolt head sheers off.

12 The remainder of installation is the reverse of removal. Tighten the steering stem nut and the fork clamp bolts in the top yoke to the torque settings specified at the beginning of Chapter 5. Make sure all wiring is correctly connected and secured by any clips or ties.

20 Handlebar switches - check

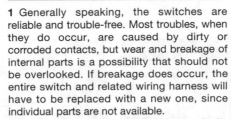

1 Generally speaking, the switches are reliable and trouble-free. Most troubles, when they do occur, are caused by dirty or corroded contacts, but wear and breakage of internal parts is a possibility that should not be overlooked. If breakage does occur, the entire switch and related wiring harness will have to be replaced with a new one, since individual parts are not available.

2 The switches can be checked for continuity using an ohmmeter or a continuity test light. Always disconnect the battery negative (-ve) cable, which will prevent the possibility of a short circuit, before making the checks.

3 Trace the wiring harness of the switch in question back to its connector and disconnect it (right-hand switch - black connector; left-hand switch - yellow connector). On models without a fairing, the connectors are in the headlight housing; remove the two screws securing the headlight rim to the headlight shell, and ease the rim out of the shell **(see illustrations 7.1a and b)**. On

S models, the connectors are in a cover which sits on top of the headlight inside the fairing **(see illustration 15.1b)**.

4 Check for continuity between the terminals of the switch harness with the switch in the various positions (ie switch off - no continuity, switch on - continuity) - see the *wiring diagrams* at the end of this Chapter.

5 If the continuity check indicates a problem exists, refer to Section 21, remove the switch and spray the switch contacts with electrical contact cleaner. If they are accessible, the contacts can be scraped clean with a knife or polished with crocus cloth. If switch components are damaged or broken, it will be obvious when the switch is disassembled.

21 Handlebar switches - removal and installation

Right-hand handlebar switch

Removal

1 If the switch is to be removed from the bike, rather than just displaced from the handlebar, trace the wiring harness back from the switch to the wiring connector and disconnect it (black connector). On models without a fairing, the connectors are in the headlight housing; remove the two screws securing the headlight rim to the headlight shell, and ease the rim out of the shell **(see illustrations 7.1a and b)**. On S models, the connectors are in a cover which sits on top of the headlight inside the fairing **(see illustration 15.1b)**. Work back along the harness, freeing it from all the relevant clips and ties, whilst noting its correct routing.

2 Disconnect the two wires from the brake light switch **(see illustration 14.5)**.

3 Remove the throttle cables from the switch (see Chapter 4 - this procedure incorporates switch removal).

Installation

4 Installation is the reverse of removal. Make sure the locating pin in the upper half of the switch fits into hole in the top of the handlebar. Refer to Chapter 4 for installation of the throttle cables.

Left-hand handlebar switch

Removal

5 If the switch is to be removed from the bike, rather than just displaced from the handlebar, trace the wiring harness back from the switch to the wiring connector and disconnect it (yellow connector). On models without a fairing, the connectors are in the headlight housing; remove the two screws securing the headlight rim to the headlight shell, and ease the rim out of the shell **(see illustrations 7.1a and b)**. On S models, the connectors are in a cover which sits on top of the headlight inside the fairing **(see illustration 15.1b)**. Work back

21.6 Disconnect the clutch switch wiring connectors

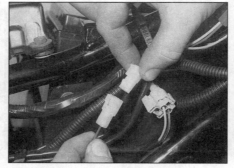

22.2 Disconnect the neutral switch wiring connector

22.6a Remove the bolt and slide the gearchange arm off the shaft

along the harness, freeing it from all the relevant clips and ties, whilst noting its correct routing.

6 Disconnect the two wires from the clutch switch **(see illustration)**.

7 Remove the choke cable from the switch (see Chapter 4 - this procedure incorporates switch removal).

Installation

8 Installation is the reverse of removal. Make sure the locating pin in the upper half of the switch fits into hole in the top of the handlebar. Refer to Chapter 4 for installation of the choke cable.

---

22 Neutral switch - check, removal and installation

Check

1 Before checking the electrical circuit, check the bulb (see Section 17) and fuse (see Section 5).

2 The switch is located in the left-hand side of the crankcase behind the engine sprocket cover. Trace the switch wiring from the grommet on top of the engine sprocket cover and disconnect it at its connector (white) behind the left-hand side panel **(see illustration)**. Make sure the transmission is in neutral.

3 With the connector disconnected and the ignition switched ON, the neutral light should be out. If not, the wire between the connector and instrument cluster must be earthed (grounded) at some point.

4 Check for continuity between the switch side of the wiring connector and the crankcase. With the transmission in neutral, there should be continuity. With the transmission in gear, there should be no continuity. If the tests prove otherwise, then either the switch is faulty or the spring and plunger mechanism in the selector drum is faulty. Remove the switch (see below) and check the condition of the spring and plunger; make sure that the plunger moves freely in its hole. If there is any sign of wear or damage, replace the spring and plunger and check the operation of the switch before buying a new switch.

5 If the continuity tests prove the switch is good, check for voltage at the wire terminal using a test light. If there's no voltage present, check the wire between the switch, the instrument cluster and fusebox (see the *wiring diagrams* at the end of this Chapter).

Removal

6 Unscrew the gearchange linkage arm pinch bolt and remove the arm from the shaft, noting any alignment marks **(see illustration)**. If no marks are visible, make your own before removing the lever so that it can be correctly aligned with the shaft on installation. Unscrew the bolts securing the engine sprocket cover to the crankcase, and free the wiring grommet from the cover as you remove it **(see illustration)**. There is no need to detach the clutch cable or release cylinder from the cover.

7 Trace the switch wiring from the switch and disconnect it at its connector behind the left-hand side panel **(see illustration 22.2)**. Free the wiring from any clips or ties, noting its routing.

8 Remove the two screws securing the switch to the crankcase and carefully remove it, together with the contact plunger and spring **(see illustration)**. Discard the O-ring as a new one must be used.

Installation

9 Install the spring and plunger into the hole

22.6b Free the grommet (arrow) from the cover as you remove it

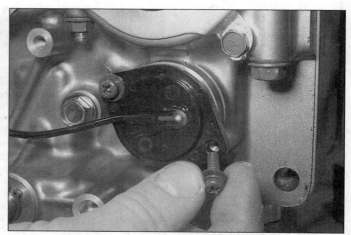

22.8 The switch is secured by two screws

22.9a Fit the spring and plunger (arrow), and a new O-ring . . .

22.9b . . . then fit the cover

22.10 Route the wire behind the tab (arrow) on the seal retainer plate

in the end of the selector drum, then install the switch using a new O-ring and tighten its screws securely **(see illustrations)**.
10 Route the wiring up to its connector behind the left-hand side panel and reconnect it **(see illustration)**. Secure the wiring with any clips or ties.
11 Check the operation of the neutral light.
12 Install the sprocket cover and the gearchange linkage arm, aligning the marks made on removal.

23 Sidestand switch -
check and replacement

Check

1 The sidestand switch is mounted on the frame just ahead of the sidestand **(see illustration 23.8)**. The switch is part of the safety circuit which prevents or stops the engine running if the transmission is in gear whilst the sidestand is down, and prevents the engine from starting if the transmission is in gear unless the sidestand is up, and unless the clutch is pulled in (models with clutch switch - see Section 25). Before checking the electrical circuit, check the bulb (see Section 17) and fuse (see Section 5).
2 Trace the wiring back from the switch to its connector behind the left-hand side panel and disconnect it **(see illustration)**.
3 Check the operation of the switch using an ohmmeter or continuity test light. Connect the meter to the black/white and green wires on the switch side of the connector. With the sidestand up there should be continuity (zero

resistance) between the terminals, and with the stand down there should be no continuity (infinite resistance).
4 If the switch does not perform as expected, it is defective and must be replaced. Check first that the fault is not caused by a sticking switch plunger due to the ingress of road dirt; spray the switch with a water dispersant aerosol.
5 If the switch is good, check the sidestand relay and diode as described in the relevant sections of this Chapter. Also check the wiring between the various components (see the *wiring diagrams* at the end of this book).

Replacement

6 The sidestand switch is mounted on the frame just ahead of the sidestand. Trace the wiring back from the switch to its connector behind the left-hand side panel and disconnect it **(see illustration 23.2)**.
7 Work back along the switch wiring, freeing it from any relevant retaining clips and ties, noting its correct routing.
8 Remove the two screws securing the switch to the frame **(see illustration)**.
9 Fit the new switch to the frame and install

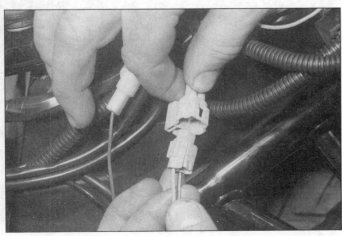

23.2 Disconnect the sidestand switch wiring connector

23.8 The sidestand switch is secured by two screws (arrows)

8

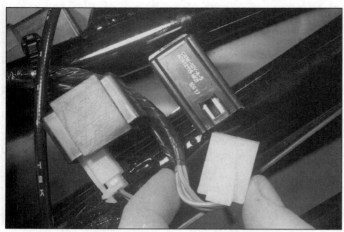

24.2a Disconnect the wiring connector from the sidestand relay

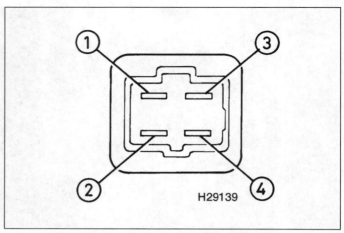

24.2b Sidestand relay terminal identification

the retaining screws, tightening them securely.

10 Make sure the wiring is correctly routed up to the connector and retained by all the necessary clips and ties.

11 Reconnect the wiring connector and check the operation of the sidestand switch.

24 Sidestand relay - check and replacement

Check

1 If the sidestand switch and wiring are good, the sidestand relay may be at fault. The relay is located behind the left-hand side panel.

2 Disconnect the relay wiring connector and remove the relay from its mounting **(see illustration)**. Using an ohmmeter or continuity tester, connect the positive (+ve) lead to the no. 1 terminal on the relay and the

negative (-ve) lead to the no. 2 terminal on the relay **(see illustration)**. There should be no continuity between the terminals.

3 Using an auxiliary 12V battery and a set of leads, connect the battery positive (+ve) lead to the no. 3 terminal on the relay, and the battery negative (-ve) lead to the no. 4 terminal on the relay. With the battery connected, there should be continuity (zero resistance) between nos. 1 and 2 terminals. If either of the above conditions do not exist, replace the relay.

4 If the relay is good, check the other components in the starter circuit as described in the relevant sections of this Chapter. If all components are good, check the wiring between the various components (see the *wiring diagrams* at the end of this book).

Replacement

5 Remove the side panels (see Chapter 7).

6 Disconnect the relay wiring connector and remove the relay from its mounting **(see illustration 24.2a)**.

7 Connect the wiring connector to the new relay and check the operation of the sidestand switch.

25 Clutch switch - check and replacement

Check

1 The clutch switch is situated on the base of the clutch lever bracket (600 models) or master cylinder (1200 models). The switch is part of the safety circuit which prevents or stops the engine running if the transmission is in gear whilst the sidestand is down, and prevents the engine from starting if the transmission is in gear unless the sidestand is up and the clutch lever is pulled in.

2 To check the switch, disconnect the wiring connectors from the switch **(see illustration)**. Connect the probes of an ohmmeter or a continuity test light to the two switch terminals. With the clutch lever pulled in,

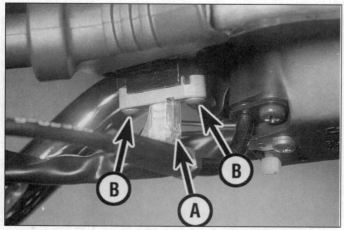

25.2 Clutch switch wiring connectors (A) and mounting screws (B)

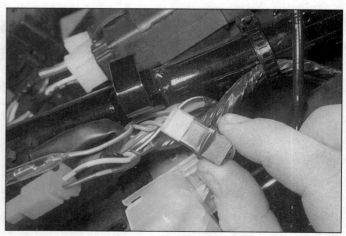

26.2 Diode location

28.2 Disconnect the horn wiring connectors

28.5 Each horn is secured by a single bolt

continuity should be indicated. With the clutch lever out, no continuity (infinite resistance) should be indicated.

3 If the switch is good, check the other components in the starter circuit as described in the relevant sections of this Chapter. If all components are good, check the wiring between the various components (see the *wiring diagrams* at the end of this book).

Replacement

4 Disconnect the wiring connectors from the clutch switch (see illustration 25.2). Remove the two retaining screws and remove the switch.

5 Installation is the reverse of removal. The switch isn't adjustable.

26 Diode -
check and replacement

Check

1 Remove the side panels (see Chapter 7).

2 The diode is a small block that plugs into a connector in the main wiring harness (see illustration). The diode is part of the safety circuit which prevents or stops the engine running if the transmission is in gear whilst the sidestand is down, and prevents the engine from starting if the transmission is in gear unless the sidestand is up and the clutch lever is pulled in (GSF1200 and GSF1200S - see Section 25). Disconnect the diode from the harness.

3 Using an ohmmeter or continuity tester, connect the positive (+ve) probe to one of the outer terminals of the diode and the negative (-ve) probe to the middle terminal of the diode. The diode should show continuity. Now reverse the probes. The diode should show no continuity. Repeat the tests between the other outer terminal and the middle terminal. The same results should be achieved. If it doesn't behave as stated, replace the diode.

4 If the diode is good, check the other components in the starter circuit as described in the relevant sections of this Chapter. If all components are good, check the wiring between the various components (see the *wiring diagrams* at the end of this book).

Replacement

5 Remove the side panels (see Chapter 7).

6 The diode is a small block that plugs into a connector in the main wiring harness (see illustration 26.2). Disconnect the diode and connect the new one.

27 Fuel level sender (GSF1200 and GSF1200S) - check and replacement

⚠️ **Warning: Petrol (gasoline) is extremely flammable, so take extra precautions when you work on any part of the fuel system. Don't smoke or allow open flames or bare light bulbs near the work area, and don't work in a garage where a natural gas-type appliance is present. If you spill any fuel on your skin, rinse it off immediately with soap and water. When you perform any kind of work on the fuel system, wear safety glasses and have a fire extinguisher suitable for a class B type fire (flammable liquids) on hand.**

Check

1 If the fuel gauge fails to operate, trace the wiring back from the fuel level sender in the base of the fuel tank and disconnect it at the connector.

2 Using an ohmmeter set to ohms x 100 scale, connect its probes to the terminals on the sender side of the connector. Check the resistance reading with the tank empty and full. Compare the readings with those listed in the specifications at the beginning of this Chapter. Alternatively, remove the sender from the tank (see Steps 4 and 5 below) and,

with the meter connected as above, manually move the float up and down to emulate the different positions.

3 If the readings taken differ to those listed in the specifications, replace the sender.

Replacement

4 Drain and remove the fuel tank (see Chapter 3).

5 Unscrew the five bolts securing the sender to the base of the tank and withdraw it, taking care not to bend the float arm. Discard the gasket as a new one must be used.

6 Install the sender by reversing the removal process, using a new gasket.

28 Horn(s) -
check and replacement

Check

1 The horns are mounted on the front of the frame below the steering head (see illustration 28.5). Either a single horn or high and low twin horns are fitted, depending on the model.

2 Unplug the wiring connectors from the horn being tested (see illustration). Using two jumper wires, apply battery voltage directly to the terminals on the horn. If the horn sounds, check the switch (see Section 21) and the wiring between the switch and the horn (see the *wiring diagrams* at the end of this Chapter).

3 If the horn doesn't sound, replace it.

Replacement

4 The horns are mounted on the front of the machine below the steering head.

5 Unplug the wiring connectors from the horns (see illustration 28.2), then unscrew the bolt securing the horn and remove it from the bike (see illustration).

6 Install the horn and securely tighten the bolt. Connect the wiring connectors to the horn.

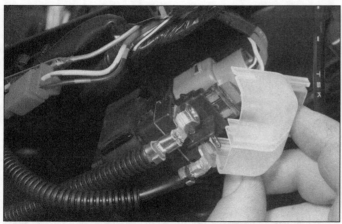

29.2a The starter relay has a white plastic cover

29.2b Remove the starter motor lead (arrow)

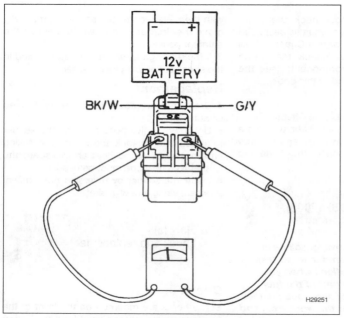

29.4 Starter relay test connections

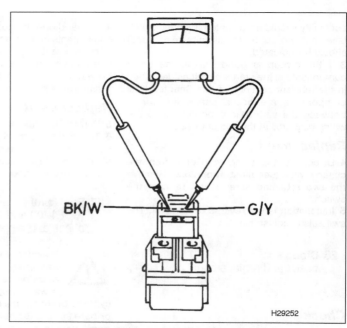

29.5 Starter relay resistance check

29.9a Disconnect the wiring connector and the starter motor and battery leads (arrows)

29.9b The relay is mounted on lugs on the frame (arrow)

30.2 Peel back the cover to expose the terminal screw

30.3 The starter motor is secured by two bolts

29 Starter relay - check and replacement

Check

1 If the starter circuit is faulty, first check the fuse (see Section 5).
2 The starter relay is located behind the left-hand side panel **(see illustration)**. Remove the side panels for access to the relay (see Chapter 7). Remove the plastic cover on the top of the relay. Unscrew the nut securing the starter motor lead to its terminal and disconnect the lead **(see illustration)**; position the lead away from the relay terminal. With the ignition switch ON, the engine kill switch in the RUN position, the transmission in neutral and the clutch pulled in (GSF1200 and GSF1200S), press the starter switch. The relay should be heard to click.
3 If the relay doesn't click, switch off the ignition and remove the relay as described below; test it as follows.
4 Set a multimeter to the ohms x 1 scale and connect it across the relay's starter motor and battery lead terminals. Using a fully-charged 12 volt battery and two insulated jumper wires, connect the positive (+ve) terminal of

the battery to the yellow/green wire terminal of the relay, and the negative (-ve) terminal to the black/white wire terminal of the relay **(see illustration)**. At this point the relay should be heard to click and the multimeter read 0 ohms (continuity). If this is the case the relay is proved good. If the relay does not click when battery voltage is applied and indicates no continuity (infinite resistance) across its terminals, it is faulty and must be replaced.
5 To check the internal resistance of the relay, use a multimeter set to the ohms x 1 scale and connect the probes to the yellow/green and black/white terminals of the relay **(see illustration)**. The resistance reading obtained should be as specified at the beginning of the Chapter.
6 If the relay is good, check for battery voltage between the yellow/green wire and the black/white wire when the starter button is pressed. Check the other components in the starter circuit as described in the relevant sections of this Chapter. If all components are good, check the wiring between the various components (see the *wiring diagrams* at the end of this book).

Replacement

7 Remove the side panels (see Chapter 7).
8 Disconnect the battery terminals,

remembering to disconnect the negative (-ve) terminal first.
9 Disconnect the relay wiring connector, then unscrew the two nuts securing the starter motor and battery leads to the relay and detach the leads **(see illustration)**. Remove the relay with its rubber sleeve from its mounting lugs on the frame **(see illustration)**.
10 Installation is the reverse of removal, ensuring the terminal nuts are securely tightened. Connect the negative (-ve) lead last when reconnecting the battery.

30 Starter motor - removal and installation

Removal

1 Remove the seat (see Chapter 7). Disconnect the battery negative (-ve) lead.
2 Peel back the rubber cover and remove the screw (600 models) or nut (1200 models) securing the starter lead to the motor **(see illustration)**.
3 Unscrew the two bolts securing the starter motor to the crankcase **(see illustration)**.
4 Slide the starter motor out from the crankcase and remove it from the machine.
5 Remove the O-ring on the end of the starter motor and discard it as a new one must be used.

Installation

6 Install a new O-ring on the end of the starter motor and ensure it is seated in its groove **(see illustration)**. Apply a smear of engine oil to the O-ring to aid installation.
7 Manoeuvre the motor into position and slide it into the crankcase **(see illustration)**. Ensure that the starter motor teeth mesh correctly with those of the starter idle/reduction gear.

30.6 Fit a new O-ring into the starter motor groove

30.7 Fit the starter motor into the crankcase . . .

8

30.8 . . . and install the bolts

8 Install the retaining bolts and tighten them securely (see illustration).

9 Connect the starter lead to the motor and secure it with the screw (600 models) or nut (1200 models). Make sure the rubber cover is correctly seated over the terminal.

10 Connect the battery negative (-ve) lead and install the seat.

31 Starter motor - disassembly, inspection and reassembly

Disassembly

1 Remove the starter motor (see Section 30).

2 Check for matchmarks between the main housing and the front and rear covers. If none are found, make your own as an aid to installation.

3 Unscrew the two long bolts and withdraw them from the starter motor (see illustrations). Remove the rear cover from the motor along with its O-ring and, on 600 models, the brushplate assembly. Retrieve any shims from the armature shaft.

4 Wrap some insulating tape around the teeth on the end of the starter motor shaft - this will protect the oil seal from damage as the front cover is removed. Remove the front cover from the motor along with its O-ring. Remove the shim(s) from the front end of the armature

shaft and the special washer from inside the front cover, noting their correct fitted locations.

5 Withdraw the armature from the main housing. On 1200 models slide the brush springs up far enough for the brushes to be slipped out of their holders, then remove the brushplate assembly.

6 On 1200 models, noting the correct fitted location of each component, unscrew the terminal nut and withdraw the terminal bolt and brush assembly from the main housing.

Inspection

7 The parts of the starter motor that are most likely to require attention are the brushes. Measure the length of the brushes and compare the results to the brush length listed in this Chapter's Specifications (see illustration). If any of the brushes are worn beyond the service limit, replace the brush assembly with a new one. If the brushes are not worn excessively, nor cracked, chipped,

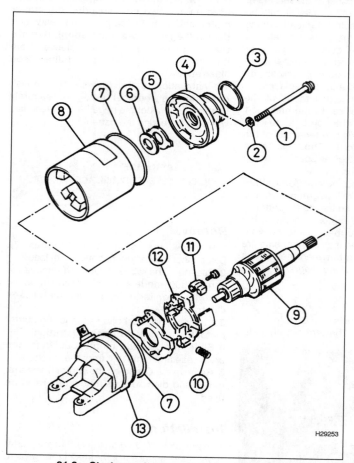

31.3a Starter motor components - 600 models

1 Long bolt
2 O-ring
3 O-ring
4 Front cover
5 Special washer
6 Shim
7 O-ring
8 Main housing
9 Armature
10 Spring
11 Brush
12 Brushplate
13 Rear cover

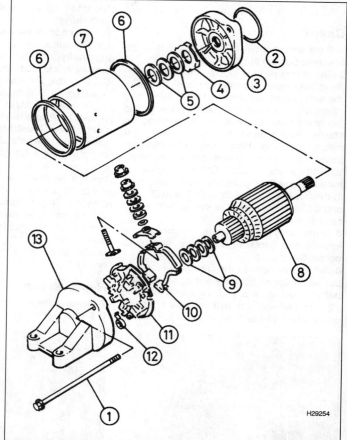

31.3b Starter motor components - 1200 models

1 Long bolt
2 O-ring
3 Front cover
4 Special washer
5 Shims
6 O-ring
7 Main housing
8 Armature
9 Shims
10 Brush assembly
11 Brush plate
12 Brush spring
13 Rear cover

31.8 Measure the length of each brush

31.9 Check the commutator bars as described

or otherwise damaged, they may be re-used.
8 Inspect the commutator bars on the armature for scoring, scratches and discoloration **(see illustration)**. The commutator can be cleaned and polished with crocus cloth, but do not use sandpaper or emery paper. After cleaning, wipe away any residue with a cloth soaked in electrical system cleaner or denatured alcohol.
9 Check for continuity between the commutator bars **(see illustration)**. Continuity should exist between each bar and all of the others. Also, check for continuity between the commutator bars and the armature shaft **(see illustration)**. There should be no continuity (infinite resistance) between the commutator and the shaft. If the checks indicate otherwise, the armature is defective.
10 Check for continuity between each brush and the terminal bolt. There should be continuity (zero resistance). Check for continuity between the terminal bolt and the housing (when assembled). There should be no continuity (infinite resistance).
11 Check the front end of the armature shaft for worn, cracked, chipped and broken teeth. If the shaft is damaged or worn, replace the armature.
12 Inspect the end covers for signs of cracks

31.10a Continuity should exist between the commutator bars

or wear. Inspect the magnets in the main housing and the housing itself for cracks.
13 Inspect the insulating washers and front cover oil seal for signs of damage and replace them if necessary. Note that it may not be possible to purchase the oil seal separately from the front cover - check first with a Suzuki dealer.

Reassembly

600 models

14 Slide the springs and brushes back into

31.10b There should be no continuity between the commutator bars and the armature shaft

position in their holders **(see illustration)**. Fit the O-ring onto the rear cover.
15 Insert the armature and pull each brush back against its spring to provide clearance, then locate the brushes on the commutator bars **(see illustration)**. Check that each brush is securely pressed against the commutator by its spring and is free to move easily in its holder.
16 Fit the main housing over the armature, aligning the matchmarks on the housing and rear cover **(see illustration)**.

31.14 Insert the brush springs and slip the brushes in their holders

31.15 Hold the brushes back whilst installing the commutator

31.16 Align the notch in the main housing with the cutout in the rear cover

8

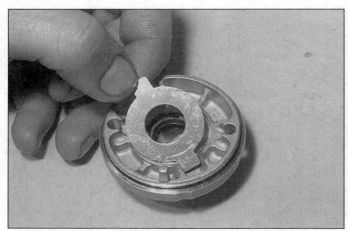

31.17a Special washer tabs locate in front cover cutouts

31.17b Install the front cover on the armature end

17 Apply a smear of grease to the lips of the front cover oil seal and fit a new O-ring onto the cover. Fit the shim onto the shaft and the special washer onto the front cover, making sure that its tabs locate correctly in the cover cutouts **(see illustration)**. Install the cover,

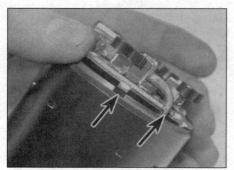

31.21 Brushplate tab and brush lead cutout (arrows)

aligning the matchmarks **(see illustration)**. Remove the protective tape from the shaft end.

18 Make sure that the O-ring is in place on each of the long bolts. Apply a suitable non-permanent thread locking compound to the threads of the long bolts and tighten them securely.

19 Install the starter motor (see Section 30).

1200 models

20 Fit the brush assembly and the inner rubber insulator on the terminal bolt, then insert the bolt through the hole in the main housing. Fit the O-ring and the outer rubber insulator and washers over the terminal bolt and secure it with the nut.

21 Install the brushplate assembly into the main housing, making sure its tab is correctly located in the slot in the cover **(see illustration)**. Note that the brush leads must be routed through the cutouts in the brushplate. Do not yet place the brush spring

ends onto the brushes. This makes it much easier to install the armature.

22 Slide the armature into place and install the brush springs **(see illustrations)**.

23 Install the shims on the front end of the armature shaft, returning them to their original locations **(see illustration)**. Apply a smear of grease to the lips of the front cover oil seal and fit the special washer on the inside of the front cover so that its tabs engage the cover webs **(see illustration)**. Install the front cover with its O-ring and remove any protective tape from the shaft end; align the cover matchmarks with those on the main housing.

24 Install the shims on the rear end of the armature shaft, returning them to their original locations **(see illustration)**. Install the rear cover with its O-ring and align the matchmarks **(see illustration)**. Apply a suitable non-permanent thread locking compound to the threads of the two long bolts and tighten them securely.

25 Install the starter motor (see Section 30).

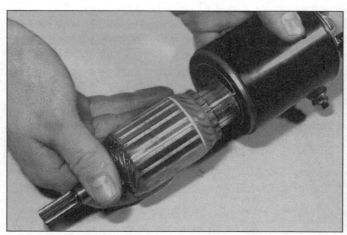

31.22a Slide the armature into the main housing . . .

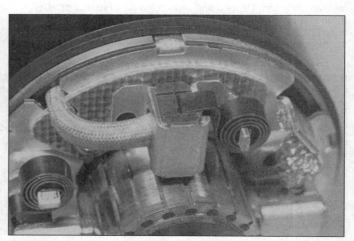

31.22b . . . and engage the brush spring ends in the groove in the end of each brush

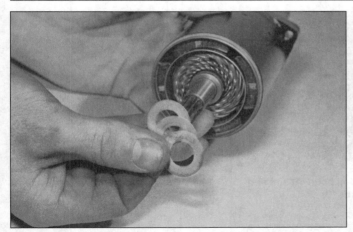

31.23a Install the shims on the front end of the armature shaft . . .

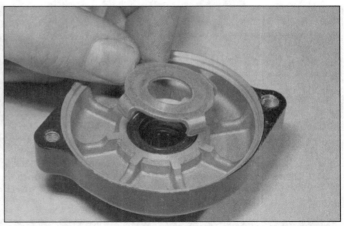

31.23b . . . and fit the special washer on the inside of the front cover

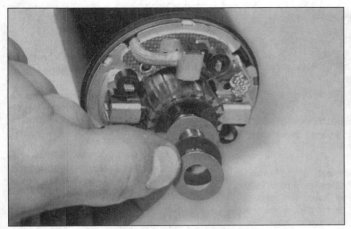

31.24a Install the shims on the rear end of the armature shaft . . .

31.24b . . . and install the rear cover

32 Charging system testing - general information and precautions

1 If the performance of the charging system is suspect, the system as a whole should be checked first, followed by testing of the individual components. **Note:** *Before beginning the checks, make sure the battery is fully charged and that all system connections are clean and tight.*

2 Checking the output of the charging system and the performance of the various components within the charging system requires the use of a multimeter (with voltage, current and resistance checking facilities).

3 When making the checks, follow the procedures carefully to prevent incorrect connections or short circuits, as irreparable damage to electrical system components may result if short circuits occur.

4 If a multimeter is not available, the job of checking the charging system should be left to a Suzuki dealer.

33 Charging system - leakage and output test

1 If the charging system of the machine is thought to be faulty, remove the seat (see Chapter 7) and perform the following checks.

Leakage test

Caution: Always connect an ammeter in series, never in parallel with the battery, otherwise it will be damaged. Do not turn the ignition ON or operate the starter motor when the ammeter is connected - a sudden surge in current will blow the meter's fuse.

2 Turn the ignition switch OFF and disconnect the lead from the battery negative (-ve) terminal.

3 Set the multimeter to the Amps function and connect its negative (-ve) probe to the battery negative (-ve) terminal, and positive (+ve) probe to the disconnected negative (-ve) lead **(see illustration)**. Always set the meter to a high amps range initially and then bring it down to the mA (milli Amps) range; if there is a high current flow in the circuit it may blow the meter's fuse.

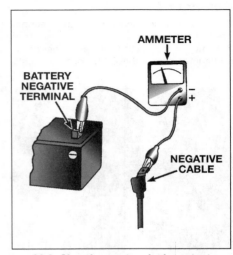

33.3 Charging system leakage test ammeter connections

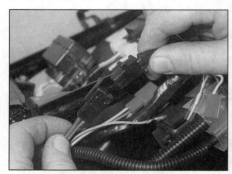

34.1 Disconnect the alternator wiring connector

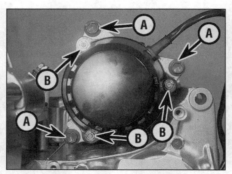

34.2 Alternator mounting bolts (A) and end cover nuts (B)

34.4a Brush holder screws (arrows)

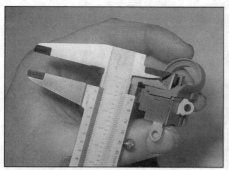

34.4b Measure the brush lengths and replace them if necessary

34.4c Clean the slip rings and check their diameter

4 No current flow should be indicated. If current leakage is indicated (generally greater than 0.1 mA), there is a short circuit in the wiring. Disconnect the meter and connect the negative (-ve) lead to the battery, tightening it securely.

5 If leakage is indicated, use the wiring diagrams at the end of this book to systematically disconnect individual electrical components and repeat the test until the source is identified.

Output test

6 Start the engine and warm it up to normal operating temperature.

7 Allow the engine to idle and connect a multimeter set to the 0-20 volts DC scale

(voltmeter) across the terminals of the battery (positive (+ve) lead to battery positive (+ve) terminal, negative (-ve) lead to battery negative (-ve) terminal). Slowly increase the engine speed to 5000 rpm and note the reading obtained. At this speed the voltage should be 13.5 volts. If the voltage is outside these limits, check the alternator and the regulator (see Section 34).

 HAYNES HiNT *Clues to a faulty regulator are constantly blowing bulbs, with brightness varying considerably with engine speed, and battery overheating.*

34 Alternator/regulator/rectifier - removal, inspection and installation

Removal

1 Trace the alternator wiring to its connector behind the left-hand side panel and disconnect it **(see illustration)**.

2 Unscrew the three alternator mounting bolts and remove the alternator **(see illustration)**. Remove the O-ring and discard it as a new one must be used.

Inspection

3 Unscrew the three nuts securing the alternator end cover and remove the cover **(see illustration 34.2)**.

4 Remove the three screws securing the brush holder to the regulator and rectifier and remove the holder, noting the position of the wire **(see illustration)**. Inspect the holder for any signs of damage. Measure the brush lengths and compare the measurements with the figures given in the Specifications at the beginning of the Chapter **(see illustration)**. Clean the slip rings with a rag moistened with some solvent **(see illustration)**. Slip ring diameter can be measured and compared with the figures given in the Specifications at the beginning of the Chapter, although access is difficult with the rotor installed in the alternator body.

5 Check for continuity between the slip rings **(see illustration)**. There should be continuity (zero resistance). If there is no continuity, replace the rotor.

6 Remove the two screws securing the regulator to the alternator and remove the regulator **(see illustration)**. Testing the regulator requires a variable DC power source, a voltmeter, a switch, a 3.4W 12V bulb and connecting wires. Identify the regulator terminals and set up the circuit as shown **(see illustrations)**. Set the power source to 12V and turn the switch on. The bulb should light. Increase the voltage to 14.5V - the bulb should go out. If it doesn't, replace the regulator.

34.5 Check for continuity between the slip rings

34.6a Regulator screws (arrows)

7 To test the rectifier it is necessary to unsolder the rectifier connections and remove it from the alternator **(see illustration)**.
Caution: The rectifier wires must be unsoldered quickly, otherwise the heat from the soldering iron will damage the rectifier diodes.
With the rectifier removed from the alternator, use a multimeter set to the ohms x 1 scale to check its six diodes **(see illustration)**. Each diode is checked in both directions by reversing the meter probes. Continuity should only exist in one direction only; if no continuity is shown in both directions, or continuity is shown if both directions, the diode is fault. When installing the rectifier, solder its connections quickly to avoid damage (see **Caution**).

B to P1	P1 to B
B to P2	P2 to B
B to P3	P3 to B
E to P1	P1 to E
E to P2	P2 to E
E to P3	P3 to E

8 Place the alternator driven gear in a vice with two pieces of wood to protect the gear teeth **(see illustration)** - do not clamp the damper housing behind the gear otherwise it

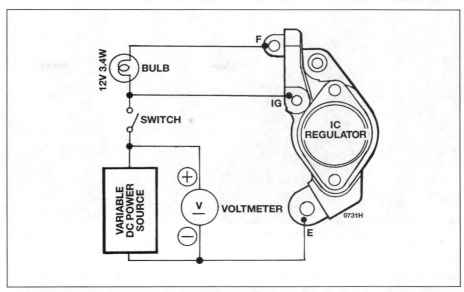
34.6b Identify the regulator terminals and set up the circuit as shown to test the regulator

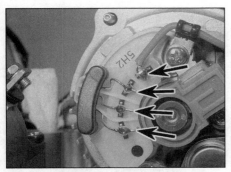
34.7a Rectifier soldered connections (arrows)

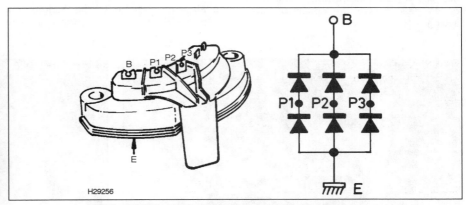
34.7b Rectifier test connections and diode arrangement

34.8a Clamp the driven gear between wood blocks in a vice

34.8b Remove the nut and washer . . .

8

34.8c . . . and lift off the driven gear

34.8d Inspect the rubber damper segments

will distort. Remove the nut and washer from the shaft end, followed by the driven gear **(see illustrations)**. Inspect the rubber damper for damage or deterioration and replace it if necessary **(see illustration)**. Tighten the driven gear nut to the specified torque setting.

9 Any further testing or dismantling of the alternator assembly must be carried out by an electrical specialist or Suzuki dealer.

Installation

10 Fit a new O-ring to the front of the alternator and smear it with oil **(see illustration)**. Install the end cover **(see illustration 34.2)**.

11 Install the alternator on the engine and tighten its mounting bolts to the specified torque setting **(see illustration)**. Route the wiring correctly and connect it at the connector **(see illustration 34.1)**.

34.10 Fit a new O-ring . . .

34.11 . . . and install the alternator

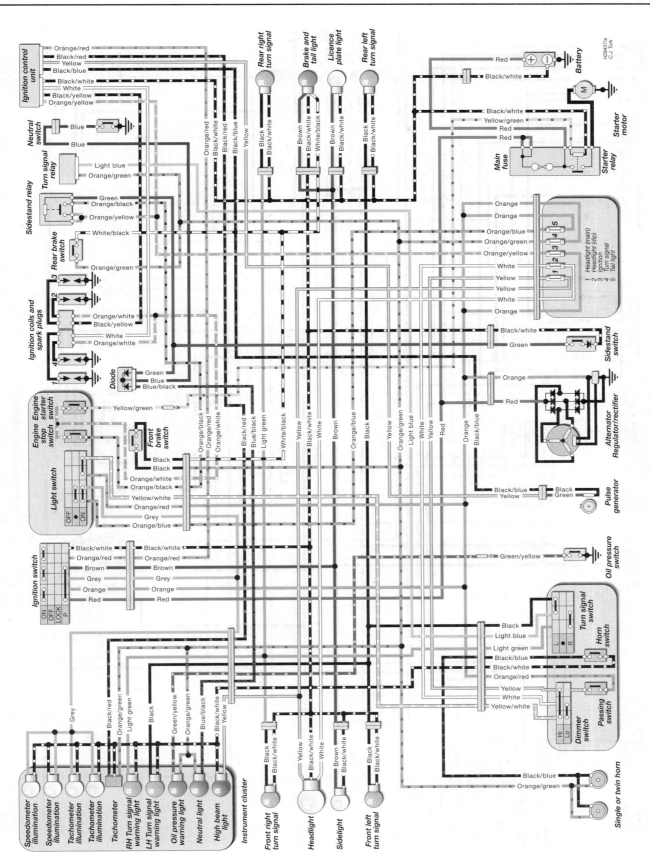

Wiring diagram - UK GSF600

Ignition control unit

Orange/red
Black/red
Yellow
Black/blue
Black/white
White
Black/yellow
Orange/yellow

Rear right turn signal
Brake and tail light
Licence plate light
Rear left turn signal

Red — Battery
Black/white

Starter motor

Yellow/green
Red
Red

Main fuse
Starter relay

Neutral switch
Blue
Blue

Turn signal relay
Light blue
Orange/green

Orange/red
Black/red
Black/blue
Yellow

Black
Black/white
Brown
Black/white
White/black
Brown
Black/blue
Black
Black/white

Sidestand relay
Green
Orange/black
Orange/yellow

Rear brake switch
White/black
Orange/green

Orange
Orange
Orange/blue
Orange/green
Orange/yellow
White
Yellow
Yellow
White
Orange

1 Headlight (main)
2 Headlight (dip)
3 Ignition
4 Turn signal
5 Tail light

Ignition coils and spark plugs
Orange/white
Black/yellow
White
Orange/white

Black/white
Green
Sidestand switch

Diode
Green
Blue
Blue/black

Orange
Red
Alternator Regulator/rectifier

Engine stop switch / Engine starter switch
Yellow/green

Front brake switch
Black
Black/Red

Orange/black
Orange/red
Orange/white
Black/red
Yellow/black
Black
White/black
Yellow
Black/white
White
Brown
Orange/blue
Black
Yellow
Orange/green
Light blue
White
Red
Yellow/green
Orange
Black/blue

Black/blue
Yellow
Black
Green
Pulse generator

Orange/white
Orange/black
Yellow/white
Orange
Grey
Orange/blue

Yellow/green
Yellow/green
Clutch switch

Ignition switch
Black/white
Orange/red
Brown
Grey
Orange
Red

Black/white
Orange/red
Brown
Grey
Orange
Red

Green/yellow
Oil pressure switch

ON
OFF
LOCK
P

Turn signal switch
Black
Light blue
Light green
Black/blue
Black/white

Horn switch
L PUSH R

Yellow
White
Yellow/white

Dimmer switch
Hi LO

Grey
Black/red
Orange/green
Light green
Black
Green/yellow
Orange/green
Blue/black
Black/white
Yellow

Black/blue
Orange/green
Horn

Speedometer illumination
Speedometer illumination
Tachometer illumination
Tachometer illumination
Tachometer
RH Turn signal warning light
LH Turn signal warning light
Oil pressure warning light
Neutral light
High beam light

Instrument cluster

Front right turn signal
Black
Black/white

Headlight
Yellow
Black/white
White

Brown
Black/white

Front left turn signal
Black
Black/white

Wiring diagram – US GSF600

H29438/a
C.J. Turk

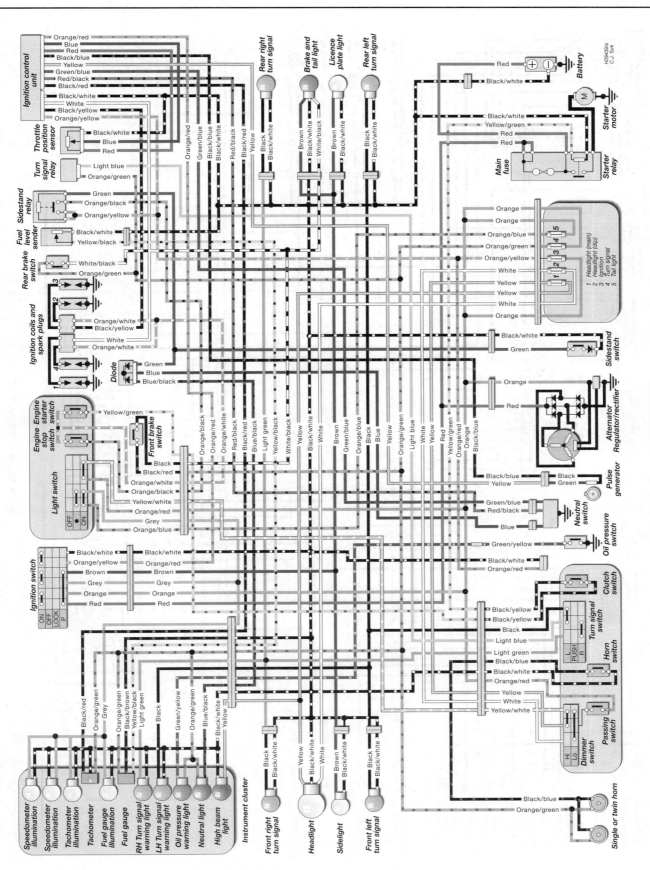

Wiring diagram - UK GSF1200

8

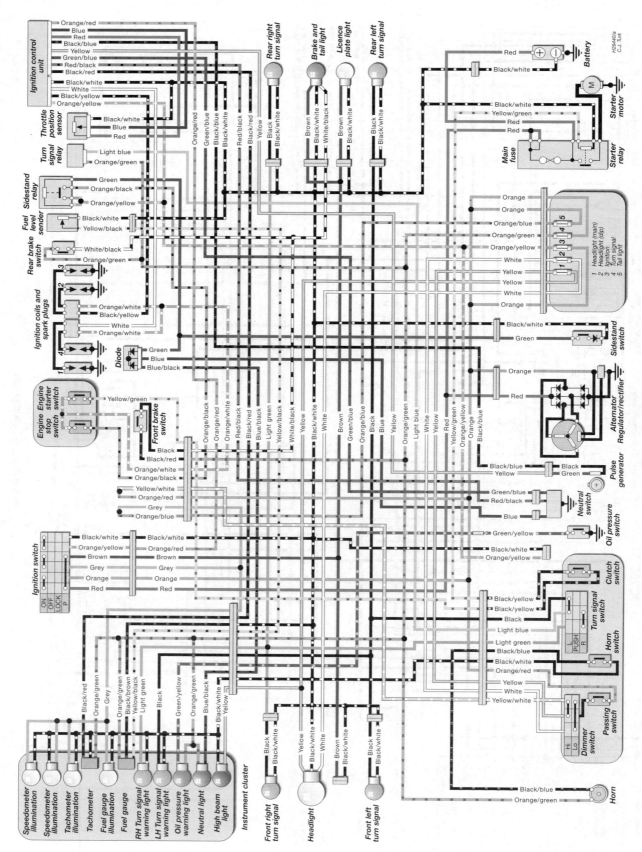

Wiring diagram - US GSF1200

Dimensions and Weights

	600 models	1200 models
Wheelbase (W)	1430 mm	1435 mm
Overall length (L)	2085 mm	2095 mm
Overall width	745 mm	790 mm
Overall height (H)		
Non-faired model	1100 mm	1100 mm
Faired model	1205 mm	1215 mm
Seat height (S)	805 mm	835 mm
Minimum ground clearance	125 mm	130 mm
Weight (dry)		
Non-faired model	196 kg	211 kg
Faired model	202 kg	214 kg

Buying tools

A toolkit is a fundamental requirement for servicing and repairing a motorcycle. Although there will be an initial expense in building up enough tools for servicing, this will soon be offset by the savings made by doing the job yourself. As experience and confidence grow, additional tools can be added to enable the repair and overhaul of the motorcycle. Many of the specialist tools are expensive and not often used so it may be preferable to hire them, or for a group of friends or motorcycle club to join in the purchase.

As a rule, it is better to buy more expensive, good quality tools. Cheaper tools are likely to wear out faster and need to be renewed more often, nullifying the original saving.

> **Warning: To avoid the risk of a poor quality tool breaking in use, causing injury or damage to the component being worked on, always aim to purchase tools which meet the relevant national safety standards.**

The following lists of tools do not represent the manufacturer's service tools, but serve as a guide to help the owner decide which tools are needed for this level of work. In addition, items such as an electric drill, hacksaw, files, soldering iron and a workbench equipped with a vice, may be needed. Although not classed as tools, a selection of bolts, screws, nuts, washers and pieces of tubing always come in useful.

For more information about tools, refer to the Haynes *Motorcycle Workshop Practice TechBook* (Bk. No. 3470).

Manufacturer's service tools

Inevitably certain tasks require the use of a service tool. Where possible an alternative tool or method of approach is recommended, but sometimes there is no option if personal injury or damage to the component is to be avoided. Where required, service tools are referred to in the relevant procedure.

Service tools can usually only be purchased from a motorcycle dealer and are identified by a part number. Some of the commonly-used tools, such as rotor pullers, are available in aftermarket form from mail-order motorcycle tool and accessory suppliers.

Maintenance and minor repair tools

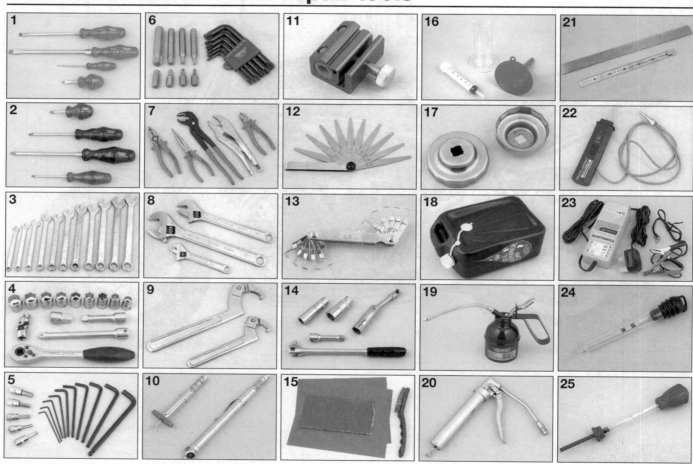

1 Set of flat-bladed screwdrivers
2 Set of Phillips head screwdrivers
3 Combination open-end and ring spanners
4 Socket set (3/8 inch or 1/2 inch drive)
5 Set of Allen keys or bits
6 Set of Torx keys or bits
7 Pliers, cutters and self-locking grips (Mole grips)
8 Adjustable spanners
9 C-spanners
10 Tread depth gauge and tyre pressure gauge
11 Cable oiler clamp
12 Feeler gauges
13 Spark plug gap measuring tool
14 Spark plug spanner or deep plug sockets
15 Wire brush and emery paper
16 Calibrated syringe, measuring vessel and funnel
17 Oil filter adapters
18 Oil drainer can or tray
19 Pump type oil can
20 Grease gun
21 Straight-edge and steel rule
22 Continuity tester
23 Battery charger
24 Hydrometer (for battery specific gravity check)
25 Anti-freeze tester (for liquid-cooled engines)

Tools and Workshop Tips REF•3

Repair and overhaul tools

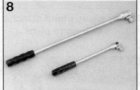

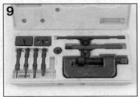

1 Torque wrench (small and mid-ranges)
2 Conventional, plastic or soft-faced hammers
3 Impact driver set
4 Vernier gauge
5 Circlip pliers (internal and external, or combination)
6 Set of cold chisels and punches
7 Selection of pullers
8 Breaker bars
9 Chain breaking/riveting tool set
10 Wire stripper and crimper tool
11 Multimeter (measures amps, volts and ohms)
12 Stroboscope (for dynamic timing checks)
13 Hose clamp (wingnut type shown)
14 Clutch holding tool
15 One-man brake/clutch bleeder kit

Specialist tools

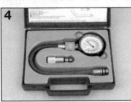
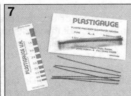

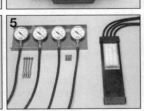
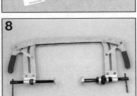
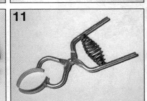

1 Micrometers (external type)
2 Telescoping gauges
3 Dial gauge
4 Cylinder compression gauge
5 Vacuum gauges (left) or manometer (right)
6 Oil pressure gauge
7 Plastigauge kit
8 Valve spring compressor (4-stroke engines)
9 Piston pin drawbolt tool
10 Piston ring removal and installation tool
11 Piston ring clamp
12 Cylinder bore hone (stone type shown)
13 Stud extractor
14 Screw extractor set
15 Bearing driver set

1 Workshop equipment and facilities

The workbench

● Work is made much easier by raising the bike up on a ramp - components are much more accessible if raised to waist level. The hydraulic or pneumatic types seen in the dealer's workshop are a sound investment if you undertake a lot of repairs or overhauls **(see illustration 1.1)**.

1.1 Hydraulic motorcycle ramp

● If raised off ground level, the bike must be supported on the ramp to avoid it falling. Most ramps incorporate a front wheel locating clamp which can be adjusted to suit different diameter wheels. When tightening the clamp, take care not to mark the wheel rim or damage the tyre - use wood blocks on each side to prevent this.
● Secure the bike to the ramp using tie-downs **(see illustration 1.2)**. If the bike has only a sidestand, and hence leans at a dangerous angle when raised, support the bike on an auxiliary stand.

1.2 Tie-downs are used around the passenger footrests to secure the bike

● Auxiliary (paddock) stands are widely available from mail order companies or motorcycle dealers and attach either to the wheel axle or swingarm pivot **(see illustration 1.3)**. If the motorcycle has a centrestand, you can support it under the crankcase to prevent it toppling whilst either wheel is removed **(see illustration 1.4)**.

1.3 This auxiliary stand attaches to the swingarm pivot

1.4 Always use a block of wood between the engine and jack head when supporting the engine in this way

Fumes and fire

● Refer to the Safety first! page at the beginning of the manual for full details. Make sure your workshop is equipped with a fire extinguisher suitable for fuel-related fires (Class B fire - flammable liquids) - it is not sufficient to have a water-filled extinguisher.
● Always ensure adequate ventilation is available. Unless an exhaust gas extraction system is available for use, ensure that the engine is run outside of the workshop.
● If working on the fuel system, make sure the workshop is ventilated to avoid a build-up of fumes. This applies equally to fume build-up when charging a battery. Do not smoke or allow anyone else to smoke in the workshop.

Fluids

● If you need to drain fuel from the tank, store it in an approved container marked as suitable for the storage of petrol (gasoline) **(see illustration 1.5)**. Do not store fuel in glass jars or bottles.

1.5 Use an approved can only for storing petrol (gasoline)

● Use proprietary engine degreasers or solvents which have a high flash-point, such as paraffin (kerosene), for cleaning off oil, grease and dirt - never use petrol (gasoline) for cleaning. Wear rubber gloves when handling solvent and engine degreaser. The fumes from certain solvents can be dangerous - always work in a well-ventilated area.

Dust, eye and hand protection

● Protect your lungs from inhalation of dust particles by wearing a filtering mask over the nose and mouth. Many frictional materials still contain asbestos which is dangerous to your health. Protect your eyes from spouts of liquid and sprung components by wearing a pair of protective goggles **(see illustration 1.6)**.

1.6 A fire extinguisher, goggles, mask and protective gloves should be at hand in the workshop

● Protect your hands from contact with solvents, fuel and oils by wearing rubber gloves. Alternatively apply a barrier cream to your hands before starting work. If handling hot components or fluids, wear suitable gloves to protect your hands from scalding and burns.

What to do with old fluids

● Old cleaning solvent, fuel, coolant and oils should not be poured down domestic drains or onto the ground. Package the fluid up in old oil containers, label it accordingly, and take it to a garage or disposal facility. Contact your local authority for location of such sites or ring the oil care hotline.

OIL CARE
FOLLOW THE CODE
OIL BANK LINE
0800 66 33 66

Note: It is antisocial and illegal to dump oil down the drain. To find the location of your local oil recycling bank, call this number free.

In the USA, note that any oil supplier must accept used oil for recycling.

2 Fasteners -
screws, bolts and nuts

Fastener types and applications

Bolts and screws

● Fastener head types are either of hexagonal, Torx or splined design, with internal and external versions of each type (see illustrations 2.1 and 2.2); splined head fasteners are not in common use on motorcycles. The conventional slotted or Phillips head design is used for certain screws. Bolt or screw length is always measured from the underside of the head to the end of the item (see illustration 2.11).

2.1 Internal hexagon/Allen (A), Torx (B) and splined (C) fasteners, with corresponding bits

2.2 External Torx (A), splined (B) and hexagon (C) fasteners, with corresponding sockets

● Certain fasteners on the motorcycle have a tensile marking on their heads, the higher the marking the stronger the fastener. High tensile fasteners generally carry a 10 or higher marking. Never replace a high tensile fastener with one of a lower tensile strength.

Washers (see illustration 2.3)

● Plain washers are used between a fastener head and a component to prevent damage to the component or to spread the load when torque is applied. Plain washers can also be used as spacers or shims in certain assemblies. Copper or aluminium plain washers are often used as sealing washers on drain plugs.

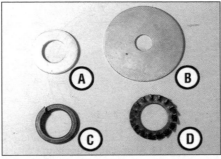

2.3 Plain washer (A), penny washer (B), spring washer (C) and serrated washer (D)

● The split-ring spring washer works by applying axial tension between the fastener head and component. If flattened, it is fatigued and must be renewed. If a plain (flat) washer is used on the fastener, position the spring washer between the fastener and the plain washer.
● Serrated star type washers dig into the fastener and component faces, preventing loosening. They are often used on electrical earth (ground) connections to the frame.
● Cone type washers (sometimes called Belleville) are conical and when tightened apply axial tension between the fastener head and component. They must be installed with the dished side against the component and often carry an OUTSIDE marking on their outer face. If flattened, they are fatigued and must be renewed.
● Tab washers are used to lock plain nuts or bolts on a shaft. A portion of the tab washer is bent up hard against one flat of the nut or bolt to prevent it loosening. Due to the tab washer being deformed in use, a new tab washer should be used every time it is disturbed.
● Wave washers are used to take up endfloat on a shaft. They provide light springing and prevent excessive side-to-side play of a component. Can be found on rocker arm shafts.

Nuts and split pins

● Conventional plain nuts are usually six-sided (see illustration 2.4). They are sized by thread diameter and pitch. High tensile nuts carry a number on one end to denote their tensile strength.

2.4 Plain nut (A), shouldered locknut (B), nylon insert nut (C) and castellated nut (D)

● Self-locking nuts either have a nylon insert, or two spring metal tabs, or a shoulder which is staked into a groove in the shaft - their advantage over conventional plain nuts is a resistance to loosening due to vibration. The nylon insert type can be used a number of times, but must be renewed when the friction of the nylon insert is reduced, ie when the nut spins freely on the shaft. The spring tab type can be reused unless the tabs are damaged. The shouldered type must be renewed every time it is disturbed.
● Split pins (cotter pins) are used to lock a castellated nut to a shaft or to prevent slackening of a plain nut. Common applications are wheel axles and brake torque arms. Because the split pin arms are deformed to lock around the nut a new split pin must always be used on installation - always fit the correct size split pin which will fit snugly in the shaft hole. Make sure the split pin arms are correctly located around the nut (see illustrations 2.5 and 2.6).

2.5 Bend split pin (cotter pin) arms as shown (arrows) to secure a castellated nut

2.6 Bend split pin (cotter pin) arms as shown to secure a plain nut

Caution: If the castellated nut slots do not align with the shaft hole after tightening to the torque setting, tighten the nut until the next slot aligns with the hole - never slacken the nut to align its slot.

● R-pins (shaped like the letter R), or slip pins as they are sometimes called, are sprung and can be reused if they are otherwise in good condition. Always install R-pins with their closed end facing forwards (see illustration 2.7).

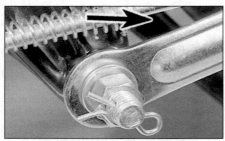

2.7 Correct fitting of R-pin. Arrow indicates forward direction

Circlips (see illustration 2.8)

● Circlips (sometimes called snap-rings) are used to retain components on a shaft or in a housing and have corresponding external or internal ears to permit removal. Parallel-sided (machined) circlips can be installed either way round in their groove, whereas stamped circlips (which have a chamfered edge on one face) must be installed with the chamfer facing away from the direction of thrust load **(see illustration 2.9)**.

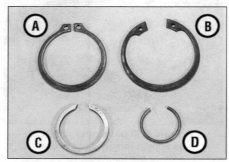

2.8 External stamped circlip (A), internal stamped circlip (B), machined circlip (C) and wire circlip (D)

● Always use circlip pliers to remove and install circlips; expand or compress them just enough to remove them. After installation, rotate the circlip in its groove to ensure it is securely seated. If installing a circlip on a splined shaft, always align its opening with a shaft channel to ensure the circlip ends are well supported and unlikely to catch **(see illustration 2.10)**.

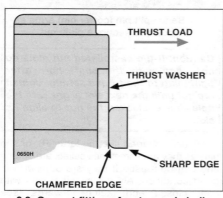

2.9 Correct fitting of a stamped circlip

THRUST LOAD

THRUST WASHER

SHARP EDGE

CHAMFERED EDGE

0650H

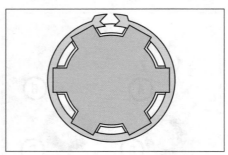

2.10 Align circlip opening with shaft channel

● Circlips can wear due to the thrust of components and become loose in their grooves, with the subsequent danger of becoming dislodged in operation. For this reason, renewal is advised every time a circlip is disturbed.

● Wire circlips are commonly used as piston pin retaining clips. If a removal tang is provided, long-nosed pliers can be used to dislodge them, otherwise careful use of a small flat-bladed screwdriver is necessary. Wire circlips should be renewed every time they are disturbed.

Thread diameter and pitch

● Diameter of a male thread (screw, bolt or stud) is the outside diameter of the threaded portion **(see illustration 2.11)**. Most motorcycle manufacturers use the ISO (International Standards Organisation) metric system expressed in millimetres, eg M6 refers to a 6 mm diameter thread. Sizing is the same for nuts, except that the thread diameter is measured across the valleys of the nut.

● Pitch is the distance between the peaks of the thread **(see illustration 2.11)**. It is expressed in millimetres, thus a common bolt size may be expressed as 6.0 x 1.0 mm (6 mm thread diameter and 1 mm pitch). Generally pitch increases in proportion to thread diameter, although there are always exceptions.

● Thread diameter and pitch are related for conventional fastener applications and the accompanying table can be used as a guide. Additionally, the AF (Across Flats), spanner or socket size dimension of the bolt or nut **(see illustration 2.11)** is linked to thread and pitch specification. Thread pitch can be measured with a thread gauge **(see illustration 2.12)**.

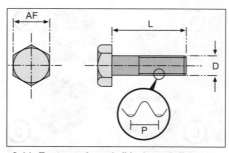

AF

L

D

P

2.11 Fastener length (L), thread diameter (D), thread pitch (P) and head size (AF)

2.12 Using a thread gauge to measure pitch

AF size	Thread diameter x pitch (mm)
8 mm	M5 x 0.8
8 mm	M6 x 1.0
10 mm	M6 x 1.0
12 mm	M8 x 1.25
14 mm	M10 x 1.25
17 mm	M12 x 1.25

● The threads of most fasteners are of the right-hand type, ie they are turned clockwise to tighten and anti-clockwise to loosen. The reverse situation applies to left-hand thread fasteners, which are turned anti-clockwise to tighten and clockwise to loosen. Left-hand threads are used where rotation of a component might loosen a conventional right-hand thread fastener.

Seized fasteners

● Corrosion of external fasteners due to water or reaction between two dissimilar metals can occur over a period of time. It will build up sooner in wet conditions or in countries where salt is used on the roads during the winter. If a fastener is severely corroded it is likely that normal methods of removal will fail and result in its head being ruined. When you attempt removal, the fastener thread should be heard to crack free and unscrew easily - if it doesn't, stop there before damaging something.

● A smart tap on the head of the fastener will often succeed in breaking free corrosion which has occurred in the threads **(see illustration 2.13)**.

● An aerosol penetrating fluid (such as WD-40) applied the night beforehand may work its way down into the thread and ease removal. Depending on the location, you may be able to make up a Plasticine well around the fastener head and fill it with penetrating fluid.

2.13 A sharp tap on the head of a fastener will often break free a corroded thread

● If you are working on an engine internal component, corrosion will most likely not be a problem due to the well lubricated environment. However, components can be very tight and an impact driver is a useful tool in freeing them **(see illustration 2.14)**.

2.14 Using an impact driver to free a fastener

● Where corrosion has occurred between dissimilar metals (eg steel and aluminium alloy), the application of heat to the fastener head will create a disproportionate expansion rate between the two metals and break the seizure caused by the corrosion. Whether heat can be applied depends on the location of the fastener - any surrounding components likely to be damaged must first be removed **(see illustration 2.15)**. Heat can be applied using a paint stripper heat gun or clothes iron, or by immersing the component in boiling water - wear protective gloves to prevent scalding or burns to the hands.

2.15 Using heat to free a seized fastener

● As a last resort, it is possible to use a hammer and cold chisel to work the fastener head unscrewed **(see illustration 2.16)**. This will damage the fastener, but more importantly extreme care must be taken not to damage the surrounding component.

> *Caution: Remember that the component being secured is generally of more value than the bolt, nut or screw - when the fastener is freed, do not unscrew it with force, instead work the fastener back and forth when resistance is felt to prevent thread damage.*

2.16 Using a hammer and chisel to free a seized fastener

Broken fasteners and damaged heads

● If the shank of a broken bolt or screw is accessible you can grip it with self-locking grips. The knurled wheel type stud extractor tool or self-gripping stud puller tool is particularly useful for removing the long studs which screw into the cylinder mouth surface of the crankcase or bolts and screws from which the head has broken off **(see illustration 2.17)**. Studs can also be removed by locking two nuts together on the threaded end of the stud and using a spanner on the lower nut **(see illustration 2.18)**.

2.17 Using a stud extractor tool to remove a broken crankcase stud

2.18 Two nuts can be locked together to unscrew a stud from a component

● A bolt or screw which has broken off below or level with the casing must be extracted using a screw extractor set. Centre punch the fastener to centralise the drill bit, then drill a hole in the fastener **(see illustration 2.19)**. Select a drill bit which is approximately half to three-quarters the

2.19 When using a screw extractor, first drill a hole in the fastener . . .

diameter of the fastener and drill to a depth which will accommodate the extractor. Use the largest size extractor possible, but avoid leaving too small a wall thickness otherwise the extractor will merely force the fastener walls outwards wedging it in the casing thread.

● If a spiral type extractor is used, thread it anti-clockwise into the fastener. As it is screwed in, it will grip the fastener and unscrew it from the casing **(see illustration 2.20)**.

2.20 . . . then thread the extractor anti-clockwise into the fastener

● If a taper type extractor is used, tap it into the fastener so that it is firmly wedged in place. Unscrew the extractor (anti-clockwise) to draw the fastener out.

>  *Warning: Stud extractors are very hard and may break off in the fastener if care is not taken - ask an engineer about spark erosion if this happens.*

● Alternatively, the broken bolt/screw can be drilled out and the hole retapped for an oversize bolt/screw or a diamond-section thread insert. It is essential that the drilling is carried out squarely and to the correct depth, otherwise the casing may be ruined - if in doubt, entrust the work to an engineer.
● Bolts and nuts with rounded corners cause the correct size spanner or socket to slip when force is applied. Of the types of spanner/socket available always use a six-point type rather than an eight or twelve-point type - better grip

2.21 Comparison of surface drive ring spanner (left) with 12-point type (right)

is obtained. Surface drive spanners grip the middle of the hex flats, rather than the corners, and are thus good in cases of damaged heads **(see illustration 2.21)**.

● Slotted-head or Phillips-head screws are often damaged by the use of the wrong size screwdriver. Allen-head and Torx-head screws are much less likely to sustain damage. If enough of the screw head is exposed you can use a hacksaw to cut a slot in its head and then use a conventional flat-bladed screwdriver to remove it. Alternatively use a hammer and cold chisel to tap the head of the fastener around to slacken it. Always replace damaged fasteners with new ones, preferably Torx or Allen-head type.

HAYNES HINT

A dab of valve grinding compound between the screw head and screw-driver tip will often give a good grip.

Thread repair

● Threads (particularly those in aluminium alloy components) can be damaged by overtightening, being assembled with dirt in the threads, or from a component working loose and vibrating. Eventually the thread will fail completely, and it will be impossible to tighten the fastener.

● If a thread is damaged or clogged with old locking compound it can be renovated with a thread repair tool (thread chaser) **(see illustrations 2.22 and 2.23)**; special thread

2.22 A thread repair tool being used to correct an internal thread

2.23 A thread repair tool being used to correct an external thread

chasers are available for spark plug hole threads. The tool will not cut a new thread, but clean and true the original thread. Make sure that you use the correct diameter and pitch tool. Similarly, external threads can be cleaned up with a die or a thread restorer file **(see illustration 2.24)**.

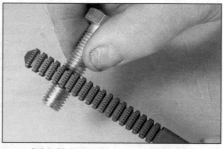

2.24 Using a thread restorer file

● It is possible to drill out the old thread and retap the component to the next thread size. This will work where there is enough surrounding material and a new bolt or screw can be obtained. Sometimes, however, this is not possible - such as where the bolt/screw passes through another component which must also be suitably modified, also in cases where a spark plug or oil drain plug cannot be obtained in a larger diameter thread size.

● The diamond-section thread insert (often known by its popular trade name of Heli-Coil) is a simple and effective method of renewing the thread and retaining the original size. A kit can be purchased which contains the tap, insert and installing tool **(see illustration 2.25)**. Drill out the damaged thread with the size drill specified **(see illustration 2.26)**. Carefully retap the thread **(see illustration 2.27)**. Install the

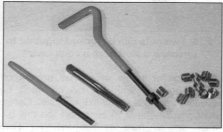

2.25 Obtain a thread insert kit to suit the thread diameter and pitch required

2.26 To install a thread insert, first drill out the original thread . . .

2.27 . . . tap a new thread . . .

2.28 . . . fit insert on the installing tool . . .

2.29 . . . and thread into the component . . .

2.30 . . . break off the tang when complete

insert on the installing tool and thread it slowly into place using a light downward pressure **(see illustrations 2.28 and 2.29)**. When positioned between a 1/4 and 1/2 turn below the surface withdraw the installing tool and use the break-off tool to press down on the tang, breaking it off **(see illustration 2.30)**.

● There are epoxy thread repair kits on the market which can rebuild stripped internal threads, although this repair should not be used on high load-bearing components.

Thread locking and sealing compounds

● Locking compounds are used in locations where the fastener is prone to loosening due to vibration or on important safety-related items which might cause loss of control of the motorcycle if they fail. It is also used where important fasteners cannot be secured by other means such as lockwashers or split pins.

● Before applying locking compound, make sure that the threads (internal and external) are clean and dry with all old compound removed. Select a compound to suit the component being secured - a non-permanent general locking and sealing type is suitable for most applications, but a high strength type is needed for permanent fixing of studs in castings. Apply a drop or two of the compound to the first few threads of the fastener, then thread it into place and tighten to the specified torque. Do not apply excessive thread locking compound otherwise the thread may be damaged on subsequent removal.

● Certain fasteners are impregnated with a dry film type coating of locking compound on their threads. Always renew this type of fastener if disturbed.

● Anti-seize compounds, such as copper-based greases, can be applied to protect threads from seizure due to extreme heat and corrosion. A common instance is spark plug threads and exhaust system fasteners.

3 Measuring tools and gauges

Feeler gauges

● Feeler gauges (or blades) are used for measuring small gaps and clearances (see illustration 3.1). They can also be used to measure endfloat (sideplay) of a component on a shaft where access is not possible with a dial gauge.

● Feeler gauge sets should be treated with care and not bent or damaged. They are etched with their size on one face. Keep them clean and very lightly oiled to prevent corrosion build-up.

3.1 Feeler gauges are used for measuring small gaps and clearances - thickness is marked on one face of gauge

● When measuring a clearance, select a gauge which is a light sliding fit between the two components. You may need to use two gauges together to measure the clearance accurately.

Micrometers

● A micrometer is a precision tool capable of measuring to 0.01 or 0.001 of a millimetre. It should always be stored in its case and not in the general toolbox. It must be kept clean and never dropped, otherwise its frame or measuring anvils could be distorted resulting in inaccurate readings.

● External micrometers are used for measuring outside diameters of components and have many more applications than internal micrometers. Micrometers are available in different size ranges, eg 0 to 25 mm, 25 to 50 mm, and upwards in 25 mm steps; some large micrometers have interchangeable anvils to allow a range of measurements to be taken. Generally the largest precision measurement you are likely to take on a motorcycle is the piston diameter.

● Internal micrometers (or bore micrometers) are used for measuring inside diameters, such as valve guides and cylinder bores. Telescoping gauges and small hole gauges are used in conjunction with an external micrometer, whereas the more expensive internal micrometers have their own measuring device.

External micrometer

Note: *The conventional analogue type instrument is described. Although much easier to read, digital micrometers are considerably more expensive.*

● Always check the calibration of the micrometer before use. With the anvils closed (0 to 25 mm type) or set over a test gauge (for

3.2 Check micrometer calibration before use

the larger types) the scale should read zero (see illustration 3.2); make sure that the anvils (and test piece) are clean first. Any discrepancy can be adjusted by referring to the instructions supplied with the tool. Remember that the micrometer is a precision measuring tool - don't force the anvils closed, use the ratchet (4) on the end of the micrometer to close it. In this way, a measured force is always applied.

● To use, first make sure that the item being measured is clean. Place the anvil of the micrometer (1) against the item and use the thimble (2) to bring the spindle (3) lightly into contact with the other side of the item (see illustration 3.3). Don't tighten the thimble down because this will damage the micrometer - instead use the ratchet (4) on the end of the micrometer. The ratchet mechanism applies a measured force preventing damage to the instrument.

● The micrometer is read by referring to the linear scale on the sleeve and the annular scale on the thimble. Read off the sleeve first to obtain the base measurement, then add the fine measurement from the thimble to obtain the overall reading. The linear scale on the sleeve represents the measuring range of the micrometer (eg 0 to 25 mm). The annular scale

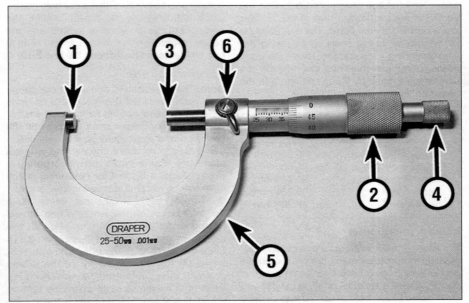

3.3 Micrometer component parts

1 Anvil	3 Spindle	5 Frame
2 Thimble	4 Ratchet	6 Locking lever

on the thimble will be in graduations of 0.01 mm (or as marked on the frame) - one full revolution of the thimble will move 0.5 mm on the linear scale. Take the reading where the datum line on the sleeve intersects the thimble's scale. Always position the eye directly above the scale otherwise an inaccurate reading will result.

In the example shown the item measures 2.95 mm (see illustration 3.4):

Linear scale	2.00 mm
Linear scale	0.50 mm
Annular scale	0.45 mm
Total figure	**2.95 mm**

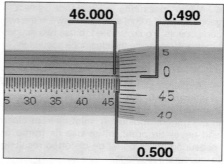

3.5 Micrometer reading of 46.99 mm on linear and annular scales . . .

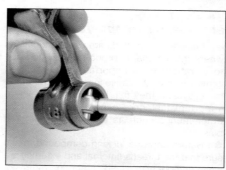

3.7 Expand the telescoping gauge in the bore, lock its position . . .

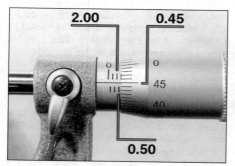

3.4 Micrometer reading of 2.95 mm

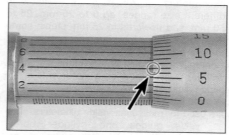

3.6 . . . and 0.004 mm on vernier scale

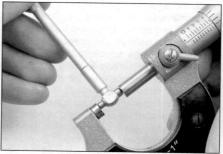

3.8 . . . then measure the gauge with a micrometer

Most micrometers have a locking lever (6) on the frame to hold the setting in place, allowing the item to be removed from the micrometer.
● Some micrometers have a vernier scale on their sleeve, providing an even finer measurement to be taken, in 0.001 increments of a millimetre. Take the sleeve and thimble measurement as described above, then check which graduation on the vernier scale aligns with that of the annular scale on the thimble **Note:** *The eye must be perpendicular to the scale when taking the vernier reading - if necessary rotate the body of the micrometer to ensure this.* Multiply the vernier scale figure by 0.001 and add it to the base and fine measurement figures.

In the example shown the item measures 46.994 mm (see illustrations 3.5 and 3.6):

Linear scale (base)	46.000 mm
Linear scale (base)	00.500 mm
Annular scale (fine)	00.490 mm
Vernier scale	00.004 mm
Total figure	**46.994 mm**

Internal micrometer

● Internal micrometers are available for measuring bore diameters, but are expensive and unlikely to be available for home use. It is suggested that a set of telescoping gauges and small hole gauges, both of which must be used with an external micrometer, will suffice for taking internal measurements on a motorcycle.
● Telescoping gauges can be used to

measure internal diameters of components. Select a gauge with the correct size range, make sure its ends are clean and insert it into the bore. Expand the gauge, then lock its position and withdraw it from the bore (see illustration 3.7). Measure across the gauge ends with a micrometer (see illustration 3.8).
● Very small diameter bores (such as valve guides) are measured with a small hole gauge. Once adjusted to a slip-fit inside the component, its position is locked and the gauge withdrawn for measurement with a micrometer (see illustrations 3.9 and 3.10).

Vernier caliper

Note: *The conventional linear and dial gauge type instruments are described. Digital types are easier to read, but are far more expensive.*
● The vernier caliper does not provide the precision of a micrometer, but is versatile in being able to measure internal and external diameters. Some types also incorporate a depth gauge. It is ideal for measuring clutch plate friction material and spring free lengths.
● To use the conventional linear scale vernier, slacken off the vernier clamp screws (1) and set its jaws over (2), or inside (3), the item to be measured (see illustration 3.11). Slide the jaw into contact, using the thumb-wheel (4) for fine movement of the sliding scale (5) then tighten the clamp screws (1). Read off the main scale (6) where the zero on the sliding scale (5) intersects it, taking the whole number to the left of the zero; this provides the base measurement. View along the sliding scale and select the division which

3.9 Expand the small hole gauge in the bore, lock its position . . .

3.10 . . . then measure the gauge with a micrometer

lines up exactly with any of the divisions on the main scale, noting that the divisions usually represents 0.02 of a millimetre. Add this fine measurement to the base measurement to obtain the total reading.

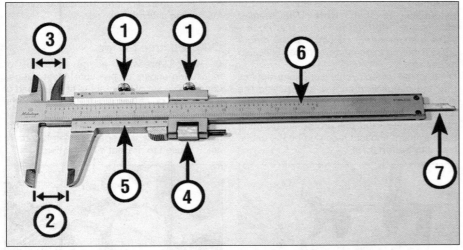

3.11 Vernier component parts (linear gauge)

1 *Clamp screws*	3 *Internal jaws*	5 *Sliding scale*	7 *Depth gauge*
2 *External jaws*	4 *Thumbwheel*	6 *Main scale*	

In the example shown the item measures 55.92 mm **(see illustration 3.12)**:

Base measurement	55.00 mm
Fine measurement	00.92 mm
Total figure	**55.92 mm**

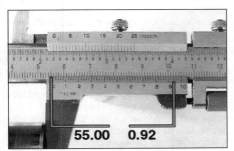

3.12 Vernier gauge reading of 55.92 mm

● Some vernier calipers are equipped with a dial gauge for fine measurement. Before use, check that the jaws are clean, then close them fully and check that the dial gauge reads zero. If necessary adjust the gauge ring accordingly. Slacken the vernier clamp screw (1) and set its jaws over (2), or inside (3), the item to be measured **(see illustration 3.13)**. Slide the jaws into contact, using the thumbwheel (4) for fine movement. Read off the main scale (5) where the edge of the sliding scale (6) intersects it, taking the whole number to the left of the zero; this provides the base measurement. Read off the needle position on the dial gauge (7) scale to provide the fine measurement; each division represents 0.05 of a millimetre. Add this fine measurement to the base measurement to obtain the total reading.

In the example shown the item measures 55.95 mm **(see illustration 3.14)**:

Base measurement	55.00 mm
Fine measurement	00.95 mm
Total figure	**55.95 mm**

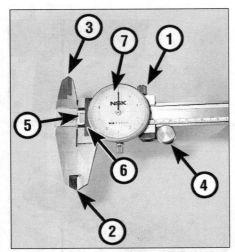

3.13 Vernier component parts (dial gauge)

1 *Clamp screw*	5 *Main scale*
2 *External jaws*	6 *Sliding scale*
3 *Internal jaws*	7 *Dial gauge*
4 *Thumbwheel*	

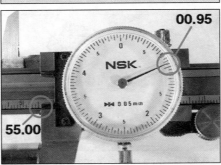

3.14 Vernier gauge reading of 55.95 mm

Plastigauge

● Plastigauge is a plastic material which can be compressed between two surfaces to measure the oil clearance between them. The width of the compressed Plastigauge is measured against a calibrated scale to determine the clearance.

● Common uses of Plastigauge are for measuring the clearance between crankshaft journal and main bearing inserts, between crankshaft journal and big-end bearing inserts, and between camshaft and bearing surfaces. The following example describes big-end oil clearance measurement.

● Handle the Plastigauge material carefully to prevent distortion. Using a sharp knife, cut a length which corresponds with the width of the bearing being measured and place it carefully across the journal so that it is parallel with the shaft **(see illustration 3.15)**. Carefully install both bearing shells and the connecting rod. Without rotating the rod on the journal tighten its bolts or nuts (as applicable) to the specified torque. The connecting rod and bearings are then disassembled and the crushed Plastigauge examined.

3.15 Plastigauge placed across shaft journal

● Using the scale provided in the Plastigauge kit, measure the width of the material to determine the oil clearance **(see illustration 3.16)**. Always remove all traces of Plastigauge after use using your fingernails.

> *Caution: Arriving at the correct clearance demands that the assembly is torqued correctly, according to the settings and sequence (where applicable) provided by the motorcycle manufacturer.*

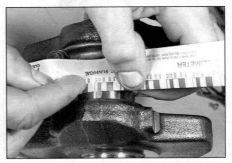

3.16 Measuring the width of the crushed Plastigauge

Dial gauge or DTI (Dial Test Indicator)

● A dial gauge can be used to accurately measure small amounts of movement. Typical uses are measuring shaft runout or shaft endfloat (sideplay) and setting piston position for ignition timing on two-strokes. A dial gauge set usually comes with a range of different probes and adapters and mounting equipment.

● The gauge needle must point to zero when at rest. Rotate the ring around its periphery to zero the gauge.

● Check that the gauge is capable of reading the extent of movement in the work. Most gauges have a small dial set in the face which records whole millimetres of movement as well as the fine scale around the face periphery which is calibrated in 0.01 mm divisions. Read off the small dial first to obtain the base measurement, then add the measurement from the fine scale to obtain the total reading.

In the example shown the gauge reads 1.48 mm **(see illustration 3.17)**:

Base measurement	1.00 mm
Fine measurement	0.48 mm
Total figure	**1.48 mm**

3.17 Dial gauge reading of 1.48 mm

● If measuring shaft runout, the shaft must be supported in vee-blocks and the gauge mounted on a stand perpendicular to the shaft. Rest the tip of the gauge against the centre of the shaft and rotate the shaft slowly whilst watching the gauge reading **(see illustration 3.18)**. Take several measurements along the length of the shaft and record the

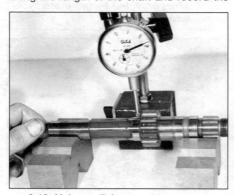

3.18 Using a dial gauge to measure shaft runout

maximum gauge reading as the amount of runout in the shaft. **Note:** *The reading obtained will be total runout at that point - some manufacturers specify that the runout figure is halved to compare with their specified runout limit.*

● Endfloat (sideplay) measurement requires that the gauge is mounted securely to the surrounding component with its probe touching the end of the shaft. Using hand pressure, push and pull on the shaft noting the maximum endfloat recorded on the gauge **(see illustration 3.19)**.

3.19 Using a dial gauge to measure shaft endfloat

● A dial gauge with suitable adapters can be used to determine piston position BTDC on two-stroke engines for the purposes of ignition timing. The gauge, adapter and suitable length probe are installed in the place of the spark plug and the gauge zeroed at TDC. If the piston position is specified as 1.14 mm BTDC, rotate the engine back to 2.00 mm BTDC, then slowly forwards to 1.14 mm BTDC.

Cylinder compression gauges

● A compression gauge is used for measuring cylinder compression. Either the rubber-cone type or the threaded adapter type can be used. The latter is preferred to ensure a perfect seal against the cylinder head. A 0 to 300 psi (0 to 20 Bar) type gauge (for petrol/gasoline engines) will be suitable for motorcycles.

● The spark plug is removed and the gauge either held hard against the cylinder head (cone type) or the gauge adapter screwed into the cylinder head (threaded type) **(see illustration 3.20)**. Cylinder compression is measured with the engine turning over, but not running - carry out the compression test as described in

3.20 Using a rubber-cone type cylinder compression gauge

Fault Finding Equipment. The gauge will hold the reading until manually released.

Oil pressure gauge

● An oil pressure gauge is used for measuring engine oil pressure. Most gauges come with a set of adapters to fit the thread of the take-off point **(see illustration 3.21)**. If the take-off point specified by the motorcycle manufacturer is an external oil pipe union, make sure that the specified replacement union is used to prevent oil starvation.

3.21 Oil pressure gauge and take-off point adapter (arrow)

● Oil pressure is measured with the engine running (at a specific rpm) and often the manufacturer will specify pressure limits for a cold and hot engine.

Straight-edge and surface plate

● If checking the gasket face of a component for warpage, place a steel rule or precision straight-edge across the gasket face and measure any gap between the straight-edge and component with feeler gauges **(see illustration 3.22)**. Check diagonally across the component and between mounting holes **(see illustration 3.23)**.

3.22 Use a straight-edge and feeler gauges to check for warpage

3.23 Check for warpage in these directions

● Checking individual components for warpage, such as clutch plain (metal) plates, requires a perfectly flat plate or piece or plate glass and feeler gauges.

4 Torque and leverage

What is torque?

● Torque describes the twisting force about a shaft. The amount of torque applied is determined by the distance from the centre of the shaft to the end of the lever and the amount of force being applied to the end of the lever; distance multiplied by force equals torque.

● The manufacturer applies a measured torque to a bolt or nut to ensure that it will not slacken in use and to hold two components securely together without movement in the joint. The actual torque setting depends on the thread size, bolt or nut material and the composition of the components being held.

● Too little torque may cause the fastener to loosen due to vibration, whereas too much torque will distort the joint faces of the component or cause the fastener to shear off. Always stick to the specified torque setting.

Using a torque wrench

● Check the calibration of the torque wrench and make sure it has a suitable range for the job. Torque wrenches are available in Nm (Newton-metres), kgf m (kilograms-force metre), lbf ft (pounds-feet), lbf in (inch-pounds). Do not confuse lbf ft with lbf in.

● Adjust the tool to the desired torque on the scale (see illustration 4.1). If your torque wrench is not calibrated in the units specified, carefully convert the figure (see *Conversion Factors*). A manufacturer sometimes gives a torque setting as a range (8 to 10 Nm) rather than a single figure - in this case set the tool midway between the two settings. The same torque may be expressed as 9 Nm ± 1 Nm. Some torque wrenches have a method of locking the setting so that it isn't inadvertently altered during use.

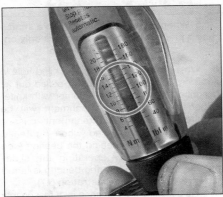

4.1 Set the torque wrench index mark to the setting required, in this case 12 Nm

● Install the bolts/nuts in their correct location and secure them lightly. Their threads must be clean and free of any old locking compound. Unless specified the threads and flange should be dry - oiled threads are necessary in certain circumstances and the manufacturer will take this into account in the specified torque figure. Similarly, the manufacturer may also specify the application of thread-locking compound.

● Tighten the fasteners in the specified sequence until the torque wrench clicks, indicating that the torque setting has been reached. Apply the torque again to double-check the setting. Where different thread diameter fasteners secure the component, as a rule tighten the larger diameter ones first.

● When the torque wrench has been finished with, release the lock (where applicable) and fully back off its setting to zero - do not leave the torque wrench tensioned. Also, do not use a torque wrench for slackening a fastener.

Angle-tightening

● Manufacturers often specify a figure in degrees for final tightening of a fastener. This usually follows tightening to a specific torque setting.

● A degree disc can be set and attached to the socket (see illustration 4.2) or a protractor can be used to mark the angle of movement on the bolt/nut head and the surrounding casting (see illustration 4.3).

4.2 Angle tightening can be accomplished with a torque-angle gauge . . .

4.3 . . . or by marking the angle on the surrounding component

Loosening sequences

● Where more than one bolt/nut secures a component, loosen each fastener evenly a little at a time. In this way, not all the stress of the joint is held by one fastener and the components are not likely to distort.

● If a tightening sequence is provided, work in the REVERSE of this, but if not, work from the outside in, in a criss-cross sequence (see illustration 4.4).

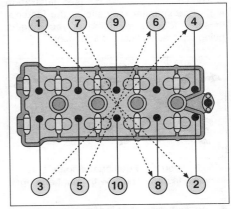

4.4 When slackening, work from the outside inwards

Tightening sequences

● If a component is held by more than one fastener it is important that the retaining bolts/nuts are tightened evenly to prevent uneven stress build-up and distortion of sealing faces. This is especially important on high-compression joints such as the cylinder head.

● A sequence is usually provided by the manufacturer, either in a diagram or actually marked in the casting. If not, always start in the centre and work outwards in a criss-cross pattern (see illustration 4.5). Start off by securing all bolts/nuts finger-tight, then set the torque wrench and tighten each fastener by a small amount in sequence until the final torque is reached. By following this practice,

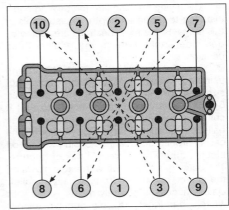

4.5 When tightening, work from the inside outwards

the joint will be held evenly and will not be distorted. Important joints, such as the cylinder head and big-end fasteners often have two- or three-stage torque settings.

Applying leverage

● Use tools at the correct angle. Position a socket wrench or spanner on the bolt/nut so that you pull it towards you when loosening. If this can't be done, push the spanner without curling your fingers around it **(see illustration 4.6)** - the spanner may slip or the fastener loosen suddenly, resulting in your fingers being crushed against a component.

4.6 If you can't pull on the spanner to loosen a fastener, push with your hand open

● Additional leverage is gained by extending the length of the lever. The best way to do this is to use a breaker bar instead of the regular length tool, or to slip a length of tubing over the end of the spanner or socket wrench.
● If additional leverage will not work, the fastener head is either damaged or firmly corroded in place (see *Fasteners*).

5 Bearings

Bearing removal and installation

Drivers and sockets

● Before removing a bearing, always inspect the casing to see which way it must be driven out - some casings will have retaining plates or a cast step. Also check for any identifying markings on the bearing and if installed to a certain depth, measure this at this stage. Some roller bearings are sealed on one side - take note of the original fitted position.
● Bearings can be driven out of a casing using a bearing driver tool (with the correct size head) or a socket of the correct diameter. Select the driver head or socket so that it contacts the outer race of the bearing, not the balls/rollers or inner race. Always support the casing around the bearing housing with wood blocks, otherwise there is a risk of fracture. The bearing is driven out with a few blows on the driver or socket from a heavy mallet. Unless access is severely restricted (as with wheel bearings), a pin-punch is not recommended unless it is moved around the bearing to keep it square in its housing.

● The same equipment can be used to install bearings. Make sure the bearing housing is supported on wood blocks and line up the bearing in its housing. Fit the bearing as noted on removal - generally they are installed with their marked side facing outwards. Tap the bearing squarely into its housing using a driver or socket which bears only on the bearing's outer race - contact with the bearing balls/rollers or inner race will destroy it **(see illustrations 5.1 and 5.2)**.
● Check that the bearing inner race and balls/rollers rotate freely.

5.1 Using a bearing driver against the bearing's outer race

5.2 Using a large socket against the bearing's outer race

Pullers and slide-hammers

● Where a bearing is pressed on a shaft a puller will be required to extract it **(see illustration 5.3)**. Make sure that the puller clamp or legs fit securely behind the bearing and are unlikely to slip out. If pulling a bearing

5.3 This bearing puller clamps behind the bearing and pressure is applied to the shaft end to draw the bearing off

off a gear shaft for example, you may have to locate the puller behind a gear pinion if there is no access to the race and draw the gear pinion off the shaft as well **(see illustration 5.4)**.

> *Caution: Ensure that the puller's centre bolt locates securely against the end of the shaft and will not slip when pressure is applied. Also ensure that puller does not damage the shaft end.*

5.4 Where no access is available to the rear of the bearing, it is sometimes possible to draw off the adjacent component

● Operate the puller so that its centre bolt exerts pressure on the shaft end and draws the bearing off the shaft.
● When installing the bearing on the shaft, tap only on the bearing's inner race - contact with the balls/rollers or outer race with destroy the bearing. Use a socket or length of tubing as a drift which fits over the shaft end **(see illustration 5.5)**.

5.5 When installing a bearing on a shaft use a piece of tubing which bears only on the bearing's inner race

● Where a bearing locates in a blind hole in a casing, it cannot be driven or pulled out as described above. A slide-hammer with knife-edged bearing puller attachment will be required. The puller attachment passes through the bearing and when tightened expands to fit firmly behind the bearing **(see illustration 5.6)**. By operating the slide-hammer part of the tool the bearing is jarred out of its housing **(see illustration 5.7)**.
● It is possible, if the bearing is of reasonable weight, for it to drop out of its housing if the casing is heated as described opposite. If this

5.6 Expand the bearing puller so that it locks behind the bearing . . .

5.7 . . . attach the slide hammer to the bearing puller

method is attempted, first prepare a work surface which will enable the casing to be tapped face down to help dislodge the bearing - a wood surface is ideal since it will not damage the casing's gasket surface. Wearing protective gloves, tap the heated casing several times against the work surface to dislodge the bearing under its own weight (see illustration 5.8).

5.8 Tapping a casing face down on wood blocks can often dislodge a bearing

● Bearings can be installed in blind holes using the driver or socket method described above.

Drawbolts

● Where a bearing or bush is set in the eye of a component, such as a suspension linkage arm or connecting rod small-end, removal by drift may damage the component. Furthermore, a rubber bushing in a shock absorber eye cannot successfully be driven out of position. If access is available to a engineering press, the task is straightforward. If not, a drawbolt can be fabricated to extract the bearing or bush.

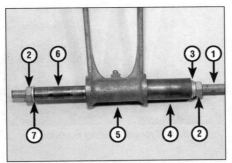

5.9 Drawbolt component parts assembled on a suspension arm

1 Bolt or length of threaded bar
2 Nuts
3 Washer (external diameter greater than tubing internal diameter)
4 Tubing (internal diameter sufficient to accommodate bearing)
5 Suspension arm with bearing
6 Tubing (external diameter slightly smaller than bearing)
7 Washer (external diameter slightly smaller than bearing)

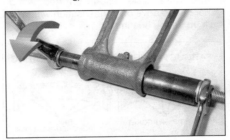

5.10 Drawing the bearing out of the suspension arm

● To extract the bearing/bush you will need a long bolt with nut (or piece of threaded bar with two nuts), a piece of tubing which has an internal diameter larger than the bearing/bush, another piece of tubing which has an external diameter slightly smaller than the bearing/bush, and a selection of washers (see illustrations 5.9 and 5.10). Note that the pieces of tubing must be of the same length, or longer, than the bearing/bush.
● The same kit (without the pieces of tubing) can be used to draw the new bearing/bush back into place (see illustration 5.11).

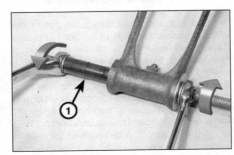

5.11 Installing a new bearing (1) in the suspension arm

Temperature change

● If the bearing's outer race is a tight fit in the casing, the aluminium casing can be heated to release its grip on the bearing. Aluminium will expand at a greater rate than the steel bearing outer race. There are several ways to do this, but avoid any localised extreme heat (such as a blow torch) - aluminium alloy has a low melting point.
● Approved methods of heating a casing are using a domestic oven (heated to 100°C) or immersing the casing in boiling water (see illustration 5.12). Low temperature range localised heat sources such as a paint stripper heat gun or clothes iron can also be used (see illustration 5.13). Alternatively, soak a rag in boiling water, wring it out and wrap it around the bearing housing.

> ⚠️ **Warning: All of these methods require care in use to prevent scalding and burns to the hands. Wear protective gloves when handling hot components.**

5.12 A casing can be immersed in a sink of boiling water to aid bearing removal

5.13 Using a localised heat source to aid bearing removal

● If heating the whole casing note that plastic components, such as the neutral switch, may suffer - remove them beforehand.
● After heating, remove the bearing as described above. You may find that the expansion is sufficient for the bearing to fall out of the casing under its own weight or with a light tap on the driver or socket.
● If necessary, the casing can be heated to aid bearing installation, and this is sometimes the recommended procedure if the motorcycle manufacturer has designed the housing and bearing fit with this intention.

● Installation of bearings can be eased by placing them in a freezer the night before installation. The steel bearing will contract slightly, allowing easy insertion in its housing. This is often useful when installing steering head outer races in the frame.

Bearing types and markings

● Plain shell bearings, ball bearings, needle roller bearings and tapered roller bearings will all be found on motorcycles (see illustrations 5.14 and 5.15). The ball and roller types are usually caged between an inner and outer race, but uncaged variations may be found.

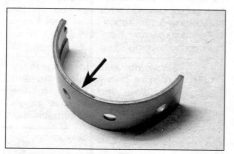

5.14 Shell bearings are either plain or grooved. They are usually identified by colour code (arrow)

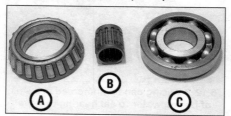

5.15 Tapered roller bearing (A), needle roller bearing (B) and ball journal bearing (C)

● Shell bearings (often called inserts) are usually found at the crankshaft main and connecting rod big-end where they are good at coping with high loads. They are made of a phosphor-bronze material and are impregnated with self-lubricating properties.

● Ball bearings and needle roller bearings consist of a steel inner and outer race with the balls or rollers between the races. They require constant lubrication by oil or grease and are good at coping with axial loads. Taper roller bearings consist of rollers set in a tapered cage set on the inner race; the outer race is separate. They are good at coping with axial loads and prevent movement along the shaft - a typical application is in the steering head.

● Bearing manufacturers produce bearings to ISO size standards and stamp one face of the bearing to indicate its internal and external diameter, load capacity and type (see illustration 5.16).

● Metal bushes are usually of phosphor-bronze material. Rubber bushes are used in suspension mounting eyes. Fibre bushes have also been used in suspension pivots.

5.16 Typical bearing marking

Bearing fault finding

● If a bearing outer race has spun in its housing, the housing material will be damaged. You can use a bearing locking compound to bond the outer race in place if damage is not too severe.

● Shell bearings will fail due to damage of their working surface, as a result of lack of lubrication, corrosion or abrasive particles in the oil (see illustration 5.17). Small particles of dirt in the oil may embed in the bearing material whereas larger particles will score the bearing and shaft journal. If a number of short journeys are made, insufficient heat will be generated to drive off condensation which has built up on the bearings.

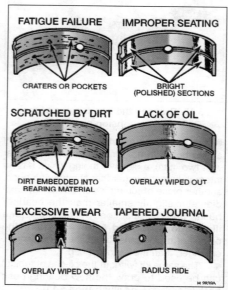

5.17 Typical bearing failures

● Ball and roller bearings will fail due to lack of lubrication or damage to the balls or rollers. Tapered-roller bearings can be damaged by overloading them. Unless the bearing is sealed on both sides, wash it in paraffin (kerosene) to remove all old grease then allow it to dry. Make a visual inspection looking to dented balls or rollers, damaged cages and worn or pitted races (see illustration 5.18).

● A ball bearing can be checked for wear by listening to it when spun. Apply a film of light oil to the bearing and hold it close to the ear - hold the outer race with one hand and spin the inner

5.18 Example of ball journal bearing with damaged balls and cages

5.19 Hold outer race and listen to inner race when spun

race with the other hand (see illustration 5.19). The bearing should be almost silent when spun; if it grates or rattles it is worn.

6 Oil seals

Oil seal removal and installation

● Oil seals should be renewed every time a component is dismantled. This is because the seal lips will become set to the sealing surface and will not necessarily reseal.

● Oil seals can be prised out of position using a large flat-bladed screwdriver (see illustration 6.1). In the case of crankcase seals, check first that the seal is not lipped on the inside, preventing its removal with the crankcases joined.

6.1 Prise out oil seals with a large flat-bladed screwdriver

● New seals are usually installed with their marked face (containing the seal reference code) outwards and the spring side towards the fluid being retained. In certain cases, such as a two-stroke engine crankshaft seal, a double lipped seal may be used due to there being fluid or gas on each side of the joint.

● Use a bearing driver or socket which bears only on the outer hard edge of the seal to install it in the casing - tapping on the inner edge will damage the sealing lip.

Oil seal types and markings

● Oil seals are usually of the single-lipped type. Double-lipped seals are found where a liquid or gas is on both sides of the joint.

● Oil seals can harden and lose their sealing ability if the motorcycle has been in storage for a long period - renewal is the only solution.

● Oil seal manufacturers also conform to the ISO markings for seal size - these are moulded into the outer face of the seal **(see illustration 6.2)**.

6.2 These oil seal markings indicate inside diameter, outside diameter and seal thickness

7 Gaskets and sealants

Types of gasket and sealant

● Gaskets are used to seal the mating surfaces between components and keep lubricants, fluids, vacuum or pressure contained within the assembly. Aluminium gaskets are sometimes found at the cylinder joints, but most gaskets are paper-based. If the mating surfaces of the components being joined are undamaged the gasket can be installed dry, although a dab of sealant or grease will be useful to hold it in place during assembly.

● RTV (Room Temperature Vulcanising) silicone rubber sealants cure when exposed to moisture in the atmosphere. These sealants are good at filling pits or irregular gasket faces, but will tend to be forced out of the joint under very high torque. They can be used to replace a paper gasket, but first make sure that the width of the paper gasket is not essential to the shimming of internal components. RTV sealants should not be used on components containing petrol (gasoline).

● Non-hardening, semi-hardening and hard setting liquid gasket compounds can be used with a gasket or between a metal-to-metal joint. Select the sealant to suit the application: universal non-hardening sealant can be used on virtually all joints; semi-hardening on joint faces which are rough or damaged; hard setting sealant on joints which require a permanent bond and are subjected to high temperature and pressure. **Note:** *Check first if the paper gasket has a bead of sealant*

impregnated in its surface before applying additional sealant.

● When choosing a sealant, make sure it is suitable for the application, particularly if being applied in a high-temperature area or in the vicinity of fuel. Certain manufacturers produce sealants in either clear, silver or black colours to match the finish of the engine. This has a particular application on motorcycles where much of the engine is exposed.

● Do not over-apply sealant. That which is squeezed out on the outside of the joint can be wiped off, whereas an excess of sealant on the inside can break off and clog oilways.

Breaking a sealed joint

● Age, heat, pressure and the use of hard setting sealant can cause two components to stick together so tightly that they are difficult to separate using finger pressure alone. Do not resort to using levers unless there is a pry point provided for this purpose **(see illustration 7.1)** or else the gasket surfaces will be damaged.

● Use a soft-faced hammer **(see illustration 7.2)** or a wood block and conventional hammer to strike the component near the mating surface. Avoid hammering against cast extremities since they may break off. If this method fails, try using a wood wedge between the two components.

Caution: If the joint will not separate, double-check that you have removed all the fasteners.

7.1 If a pry point is provided, apply gently pressure with a flat-bladed screwdriver

7.2 Tap around the joint with a soft-faced mallet if necessary - don't strike cooling fins

Removal of old gasket and sealant

● Paper gaskets will most likely come away complete, leaving only a few traces stuck on

Most components have one or two hollow locating dowels between the two gasket faces. If a dowel cannot be removed, do not resort to gripping it with pliers - it will almost certainly be distorted. Install a close-fitting socket or Phillips screwdriver into the dowel and then grip the outer edge of the dowel to free it.

the sealing faces of the components. It is imperative that all traces are removed to ensure correct sealing of the new gasket.

● Very carefully scrape all traces of gasket away making sure that the sealing surfaces are not gouged or scored by the scraper **(see illustrations 7.3, 7.4 and 7.5)**. Stubborn deposits can be removed by spraying with an aerosol gasket remover. Final preparation of

7.3 Paper gaskets can be scraped off with a gasket scraper tool . . .

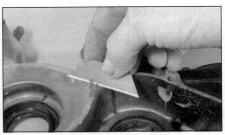

7.4 . . . a knife blade . . .

7.5 . . . or a household scraper

7.6 Fine abrasive paper is wrapped around a flat file to clean up the gasket face

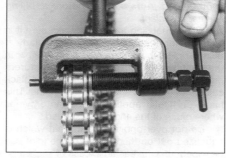

8.1 Tighten the chain breaker to push the pin out of the link . . .

8.4 Insert the new soft link, with O-rings, through the chain ends . . .

7.7 A kitchen scourer can be used on stubborn deposits

8.2 . . . withdraw the pin, remove the tool . . .

8.5 . . . install the O-rings over the pin ends . . .

8.6 . . . followed by the sideplate

the gasket surface can be made with very fine abrasive paper or a plastic kitchen scourer (see illustrations 7.6 and 7.7).

● Old sealant can be scraped or peeled off components, depending on the type originally used. Note that gasket removal compounds are available to avoid scraping the components clean; make sure the gasket remover suits the type of sealant used.

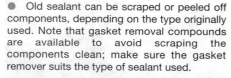

8 Chains

Breaking and joining final drive chains

● Drive chains for all but small bikes are continuous and do not have a clip-type connecting link. The chain must be broken using a chain breaker tool and the new chain securely riveted together using a new soft rivet-type link. Never use a clip-type connecting link instead of a rivet-type link, except in an emergency. Various chain breaking and riveting tools are available, either as separate tools or combined as illustrated in the accompanying photographs - read the instructions supplied with the tool carefully.

> ⚠ **Warning: The need to rivet the new link pins correctly cannot be overstressed - loss of control of the motorcycle is very likely to result if the chain breaks in use.**

● Rotate the chain and look for the soft link. The soft link pins look like they have been

8.3 . . . and separate the chain link

deeply centre-punched instead of peened over like all the other pins (see illustration 8.9) and its sideplate may be a different colour. Position the soft link midway between the sprockets and assemble the chain breaker tool over one of the soft link pins (see illustration 8.1). Operate the tool to push the pin out through the chain (see illustration 8.2). On an O-ring chain, remove the O-rings (see illustration 8.3). Carry out the same procedure on the other soft link pin.

> *Caution: Certain soft link pins (particularly on the larger chains) may require their ends to be filed or ground off before they can be pressed out using the tool.*

● Check that you have the correct size and strength (standard or heavy duty) new soft link - do not reuse the old link. Look for the size marking on the chain sideplates (see illustration 8.10).

● Position the chain ends so that they are engaged over the rear sprocket. On an O-ring

chain, install a new O-ring over each pin of the link and insert the link through the two chain ends (see illustration 8.4). Install a new O-ring over the end of each pin, followed by the sideplate (with the chain manufacturer's marking facing outwards) (see illustrations 8.5 and 8.6). On an unsealed chain, insert the link through the two chain ends, then install the sideplate with the chain manufacturer's marking facing outwards.

● Note that it may not be possible to install the sideplate using finger pressure alone. If using a joining tool, assemble it so that the plates of the tool clamp the link and press the sideplate over the pins (see illustration 8.7). Otherwise, use two small sockets placed over

8.7 Push the sideplate into position using a clamp

8.8 Assemble the chain riveting tool over one pin at a time and tighten it fully

8.9 Pin end correctly riveted (A), pin end unriveted (B)

the rivet ends and two pieces of the wood between a G-clamp. Operate the clamp to press the sideplate over the pins.

● Assemble the joining tool over one pin (following the maker's instructions) and tighten the tool down to spread the pin end securely **(see illustrations 8.8 and 8.9)**. Do the same on the other pin.

 Warning: Check that the pin ends are secure and that there is no danger of the sideplate coming loose. If the pin ends are cracked the soft link must be renewed.

Final drive chain sizing

● Chains are sized using a three digit number, followed by a suffix to denote the chain type **(see illustration 8.10)**. Chain type is either standard or heavy duty (thicker sideplates), and also unsealed or O-ring/X-ring type.

● The first digit of the number relates to the pitch of the chain, ie the distance from the centre of one pin to the centre of the next pin **(see illustration 8.11)**. Pitch is expressed in eighths of an inch, as follows:

8.10 Typical chain size and type marking

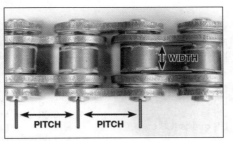

8.11 Chain dimensions

| Sizes commencing with a 4 (eg 428) have a pitch of 1/2 inch (12.7 mm) |
| Sizes commencing with a 5 (eg 520) have a pitch of 5/8 inch (15.9 mm) |
| Sizes commencing with a 6 (eg 630) have a pitch of 3/4 inch (19.1 mm) |

● The second and third digits of the chain size relate to the width of the rollers, again in imperial units, eg the 525 shown has 5/16 inch (7.94 mm) rollers **(see illustration 8.11)**.

9 Hoses

Clamping to prevent flow

● Small-bore flexible hoses can be clamped to prevent fluid flow whilst a component is worked on. Whichever method is used, ensure that the hose material is not permanently distorted or damaged by the clamp.

a) A brake hose clamp available from auto accessory shops **(see illustration 9.1)**.
b) A wingnut type hose clamp **(see illustration 9.2)**.

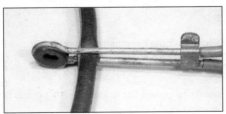

9.1 Hoses can be clamped with an automotive brake hose clamp . . .

9.2 . . . a wingnut type hose clamp . . .

c) Two sockets placed each side of the hose and held with straight-jawed self-locking grips **(see illustration 9.3)**.
d) Thick card each side of the hose held between straight-jawed self-locking grips **(see illustration 9.4)**.

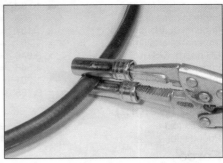

9.3 . . . two sockets and a pair of self-locking grips . . .

9.4 . . . or thick card and self-locking grips

Freeing and fitting hoses

● Always make sure the hose clamp is moved well clear of the hose end. Grip the hose with your hand and rotate it whilst pulling it off the union. If the hose has hardened due to age and will not move, slit it with a sharp knife and peel its ends off the union **(see illustration 9.5)**.

● Resist the temptation to use grease or soap on the unions to aid installation; although it helps the hose slip over the union it will equally aid the escape of fluid from the joint. It is preferable to soften the hose ends in hot water and wet the inside surface of the hose with water or a fluid which will evaporate.

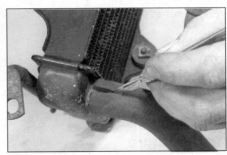

9.5 Cutting a coolant hose free with a sharp knife

Conversion Factors

Length (distance)

Inches (in)	x 25.4	= Millimetres (mm)	x 0.0394	= Inches (in)
Feet (ft)	x 0.305	= Metres (m)	x 3.281	= Feet (ft)
Miles	x 1.609	= Kilometres (km)	x 0.621	= Miles

Volume (capacity)

Cubic inches (cu in; in^3)	x 16.387	= Cubic centimetres (cc; cm^3)	x 0.061	= Cubic inches (cu in; in^3)
Imperial pints (Imp pt)	x 0.568	= Litres (l)	x 1.76	= Imperial pints (Imp pt)
Imperial quarts (Imp qt)	x 1.137	= Litres (l)	x 0.88	= Imperial quarts (Imp qt)
Imperial quarts (Imp qt)	x 1.201	= US quarts (US qt)	x 0.833	= Imperial quarts (Imp qt)
US quarts (US qt)	x 0.946	= Litres (l)	x 1.057	= US quarts (US qt)
Imperial gallons (Imp gal)	x 4.546	= Litres (l)	x 0.22	= Imperial gallons (Imp gal)
Imperial gallons (Imp gal)	x 1.201	= US gallons (US gal)	x 0.833	= Imperial gallons (Imp gal)
US gallons (US gal)	x 3.785	= Litres (l)	x 0.264	= US gallons (US gal)

Mass (weight)

Ounces (oz)	x 28.35	= Grams (g)	x 0.035	= Ounces (oz)
Pounds (lb)	x 0.454	= Kilograms (kg)	x 2.205	= Pounds (lb)

Force

Ounces-force (ozf; oz)	x 0.278	= Newtons (N)	x 3.6	= Ounces-force (ozf; oz)
Pounds-force (lbf; lb)	x 4.448	= Newtons (N)	x 0.225	= Pounds-force (lbf; lb)
Newtons (N)	x 0.1	= Kilograms-force (kgf; kg)	x 9.81	= Newtons (N)

Pressure

Pounds-force per square inch (psi; lbf/in^2; lb/in^2)	x 0.070	= Kilograms-force per square centimetre (kgf/cm^2; kg/cm^2)	x 14.223	= Pounds-force per square inch (psi; lbf/in^2; lb/in^2)
Pounds-force per square inch (psi; lbf/in^2; lb/in^2)	x 0.068	= Atmospheres (atm)	x 14.696	= Pounds-force per square inch (psi; lbf/in^2; lb/in^2)
Pounds-force per square inch (psi; lbf/in^2; lb/in^2)	x 0.069	= Bars	x 14.5	= Pounds-force per square inch (psi; lbf/in^2; lb/in^2)
Pounds-force per square inch (psi; lbf/in^2; lb/in^2)	x 6.895	= Kilopascals (kPa)	x 0.145	= Pounds-force per square inch (psi; lbf/in^2; lb/in^2)
Kilopascals (kPa)	x 0.01	= Kilograms-force per square centimetre (kgf/cm^2; kg/cm^2)	x 98.1	= Kilopascals (kPa)
Millibar (mbar)	x 100	= Pascals (Pa)	x 0.01	= Millibar (mbar)
Millibar (mbar)	x 0.0145	= Pounds-force per square inch (psi; lbf/in^2; lb/in^2)	x 68.947	= Millibar (mbar)
Millibar (mbar)	x 0.75	= Millimetres of mercury (mmHg)	x 1.333	= Millibar (mbar)
Millibar (mbar)	x 0.401	= Inches of water (inH$_2$O)	x 2.491	= Millibar (mbar)
Millimetres of mercury (mmHg)	x 0.535	= Inches of water (inH$_2$O)	x 1.868	= Millimetres of mercury (mmHg)
Inches of water (inH$_2$O)	x 0.036	= Pounds-force per square inch (psi; lbf/in^2; lb/in^2)	x 27.68	= Inches of water (inH$_2$O)

Torque (moment of force)

Pounds-force inches (lbf in; lb in)	x 1.152	= Kilograms-force centimetre (kgf cm; kg cm)	x 0.868	= Pounds-force inches (lbf in; lb in)
Pounds-force inches (lbf in; lb in)	x 0.113	= Newton metres (Nm)	x 8.85	= Pounds-force inches (lbf in; lb in)
Pounds-force inches (lbf in; lb in)	x 0.083	= Pounds-force feet (lbf ft; lb ft)	x 12	= Pounds-force inches (lbf in; lb in)
Pounds-force feet (lbf ft; lb ft)	x 0.138	= Kilograms-force metres (kgf m; kg m)	x 7.233	= Pounds-force feet (lbf ft; lb ft)
Pounds-force feet (lbf ft; lb ft)	x 1.356	= Newton metres (Nm)	x 0.738	= Pounds-force feet (lbf ft; lb ft)
Newton metres (Nm)	x 0.102	= Kilograms-force metres (kgf m; kg m)	x 9.804	= Newton metres (Nm)

Power

Horsepower (hp)	x 745.7	= Watts (W)	x 0.0013	= Horsepower (hp)

Velocity (speed)

Miles per hour (miles/hr; mph)	x 1.609	= Kilometres per hour (km/hr; kph)	x 0.621	= Miles per hour (miles/hr; mph)

Fuel consumption*

Miles per gallon (mpg)	x 0.354	= Kilometres per litre (km/l)	x 2.825	= Miles per gallon (mpg)

Temperature

Degrees Fahrenheit = (°C x 1.8) + 32   Degrees Celsius (Degrees Centigrade; °C) = (°F - 32) x 0.56

It is common practice to convert from miles per gallon (mpg) to litres/100 kilometres (l/100km), where mpg x l/100 km = 282

A number of chemicals and lubricants are available for use in motorcycle maintenance and repair. They include a wide variety of products ranging from cleaning solvents and degreasers to lubricants and protective sprays for rubber, plastic and vinyl.

● **Contact point/spark plug cleaner** is a solvent used to clean oily film and dirt from points, grime from electrical connectors and oil deposits from spark plugs. It is oil free and leaves no residue. It can also be used to remove gum and varnish from carburettor jets and other orifices.

● **Carburettor cleaner** is similar to contact point/spark plug cleaner but it usually has a stronger solvent and may leave a slight oily reside. It is not recommended for cleaning electrical components or connections.

● **Brake system cleaner** is used to remove grease or brake fluid from brake system components (where clean surfaces are absolutely necessary and petroleum-based solvents cannot be used); it also leaves no residue.

● **Silicone-based lubricants** are used to protect rubber parts such as hoses and grommets, and are used as lubricants for hinges and locks.

● **Multi-purpose grease** is an all purpose lubricant used wherever grease is more practical than a liquid lubricant such as oil. Some multi-purpose grease is coloured white and specially formulated to be more resistant to water than ordinary grease.

● **Gear oil** (sometimes called gear lube) is a specially designed oil used in transmissions and final drive units, as well as other areas where high friction, high temperature lubrication is required. It is available in a number of viscosities (weights) for various applications.

● **Motor oil**, of course, is the lubricant specially formulated for use in the engine. It normally contains a wide variety of additives to prevent corrosion and reduce foaming and wear. Motor oil comes in various weights (viscosity ratings) of from 5 to 80. The recommended weight of the oil depends on the seasonal temperature and the demands on the engine. Light oil is used in cold climates and under light load conditions; heavy oil is used in hot climates and where high loads are encountered. Multi-viscosity oils are designed to have characteristics of both light and heavy oils and are available in a number of weights from 5W-20 to 20W-50.

● **Petrol additives** perform several functions, depending on their chemical makeup. They usually contain solvents that help dissolve gum and varnish that build up on carburettor and inlet parts. They also serve to break down carbon deposits that form on the inside surfaces of the combustion chambers. Some additives contain upper cylinder lubricants for valves and piston rings.

● **Brake and clutch fluid** is a specially formulated hydraulic fluid that can withstand the heat and pressure encountered in brake/clutch systems. Care must be taken that this fluid does not come in contact with painted surfaces or plastics. An opened container should always be resealed to prevent contamination by water or dirt.

● **Chain lubricants** are formulated especially for use on motorcycle final drive chains. A good chain lube should adhere well and have good penetrating qualities to be effective as a lubricant inside the chain and on the side plates, pins and rollers. Most chain lubes are either the foaming type or quick drying type and are usually marketed as sprays. Take care to use a lubricant marked as being suitable for O-ring chains.

● **Degreasers** are heavy duty solvents used to remove grease and grime that may accumulate on engine and frame components. They can be sprayed or brushed on and, depending on the type, are rinsed with either water or solvent.

● **Solvents** are used alone or in combination with degreasers to clean parts and assemblies during repair and overhaul. The home mechanic should use only solvents that are non-flammable and that do not produce irritating fumes.

● **Gasket sealing compounds** may be used in conjunction with gaskets, to improve their sealing capabilities, or alone, to seal metal-to-metal joints. Many gasket sealers can withstand extreme heat, some are impervious to petrol and lubricants, while others are capable of filling and sealing large cavities. Depending on the intended use, gasket sealers either dry hard or stay relatively soft and pliable. They are usually applied by hand, with a brush, or are sprayed on the gasket sealing surfaces.

● **Thread locking compound** is an adhesive locking compound that prevents threaded fasteners from loosening because of vibration. It is available in a variety of types for different applications.

● **Moisture dispersants** are usually sprays that can be used to dry out electrical components such as the fuse block and wiring connectors. Some types can also be used as treatment for rubber and as a lubricant for hinges, cables and locks.

● **Waxes and polishes** are used to help protect painted and plated surfaces from the weather. Different types of paint may require the use of different types of wax polish. Some polishes utilise a chemical or abrasive cleaner to help remove the top layer of oxidised (dull) paint on older vehicles. In recent years, many non-wax polishes (that contain a wide variety of chemicals such as polymers and silicones) have been introduced. These non-wax polishes are usually easier to apply and last longer than conventional waxes and polishes.

About the MOT Test

In the UK, all vehicles more than three years old are subject to an annual test to ensure that they meet minimum safety requirements. A current test certificate must be issued before a machine can be used on public roads, and is required before a road fund licence can be issued. Riding without a current test certificate will also invalidate your insurance.

For most owners, the MOT test is an annual cause for anxiety, and this is largely due to owners not being sure what needs to be checked prior to submitting the motorcycle for testing. The simple answer is that a fully roadworthy motorcycle will have no difficulty in passing the test.

This is a guide to getting your motorcycle through the MOT test. Obviously it will not be possible to examine the motorcycle to the same standard as the professional MOT

tester, particularly in view of the equipment required for some of the checks. However, working through the following procedures will enable you to identify any problem areas before submitting the motorcycle for the test.

It has only been possible to summarise the test requirements here, based on the regulations in force at the time of printing. Test standards are becoming increasingly stringent, although there are some exemptions for older vehicles. More information about the MOT test can be obtained from the TSO publications, *How Safe is your Motorcycle* and *The MOT Inspection Manual for Motorcycle Testing*.

Many of the checks require that one of the wheels is raised off the ground. If the motorcycle doesn't have a centre stand, note that an auxiliary stand will be required. Additionally, the help of an assistant may prove useful.

Certain exceptions apply to machines under 50 cc, machines without a lighting system, and Classic bikes - if in doubt about any of the requirements listed below seek confirmation from an MOT tester prior to submitting the motorcycle for the test.

Check that the frame number is clearly visible.

> **HAYNES HINT** *If a component is in borderline condition, the tester has discretion in deciding whether to pass or fail it. If the motorcycle presented is clean and evidently well cared for, the tester may be more inclined to pass a borderline component than if the motorcycle is scruffy and apparently neglected.*

Electrical System

Lights, turn signals, horn and reflector

✔ With the ignition on, check the operation of the following electrical components. **Note:** *The electrical components on certain small-capacity machines are powered by the generator, requiring that the engine is run for this check.*

a) *Headlight and tail light. Check that both illuminate in the low and high beam switch positions.*

b) *Position lights. Check that the front position (or sidelight) and tail light illuminate in this switch position.*

c) *Turn signals. Check that all flash at the correct rate, and that the warning light(s) function correctly. Check that the turn signal switch works correctly.*

d) *Hazard warning system (where fitted). Check that all four turn signals flash in this switch position.*

e) *Brake stop light. Check that the light comes on when the front and rear brakes are independently applied. Models first used on or after 1st April 1986 must have a brake light switch on each brake.*

f) *Horn. Check that the sound is continuous and of reasonable volume.*

✔ Check that there is a red reflector on the rear of the machine, either mounted separately or as part of the tail light lens.

✔ Check the condition of the headlight, tail light and turn signal lenses.

Headlight beam height

✔ The MOT tester will perform a headlight beam height check using specialised beam setting equipment **(see illustration 1)**. This equipment will not be available to the home mechanic, but if you suspect that the headlight is incorrectly set or may have been maladjusted in the past, you can perform a rough test as follows.

✔ Position the bike in a straight line facing a brick wall. The bike must be off its stand, upright and with a rider seated. Measure the height from the ground to the centre of the headlight and mark a horizontal line on the wall at this height. Position the motorcycle 3.8 metres from the wall and draw a vertical

Headlight beam height checking equipment

line up the wall central to the centreline of the motorcycle. Switch to dipped beam and check that the beam pattern falls slightly lower than the horizontal line and to the left of the vertical line **(see illustration 2)**.

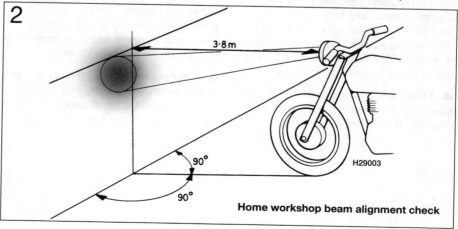

Home workshop beam alignment check

Exhaust System and Final Drive

Exhaust

✔ Check that the exhaust mountings are secure and that the system does not foul any of the rear suspension components.

✔ Start the motorcycle. When the revs are increased, check that the exhaust is neither holed nor leaking from any of its joints. On a linked system, check that the collector box is not leaking due to corrosion.

✔ Note that the exhaust decibel level ("loudness" of the exhaust) is assessed at the discretion of the tester. If the motorcycle was first used on or after 1st January 1985 the silencer must carry the BSAU 193 stamp, or a marking relating to its make and model, or be of OE (original equipment) manufacture. If the silencer is marked NOT FOR ROAD USE, RACING USE ONLY or similar, it will fail the MOT.

Final drive

✔ On chain or belt drive machines, check that the chain/belt is in good condition and does not have excessive slack. Also check that the sprocket is securely mounted on the rear wheel hub. Check that the chain/belt guard is in place.

✔ On shaft drive bikes, check for oil leaking from the drive unit and fouling the rear tyre.

Steering and Suspension

Steering

✔ With the front wheel raised off the ground, rotate the steering from lock to lock. The handlebar or switches must not contact the fuel tank or be close enough to trap the rider's hand. Problems can be caused by damaged lock stops on the lower yoke and frame, or by the fitting of non-standard handlebars.

✔ When performing the lock to lock check, also ensure that the steering moves freely without drag or notchiness. Steering movement can be impaired by poorly routed cables, or by overtight head bearings or worn bearings. The tester will perform a check of the steering head bearing lower race by mounting the front wheel on a surface plate, then performing a lock to lock check with the weight of the machine on the lower bearing (see illustration 3).

✔ Grasp the fork sliders (lower legs) and attempt to push and pull on the forks (see

Front wheel mounted on a surface plate for steering head bearing lower race check

illustration 4). Any play in the steering head bearings will be felt. Note that in extreme cases, wear of the front fork bushes can be misinterpreted for head bearing play.

✔ Check that the handlebars are securely mounted.

✔ Check that the handlebar grip rubbers are secure. They should by bonded to the bar left end and to the throttle cable pulley on the right end.

Front suspension

✔ With the motorcycle off the stand, hold the front brake on and pump the front forks up and down (see illustration 5). Check that they are adequately damped.

Checking the steering head bearings for freeplay

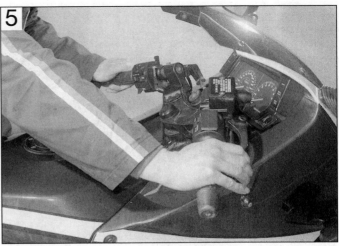

Hold the front brake on and pump the front forks up and down to check operation

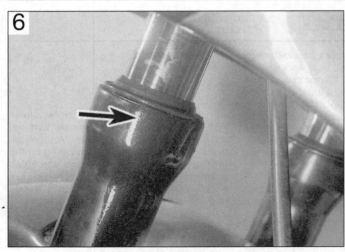

Inspect the area around the fork dust seal for oil leakage (arrow)

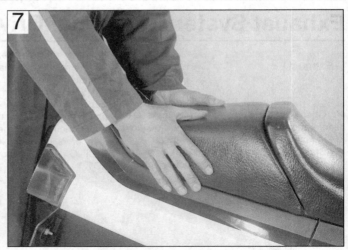

Bounce the rear of the motorcycle to check rear suspension operation

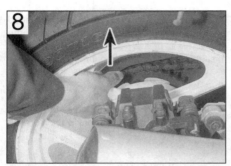

Checking for rear suspension linkage play

✔ Inspect the area above and around the front fork oil seals **(see illustration 6)**. There should be no sign of oil on the fork tube (stanchion) nor leaking down the slider (lower leg). On models so equipped, check that there is no oil leaking from the anti-dive units.

✔ On models with swingarm front suspension, check that there is no freeplay in the linkage when moved from side to side.

Rear suspension

✔ With the motorcycle off the stand and an assistant supporting the motorcycle by its handlebars, bounce the rear suspension **(see illustration 7)**. Check that the suspension components do not foul on any of the cycle parts and check that the shock absorber(s) provide adequate damping.

✔ Visually inspect the shock absorber(s) and check that there is no sign of oil leakage from its damper. This is somewhat restricted on certain single shock models due to the location of the shock absorber.

✔ With the rear wheel raised off the ground, grasp the wheel at the highest point and attempt to pull it up **(see illustration 8)**. Any play in the swingarm pivot or suspension linkage bearings will be felt as movement. **Note:** *Do not confuse play with actual suspension movement.* Failure to lubricate suspension linkage bearings can lead to bearing failure **(see illustration 9)**.

✔ With the rear wheel raised off the ground, grasp the swingarm ends and attempt to move the swingarm from side to side and forwards and backwards - any play indicates wear of the swingarm pivot bearings **(see illustration 10)**.

Worn suspension linkage pivots (arrows) are usually the cause of play in the rear suspension

Grasp the swingarm at the ends to check for play in its pivot bearings

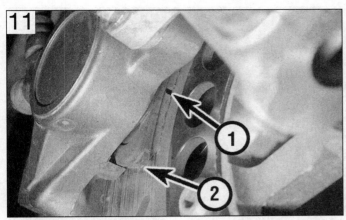

Brake pad wear can usually be viewed without removing the caliper. Most pads have wear indicator grooves (1) and some also have indicator tangs (2)

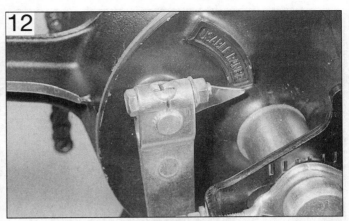

On drum brakes, check the angle of the operating lever with the brake fully applied. Most drum brakes have a wear indicator pointer and scale.

Brakes, Wheels and Tyres

Brakes

✔ With the wheel raised off the ground, apply the brake then free it off, and check that the wheel is about to revolve freely without brake drag.

✔ On disc brakes, examine the disc itself. Check that it is securely mounted and not cracked.

✔ On disc brakes, view the pad material through the caliper mouth and check that the pads are not worn down beyond the limit (see illustration 11).

✔ On drum brakes, check that when the brake is applied the angle between the operating lever and cable or rod is not too great (see illustration 12). Check also that the operating lever doesn't foul any other components.

✔ On disc brakes, examine the flexible hoses from top to bottom. Have an assistant hold the brake on so that the fluid in the hose is under pressure, and check that there is no sign of fluid leakage, bulges or cracking. If there are any metal brake pipes or unions, check that these are free from corrosion and damage. Where a brake-linked anti-dive system is fitted, check the hoses to the anti-dive in a similar manner.

✔ Check that the rear brake torque arm is secure and that its fasteners are secured by self-locking nuts or castellated nuts with split-pins or R-pins (see illustration 13).

✔ On models with ABS, check that the self-check warning light in the instrument panel works.

✔ The MOT tester will perform a test of the motorcycle's braking efficiency based on a calculation of rider and motorcycle weight. Although this cannot be carried out at home, you can at least ensure that the braking systems are properly maintained. For hydraulic disc brakes, check the fluid level, lever/pedal feel (bleed of air if its spongy) and pad material. For drum brakes, check adjustment, cable or rod operation and shoe lining thickness.

Wheels and tyres

✔ Check the wheel condition. Cast wheels should be free from cracks and if of the built-up design, all fasteners should be secure. Spoked wheels should be checked for broken, corroded, loose or bent spokes.

✔ With the wheel raised off the ground, spin the wheel and visually check that the tyre and wheel run true. Check that the tyre does not foul the suspension or mudguards.

✔ With the wheel raised off the ground, grasp the wheel and attempt to move it about the axle (spindle) (see illustration 14). Any play felt here indicates wheel bearing failure.

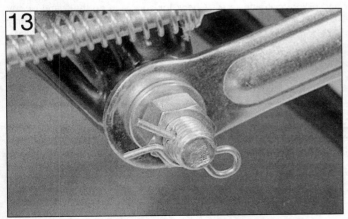

Brake torque arm must be properly secured at both ends

Check for wheel bearing play by trying to move the wheel about the axle (spindle)

Checking the tyre tread depth

Tyre direction of rotation arrow can be found on tyre sidewall

Castellated type wheel axle (spindle) nut must be secured by a split pin or R-pin

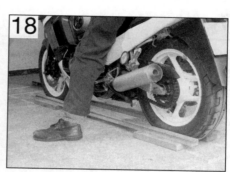

Two straightedges are used to check wheel alignment

✔ Check the tyre tread depth, tread condition and sidewall condition (see illustration 15).
✔ Check the tyre type. Front and rear tyre types must be compatible and be suitable for road use. Tyres marked NOT FOR ROAD USE, COMPETITION USE ONLY or similar, will fail the MOT.

✔ If the tyre sidewall carries a direction of rotation arrow, this must be pointing in the direction of normal wheel rotation (see illustration 16).
✔ Check that the wheel axle (spindle) nuts (where applicable) are properly secured. A self-locking nut or castellated nut with a split-pin or R-pin can be used (see illustration 17).
✔ Wheel alignment is checked with the motorcycle off the stand and a rider seated. With the front wheel pointing straight ahead, two perfectly straight lengths of metal or wood and placed against the sidewalls of both tyres (see illustration 18). The gap each side of the front tyre must be equidistant on both sides. Incorrect wheel alignment may be due to a cocked rear wheel (often as the result of poor chain adjustment) or in extreme cases, a bent frame.

General checks and condition

✔ Check the security of all major fasteners, bodypanels, seat, fairings (where fitted) and mudguards.

✔ Check that the rider and pillion footrests, handlebar levers and brake pedal are securely mounted.

✔ Check for corrosion on the frame or any load-bearing components. If severe, this may affect the structure, particularly under stress.

Sidecars

A motorcycle fitted with a sidecar requires additional checks relating to the stability of the machine and security of attachment and swivel joints, plus specific wheel alignment (toe-in) requirements. Additionally, tyre and lighting requirements differ from conventional motorcycle use. Owners are advised to check MOT test requirements with an official test centre.

Preparing for storage

Before you start

If repairs or an overhaul is needed, see that this is carried out now rather than left until you want to ride the bike again.

Give the bike a good wash and scrub all dirt from its underside. Make sure the bike dries completely before preparing for storage.

Engine

● Remove the spark plug(s) and lubricate the cylinder bores with approximately a teaspoon of motor oil using a spout-type oil can **(see illustration 1)**. Reinstall the spark plug(s). Crank the engine over a couple of times to coat the piston rings and bores with oil. If the bike has a kickstart, use this to turn the engine over. If not, flick the kill switch to the OFF position and crank the engine over on the starter **(see illustration 2)**. If the nature on the ignition system prevents the starter operating with the kill switch in the OFF position,

remove the spark plugs and fit them back in their caps; ensure that the plugs are earthed (grounded) against the cylinder head when the starter is operated **(see illustration 3)**.

⚠️ **_Warning: It is important that the plugs are earthed (grounded) away from the spark plug holes otherwise there is a risk of atomised fuel from the cylinders igniting._**

> **HAYNES HiNT** *On a single cylinder four-stroke engine, you can seal the combustion chamber completely by positioning the piston at TDC on the compression stroke.*

● Drain the carburettor(s) otherwise there is a risk of jets becoming blocked by gum deposits from the fuel **(see illustration 4)**.

● If the bike is going into long-term storage, consider adding a fuel stabiliser to the fuel in the tank. If the tank is drained completely, corrosion of its internal surfaces may occur if left unprotected for a long period. The tank can be treated with a rust preventative especially for this purpose. Alternatively, remove the tank and pour half a litre of motor oil into it, install the filler cap and shake the tank to coat its internals with oil before draining off the excess. The same effect can also be achieved by spraying WD40 or a similar water-dispersant around the inside of the tank via its flexible nozzle.

● Make sure the cooling system contains the correct mix of antifreeze. Antifreeze also contains important corrosion inhibitors.

● The air intakes and exhaust can be sealed off by covering or plugging the openings. Ensure that you do not seal in any condensation; run the engine until it is hot,

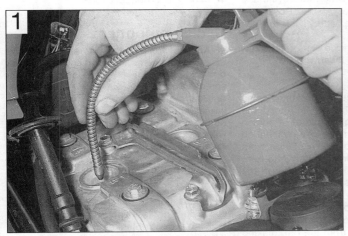

Squirt a drop of motor oil into each cylinder

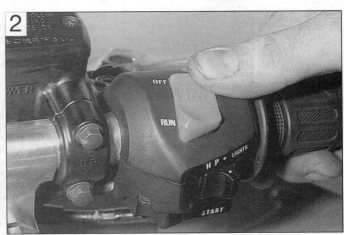

Flick the kill switch to OFF . . .

. . . and ensure that the metal bodies of the plugs (arrows) are earthed against the cylinder head

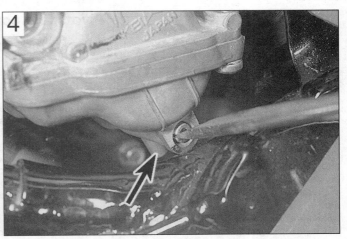

Connect a hose to the carburettor float chamber drain stub (arrow) and unscrew the drain screw

Exhausts can be sealed off with a plastic bag

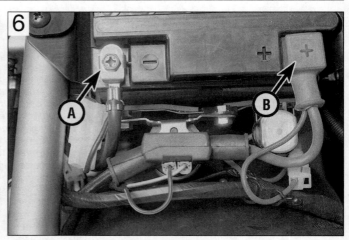

Disconnect the negative lead (A) first, followed by the positive lead (B)

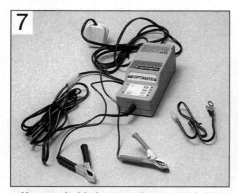

Use a suitable battery charger - this kit also assess battery condition

then switch off and allow to cool. Tape a piece of thick plastic over the silencer end(s) **(see illustration 5)**. Note that some advocate pouring a tablespoon of motor oil into the silencer(s) before sealing them off.

Battery

● Remove it from the bike - in extreme cases of cold the battery may freeze and crack its case **(see illustration 6)**.

● Check the electrolyte level and top up if necessary (conventional refillable batteries). Clean the terminals.
● Store the battery off the motorcycle and away from any sources of fire. Position a wooden block under the battery if it is to sit on the ground.
● Give the battery a trickle charge for a few hours every month **(see illustration 7)**.

Tyres

● Place the bike on its centrestand or an auxiliary stand which will support the motorcycle in an upright position. Position wood blocks under the tyres to keep them off the ground and to provide insulation from damp. If the bike is being put into long-term storage, ideally both tyres should be off the ground; not only will this protect the tyres, but will also ensure that no load is placed on the steering head or wheel bearings.
● Deflate each tyre by 5 to 10 psi, no more or the beads may unseat from the rim, making subsequent inflation difficult on tubeless tyres.

Pivots and controls

● Lubricate all lever, pedal, stand and

footrest pivot points. If grease nipples are fitted to the rear suspension components, apply lubricant to the pivots.
● Lubricate all control cables.

Cycle components

● Apply a wax protectant to all painted and plastic components. Wipe off any excess, but don't polish to a shine. Where fitted, clean the screen with soap and water.
● Coat metal parts with Vaseline (petroleum jelly). When applying this to the fork tubes, do not compress the forks otherwise the seals will rot from contact with the Vaseline.
● Apply a vinyl cleaner to the seat.

Storage conditions

● Aim to store the bike in a shed or garage which does not leak and is free from damp.
● Drape an old blanket or bedspread over the bike to protect it from dust and direct contact with sunlight (which will fade paint). This also hides the bike from prying eyes. Beware of tight-fitting plastic covers which may allow condensation to form and settle on the bike.

Getting back on the road

Engine and transmission

● Change the oil and replace the oil filter. If this was done prior to storage, check that the oil hasn't emulsified - a thick whitish substance which occurs through condensation.
● Remove the spark plugs. Using a spout-type oil can, squirt a few drops of oil into the cylinder(s). This will provide initial lubrication as the piston rings and bores comes back into contact. Service the spark plugs, or fit new ones, and install them in the engine.

● Check that the clutch isn't stuck on. The plates can stick together if left standing for some time, preventing clutch operation. Engage a gear and try rocking the bike back and forth with the clutch lever held against the handlebar. If this doesn't work on cable-operated clutches, hold the clutch lever back against the handlebar with a strong elastic band or cable tie for a couple of hours **(see illustration 8)**.
● If the air intakes or silencer end(s) were blocked off, remove the bung or cover used.
● If the fuel tank was coated with a rust

Hold clutch lever back against the handlebar with elastic bands or a cable tie

preventative, oil or a stabiliser added to the fuel, drain and flush the tank and dispose of the fuel sensibly. If no action was taken with the fuel tank prior to storage, it is advised that the old fuel is disposed of since it will go off over a period of time. Refill the fuel tank with fresh fuel.

Frame and running gear

● Oil all pivot points and cables.
● Check the tyre pressures. They will definitely need inflating if pressures were reduced for storage.
● Lubricate the final drive chain (where applicable).
● Remove any protective coating applied to the fork tubes (stanchions) since this may well destroy the fork seals. If the fork tubes weren't protected and have picked up rust spots, remove them with very fine abrasive paper and refinish with metal polish.
● Check that both brakes operate correctly. Apply each brake hard and check that it's not possible to move the motorcycle forwards, then check that the brake frees off again once released. Brake caliper pistons can stick due to corrosion around the piston head, or on the sliding caliper types, due to corrosion of the slider pins. If the brake doesn't free after repeated operation, take the caliper off for examination. Similarly drum brakes can stick

due to a seized operating cam, cable or rod linkage.
● If the motorcycle has been in long-term storage, renew the brake fluid and clutch fluid (where applicable).
● Depending on where the bike has been stored, the wiring, cables and hoses may have been nibbled by rodents. Make a visual check and investigate disturbed wiring loom tape.

Battery

● If the battery has been previously removal and given top up charges it can simply be reconnected. Remember to connect the positive cable first and the negative cable last.
● On conventional refillable batteries, if the battery has not received any attention, remove it from the motorcycle and check its electrolyte level. Top up if necessary then charge the battery. If the battery fails to hold a charge and a visual checks show heavy white sulphation of the plates, the battery is probably defective and must be renewed. This is particularly likely if the battery is old. Confirm battery condition with a specific gravity check.
● On sealed (MF) batteries, if the battery has not received any attention, remove it from the motorcycle and charge it according to the information on the battery case - if the battery fails to hold a charge it must be renewed.

Starting procedure

● If a kickstart is fitted, turn the engine over a couple of times with the ignition OFF to distribute oil around the engine. If no kickstart is fitted, flick the engine kill switch OFF and the ignition ON and crank the engine over a couple of times to work oil around the upper cylinder components. If the nature of the ignition system is such that the starter won't work with the kill switch OFF, remove the spark plugs, fit them back into their caps and earth (ground) their bodies on the cylinder head. Reinstall the spark plugs afterwards.
● Switch the kill switch to RUN, operate the choke and start the engine. If the engine won't start don't continue cranking the engine - not only will this flatten the battery, but the starter motor will overheat. Switch the ignition off and try again later. If the engine refuses to start, go through the fault finding procedures in this manual. **Note:** *If the bike has been in storage for a long time, old fuel or a carburettor blockage may be the problem. Gum deposits in carburettors can block jets - if a carburettor cleaner doesn't prove successful the carburettors must be dismantled for cleaning.*

● Once the engine has started, check that the lights, turn signals and horn work properly.
● Treat the bike gently for the first ride and check all fluid levels on completion. Settle the bike back into the maintenance schedule.

This Section provides an easy reference-guide to the more common faults that are likely to afflict your machine. Obviously, the opportunities are almost limitless for faults to occur as a result of obscure failures, and to try and cover all eventualities would require a book. Indeed, a number have been written on the subject.

Successful troubleshooting is not a mysterious 'black art' but the application of a bit of knowledge combined with a systematic and logical approach to the problem. Approach any troubleshooting by first accurately identifying the symptom and then checking through the list of possible causes, starting with the simplest or most obvious and progressing in stages to the most complex.

Take nothing for granted, but above all apply liberal quantities of common sense.

The main symptom of a fault is given in the text as a major heading below which are listed the various systems or areas which may contain the fault. Details of each possible cause for a fault and the remedial action to be taken are given, in brief, in the paragraphs below each heading. Further information should be sought in the relevant Chapter.

1 Engine doesn't start or is difficult to start

- ☐ Starter motor doesn't rotate
- ☐ Starter motor rotates but engine does not turn over
- ☐ Starter works but engine won't turn over (seized
- ☐ No fuel flow
- ☐ Engine flooded
- ☐ No spark or weak spark
- ☐ Compression low
- ☐ Stalls after starting
- ☐ Rough idle

2 Poor running at low speed

- ☐ Spark weak
- ☐ Fuel/air mixture incorrect
- ☐ Compression low
- ☐ Poor acceleration

3 Poor running or no power at high speed

- ☐ Firing incorrect
- ☐ Fuel/air mixture incorrect
- ☐ Compression low
- ☐ Knocking or pinking
- ☐ Miscellaneous causes

4 Overheating

- ☐ Engine overheats
- ☐ Firing incorrect
- ☐ Fuel/air mixture incorrect
- ☐ Compression too high
- ☐ Engine load excessive
- ☐ Lubrication inadequate
- ☐ Miscellaneous causes

5 Clutch problems

- ☐ Clutch slipping
- ☐ Clutch not disengaging completely

6 Gearchanging problems

- ☐ Doesn't go into gear, or lever doesn't return
- ☐ Jumps out of gear
- ☐ Overselects

7 Abnormal engine noise

- ☐ Knocking or pinking
- ☐ Piston slap or rattling
- ☐ Valve noise
- ☐ Other noise

8 Abnormal driveline noise

- ☐ Clutch noise
- ☐ Transmission noise
- ☐ Final drive noise

9 Abnormal frame and suspension noise

- ☐ Front end noise
- ☐ Shock absorber noise
- ☐ Brake noise

10 Oil pressure light comes on

- ☐ Engine lubrication system
- ☐ Electrical system

11 Excessive exhaust smoke

- ☐ White smoke
- ☐ Black smoke
- ☐ Brown smoke

12 Poor handling or stability

- ☐ Handlebar hard to turn
- ☐ Handlebar shakes or vibrates excessively
- ☐ Handlebar pulls to one side
- ☐ Poor shock absorbing qualities

13 Braking problems

- ☐ Brakes are spongy, don't hold
- ☐ Brake lever or pedal pulsates
- ☐ Brakes drag

14 Electrical problems

- ☐ Battery dead or weak
- ☐ Battery overcharged

1 Engine doesn't start or is difficult to start

Starter motor doesn't rotate

- [ ] Engine kill switch OFF.
- [ ] Fuse blown. Check fuse (Chapter 8).
- [ ] Battery voltage low. Check and recharge battery (Chapter 8).
- [ ] Starter motor defective. Make sure the wiring to the starter is secure. Make sure the starter relay clicks when the start button is pushed. If the relay clicks, then the fault is in the wiring or motor.
- [ ] Starter relay faulty. Check it according to the procedure in Chapter 8.
- [ ] Starter switch not contacting. The contacts could be wet, corroded or dirty. Disassemble and clean the switch (Chapter 8).
- [ ] Wiring open or shorted. Check all wiring connections and harnesses to make sure that they are dry, tight and not corroded. Also check for broken or frayed wires that can cause a short to earth (ground) (see wiring diagram, Chapter 8).
- [ ] Ignition (main) switch defective. Check the switch according to the procedure in Chapter 8. Replace the switch with a new one if it is defective.
- [ ] Engine kill switch defective. Check for wet, dirty or corroded contacts. Clean or replace the switch as necessary (Chapter 8).
- [ ] Faulty neutral or sidestand switch. Check the wiring to each switch and the switch itself according to the procedures in Chapter 8.
- [ ] Faulty sidestand relay or diode. Check according to the procedure in Chapter 8.

Starter motor rotates but engine does not turn over

- [ ] Starter clutch defective. Inspect and repair or replace (Chapter 2).
- [ ] Damaged idle/reduction gear or starter gears. Inspect and replace the damaged parts (Chapter 2).

Starter works but engine won't turn over (seized)

- [ ] Seized engine caused by one or more internally damaged components. Failure due to wear, abuse or lack of lubrication. Damage can include seized valves, rockers, camshafts, pistons, crankshaft, connecting rod bearings, or transmission gears or bearings. Refer to Chapter 2 for engine disassembly.

No fuel flow

- [ ] No fuel in tank.
- [ ] Fuel tap filter clogged. Remove the fuel tap and clean it and the filter (Chapter 3).
- [ ] Fuel line clogged. Pull the fuel line loose and carefully blow through it.
- [ ] Float needle valve clogged. For both of the valves to be clogged, either a very bad batch of fuel with an unusual additive has been used, or some other foreign material has entered the tank. Many times after a machine has been stored for many months without running, the fuel turns to a varnish-like liquid and forms deposits on the inlet needle valves and jets. The carburettors should be removed and overhauled if draining the float chambers doesn't solve the problem (Chapter 3).

Engine flooded

- [ ] Float height incorrect. Check and adjust as necessary (Chapter 3).
- [ ] Float needle valve worn or stuck open. A piece of dirt, rust or other debris can cause the valve to seat improperly, causing excess fuel to be admitted to the float chamber. In this case, the float chamber should be cleaned and the needle valve and seat inspected. If the needle and seat are worn, then the leaking will persist and the parts should be replaced with new ones (Chapter 3).
- [ ] Starting technique incorrect. Under normal circumstances (ie, if all the carburettor functions are sound) the machine should start with little or no throttle. When the engine is cold, the choke should be operated and the engine started without opening the throttle.

When the engine is at operating temperature, only a very slight amount of throttle should be necessary. If the engine is flooded hold the throttle open while cranking the engine. This will allow additional air to reach the cylinders.

No spark or weak spark

- [ ] Ignition switch OFF.
- [ ] Engine kill switch turned to the OFF position.
- [ ] Battery voltage low. Check and recharge the battery as necessary (Chapter 8).
- [ ] Spark plugs dirty, defective or worn out. Locate reason for fouled plugs using spark plug condition chart at the end of the manual and follow the plug maintenance procedures in Chapter 1.
- [ ] Spark plug caps or HT leads faulty. Check condition. Replace either or both components if cracks or deterioration are evident (Chapter 4).
- [ ] Spark plug caps not making good contact. Make sure that the plug caps fit snugly over the plug ends.
- [ ] Ignition control unit defective. Check the unit, referring to Chapter 4 for details.
- [ ] Pulse generator coil defective. Check the coils, referring to Chapter 4 for details.
- [ ] Ignition HT coils defective. Check the coils, referring to Chapter 4 for details.
- [ ] Ignition or kill switch shorted. This is usually caused by water, corrosion, damage or excessive wear. The switches can be disassembled and cleaned with electrical contact cleaner. If cleaning does not help, replace the switches (Chapter 8).
- [ ] Wiring shorted or broken between:
    - a) Ignition (main) switch and engine kill switch (or blown fuse)
    - b) Ignition control unit and engine kill switch
    - c) Ignition control unit and ignition HT coils
    - d) Ignition HT coils and spark plugs
    - e) Ignition control unit and pulse generator coil
- [ ] Make sure that all wiring connections are clean, dry and tight. Look for chafed and broken wires (Chapters 4 and 8).

Compression low

- [ ] Spark plugs loose. Remove the plugs and inspect their threads. Reinstall and tighten to the specified torque (Chapter 1).
- [ ] Cylinder head not sufficiently tightened down. If the cylinder head is suspected of being loose, then there's a chance that the gasket or head is damaged if the problem has persisted for any length of time. The head nuts should be tightened to the proper torque in the correct sequence (Chapter 2).
- [ ] Improper valve clearance. This means that the valve is not closing completely and compression pressure is leaking past the valve. Check and adjust the valve clearances (Chapter 1).
- [ ] Cylinder and/or piston worn. Excessive wear will cause compression pressure to leak past the rings. This is usually accompanied by worn rings as well. A top-end overhaul is necessary (Chapter 2).
- [ ] Piston rings worn, weak, broken, or sticking. Broken or sticking piston rings usually indicate a lubrication or carburation problem that causes excess carbon deposits or seizures to form on the pistons and rings. Top-end overhaul is necessary (Chapter 2).
- [ ] Piston ring-to-groove clearance excessive. This is caused by excessive wear of the piston ring lands. Piston replacement is necessary (Chapter 2).
- [ ] Cylinder head gasket damaged. If the head is allowed to become loose, or if excessive carbon build-up on the piston crown and combustion chamber causes extremely high compression, the head gasket may leak. Retorquing the head is not always sufficient to restore the seal, so gasket replacement is necessary (Chapter 2).

1 Engine doesn't start or is difficult to start (continued)

☐ Cylinder head warped. This is caused by overheating or improperly tightened head nuts. Machine shop resurfacing or head replacement is necessary (Chapter 2).
☐ Valve spring broken or weak. Caused by component failure or wear; the springs must be replaced (Chapter 2).
☐ Valve not seating properly. This is caused by a bent valve (from over-revving or improper valve adjustment), burned valve or seat (improper carburation) or an accumulation of carbon deposits on the seat (from carburation or lubrication problems). The valves must be cleaned and/or replaced and the seats serviced if possible (Chapter 2).

Stalls after starting

☐ Improper choke action. Make sure the choke linkage shaft is getting a full stroke and staying in the out position (Chapter 3).
☐ Ignition malfunction (Chapter 4).
☐ Carburettor malfunction (Chapter 3).
☐ Fuel contaminated. The fuel can be contaminated with either dirt or water, or can change chemically if the machine is allowed to sit for several months or more. Drain the tank and float chambers (Chapter 3).

☐ Intake air leak. Check for loose carburettor-to-intake manifold connections, loose or missing vacuum gauge adapter caps, or loose carburettor tops (Chapter 3).
☐ Engine idle speed incorrect. Turn idle adjusting screw until the engine idles at the specified rpm (Chapter 1).

Rough idle

☐ Ignition malfunction (Chapter 4).
☐ Idle speed incorrect (Chapter 1).
☐ Carburettors not synchronised (Chapter 1).
☐ Carburettor malfunction (Chapter 3).
☐ Fuel contaminated. The fuel can be contaminated with either dirt or water, or can change chemically if the machine is allowed to sit for several months or more. Drain the tank and float chambers (Chapter 3).
☐ Intake air leak. Check for loose carburettor-to-intake manifold connections, loose or missing vacuum gauge adapter caps, or loose carburettor tops (Chapter 3).
☐ Air filter clogged. Replace the air filter element (Chapter 1).

2 Poor running at low speeds

Spark weak

☐ Battery voltage low. Check and recharge battery (Chapter 8).
☐ Spark plugs fouled, defective or worn out (Chapter 1)
☐ Spark plug cap or HT wiring defective (Chapters 1 and 4).
☐ Spark plug caps not making contact. Make sure they are properly connected.
☐ Incorrect spark plugs. Wrong type, heat range or cap configuration. Check and install correct plugs (Chapter 1).
☐ Ignition control unit defective (Chapter 4).
☐ Pulse generator coil defective (Chapter 4).
☐ Ignition HT coils defective (Chapter 4).

Fuel/air mixture incorrect

☐ Pilot screws out of adjustment (Chapter 3).
☐ Pilot jet or air passage clogged. Remove and overhaul the carburettors (Chapter 3).
☐ Air bleed holes clogged. Remove carburettor and blow out all passages (Chapter 3).
☐ Air filter clogged, poorly sealed or missing (Chapter 1).
☐ Air filter housing poorly sealed. Look for cracks, holes or loose clamps and replace or repair defective parts (Chapter 3).
☐ Fuel level too high or too low. Check the float height (Chapter 3).
☐ Carburettor intake manifolds loose. Check for cracks, breaks, tears or loose clamps. Replace the rubber intake manifold joints if split or perished (Chapter 3).

Compression low

☐ Spark plugs loose. Remove the plugs and inspect their threads. Reinstall and tighten to the specified torque (Chapter 1).
☐ Cylinder head not sufficiently tightened down. If the cylinder head is suspected of being loose, then there's a chance that the gasket or head is damaged if the problem has persisted for any length of time. The head nuts should be tightened to the proper torque in the correct sequence (Chapter 2).
☐ Improper valve clearance. This means that the valve is not closing completely and compression pressure is leaking past the valve. Check and adjust the valve clearances (Chapter 1).
☐ Cylinder and/or piston worn. Excessive wear will cause

compression pressure to leak past the rings. This is usually accompanied by worn rings as well. A top-end overhaul is necessary (Chapter 2).
☐ Piston rings worn, weak, broken, or sticking. Broken or sticking piston rings usually indicate a lubrication or carburation problem that causes excess carbon deposits or seizures to form on the pistons and rings. Top-end overhaul is necessary (Chapter 2).
☐ Piston ring-to-groove clearance excessive. This is caused by excessive wear of the piston ring lands. Piston replacement is necessary (Chapter 2).
☐ Cylinder head gasket damaged. If the head is allowed to become loose, or if excessive carbon build-up on the piston crown and combustion chamber causes extremely high compression, the head gasket may leak. Retorquing the head is not always sufficient to restore the seal, so gasket replacement is necessary (Chapter 2).
☐ Cylinder head warped. This is caused by overheating or improperly tightened head nuts. Machine shop resurfacing or head replacement is necessary (Chapter 2).
☐ Valve spring broken or weak. Caused by component failure or wear; the springs must be replaced (Chapter 2).
☐ Valve not seating properly. This is caused by a bent valve (from over-revving or improper valve adjustment), burned valve or seat (improper carburation) or an accumulation of carbon deposits on the seat (from carburation or lubrication problems). The valves must be cleaned and/or replaced and the seats serviced if possible (Chapter 2).

Poor acceleration

☐ Carburettors leaking or dirty. Overhaul the carburettors (Chapter 3).
☐ Timing not advancing. Faulty pulse generator coil or ignition control unit (Chapter 4).
☐ Carburettors not synchronised (Chapter 1).
☐ Engine oil viscosity too high. Using a heavier oil than that recommended in Chapter 1 can damage the oil pump or lubrication system and cause drag on the engine.
☐ Brakes dragging. Usually caused by debris which has entered the brake piston seals, or from a warped disc or bent axle. Repair as necessary (Chapter 6).

3 Poor running or no power at high speed

Firing incorrect

☐ Air filter restricted. Clean or replace filter (Chapter 1).
☐ Spark plugs fouled, defective or worn out (Chapter 1).
☐ Spark plug cap or HT wiring defective (Chapters 1 and 4).
☐ Spark plug caps not making contact. Make sure they are properly connected.
☐ Incorrect spark plugs. Wrong type, heat range or cap configuration. Check and install correct plugs (Chapter 1).
☐ Ignition control unit defective (Chapter 4).
☐ Pulse generator coil defective (Chapter 4).
☐ Ignition HT coils defective (Chapter 4).

Fuel/air mixture incorrect

☐ Air bleed holes clogged. Remove carburettor and blow out all passages (Chapter 3).
☐ Air filter clogged, poorly sealed or missing (Chapter 1).
☐ Air filter housing poorly sealed. Look for cracks, holes or loose clamps and replace or repair defective parts (Chapter 3).
☐ Fuel level too high or too low. Check the float height (Chapter 3).
☐ Carburettor intake manifolds loose. Check for cracks, breaks, tears or loose clamps. Replace the rubber intake manifold joints if split or perished (Chapter 3).
☐ Jet needle incorrectly positioned or worn Check and adjust or replace (Chapter 3).
☐ Main jet clogged. Dirt, water or other contaminants can clog the main jets. Clean the fuel tap filter, the float chamber area, and the jets and carburettor orifices (Chapter 3).
☐ Main jet wrong size. The standard jetting is for sea level atmospheric pressure and oxygen content. Check jet size (Chapter 3).
☐ Throttle shaft-to-carburettor body clearance excessive. Overhaul carburettors, replacing worn parts or complete carburettor if necessary (Chapter 3).

Compression low

☐ Spark plugs loose. Remove the plugs and inspect their threads. Reinstall and tighten to the specified torque (Chapter 1).
☐ Cylinder head not sufficiently tightened down. If the cylinder head is suspected of being loose, then there's a chance that the gasket or head is damaged if the problem has persisted for any length of time. The head nuts should be tightened to the proper torque in the correct sequence (Chapter 2).
☐ Improper valve clearance. This means that the valve is not closing completely and compression pressure is leaking past the valve. Check and adjust the valve clearances (Chapter 1).
☐ Cylinder and/or piston worn. Excessive wear will cause compression pressure to leak past the rings. This is usually accompanied by worn rings as well. A top-end overhaul is necessary (Chapter 2).
☐ Piston rings worn, weak, broken, or sticking. Broken or sticking piston rings usually indicate a lubrication or carburation problem that causes excess carbon deposits or seizures to form on the pistons and rings. Top-end overhaul is necessary (Chapter 2).

☐ Piston ring-to-groove clearance excessive. This is caused by excessive wear of the piston ring lands. Piston replacement is necessary (Chapter 2).
☐ Cylinder head gasket damaged. If the head is allowed to become loose, or if excessive carbon build-up on the piston crown and combustion chamber causes extremely high compression, the head gasket may leak. Retorquing the head is not always sufficient to restore the seal, so gasket replacement is necessary (Chapter 2).
☐ Cylinder head warped. This is caused by overheating or improperly tightened head nuts. Machine shop resurfacing or head replacement is necessary (Chapter 2).
☐ Valve spring broken or weak. Caused by component failure or wear; the springs must be replaced (Chapter 2).
☐ Valve not seating properly. This is caused by a bent valve (from over-revving or improper valve adjustment), burned valve or seat (improper carburation) or an accumulation of carbon deposits on the seat (from carburation or lubrication problems). The valves must be cleaned and/or replaced and the seats serviced if possible (Chapter 2).

Knocking or pinking

☐ Carbon build-up in combustion chamber. Use of a fuel additive that will dissolve the adhesive bonding the carbon particles to the crown and chamber is the easiest way to remove the build-up. Otherwise, the cylinder head will have to be removed and decarbonised (Chapter 2).
☐ Incorrect or poor quality fuel. Old or improper grades of fuel can cause detonation. This causes the piston to rattle, thus the knocking or pinking sound. Drain old fuel and always use the recommended fuel grade (Chapter 3).
☐ Spark plug heat range incorrect. Uncontrolled detonation indicates the plug heat range is too hot. The plug in effect becomes a glow plug, raising cylinder temperatures. Install the proper heat range plug (Chapter 1).
☐ Improper air/fuel mixture. This will cause the cylinder to run hot, which leads to detonation. Clogged jets or an air leak can cause this imbalance (Chapter 3).

Miscellaneous causes

☐ Throttle valve doesn't open fully. Adjust the throttle cable freeplay (Chapter 1).
☐ Clutch slipping. May be caused by loose or worn clutch components. Overhaul clutch (Chapter 2).
☐ Timing not advancing. Ignition control unit faulty (Chapter 4).
☐ Engine oil viscosity too high. Using a heavier oil than the one recommended in Chapter 1 can damage the oil pump or lubrication system and cause drag on the engine.
☐ Brakes dragging. Usually caused by debris which has entered the brake piston seals, or from a warped disc or bent axle. Repair as necessary.

4 Overheating

Firing incorrect

☐ Spark plugs fouled, defective or worn out (Chapter 1).
☐ Incorrect spark plugs (Chapter 1).
☐ Faulty ignition HT coils (Chapter 4).

Fuel/air mixture incorrect

☐ Main jet clogged. Dirt, water and other contaminants can clog the main jets. Clean the fuel tap filter, the float chamber area and the jets and carburettor orifices (Chapter 3).
☐ Main jet wrong size. The standard jetting is for sea level atmospheric pressure and oxygen content. Check jet size (Chapter 3).
☐ Air filter clogged, poorly sealed or missing (Chapter 1).
☐ Air filter housing poorly sealed. Look for cracks, holes or loose clamps and replace or repair (Chapter 3).
☐ Fuel level too low. Check float height (Chapter 3).
☐ Carburettor intake manifolds loose. Check for cracks, breaks, tears or loose clamps. Replace the rubber intake manifold joints if split or perished (Chapter 3).

Compression too high

☐ Carbon build-up in combustion chamber. Use of a fuel additive that will dissolve the adhesive bonding the carbon particles to the piston crown and chamber is the easiest way to remove the build-up. Otherwise, the cylinder head will have to be removed and decarbonised (Chapter 2).
☐ Improperly machined head surface or installation of incorrect gasket during engine assembly (Chapter 2).

Engine load excessive

☐ Clutch slipping. Can be caused by damaged, loose or worn clutch components. Overhaul clutch (Chapter 2).

☐ Engine oil level too high. The addition of too much oil will cause pressurisation of the crankcase and inefficient engine operation. (Daily (pre-ride) checks).
☐ Engine oil viscosity too high. Using a heavier oil than the one recommended in Chapter 1 can damage the oil pump or lubrication system as well as cause drag on the engine.
☐ Brakes dragging. Usually caused by debris which has entered the brake piston seals, or from a warped disc or bent axle. Repair as necessary.
☐ Excessive friction in moving engine parts due to inadequate lubrication, worn bearings or incorrect assembly. Overhaul engine (Chapter 2).

Lubrication inadequate

☐ Engine oil level too low. Friction caused by intermittent lack of lubrication or from oil that is overworked can cause overheating. The oil provides a definite cooling function in the engine. Check the oil level (Daily (pre-ride) checks).
☐ Poor quality engine oil or incorrect viscosity or type. Oil is rated not only according to viscosity but also according to type. Some oils are not rated high enough for use in this engine. Check the Specifications section and change to the correct oil (Chapter 1).
☐ Worn oil pump or clogged oil passages. Check oil pump and clean passages (Chapter 2).

Miscellaneous causes

☐ Engine cooling fins clogged with debris.
☐ Modification to exhaust system. Most aftermarket exhaust systems cause the engine to run leaner, which make them run hotter. When installing an accessory exhaust system, always rejet the carburettors.

5 Clutch problems

Clutch slipping

☐ Cable freeplay insufficient - 600 models. Check and adjust cable (Chapter 1).
☐ Excess fluid in clutch reservoir - 1200 models (Daily (pre-ride) checks).
☐ Friction plates worn or warped. Overhaul the clutch assembly (Chapter 2).
☐ Plain plates warped (Chapter 2).
☐ Clutch springs broken or weak - 600 model. Old or heat-damaged (from slipping clutch) springs should be replaced with new ones (Chapter 2).
☐ Clutch diaphragm springs fatigued - 1200 model. Measure spring height (Chapter 2).
☐ Clutch release mechanism defective - 600 model. Replace any defective parts (Chapter 2).
☐ Clutch centre or housing unevenly worn. This causes improper engagement of the plates. Replace the damaged or worn parts (Chapter 2).

Clutch not disengaging completely

☐ Cable freeplay excessive - 600 model. Check and adjust cable (Chapter 1).
☐ Insufficient fluid in master cylinder reservoir - 1200 model (Daily (pre-ride) checks).
☐ Air in hydraulic line - 1200 model. Bleed clutch line of air (Chapter 2).

☐ Clutch plates warped or damaged. This will cause clutch drag, which in turn will cause the machine to creep. Overhaul the clutch assembly (Chapter 2).
☐ Clutch spring tension uneven - 600 model. Usually caused by a sagged or broken spring. Check and replace the springs as a set (Chapter 2).
☐ Clutch diaphragm springs broken - 1200 model (Chapter 2).
☐ Engine oil deteriorated. Old, thin, worn out oil will not provide proper lubrication for the plates, causing the clutch to drag. Replace the oil and filter (Chapter 1).
☐ Engine oil viscosity too high. Using a heavier oil than recommended in Chapter 1 can cause the plates to stick together, putting a drag on the engine. Change to the correct weight oil (Chapter 1).
☐ Clutch housing seized on input shaft. Lack of lubrication, severe wear or damage can cause the bearing to seize on the shaft. Overhaul of the clutch, and perhaps transmission, may be necessary to repair the damage (Chapter 2).
☐ Clutch release mechanism defective (600 model). Overhaul the clutch cover components (Chapter 2).
☐ Master cylinder or release cylinder seals defective - 1200 model (Chapter 2).
☐ Loose clutch centre nut. Causes drum and centre misalignment putting a drag on the engine. Engagement adjustment continually varies. Overhaul the clutch assembly (Chapter 2).

6 Gearchanging problems

Doesn't go into gear or lever doesn't return

- [ ] Clutch not disengaging. See above.
- [ ] Selector fork(s) bent or seized. Overhaul the transmission (Chapter 2).
- [ ] Gear(s) stuck on shaft. Most often caused by a lack of lubrication or excessive wear in transmission bearings and bushes. Overhaul the transmission (Chapter 2).
- [ ] Selector drum binding. Caused by lubrication failure or excessive wear. Replace the drum and bearing (Chapter 2).
- [ ] Gearchange lever return spring weak or broken (Chapter 2).
- [ ] Gearchange lever broken. Splines stripped out of lever or shaft, caused by allowing the lever to get loose or from dropping the machine. Replace necessary parts (Chapter 2).
- [ ] Gearchange mechanism stopper arm broken or worn. Full engagement and rotary movement of drum results. Replace the arm (Chapter 2).
- [ ] Stopper arm spring broken. Allows arm to float, causing sporadic shift operation. Replace spring (Chapter 2).

Jumps out of gear

- [ ] Selector fork(s) worn. Overhaul the transmission (Chapter 2).
- [ ] Gear groove(s) worn. Overhaul the transmission (Chapter 2).
- [ ] Gear dogs or dog slots worn or damaged. The gears should be inspected and replaced. No attempt should be made to service the worn parts (Chapter 2).

Overselects

- [ ] Stopper arm spring weak or broken (Chapter 2).
- [ ] Gearchange shaft return spring post broken or distorted (Chapter 2).

7 Abnormal engine noise

Knocking or pinking

- [ ] Carbon build-up in combustion chamber. Use of a fuel additive that will dissolve the adhesive bonding the carbon particles to the piston crown and chamber is the easiest way to remove the build-up. Otherwise, the cylinder head will have to be removed and decarbonised (Chapter 2).
- [ ] Incorrect or poor quality fuel. Old or improper fuel can cause detonation. This causes the pistons to rattle, thus the knocking or pinking sound. Drain the old fuel and always use the recommended grade fuel (Chapter 3).
- [ ] Spark plug heat range incorrect. Uncontrolled detonation indicates that the plug heat range is too hot. The plug in effect becomes a glow plug, raising cylinder temperatures. Install the proper heat range plug (Chapter 1).
- [ ] Improper air/fuel mixture. This will cause the cylinders to run hot and lead to detonation. Clogged jets or an air leak can cause this imbalance (Chapter 3).

Piston slap or rattling

- [ ] Cylinder-to-piston clearance excessive. Caused by improper assembly. Inspect and overhaul top-end parts (Chapter 2).
- [ ] Connecting rod bent. Caused by over-revving, trying to start a badly flooded engine or from ingesting a foreign object into the combustion chamber. Replace the damaged parts (Chapter 2).
- [ ] Piston pin or piston pin bore worn or seized from wear or lack of lubrication. Replace damaged parts (Chapter 2).
- [ ] Piston ring(s) worn, broken or sticking. Overhaul the top-end (Chapter 2).
- [ ] Piston seizure damage. Usually from lack of lubrication or overheating. Replace the pistons and bore the cylinders, as necessary (Chapter 2).

- [ ] Connecting rod upper or lower end clearance excessive. Caused by excessive wear or lack of lubrication. Replace worn parts (Chapter 2).

Valve noise

- [ ] Incorrect valve clearances. Adjust the clearances (Chapter 1).
- [ ] Valve spring broken or weak. Check and replace weak valve springs (Chapter 2).
- [ ] Camshaft or cylinder head worn or damaged. Lack of lubrication at high rpm is usually the cause of damage. Insufficient oil or failure to change the oil at the recommended intervals are the chief causes. Since there are no replaceable bearings in the head, the head itself will have to be replaced if there is excessive wear or damage (Chapter 2).

Other noise

- [ ] Cylinder head gasket leaking (Chapter 1).
- [ ] Exhaust pipe leaking at cylinder head connection. Caused by improper fit of pipe(s) or loose exhaust flange. All exhaust fasteners should be tightened evenly and carefully. Failure to do this will lead to a leak (Chapter 3).
- [ ] Crankshaft runout excessive. Caused by a bent crankshaft (from over-revving) or damage from an upper cylinder component failure. Can also be attributed to dropping the machine on either of the crankshaft ends (Chapter 2).
- [ ] Engine mounting bolts loose. Tighten all engine mount bolts (Chapter 2).
- [ ] Crankshaft bearings worn (Chapter 2).
- [ ] Cam chain tensioner defective. Replace (Chapter 2).
- [ ] Cam chain, sprockets or guides worn (Chapter 2).

8 Abnormal driveline noise

Clutch noise

- [ ] Clutch housing/friction plate clearance excessive (Chapter 2).
- [ ] Loose or damaged clutch pressure plate and/or bolts (Chapter 2).

Transmission noise

- [ ] Bearings worn. Also includes the possibility that the shafts are worn. Overhaul the transmission (Chapter 2).
- [ ] Gears worn or chipped (Chapter 2).
- [ ] Metal chips jammed in gear teeth. Probably pieces from a broken clutch, gear or shift mechanism that were picked up by the gears. This will cause early bearing failure (Chapter 2).

- [ ] Engine oil level too low. Causes a howl from transmission. Also affects engine power and clutch operation (Daily (pre-ride) checks).

Final drive noise

- [ ] Chain not adjusted properly (Chapter 1).
- [ ] Front or rear sprocket loose. Tighten fasteners (Chapter 5).
- [ ] Sprockets worn. Replace sprockets (Chapter 5).
- [ ] Rear sprocket warped. Replace sprockets (Chapter 5).
- [ ] Wheel coupling damper worn. Replace damper (Chapter 5).

9 Abnormal frame and suspension noise

Front end noise

☐ Low fluid level or improper viscosity oil in forks. This can sound like spurting and is usually accompanied by irregular fork action (Chapter 5).

☐ Spring weak or broken. Makes a clicking or scraping sound. Fork oil, when drained, will have a lot of metal particles in it (Chapter 5).

☐ Steering head bearings loose or damaged. Clicks when braking. Check and adjust or replace as necessary (Chapters 1 and 5).

☐ Fork yokes loose. Make sure all clamp pinch bolts are tight (Chapter 5).

☐ Fork tube bent. Good possibility if machine has been dropped. Replace tube with a new one (Chapter 5).

☐ Front axle or axle clamp bolt loose. Tighten them to the specified torque (Chapter 6).

Shock absorber noise

☐ Fluid leakage caused by defective seal. Shock will be covered with oil. Replace shock absorber.

☐ Defective shock absorber with internal damage. This is in the body of the shock and can't be remedied. The shock must be replaced with a new one (Chapter 5).

☐ Bent or damaged shock body. Replace the shock with a new one (Chapter 5).

☐ Loose or worn linkage components. Check and replace as needed (Chapter 5).

Brake noise

☐ Squeal caused by pad shim not installed or positioned correctly (Chapter 6).

☐ Squeal caused by dust on brake pads. Usually found in combination with glazed pads. Clean using brake cleaning solvent (Chapter 6).

☐ Contamination of brake pads. Oil, brake fluid or dirt causing brake to chatter or squeal. Clean or replace pads (Chapter 6).

☐ Pads glazed. Caused by excessive heat from prolonged use or from contamination. Do not use sandpaper, emery cloth, carborundum cloth or any other abrasive to roughen the pad surfaces as abrasives will stay in the pad material and damage the disc. A very fine flat file can be used, but pad replacement is suggested as a cure (Chapter 6).

☐ Disc warped. Can cause a chattering, clicking or intermittent squeal. Usually accompanied by a pulsating lever and uneven braking. Replace the disc (Chapter 6).

☐ Loose or worn wheel bearings. Check and replace as needed (Chapter 6).

10 Oil pressure light comes on

Engine lubrication system

☐ Engine oil pump defective, blocked oil strainer gauze or failed relief valve. Carry out oil pressure check (Chapter 1).

☐ Engine oil level low. Inspect for leak or other problem causing low oil level and add recommended oil (Daily (pre-ride) checks).

☐ Engine oil viscosity too low. Very old, thin oil or an improper weight of oil used in the engine. Change to correct oil (Chapter 1).

☐ Camshaft or journals worn. Excessive wear causing drop in oil pressure. Replace cam and/or/cylinder head. Abnormal wear could be caused by oil starvation at high rpm from low oil level or improper weight or type of oil (Chapter 1).

☐ Crankshaft and/or bearings worn. Same problems as above. Check and replace crankshaft and/or bearings (Chapter 2).

Electrical system

☐ Oil pressure switch defective. Check the switch according to the procedure in Chapter 8. Replace it if it is defective.

☐ Oil pressure warning light circuit defective. Check for pinched, shorted, disconnected or damaged wiring (Chapter 8).

11 Excessive exhaust smoke

White smoke

☐ Piston oil ring worn. The ring may be broken or damaged, causing oil from the crankcase to be pulled past the piston into the combustion chamber. Replace the rings with new ones (Chapter 2).

☐ Cylinders worn, cracked, or scored. Caused by overheating or oil starvation. The cylinders will have to be rebored and new pistons installed (Chapter 2).

☐ Valve oil seal damaged or worn. Replace oil seals with new ones (Chapter 2).

☐ Valve guide worn. Measure guides (Chapter 1) and if necessary have them replaced by a Suzuki dealer.

☐ Engine oil level too high, which causes the oil to be forced past the rings. Drain oil to the proper level (Daily (pre-ride) checks).

☐ Head gasket broken between oil return and cylinder. Causes oil to be pulled into the combustion chamber. Replace the head gasket and check the head for warpage (Chapter 2).

☐ Abnormal crankcase pressurisation, which forces oil past the rings. Clogged engine breather (Chapter 2).

Black smoke

☐ Air filter clogged. Clean or replace the element (Chapter 1).

☐ Main jet too large or loose. Compare the jet size to the Specifications (Chapter 3).

☐ Choke cable or linkage shaft stuck, causing fuel to be pulled through choke circuit (Chapter 3).

☐ Fuel level too high. Check and adjust the float height(s) as necessary (Chapter 3).

☐ Float needle valve held off needle seat. Clean the float chambers and fuel line and replace the needles and seats if necessary (Chapter 3).

Brown smoke

☐ Main jet too small or clogged. Lean condition caused by wrong size main jet or by a restricted orifice. Clean float chambers and jets and compare jet size to Specifications (Chapter 3).

☐ Fuel flow insufficient. Float needle valve stuck closed due to chemical reaction with old fuel. Float height incorrect. Restricted fuel line. Clean line and float chamber and adjust floats if necessary (Chapter 3).

☐ Carburettor intake manifold clamps loose (Chapter 3).

☐ Air filter poorly sealed or not installed (Chapter 1).

12 Poor handling or stability

Handlebars hard to turn

- [ ] Steering head bearing adjuster nut too tight. Check adjustment (Chapter 1).
- [ ] Bearings damaged. Roughness can be felt as the bars are turned from side-to-side. Replace bearings and races (Chapter 5).
- [ ] Races dented or worn. Denting results from wear in only one position (eg, straight ahead), from a collision or hitting a pothole or from dropping the machine. Replace bearings (Chapter 5).
- [ ] Steering stem lubrication inadequate. Causes are grease getting hard from age or being washed out by high pressure car washes. Disassemble steering head and repack bearings (Chapter 5).
- [ ] Steering stem bent. Caused by a collision, hitting a pothole or by dropping the machine. Replace damaged part. Don't try to straighten the steering stem (Chapter 5).
- [ ] Front tyre air pressure too low (Daily (pre-ride) checks).

Handlebar shakes or vibrates excessively

- [ ] Tyres worn or out of balance (Chapter 6).
- [ ] Swingarm bearings worn. Replace worn bearings (Chapter 5).
- [ ] Rim(s) warped or damaged. Inspect wheels for runout (Chapter 6).
- [ ] Wheel bearings worn. Worn front or rear wheel bearings can cause poor tracking. Worn front bearings will cause wobble (Chapter 6).
- [ ] Handlebar clamp bolts loose (Chapter 5).
- [ ] Fork yoke bolts loose. Tighten them to the specified torque (Chapter 5).
- [ ] Engine mounting bolts loose. Will cause excessive vibration with increased engine rpm (Chapter 2).

Handlebar pulls to one side

- [ ] Frame bent. Definitely suspect this if the machine has been dropped. May or may not be accompanied by cracking near the bend. Replace the frame (Chapter 5).
- [ ] Wheels out of alignment. Caused by improper location of axle spacers or from bent steering stem or frame (Chapter 5).
- [ ] Swingarm bent or twisted. Caused by age (metal fatigue) or impact damage. Replace the arm (Chapter 5).
- [ ] Steering stem bent. Caused by impact damage or by dropping the motorcycle. Replace the steering stem (Chapter 5).
- [ ] Fork tube bent. Disassemble the forks and replace the damaged parts (Chapter 5).
- [ ] Fork oil level uneven. Check and add or drain as necessary (Chapter 5).

Poor shock absorbing qualities

- [ ] Too hard:
  a) Fork oil level excessive (Chapter 5).
  b) Fork oil viscosity too high. Use a lighter oil (see the Specifications in Chapter 5).
  c) Fork tube bent. Causes a harsh, sticking feeling (Chapter 5).
  d) Shock shaft or body bent or damaged (Chapter 5).
  e) Fork internal damage (Chapter 5).
  f) Shock internal damage.
  g) Tyre pressure too high (Chapter 1).
- [ ] Too soft:
  a) Fork or shock oil insufficient and/or leaking (Chapter 5).
  b) Fork oil level too low (Chapter 5).
  c) Fork oil viscosity too light (Chapter 5).
  d) Fork springs weak or broken (Chapter 5).
  e) Shock internal damage or leakage (Chapter 5).

13 Braking problems

Brakes are spongy, don't hold

- [ ] Air in brake line. Caused by inattention to master cylinder fluid level or by leakage. Locate problem and bleed brakes (Chapter 6).
- [ ] Pad or disc worn (Chapters 1 and 6).
- [ ] Brake fluid leak. Causes air in brake line. Locate problem and bleed brakes (Chapter 6).
- [ ] Contaminated pads. Caused by contamination with oil, grease, brake fluid, etc. Clean or replace pads. Clean disc thoroughly with brake cleaner (Chapter 6).
- [ ] Brake fluid deteriorated. Fluid is old or contaminated. Drain system, replenish with new fluid and bleed the system (Chapter 6).
- [ ] Master cylinder internal parts worn or damaged causing fluid to bypass (Chapter 6).
- [ ] Master cylinder bore scratched by foreign material or broken spring. Repair or replace master cylinder (Chapter 6).
- [ ] Disc warped. Replace disc (Chapter 6).

Brake lever or pedal pulsates

- [ ] Disc warped. Replace disc (Chapter 6).

- [ ] Axle bent. Replace axle (Chapter 6).
- [ ] Brake caliper bolts loose (Chapter 6).
- [ ] Brake caliper sliders damaged or sticking (600 model front caliper), causing caliper to bind. Lubricate the sliders or replace them if they are corroded or bent (Chapter 6).
- [ ] Wheel warped or otherwise damaged (Chapter 6).
- [ ] Wheel bearings damaged or worn (Chapter 6).

Brakes drag

- [ ] Master cylinder piston seized. Caused by wear or damage to piston or cylinder bore (Chapter 6).
- [ ] Lever balky or stuck. Check pivot and lubricate (Chapter 6).
- [ ] Brake caliper binds. Caused by inadequate lubrication or damage to caliper sliders (Chapter 6).
- [ ] Brake caliper piston seized in bore. Caused by wear or ingestion of dirt past deteriorated seal (Chapter 6).
- [ ] Brake pad damaged. Pad material separated from backing plate. Usually caused by faulty manufacturing process or from contact with chemicals. Replace pads (Chapter 6).
- [ ] Pads improperly installed (Chapter 6).

14 Electrical problems

Battery dead or weak

☐ Battery faulty. Caused by sulphated plates which are shorted through sedimentation. Also, broken battery terminal making only occasional contact (Chapter 8).

☐ Battery cables making poor contact (Chapter 1).

☐ Load excessive. Caused by addition of high wattage lights or other electrical accessories.

☐ Ignition (main) switch defective. Switch either earths (grounds) internally or fails to shut off system. Replace the switch (Chapter 8).

☐ Regulator or rectifier defective (Chapter 8).

☐ Alternator stator coil open or shorted (Chapter 8).

☐ Wiring faulty. Wiring earthed (grounded) or connections loose in ignition, charging or lighting circuits (Chapter 8).

Battery overcharged

☐ Regulator defective. Overcharging is noticed when battery gets excessively warm (Chapter 8).

☐ Battery defective. Replace battery with a new one (Chapter 8).

☐ Battery amperage too low, wrong type or size. Install manufacturer's specified amp-hour battery to handle charging load (Chapter 8).

Checking engine compression

● Low compression will result in exhaust smoke, heavy oil consumption, poor starting and poor performance. A compression test will provide useful information about an engine's condition and if performed regularly, can give warning of trouble before any other symptoms become apparent.

● A compression gauge will be required, along with an adapter to suit the spark plug hole thread size. Note that the screw-in type gauge/adapter set up is preferable to the rubber cone type.

● Before carrying out the test, first check the valve clearances as described in Chapter 1.

1 Run the engine until it reaches normal operating temperature, then stop it and remove the spark plug(s), taking care not to scald your hands on the hot components.

2 Install the gauge adapter and compression gauge in No. 1 cylinder spark plug hole (see illustration 1).

Screw the compression gauge adapter into the spark plug hole, then screw the gauge into the adapter

3 On kickstart-equipped motorcycles, make sure the ignition switch is OFF, then open the throttle fully and kick the engine over a couple of times until the gauge reading stabilises.

4 On motorcycles with electric start only, the procedure will differ depending on the nature of the ignition system. Flick the engine kill switch (engine stop switch) to OFF and turn the ignition switch ON; open the throttle fully and crank the engine over on the starter motor for a couple of revolutions until the gauge reading stabilises. If the starter will not operate with the kill switch OFF, turn the ignition switch OFF and refer to the next paragraph.

5 Install the spark plugs back into their suppressor caps and arrange the plug electrodes so that their metal bodies are earthed (grounded) against the cylinder head; this is essential to prevent damage to the ignition system as the engine is spun over (see illustration 2). Position the plugs well

All spark plugs must be earthed (grounded) against the cylinder head

away from the plug holes otherwise there is a risk of atomised fuel escaping from the combustion chambers and igniting. As a safety precaution, cover the top of the valve cover with rag. Now turn the ignition switch ON and kill switch ON, open the throttle fully and crank the engine over on the starter motor for a couple of revolutions until the gauge reading stabilises.

6 After one or two revolutions the pressure should build up to a maximum figure and then stabilise. Take a note of this reading and on multi-cylinder engines repeat the test on the remaining cylinders.

7 The correct pressures are given in Chapter 2 Specifications. If the results fall within the specified range and on multi-cylinder engines all are relatively equal, the engine is in good condition. If there is a marked difference between the readings, or if the readings are lower than specified, inspection of the top-end components will be required.

8 Low compression pressure may be due to worn cylinder bores, pistons or rings, failure of the cylinder head gasket, worn valve seals, or poor valve seating.

9 To distinguish between cylinder/piston wear and valve leakage, pour a small quantity of oil into the bore to temporarily seal the piston rings, then repeat the compression tests (see illustration 3). If the readings show

Bores can be temporarily sealed with a squirt of motor oil

a noticeable increase in pressure this confirms that the cylinder bore, piston, or rings are worn. If, however, no change is indicated, the cylinder head gasket or valves should be examined.

10 High compression pressure indicates excessive carbon build-up in the combustion chamber and on the piston crown. If this is the case the cylinder head should be removed and the deposits removed. Note that excessive carbon build-up is less likely with the used on modern fuels.

Checking battery open-circuit voltage

 Warning: The gases produced by the battery are explosive - never smoke or create any sparks in the vicinity of the battery. Never allow the electrolyte to contact your skin or clothing - if it does, wash it off and seek immediate medical attention.

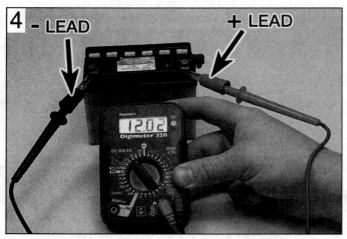

Measuring open-circuit battery voltage

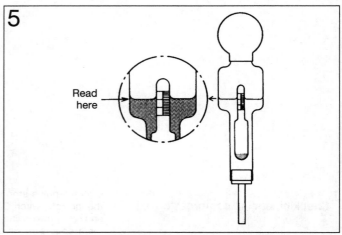

Float-type hydrometer for measuring battery specific gravity

● Before any electrical fault is investigated the battery should be checked.

● You'll need a dc voltmeter or multimeter to check battery voltage. Check that the leads are inserted in the correct terminals on the meter, red lead to positive (+ve), black lead to negative (-ve). Incorrect connections can damage the meter.

● A sound fully-charged 12 volt battery should produce between 12.3 and 12.6 volts across its terminals (12.8 volts for a maintenance-free battery). On machines with a 6 volt battery, voltage should be between 6.1 and 6.3 volts.

1 Set a multimeter to the 0 to 20 volts dc range and connect its probes across the battery terminals. Connect the meter's positive (+ve) probe, usually red, to the battery positive (+ve) terminal, followed by the meter's negative (-ve) probe, usually black, to the battery negative terminal (-ve) (see illustration 4).

2 If battery voltage is low (below 10 volts on a 12 volt battery or below 4 volts on a six volt battery), charge the battery and test the voltage again. If the battery repeatedly goes flat, investigate the motorcycle's charging system.

Checking battery specific gravity (SG)

Warning: The gases produced by the battery are explosive - never smoke or create any sparks in the vicinity of the battery. Never allow the electrolyte to contact your skin or clothing - if it does, wash it off and seek immediate medical attention.

● The specific gravity check gives an indication of a battery's state of charge.

● A hydrometer is used for measuring specific gravity. Make sure you purchase one which has a small enough hose to insert in the aperture of a motorcycle battery.

● Specific gravity is simply a measure of the electrolyte's density compared with that of water. Water has an SG of 1.000 and fully-charged battery electrolyte is about 26% heavier, at 1.260.

● Specific gravity checks are not possible on maintenance-free batteries. Testing the open-circuit voltage is the only means of determining their state of charge.

1 To measure SG, remove the battery from the motorcycle and remove the first cell cap. Draw

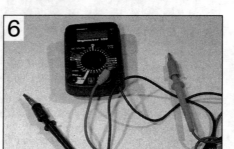

Digital multimeter can be used for all electrical tests

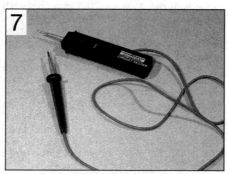

Battery-powered continuity tester

some electrolyte into the hydrometer and note the reading (see illustration 5). Return the electrolyte to the cell and install the cap.

2 The reading should be in the region of 1.260 to 1.280. If SG is below 1.200 the battery needs charging. Note that SG will vary with temperature; it should be measured at 20°C (68°F). Add 0.007 to the reading for every 10°C above 20°C, and subtract 0.007 from the reading for every 10°C below 20°C. Add 0.004 to the reading for every 10°F above 68°F, and subtract 0.004 from the reading for every 10°F below 68°F.

3 When the check is complete, rinse the hydrometer thoroughly with clean water.

Checking for continuity

● The term continuity describes the uninterrupted flow of electricity through an electrical circuit. A continuity check will determine whether an **open-circuit** situation exists.

● Continuity can be checked with an ohmmeter, multimeter, continuity tester or battery and bulb test circuit (see illustrations 6, 7 and 8).

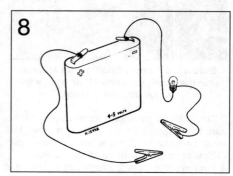

Battery and bulb test circuit

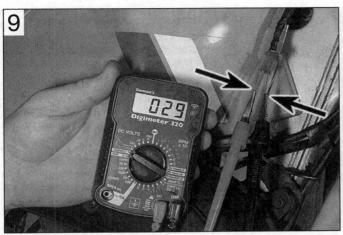

Continuity check of front brake light switch using a meter - note split pins used to access connector terminals

Continuity check of rear brake light switch using a continuity tester

● All of these instruments are self-powered by a battery, therefore the checks are made with the ignition OFF.
● As a safety precaution, always disconnect the battery negative (-ve) lead before making checks, particularly if ignition switch checks are being made.
● If using a meter, select the appropriate ohms scale and check that the meter reads infinity (∞). Touch the meter probes together and check that meter reads zero; where necessary adjust the meter so that it reads zero.
● After using a meter, always switch it OFF to conserve its battery.

Switch checks

1 If a switch is at fault, trace its wiring up to the wiring connectors. Separate the wire connectors and inspect them for security and condition. A build-up of dirt or corrosion here will most likely be the cause of the problem - clean up and apply a water dispersant such as WD40.
2 If using a test meter, set the meter to the ohms x 10 scale and connect its probes across the wires from the switch **(see illustration 9)**. Simple ON/OFF type switches, such as brake light switches, only have two

wires whereas combination switches, like the ignition switch, have many internal links. Study the wiring diagram to ensure that you are connecting across the correct pair of wires. Continuity (low or no measurable resistance - 0 ohms) should be indicated with the switch ON and no continuity (high resistance) with it OFF.
3 Note that the polarity of the test probes doesn't matter for continuity checks, although care should be taken to follow specific test procedures if a diode or solid-state component is being checked.
4 A continuity tester or battery and bulb circuit can be used in the same way. Connect its probes as described above **(see illustration 10)**. The light should come on to indicate continuity in the ON switch position, but should extinguish in the OFF position.

Wiring checks

● Many electrical faults are caused by damaged wiring, often due to incorrect routing or chaffing on frame components.
● Loose, wet or corroded wire connectors can also be the cause of electrical problems, especially in exposed locations.

1 A continuity check can be made on a single length of wire by disconnecting it at each end

and connecting a meter or continuity tester across both ends of the wire **(see illustration 11)**.
2 Continuity (low or no resistance - 0 ohms) should be indicated if the wire is good. If no continuity (high resistance) is shown, suspect a broken wire.

Checking for voltage

● A voltage check can determine whether current is reaching a component.
● Voltage can be checked with a dc voltmeter, multimeter set on the dc volts scale, test light or buzzer **(see illustrations 12 and 13)**. A meter has the advantage of being able to measure actual voltage.
● When using a meter, check that its leads are inserted in the correct terminals on the meter, red to positive (+ve), black to negative (-ve). Incorrect connections can damage the meter.
● A voltmeter (or multimeter set to the dc volts scale) should always be connected in parallel (across the load). Connecting it in series will destroy the meter.
● Voltage checks are made with the ignition ON.

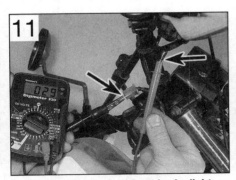

Continuity check of front brake light switch sub-harness

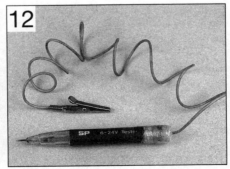

A simple test light can be used for voltage checks

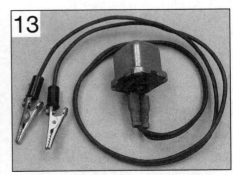

A buzzer is useful for voltage checks

Checking for voltage at the rear brake light power supply wire using a meter . . .

1 First identify the relevant wiring circuit by referring to the wiring diagram at the end of this manual. If other electrical components share the same power supply (ie are fed from the same fuse), take note whether they are working correctly - this is useful information in deciding where to start checking the circuit.

2 If using a meter, check first that the meter leads are plugged into the correct terminals on the meter (see above). Set the meter to the dc volts function, at a range suitable for the battery voltage. Connect the meter red probe (+ve) to the power supply wire and the black probe to a good metal earth (ground) on the motorcycle's frame or directly to the battery negative (-ve) terminal **(see illustration 14)**. Battery voltage should be shown on the meter

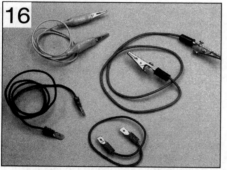

A selection of jumper wires for making earth (ground) checks

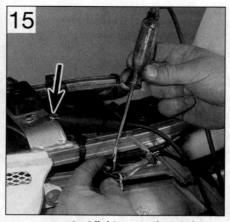

. . . or a test light - note the earth connection to the frame (arrow)

with the ignition switched ON.

3 If using a test light or buzzer, connect its positive (+ve) probe to the power supply terminal and its negative (-ve) probe to a good earth (ground) on the motorcycle's frame or directly to the battery negative (-ve) terminal **(see illustration 15)**. With the ignition ON, the test light should illuminate or the buzzer sound.

4 If no voltage is indicated, work back towards the fuse continuing to check for voltage. When you reach a point where there is voltage, you know the problem lies between that point and your last check point.

Checking the earth (ground)

● Earth connections are made either directly to the engine or frame (such as sensors, neutral switch etc. which only have a positive feed) or by a separate wire into the earth circuit of the wiring harness. Alternatively a short earth wire is sometimes run directly from the component to the motorcycle's frame.

● Corrosion is often the cause of a poor earth connection.

● If total failure is experienced, check the security of the main earth lead from the

negative (-ve) terminal of the battery and also the main earth (ground) point on the wiring harness. If corroded, dismantle the connection and clean all surfaces back to bare metal.

1 To check the earth on a component, use an insulated jumper wire to temporarily bypass its earth connection **(see illustration 16)**. Connect one end of the jumper wire between the earth terminal or metal body of the component and the other end to the motorcycle's frame.

2 If the circuit works with the jumper wire installed, the original earth circuit is faulty. Check the wiring for open-circuits or poor connections. Clean up direct earth connections, removing all traces of corrosion and remake the joint. Apply petroleum jelly to the joint to prevent future corrosion.

Tracing a short-circuit

● A short-circuit occurs where current shorts to earth (ground) bypassing the circuit components. This usually results in a blown fuse.

● A short-circuit is most likely to occur where the insulation has worn through due to wiring chafing on a component, allowing a direct path to earth (ground) on the frame.

1 Remove any bodypanels necessary to access the circuit wiring.

2 Check that all electrical switches in the circuit are OFF, then remove the circuit fuse and connect a test light, buzzer or voltmeter (set to the dc scale) across the fuse terminals. No voltage should be shown.

3 Move the wiring from side to side whilst observing the test light or meter. When the test light comes on, buzzer sounds or meter shows voltage, you have found the cause of the short. It will usually shown up as damaged or burned insulation.

4 Note that the same test can be performed on each component in the circuit, even the switch.

A

ABS (Anti-lock braking system) A system, usually electronically controlled, that senses incipient wheel lockup during braking and relieves hydraulic pressure at wheel which is about to skid.

Aftermarket Components suitable for the motorcycle, but not produced by the motorcycle manufacturer.

Allen key A hexagonal wrench which fits into a recessed hexagonal hole.

Alternating current (ac) Current produced by an alternator. Requires converting to direct current by a rectifier for charging purposes.

Alternator Converts mechanical energy from the engine into electrical energy to charge the battery and power the electrical system.

Ampere (amp) A unit of measurement for the flow of electrical current. Current = Volts ÷ Ohms.

Ampere-hour (Ah) Measure of battery capacity.

Angle-tightening A torque expressed in degrees. Often follows a conventional tightening torque for cylinder head or main bearing fasteners **(see illustration)**.

Angle-tightening cylinder head bolts

Antifreeze A substance (usually ethylene glycol) mixed with water, and added to the cooling system, to prevent freezing of the coolant in winter. Antifreeze also contains chemicals to inhibit corrosion and the formation of rust and other deposits that would tend to clog the radiator and coolant passages and reduce cooling efficiency.

Anti-dive System attached to the fork lower leg (slider) to prevent fork dive when braking hard.

Anti-seize compound A coating that reduces the risk of seizing on fasteners that are subjected to high temperatures, such as exhaust clamp bolts and nuts.

API American Petroleum Institute. A quality standard for 4-stroke motor oils.

Asbestos A natural fibrous mineral with great heat resistance, commonly used in the composition of brake friction materials. Asbestos is a health hazard and the dust created by brake systems should never be inhaled or ingested.

ATF Automatic Transmission Fluid. Often used in front forks.

ATU Automatic Timing Unit. Mechanical device for advancing the ignition timing on early engines.

ATV All Terrain Vehicle. Often called a Quad.

Axial play Side-to-side movement.

Axle A shaft on which a wheel revolves. Also known as a spindle.

B

Backlash The amount of movement between meshed components when one component is held still. Usually applies to gear teeth.

Ball bearing A bearing consisting of a hardened inner and outer race with hardened steel balls between the two races.

Bearings Used between two working surfaces to prevent wear of the components and a build-up of heat. Four types of bearing are commonly used on motorcycles: plain shell bearings, ball bearings, tapered roller bearings and needle roller bearings.

Bevel gears Used to turn the drive through 90°. Typical applications are shaft final drive and camshaft drive **(see illustration)**.

Bevel gears are used to turn the drive through 90°

BHP Brake Horsepower. The British measurement for engine power output. Power output is now usually expressed in kilowatts (kW).

Bias-belted tyre Similar construction to radial tyre, but with outer belt running at an angle to the wheel rim.

Big-end bearing The bearing in the end of the connecting rod that's attached to the crankshaft.

Bleeding The process of removing air from an hydraulic system via a bleed nipple or bleed screw.

Bottom-end A description of an engine's crankcase components and all components contained there-in.

BTDC Before Top Dead Centre in terms of piston position. Ignition timing is often expressed in terms of degrees or millimetres BTDC.

Bush A cylindrical metal or rubber component used between two moving parts.

Burr Rough edge left on a component after machining or as a result of excessive wear.

C

Cam chain The chain which takes drive from the crankshaft to the camshaft(s).

Canister The main component in an evaporative emission control system (California market only); contains activated charcoal granules to trap vapours from the fuel system rather than allowing them to vent to the atmosphere.

Castellated Resembling the parapets along the top of a castle wall. For example, a castellated wheel axle or spindle nut.

Catalytic converter A device in the exhaust system of some machines which converts certain pollutants in the exhaust gases into less harmful substances.

Charging system Description of the components which charge the battery, ie the alternator, rectifier and regulator.

Circlip A ring-shaped clip used to prevent endwise movement of cylindrical parts and shafts. An internal circlip is installed in a groove in a housing; an external circlip fits into a groove on the outside of a cylindrical piece such as a shaft. Also known as a snap-ring.

Clearance The amount of space between two parts. For example, between a piston and a cylinder, between a bearing and a journal, etc.

Coil spring A spiral of elastic steel found in various sizes throughout a vehicle, for example as a springing medium in the suspension and in the valve train.

Compression Reduction in volume, and increase in pressure and temperature, of a gas, caused by squeezing it into a smaller space.

Compression damping Controls the speed the suspension compresses when hitting a bump.

Compression ratio The relationship between cylinder volume when the piston is at top dead centre and cylinder volume when the piston is at bottom dead centre.

Continuity The uninterrupted path in the flow of electricity. Little or no measurable resistance.

Continuity tester Self-powered bleeper or test light which indicates continuity.

Cp Candlepower. Bulb rating commonly found on US motorcycles.

Crossply tyre Tyre plies arranged in a criss-cross pattern. Usually four or six plies used, hence 4PR or 6PR in tyre size codes.

Cush drive Rubber damper segments fitted between the rear wheel and final drive sprocket to absorb transmission shocks **(see illustration)**.

Cush drive rubbers dampen out transmission shocks

D

Degree disc Calibrated disc for measuring piston position. Expressed in degrees.

Dial gauge Clock-type gauge with adapters for measuring runout and piston position. Expressed in mm or inches.

Diaphragm The rubber membrane in a master cylinder or carburettor which seals the upper chamber.

Diaphragm spring A single sprung plate often used in clutches.

Direct current (dc) Current produced by a dc generator.

Decarbonisation The process of removing carbon deposits - typically from the combustion chamber, valves and exhaust port/system.

Detonation Destructive and damaging explosion of fuel/air mixture in combustion chamber instead of controlled burning.

Diode An electrical valve which only allows current to flow in one direction. Commonly used in rectifiers and starter interlock systems.

Disc valve (or rotary valve) A induction system used on some two-stroke engines.

Double-overhead camshaft (DOHC) An engine that uses two overhead camshafts, one for the intake valves and one for the exhaust valves.

Drivebelt A toothed belt used to transmit drive to the rear wheel on some motorcycles. A drivebelt has also been used to drive the camshafts. Drivebelts are usually made of Kevlar.

Driveshaft Any shaft used to transmit motion. Commonly used when referring to the final driveshaft on shaft drive motorcycles.

E

Earth return The return path of an electrical circuit, utilising the motorcycle's frame.

ECU (Electronic Control Unit) A computer which controls (for instance) an ignition system, or an anti-lock braking system.

EGO Exhaust Gas Oxygen sensor. Sometimes called a Lambda sensor.

Electrolyte The fluid in a lead-acid battery.

EMS (Engine Management System) A computer controlled system which manages the fuel injection and the ignition systems in an integrated fashion.

Endfloat The amount of lengthways movement between two parts. As applied to a crankshaft, the distance that the crankshaft can move side-to-side in the crankcase.

Endless chain A chain having no joining link. Common use for cam chains and final drive chains.

EP (Extreme Pressure) Oil type used in locations where high loads are applied, such as between gear teeth.

Evaporative emission control system Describes a charcoal filled canister which stores fuel vapours from the tank rather than allowing them to vent to the atmosphere. Usually only fitted to California models and referred to as an EVAP system.

Expansion chamber Section of two-stroke engine exhaust system so designed to improve engine efficiency and boost power.

F

Feeler blade or gauge A thin strip or blade of hardened steel, ground to an exact thickness, used to check or measure clearances between parts.

Final drive Description of the drive from the transmission to the rear wheel. Usually by chain or shaft, but sometimes by belt.

Firing order The order in which the engine cylinders fire, or deliver their power strokes, beginning with the number one cylinder.

Flooding Term used to describe a high fuel level in the carburettor float chambers, leading to fuel overflow. Also refers to excess fuel in the combustion chamber due to incorrect starting technique.

Free length The no-load state of a component when measured. Clutch, valve and fork spring lengths are measured at rest, without any preload.

Freeplay The amount of travel before any action takes place. The looseness in a linkage, or an assembly of parts, between the initial application of force and actual movement. For example, the distance the rear brake pedal moves before the rear brake is actuated.

Fuel injection The fuel/air mixture is metered electronically and directed into the engine intake ports (indirect injection) or into the cylinders (direct injection). Sensors supply information on engine speed and conditions.

Fuel/air mixture The charge of fuel and air going into the engine. See **Stoichiometric ratio**.

Fuse An electrical device which protects a circuit against accidental overload. The typical fuse contains a soft piece of metal which is calibrated to melt at a predetermined current flow (expressed as amps) and break the circuit.

G

Gap The distance the spark must travel in jumping from the centre electrode to the side electrode in a spark plug. Also refers to the distance between the ignition rotor and the pickup coil in an electronic ignition system.

Gasket Any thin, soft material - usually cork, cardboard, asbestos or soft metal - installed between two metal surfaces to ensure a good seal. For instance, the cylinder head gasket seals the joint between the block and the cylinder head.

Gauge An instrument panel display used to monitor engine conditions. A gauge with a movable pointer on a dial or a fixed scale is an analogue gauge. A gauge with a numerical readout is called a digital gauge.

Gear ratios The drive ratio of a pair of gears in a gearbox, calculated on their number of teeth.

Glaze-busting see **Honing**

Grinding Process for renovating the valve face and valve seat contact area in the cylinder head.

Gudgeon pin The shaft which connects the connecting rod small-end with the piston. Often called a piston pin or wrist pin.

H

Helical gears Gear teeth are slightly curved and produce less gear noise that straight-cut gears. Often used for primary drives.

Installing a Helicoil thread insert in a cylinder head

Helicoil A thread insert repair system. Commonly used as a repair for stripped spark plug threads **(see illustration)**.

Honing A process used to break down the glaze on a cylinder bore (also called glaze-busting). Can also be carried out to roughen a rebored cylinder to aid ring bedding-in.

HT (High Tension) Description of the electrical circuit from the secondary winding of the ignition coil to the spark plug.

Hydraulic A liquid filled system used to transmit pressure from one component to another. Common uses on motorcycles are brakes and clutches.

Hydrometer An instrument for measuring the specific gravity of a lead-acid battery.

Hygroscopic Water absorbing. In motorcycle applications, braking efficiency will be reduced if DOT 3 or 4 hydraulic fluid absorbs water from the air - care must be taken to keep new brake fluid in tightly sealed containers.

I

lbf ft Pounds-force feet. An imperial unit of torque. Sometimes written as ft-lbs.

lbf in Pound-force inch. An imperial unit of torque, applied to components where a very low torque is required. Sometimes written as in-lbs.

IC Abbreviation for Integrated Circuit.

Ignition advance Means of increasing the timing of the spark at higher engine speeds. Done by mechanical means (ATU) on early engines or electronically by the ignition control unit on later engines.

Ignition timing The moment at which the spark plug fires, expressed in the number of crankshaft degrees before the piston reaches the top of its stroke, or in the number of millimetres before the piston reaches the top of its stroke.

Infinity (∞) Description of an open-circuit electrical state, where no continuity exists.

Inverted forks (upside down forks) The sliders or lower legs are held in the yokes and the fork tubes or stanchions are connected to the wheel axle (spindle). Less unsprung weight and stiffer construction than conventional forks.

J

JASO Quality standard for 2-stroke oils.

Joule The unit of electrical energy.

Journal The bearing surface of a shaft.

K

Kickstart Mechanical means of turning the engine over for starting purposes. Only usually fitted to mopeds, small capacity motorcycles and off-road motorcycles.

Kill switch Handebar-mounted switch for emergency ignition cut-out. Cuts the ignition circuit on all models, and additionally prevent starter motor operation on others.

km Symbol for kilometre.

kmh Abbreviation for kilometres per hour.

L

Lambda (λ) sensor A sensor fitted in the exhaust system to measure the exhaust gas oxygen content (excess air factor).

Lapping see **Grinding**.
LCD Abbreviation for Liquid Crystal Display.
LED Abbreviation for Light Emitting Diode.
Liner A steel cylinder liner inserted in a aluminium alloy cylinder block.
Locknut A nut used to lock an adjustment nut, or other threaded component, in place.
Lockstops The lugs on the lower triple clamp (yoke) which abut those on the frame, preventing handlebar-to-fuel tank contact.
Lockwasher A form of washer designed to prevent an attaching nut from working loose.
LT Low Tension Description of the electrical circuit from the power supply to the primary winding of the ignition coil.

M

Main bearings The bearings between the crankshaft and crankcase.
Maintenance-free (MF) battery A sealed battery which cannot be topped up.
Manometer Mercury-filled calibrated tubes used to measure intake tract vacuum. Used to synchronise carburettors on multi-cylinder engines.
Micrometer A precision measuring instrument that measures component outside diameters **(see illustration)**.

Tappet shims are measured with a micrometer

MON (Motor Octane Number) A measure of a fuel's resistance to knock.
Monograde oil An oil with a single viscosity, eg SAE80W.
Monoshock A single suspension unit linking the swingarm or suspension linkage to the frame.
mph Abbreviation for miles per hour.
Multigrade oil Having a wide viscosity range (eg 10W40). The W stands for Winter, thus the viscosity ranges from SAE10 when cold to SAE40 when hot.
Multimeter An electrical test instrument with the capability to measure voltage, current and resistance. Some meters also incorporate a continuity tester and buzzer.

N

Needle roller bearing Inner race of caged needle rollers and hardened outer race. Examples of uncaged needle rollers can be found on some engines. Commonly used in rear suspension applications and in two-stroke engines.
Nm Newton metres.
NOx Oxides of Nitrogen. A common toxic pollutant emitted by petrol engines at higher temperatures.

O

Octane The measure of a fuel's resistance to knock.
OE (Original Equipment) Relates to components fitted to a motorcycle as standard or replacement parts supplied by the motorcycle manufacturer.
Ohm The unit of electrical resistance. Ohms = Volts ÷ Current.
Ohmmeter An instrument for measuring electrical resistance.
Oil cooler System for diverting engine oil outside of the engine to a radiator for cooling purposes.
Oil injection A system of two-stroke engine lubrication where oil is pump-fed to the engine in accordance with throttle position.
Open-circuit An electrical condition where there is a break in the flow of electricity - no continuity (high resistance).
O-ring A type of sealing ring made of a special rubber-like material; in use, the O-ring is compressed into a groove to provide the sealing action.
Oversize (OS) Term used for piston and ring size options fitted to a rebored cylinder.
Overhead cam (sohc) engine An engine with single camshaft located on top of the cylinder head.
Overhead valve (ohv) engine An engine with the valves located in the cylinder head, but with the camshaft located in the engine block or crankcase.
Oxygen sensor A device installed in the exhaust system which senses the oxygen content in the exhaust and converts this information into an electric current. Also called a Lambda sensor.

P

Plastigauge A thin strip of plastic thread, available in different sizes, used for measuring clearances. For example, a strip of Plastigauge is laid across a bearing journal. The parts are assembled and dismantled; the width of the crushed strip indicates the clearance between journal and bearing.
Polarity Either negative or positive earth (ground), determined by which battery lead is connected to the frame (earth return). Modern motorcycles are usually negative earth.
Pre-ignition A situation where the fuel/air mixture ignites before the spark plug fires. Often due to a hot spot in the combustion chamber caused by carbon build-up. Engine has a tendency to 'run-on'.
Pre-load (suspension) The amount a spring is compressed when in the unloaded state. Preload can be applied by gas, spacer or mechanical adjuster.
Premix The method of engine lubrication on older two-stroke engines. Engine oil is mixed with the petrol in the fuel tank in a specific ratio. The fuel/oil mix is sometimes referred to as "petroil".
Primary drive Description of the drive from the crankshaft to the clutch. Usually by gear or chain.
PS Pfedestärke - a German interpretation of BHP.
PSI Pounds-force per square inch. Imperial measurement of tyre pressure and cylinder pressure measurement.
PTFE Polytetrafluroethylene. A low friction substance.

Pulse secondary air injection system A process of promoting the burning of excess fuel present in the exhaust gases by routing fresh air into the exhaust ports.

Q

Quartz halogen bulb Tungsten filament surrounded by a halogen gas. Typically used for the headlight **(see illustration)**.

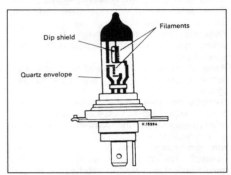

Quartz halogen headlight bulb construction

R

Rack-and-pinion A pinion gear on the end of a shaft that mates with a rack (think of a geared wheel opened up and laid flat). Sometimes used in clutch operating systems.
Radial play Up and down movement about a shaft.
Radial ply tyres Tyre plies run across the tyre (from bead to bead) and around the circumference of the tyre. Less resistant to tread distortion than other tyre types.
Radiator A liquid-to-air heat transfer device designed to reduce the temperature of the coolant in a liquid cooled engine.
Rake A feature of steering geometry - the angle of the steering head in relation to the vertical **(see illustration)**.

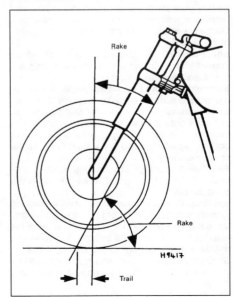

Steering geometry

Rebore Providing a new working surface to the cylinder bore by boring out the old surface. Necessitates the use of oversize piston and rings.

Rebound damping A means of controlling the oscillation of a suspension unit spring after it has been compressed. Resists the spring's natural tendency to bounce back after being compressed.

Rectifier Device for converting the ac output of an alternator into dc for battery charging.

Reed valve An induction system commonly used on two-stroke engines.

Regulator Device for maintaining the charging voltage from the generator or alternator within a specified range.

Relay A electrical device used to switch heavy current on and off by using a low current auxiliary circuit.

Resistance Measured in ohms. An electrical component's ability to pass electrical current.

RON (Research Octane Number) A measure of a fuel's resistance to knock.

rpm revolutions per minute.

Runout The amount of wobble (in-and-out movement) of a wheel or shaft as it's rotated. The amount a shaft rotates `out-of-true'. The out-of-round condition of a rotating part.

S

SAE (Society of Automotive Engineers) A standard for the viscosity of a fluid.

Sealant A liquid or paste used to prevent leakage at a joint. Sometimes used in conjunction with a gasket.

Service limit Term for the point where a component is no longer useable and must be renewed.

Shaft drive A method of transmitting drive from the transmission to the rear wheel.

Shell bearings Plain bearings consisting of two shell halves. Most often used as big-end and main bearings in a four-stroke engine. Often called bearing inserts.

Shim Thin spacer, commonly used to adjust the clearance or relative positions between two parts. For example, shims inserted into or under tappets or followers to control valve clearances. Clearance is adjusted by changing the thickness of the shim.

Short-circuit An electrical condition where current shorts to earth (ground) bypassing the circuit components.

Skimming Process to correct warpage or repair a damaged surface, eg on brake discs or drums.

Slide-hammer A special puller that screws into or hooks onto a component such as a shaft or bearing; a heavy sliding handle on the shaft bottoms against the end of the shaft to knock the component free.

Small-end bearing The bearing in the upper end of the connecting rod at its joint with the gudgeon pin.

Spalling Damage to camshaft lobes or bearing journals shown as pitting of the working surface.

Specific gravity (SG) The state of charge of the electrolyte in a lead-acid battery. A measure of the electrolyte's density compared with water.

Straight-cut gears Common type gear used on gearbox shafts and for oil pump and water pump drives.

Stanchion The inner sliding part of the front forks, held by the yokes. Often called a fork tube.

Stoichiometric ratio The optimum chemical air/fuel ratio for a petrol engine, said to be 14.7 parts of air to 1 part of fuel.

Sulphuric acid The liquid (electrolyte) used in a lead-acid battery. Poisonous and extremely corrosive.

Surface grinding (lapping) Process to correct a warped gasket face, commonly used on cylinder heads.

T

Tapered-roller bearing Tapered inner race of caged needle rollers and separate tapered outer race. Examples of taper roller bearings can be found on steering heads.

Tappet A cylindrical component which transmits motion from the cam to the valve stem, either directly or via a pushrod and rocker arm. Also called a cam follower.

TCS Traction Control System. An electronically-controlled system which senses wheel spin and reduces engine speed accordingly.

TDC Top Dead Centre denotes that the piston is at its highest point in the cylinder.

Thread-locking compound Solution applied to fastener threads to prevent slackening. Select type to suit application.

Thrust washer A washer positioned between two moving components on a shaft. For example, between gear pinions on gearshaft.

Timing chain See **Cam Chain**.

Timing light Stroboscopic lamp for carrying out ignition timing checks with the engine running.

Top-end A description of an engine's cylinder block, head and valve gear components.

Torque Turning or twisting force about a shaft.

Torque setting A prescribed tightness specified by the motorcycle manufacturer to ensure that the bolt or nut is secured correctly. Undertightening can result in the bolt or nut coming loose or a surface not being sealed. Overtightening can result in stripped threads, distortion or damage to the component being retained.

Torx key A six-point wrench.

Tracer A stripe of a second colour applied to a wire insulator to distinguish that wire from another one with the same colour insulator. For example, Br/W is often used to denote a brown insulator with a white tracer.

Trail A feature of steering geometry. Distance from the steering head axis to the tyre's central contact point.

Triple clamps The cast components which extend from the steering head and support the fork stanchions or tubes. Often called fork yokes.

Turbocharger A centrifugal device, driven by exhaust gases, that pressurises the intake air. Normally used to increase the power output from a given engine displacement.

TWI Abbreviation for Tyre Wear Indicator. Indicates the location of the tread depth indicator bars on tyres.

U

Universal joint or U-joint (UJ) A double-pivoted connection for transmitting power from a driving to a driven shaft through an angle. Typically found in shaft drive assemblies.

Unsprung weight Anything not supported by the bike's suspension (ie the wheel, tyres, brakes, final drive and bottom (moving) part of the suspension).

V

Vacuum gauges Clock-type gauges for measuring intake tract vacuum. Used for carburettor synchronisation on multi-cylinder engines.

Valve A device through which the flow of liquid, gas or vacuum may be stopped, started or regulated by a moveable part that opens, shuts or partially obstructs one or more ports or passageways. The intake and exhaust valves in the cylinder head are of the poppet type.

Valve clearance The clearance between the valve tip (the end of the valve stem) and the rocker arm or tappet/follower. The valve clearance is measured when the valve is closed. The correct clearance is important - if too small the valve won't close fully and will burn out, whereas if too large noisy operation will result.

Valve lift The amount a valve is lifted off its seat by the camshaft lobe.

Valve timing The exact setting for the opening and closing of the valves in relation to piston position.

Vernier caliper A precision measuring instrument that measures inside and outside dimensions. Not quite as accurate as a micrometer, but more convenient.

VIN Vehicle Identification Number. Term for the bike's engine and frame numbers.

Viscosity The thickness of a liquid or its resistance to flow.

Volt A unit for expressing electrical "pressure" in a circuit. Volts = current x ohms.

W

Water pump A mechanically-driven device for moving coolant around the engine.

Watt A unit for expressing electrical power. Watts = volts x current.

Wear limit see **Service limit**

Wet liner A liquid-cooled engine design where the pistons run in liners which are directly surrounded by coolant **(see illustration)**.

Wet liner arrangement

Wheelbase Distance from the centre of the front wheel to the centre of the rear wheel.

Wiring harness or loom Describes the electrical wires running the length of the motorcycle and enclosed in tape or plastic sheathing. Wiring coming off the main harness is usually referred to as a sub harness.

Woodruff key A key of semi-circular or square section used to locate a gear to a shaft. Often used to locate the alternator rotor on the crankshaft.

Wrist pin Another name for gudgeon or piston pin.

Note: *References throughout this index relate to Chapter•page number*

Haynes Motorcycle Manuals – The Complete List

Title	Book No.
BMW	
BMW 2-valve Twins (70 - 96)	0249
BMW K100 & 75 2-valve Models (83 - 96)	1373
BMW R850 & R1100 4-valve Twins (93 - 97)	3466
BSA	
BSA Bantam (48 - 71)	0117
BSA Unit Singles (58 - 72)	0127
BSA Pre-unit Singles (54 - 61)	0326
BSA A7 & A10 Twins (47 - 62)	0121
BSA A50 & A65 Twins (62 - 73)	0155
DUCATI	
Ducati 600, 750 & 900 2-valve V-Twins (91 - 96)	3290
HARLEY-DAVIDSON	
Harley-Davidson Sportsters (70 - 99)	0702
Harley-Davidson Big Twins (70 - 99)	0703
HONDA	
Honda NB, ND, NP & NS50 Melody (81 - 85) ◇	0622
Honda NE/NB50 Vision & SA50 Vision Met-in (85 - 95) ◇	1278
Honda MB, MBX, MT & MTX50 (80 - 93)	0731
Honda C50, C70 & C90 (67 - 99)	0324
Honda CR80R & CR125R (86 - 97)	2220
Honda XR80R & XR100R (85 - 96)	2218
Honda XL/XR 80, 100, 125, 185 & 200 2-valve Models (78 - 87)	0566
Honda CB100N & CB125N (78 - 86) ◇	0569
Honda H100 & H100S Singles (80 - 92) ◇	0734
Honda CB/CD125T & CM125C Twins (77 - 88) ◇	0571
Honda CG125 (76 - 99) ◇	0433
Honda NS125 (86 - 93) ◇	3056
Honda MBX/MTX125 & MTX200 (83 - 93) ◇	1132
Honda CD/CM185 200T & CM250C 2-valve Twins (77 - 85)	0572
Honda XL/XR 250 & 500 (78 - 84)	0567
Honda XR250L, XR250R & XR400R (86 - 97)	2219
Honda CB250 & CB400N Super Dreams (78 - 84) ◇	0540
Honda CR250R & CR500R (86 - 97)	2222
Honda Elsinore 250 (73 - 75)	0217
Honda CBR400RR Fours (88 - 99)	3552
Honda VFR400 (NC30) & RVF400 (NC35) V-Fours (89 - 98)	3496
Honda CB400 & CB550 Fours (73 - 77)	0262
Honda CX/GL500 & 650 V-Twins (78 - 86)	0442
Honda CBX550 Four (82 - 86) ◇	0940
Honda XL600R & XR600R (83 - 96)	2183
Honda CBR600F1 & 1000F Fours (87 - 96)	1730
Honda CBR600F2 & F3 Fours (91 - 98)	2070
Honda CB650 sohc Fours (78 - 84)	0665
Honda NTV600 & 650 V-Twins (88 - 96)	3243
Honda Shadow VT600 & 750 (USA) (88 - 99)	2312
Honda CB750 sohc Four (69 - 79)	0131
Honda V45/65 Sabre & Magna (82 - 88)	0820
Honda VFR750 & 700 V-Fours (86 - 97)	2101
Honda VFR800 V-Fours (97 - 00)	3703
Honda CB750 & CB900 dohc Fours (78 - 84)	0535
Honda CBR900RR FireBlade (92 - 99)	2161
Honda ST1100 Pan European V-Fours (90 - 97)	3384
Honda Shadow VT1100 (USA) (85 - 98)	2313
Honda GL1000 Gold Wing (75 - 79)	0309
Honda GL1100 Gold Wing (79 - 81)	0669
Honda Gold Wing 1200 (USA) (84 - 87)	2199
Honda Gold Wing 1500 (USA) (88 - 98)	2225
KAWASAKI	
Kawasaki AE/AR 50 & 80 (81 - 95)	1007

Title	Book No.
Kawasaki KC, KE & KH100 (75 - 99)	1371
Kawasaki KMX125 & 200 (86 - 96) ◇	3046
Kawasaki 250, 350 & 400 Triples (72 - 79)	0134
Kawasaki 400 & 440 Twins (74 - 81)	0281
Kawasaki 400, 500 & 550 Fours (79 - 91)	0910
Kawasaki EN450 & 500 Twins (Ltd/Vulcan) (85 - 93)	2053
Kawasaki EX & ER500 (GPZ500S & ER-5) Twins (87 - 99)	2052
Kawasaki ZX600 (Ninja ZX-6, ZZ-R600) Fours (90 - 97)	2146
Kawasaki ZX-6R Ninja Fours (95 - 98)	3541
Kawasaki ZX600 (GPZ600R, GPX600R, Ninja 600R & RX) & ZX750 (GPX750R, Ninja 750R) Fours (85 - 97)	1780
Kawasaki 650 Four (76 - 78)	0373
Kawasaki 750 Air-cooled Fours (80 - 91)	0574
Kawasaki ZR550 & 750 Zephyr Fours (90 - 97)	3382
Kawasaki ZX750 (Ninja ZX-7 & ZXR750) Fours (89 - 96)	2054
Kawasaki 900 & 1000 Fours (73 - 77)	0222
Kawasaki ZX900, 1000 & 1100 Liquid-cooled Fours (83 - 97)	1681
MOTO GUZZI	
Moto Guzzi 750, 850 & 1000 V-Twins (74 - 78)	0339
MZ	
MZ ETZ Models (81 - 95) ◇	1680
NORTON	
Norton 500, 600, 650 & 750 Twins (57 - 70)	0187
Norton Commando (68 - 77)	0125
PIAGGIO	
Piaggio (Vespa) Scooters (91 - 98)	3492
SUZUKI	
Suzuki GT, ZR & TS50 (77 - 90) ◇	0799
Suzuki TS50X (83 - 99) ◇	1599
Suzuki 100, 125, 185 & 250 Air-cooled Trail bikes (79 - 89)	0797
Suzuki GP100 & 125 Singles (78 - 93) ◇	0576
Suzuki GS, GN, GZ & DR125 Singles (82 - 99) ◇	0888
Suzuki 250 & 350 Twins (68 - 78)	0120
Suzuki GT250X7, GT200X5 & SB200 Twins (78 - 83) ◇	0469
Suzuki GS/GSX250, 400 & 450 Twins (79 - 85)	0736
Suzuki GS500E Twin (89 - 97)	3238
Suzuki GS550 (77 - 82) & GS750 Fours (76 - 79)	0363
Suzuki GS/GSX550 4-valve Fours (83 - 88)	1133
Suzuki GSX-R600 & 750 (96 - 99)	3553
Suzuki GSF600 & 1200 Bandit Fours (95 - 97)	3367
Suzuki GS850 Fours (78 - 88)	0536
Suzuki GS1000 Four (77 - 79)	0484
Suzuki GSX-R750, GSX-R1100 (85 - 92), GSX600F, GSX750F, GSX1100F (Katana) Fours (88 - 96)	2055
Suzuki GS/GSX1000, 1100 & 1150 4-valve Fours (79 - 88)	0737
TRIUMPH	
Triumph Tiger Cub & Terrier (52 - 68)	0414
Triumph 350 & 500 Unit Twins (58 - 73)	0137
Triumph Pre-Unit Twins (47 - 62)	0251
Triumph 650 & 750 2-valve Unit Twins (63 - 83)	0122
Triumph Trident & BSA Rocket 3 (69 - 75)	0136
Triumph Triples & Fours (carburettor engines) (91 - 99)	2162
VESPA	
Vespa P/PX125, 150 & 200 Scooters (78 - 95)	0707
Vespa Scooters (59 - 78)	0126
YAMAHA	
Yamaha DT50 & 80 Trail Bikes (78 - 95) ◇	0800
Yamaha T50 & 80 Townmate (83 - 95) ◇	1247
Yamaha YB100 Singles (73 - 91) ◇	0474

Title	Book No.
Yamaha RS/RXS100 & 125 Singles (74 - 95)	0331
Yamaha RD & DT125LC (82 - 87) ◇	0887
Yamaha TZR125 (87 - 93) & DT125R (88 - 97) ◇	1655
Yamaha TY50, 80, 125 & 175 (74 - 84) ◇	0464
Yamaha XT & SR125 (82 - 96)	1021
Yamaha 250 & 350 Twins (70 - 79)	0040
Yamaha XS250, 360 & 400 sohc Twins (75 - 84)	0378
Yamaha RD250 & 350LC Twins (80 - 82)	0803
Yamaha RD350 YPVS Twins (83 - 95)	1158
Yamaha RD400 Twin (75 - 79)	0333
Yamaha XT, TT & SR500 Singles (75 - 83)	0342
Yamaha XZ550 Vision V-Twins (82 - 85)	0821
Yamaha FJ, FZ, XJ & YX600 Radian (84 - 92)	2100
Yamaha XJ600S (Diversion, Seca II) & XJ600N Fours (92 - 99)	2145
Yamaha YZF600R Thundercat & FZS600 Fazer (96 - 99)	3702
Yamaha 650 Twins (70 - 83)	0341
Yamaha XJ650 & 750 Fours (80 - 84)	0738
Yamaha XS750 & 850 Triples (76 - 85)	0340
Yamaha TDM850, TRX850 & XTZ750 (89 - 99)	3540
Yamaha FZR600, 750 & 1000 Fours (87 - 96)	2056
Yamaha XV V-Twins (81 - 96)	0802
Yamaha XJ900F Fours (83 - 94)	3239
Yamaha FJ1100 & 1200 Fours (84 - 96)	2057
ATVS	
Honda ATC70, 90, 110, 185 & 200 (71 - 85)	0565
Honda TRX300 Shaft Drive ATVs (88 - 95)	2125
Honda TRX300EX & TRX400EX ATVs (93 - 99)	2318
Polaris ATVs (85 to 97)	2302
Yamaha YT, YFM, YTM & YTZ ATVs (80 - 85)	1154
Yamaha YFS200 Blaster ATV (88 - 98)	2317
Yamaha YFB250 Timberwolf ATV (92 - 96)	2217
Yamaha YFM350 Big Bear and ER ATVs (87 - 95)	2126
Yamaha Warrior and Banshee ATVs (87 - 99)	2314
ATV Basics	10450
TECHNICAL TITLES	
Motorcycle Basics Manual	1083
MOTORCYCLE TECHBOOKS	
Motorcycle Electrical TechBook (3rd Edition)	3471
Motorcycle Fuel Systems TechBook	3514
Motorcycle Workshop Practice TechBook (2nd Edition)	3470

◇ = not available in the USA   **Bold type** = *Superbike*

The manuals on this page are available through good motorcycle dealers and accessory shops.
In case of difficulty, contact: **Haynes Publishing**
(UK) +44 1963 440635   (USA) +1 805 4986703
(FR) +33 1 47 78 50 50   (SV) +46 18 124016
(Australia/New Zealand) +61 3 9763 8100

MCL08.09/99

Preserving Our Motoring Heritage

> The Model J Duesenberg Derham Tourster. Only eight of these magnificent cars were ever built – this is the only example to be found outside the United States of America

Almost every car you've ever loved, loathed or desired is gathered under one roof at the Haynes Motor Museum. Over 300 immaculately presented cars and motorbikes represent every aspect of our motoring heritage, from elegant reminders of bygone days, such as the superb Model J Duesenberg to curiosities like the bug-eyed BMW Isetta. There are also many old friends and flames. Perhaps you remember the 1959 Ford Popular that you did your courting in? The magnificent 'Red Collection' is a spectacle of classic sports cars including AC, Alfa Romeo, Austin Healey, Ferrari, Lamborghini, Maserati, MG, Riley, Porsche and Triumph.

A Perfect Day Out

Each and every vehicle at the Haynes Motor Museum has played its part in the history and culture of Motoring. Today, they make a wonderful spectacle and a great day out for all the family. Bring the kids, bring Mum and Dad, but above all bring your camera to capture those golden memories for ever. You will also find an impressive array of motoring memorabilia, a comfortable 70 seat video cinema and one of the most extensive transport book shops in Britain. The Pit Stop Cafe serves everything from a cup of tea to wholesome, home-made meals or, if you prefer, you can enjoy the large picnic area nestled in the beautiful rural surroundings of Somerset.

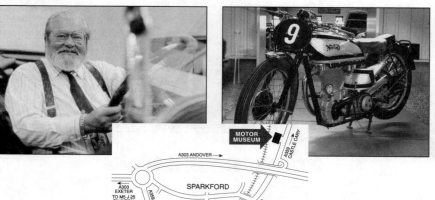

John Haynes O.B.E., Founder and Chairman of the museum at the wheel of a Haynes Light 12.

The 1936 490cc sohc-engined International Norton – well known for its racing success

The Museum is situated on the A359 Yeovil to Frome road at Sparkford, just off the A303 in Somerset. It is about 40 miles south of Bristol, and 25 minutes drive from the M5 intersection at Taunton.

Open 9.30am - 5.30pm (10.00am - 4.00pm Winter) 7 days a week, *except Christmas Day, Boxing Day and New Years Day*
Special rates available for schools, coach parties and outings Charitable Trust No. 292048